Hymns for the Family of God

Hymns for the Family of God

Paragon Associates, Inc.
Nashville, Tennessee 37202

288NEMO
SS6
ISBN 0-89477-000-4

*C*reating a new hymnal brings many rewards. For two thousand years, Christians have been a singing people. From early chants to sung Scriptures, from versified Psalms to original words and music written in our own time, our musical heritage is as varied as it is long. Different musical styles have spoken the eternal truths of God's Word. The great advantage we have over our forefathers is being able to enjoy the richness of the past together with the creativity of the present. Whereas it used to take decades or centuries for a hymn or song-style to become an established part of the Christian's repertoire, today this can happen in a matter of a few month's time. For example "Alleluia " and "They'll Know We are Christians by our Love" are sung almost everywhere by almost everyone. They stand as a symbol of the legacy we shall leave to future generations.

It was rewarding to all of us who worked on this hymnal to appreciate the work of earlier hymnologists and compilers. The responsibility of accuracy in crediting correct sources of music and text lay heavily upon us as we aimed for a thoroughly researched hymnal in all areas. In compiling the music and reading selections for this book, we sought assistance from over forty pastors, musicians and laymen. We received a wide response, and from these leaders developed a core of hymnody common to us all. As you might expect, the most popular titles were predictable: "Holy, Holy, Holy"; "How Great Thou Art;" "O For a Thousand Tongues;" and "When I Survey the Wondrous Cross." Also from this body of supporters came eclectic denominational, cultural and geographical favorites necessary to make a complete lexicon of music for the Church today. We wanted representation from each member of the family of God. Then came the difficult part: creating a hymnal that would be inspirational and functional to each member of that diverse family of believers.

As we made our list of hymns we found we had music from many sources and many traditions. We had that in the back of our minds all along: our hymnal must have variety. As we began the task of locating the owners of these words and music we found ourselves writing requests all over the world. The composers, authors, publishers, and copyright owners were very cooperative, and we thank them all for their consideration in this venture.

As recently as twenty years ago, there were only two or three major translations of the Scriptures. Hymnals of the past usually chose to use the King James Bible, which dates back to the 1600's. Today there are close to twenty highly regarded versions, paraphrases or new translations of the original Hebrew and Greek. What an enjoyable reward to search for the best possible edition. By comparing each passage in many versions, we were able to select the best one: easiest to understand, and the one that read well when spoken aloud by a congregation.

A major reward was being allowed the freedom to be innovative. From the very beginning, we knew we wanted a hymnal that was like no other. For this, I am greatly indebted to my good friends and colleagues, Robert MacKenzie and William Gaither. They have given loving support and criticism, and as publishers, have made it possible for us to incorporate many new and hitherto untried features. These include numbering each stanza on each staff, and italicizing every other verse for clarity and to help congregations keep their place. We also beamed continuous eighth-notes so that they appear in units of beat, and provided over fifty last-verse harmonizations and/or descants. It is our sincere desire that congregational singing will improve through utilization of these features.

But not only is this hymnal a worship book, it is a devotional tool as well. By interspersing Scripture between hymns of the same topical theme, together with readings by various Christian leaders, a Sunday hymnbook is transformed into a seven-days-a-week devotional book of Scripture, hymnody, and contemporary religious thought. We feel strongly that the readings belong with the hymns, not tucked away in the back of the book.

We have divided our hymnal into four major sections: **God's Love for Us, Our Love for God, Our Love for the Family of God**, and **Our Love for Others.** This seems a logical and theologically oriented sequence. As we are made aware of God's love for us, we respond to His love with our own love. Once we know His love and acknowledge it by giving Him our love, we are then free to love each other and those beyond the family of God. It is our hope that this plan will help us all to know **why** we are singing, and to **whom** we are singing.

Right from the start we set our goals high in the area of quality-control. We wanted the very best music, Scripture sources, readings, music engravings, typefaces, paper, and binding. Our responsibility before God demands excellence, and the family of God deserves excellence. Many people have assisted in the creation of this hymnal, and I want to recognize them properly. Our editorial board of reference, our suppliers, proofreaders, printers, designers and engravers – thank you for your support and interest. Bryan Jeffery Leech, a friend, a minister, a musician, and a very capable Assistant Editor, did his work superbly and also counseled, challenged and admonished us to keep with the task that lay before us; my secretary, Marilyn Powell Austin, who typed, and retyped, and retyped again and again, list after list after list, and briefed us throughout the project on current practices with regard to capitalization and proper use of the semi-colon. I must also share how pleasant it is to be involved in a business where competitors are friends. How good to be able to pick up the phone and call fellow hymnal publishers and find them more than willing to help and share their experience and expertise without reservation. Messrs George and William Shorney, Peter Kladder, James Hawkinson, P.J. Zondervan and Bruce Howe are fine Christian gentlemen. The love of my wife, Lois, and of our family is evidenced in how supportive they've been toward this endeavor, allowing me many hours away from them writing, thinking, phoning, traveling, arranging or planning, while they kept everything running smoothly at home. They love me, I know that, and I love them for giving me this freedom in my work.

Our final reward is not in how many copies of this book are in print, but from the discovery that Christians from many churches will find this a useful tool in their personal lives, the life of their local church, and in the ministries we have as individuals, and as members of His family.

Let the Church continue to be His Church, let God's people rejoice: songs of praise and power, majesty and might, worship and witness, testimony and teaching–let them fill the air. Organs, hymns, readings, drums, guitars, and anthems swell! For His Church is triumphant, alive and well!

FRED BOCK

Acknowledgements

EDITORIAL BOARD: Fred Bock, General Editor; Bryan Jeffery Leech, Assistant Editor; William J. Gaither, Gloria Gaither, Ronn Huff, Wayne Erickson, Robert MacKenzie, Dorothy Sickal.
DESIGN AND LAYOUT: Michael Harris and Illustrated Design, Sherman Oaks, California: Allen D. Eckman, Patricia A. Eckman.
MUSIC TYPOGRAPHY: Musictype, Inc., Omaha, Arkansas: Don Ellingson, Robert Abbott, Jr.
MUSIC ARRANGING, PROOFREADING, and SECRETARIAL ASSISTANTS: Tom Keene, Cinda Goold Redman, Paul Sjolund, John Hall, Fred Bock, Darlene Lawrence, Marilyn Austin, Virginia Watts, Louise Bock, Fred Tulan, Bryan Jeffery Leech, Lois Bock, David Dunham, Diane Zagnoli.

Hymns for the Family of God

The hymns and readings are located together in the following topical areas:

III. Our Love for the Family of God 525-617

IV. Our Love for Others   618-699

Indexes

The following indexes are found in the **Hymnal Companion:**
   Alphabetical index of tunes
   Metrical index of tunes
   Composer/author index
   First lines of all stanzas of all hymns

*God's
Love for Us*

A Fair and Glorious Gift

I wish to see all arts, principally music, in the service of Him who gave and created them. Music is a fair and glorious gift of God. I would not for the world forego my humble share of music. Singers are never sorrowful, but are merry, and smile through their troubles in song. Music makes people kinder, gentler, more staid and reasonable. I am strongly persuaded that after theology there is no art than can be placed on a level with music; for besides theology, music is the only art capable of affording peace and joy of the heart . . . the devil flees before the sound of music almost as much as before the Word of God.

—Martin Luther

For the Beauty of the Earth

He hath made all things beautiful. — Ecclesiastes 3:11

Folliott S. Pierpoint, alt.

DIX
Adapted by Conrad Kocher

1

1 For the beau - ty of the earth, For the glo - ry of the skies,
2 *For the won - der of each hour Of the day and of the night,*
3 For the joy of hu - man love, Broth - er, sis - ter, par - ent, child;
4 *For Thy Church that ev - er - more Lift - eth ho - ly hands a - bove,*
5 For Thy-self, best gift di - vine, To our race so free - ly given;

1 For the love which from our birth O - ver and a - round us lies:
2 *Hill and vale and tree and flower, Sun and moon and stars of light:*
3 Friends on earth and friends a - bove; For all gen - tle thoughts and mild:
4 *Off - ering up on ev - ery shore Her pure sac - ri - fice of love:*
5 For that great, great love of Thine, Peace on earth and joy in heaven:

Lord of all, to Thee we raise This our hymn of grate - ful praise. A - men.

GOD'S HAND IN NATURE

2

How Great Thou Art

Great is the Lord and greatly to be praised. — Psalm 48:1

Stuart K. Hine

O STORE GUD
Stuart K. Hine

1 O Lord my God! when I in awe-some won-der Con-sid-er
2 *When through the woods and for-est glades I wan-der And hear the*
3 And when I think that God, His Son not spar-ing, Sent Him to
4 *When Christ shall come with shout of ac-cla-ma-tion And take me*

1 all the worlds Thy hands have made, I see the stars, I
2 *birds sing sweet-ly in the trees; When I look down from*
3 die, I scarce can take it in; That on the cross, my
4 *home, what joy shall fill my heart! Then I shall bow in*

1 hear the roll-ing thun-der, Thy power through-out the u-ni-verse dis-
2 *loft-y moun-tain gran-deur And hear the brook and feel the gen-tle*
3 bur-den glad-ly bear-ing, He bled and died to take a-way my
4 *hum-ble ad-o-ra-tion, And there pro-claim, my God, how great Thou*

1 played:
2 *breeze:*
3 sin:
4 *art!*

Then sings my soul, my Sav-ior God, to Thee;

GOD'S HAND IN NATURE

How great Thou art, how great Thou art! Then sings my soul, my
Sav-ior God, to Thee: How great Thou art, how great Thou art!

Praise Hymn 3

Praise the Lord!
　　Praise the Lord from the heavens!
　　　　Praise Him from the skies!
Praise the Lord!
　　Praise the Lord, O heavens!
　　　　Praise Him from the skies!
All of His angels,
All of the armies of heaven,
　　　　Praise Him! Praise Him!
Praise Him, sun, and moon, and shining stars.
　　Let everything He has made give thanks to Him;
　　Let everything God has made give praise to Him!
　　　　Mountains and hills, the fruit trees and cedars,
　　　　　Beasts of the fields, and fish of the oceans;
　　　　　Fire and hail, and snow and rain,
　　　　　　And wind and weather obey Him.

The young men and women,
　　The old men and children
All praise the Lord together!
　　　　Sing out your thanks to Him,
　　　　　Sing praises to God!
　　　　Sing out your thanks to Him,
　　　　　Sing praises to God!
　　Sing out your praises with cymbals and harp,
　　　　And with timbrel and voices and organ!
Let them praise the name of the Lord,
　　For His name alone is exalted;
　　　His glory is above earth and heaven.
He raised up a horn for His people,
　　Praise for all His saints.
　　Praise the Lord! Praise the Lord!

　　　　　　　　　　　　　−Psalm 148. Fred Bock, alt.

　　　　　　　　　　　　GOD'S HAND IN NATURE

4 God, Who Made the Earth and Heaven

Let the sea roar, let the floods clap their hands, let the hills be joyful together. — Psalm 98: 7-8

Reginald Heber, stanza 1
Frederick L. Hosmer, stanza 2

AR HYD Y NOS
Traditional Welsh Melody

1 God, who made the earth and heav - en, Dark - ness and light,
2 When the con - stant sun re - turn - ing Un - seals our eyes,

1 Who the day for toil has giv - en, For rest the night,
2 May we, born a - new like morn - ing, To la - bor rise;

1 May Your an - gels guard, de - fend us, Slum - ber sweet Your mer - cy send us,
2 Fit us for the task that calls us, Let not ease and self en - thrall us,

1 Ho - ly dreams and hopes at - tend us, All through the night.
2 Strong through You what - e'er be - fall us, O God most wise!

GOD'S HAND IN NATURE

Morning Has Broken

This is the day that the Lord hath made; we shall rejoice . . . . — Psalm 118: 24

5

BUNESSAN
Traditional Gaelic Melody
Arranged by David Evans

Eleanor Farjeon

1 Morn-ing has bro — ken   Like the first morn — ing,
2 *Sweet the rain's new fall   Sun - lit from heav — en,*
3 Mine is the sun - light!   Mine is the morn — ing

1 Black - bird has spo — ken   Like the first bird.
2 *Like the first dew - fall   On the first grass.*
3 Born of the one light   E - den saw play!

1 Praise for the sing — ing!   Praise for the morn — ing!
2 *Praise for the sweet - ness   Of the wet gar - den,*
3 Praise with e - la - tion,   Praise ev - ery morn — ing,

1 Praise for them, spring — ing   Fresh from the Word!
2 *Sprung in com - plete - ness   Where His feet pass.*
3 God's re - cre - a - tion   Of the new day!   A - men.

GOD'S HAND IN NATURE

6 This Is My Father's World

The earth is the Lord's and the fullness thereof.... — Psalm 24:1

TERRA BEATA
English Melody
Adapted by Franklin L. Sheppard

Maltbie D. Babcock

1 This is my Fa-ther's world, And to my lis-ten-ing ears
2 *This is my Fa-ther's world, The birds their car - ols raise,*
3 This is my Fa-ther's world, O let me ne'er for - get

1 All na-ture sings, and 'round me rings The mu - sic of the spheres.
2 *The morn-ing light, the lil - y white, De - clare their Mak-er's praise.*
3 That though the wrong seems oft so strong, God is the rul - er yet.

1 This is my Fa-ther's world: I rest me in the thought Of
2 *This is my Fa-ther's world: He shines in all that's fair; In the*
3 This is my Fa-ther's world: The bat - tle is not done; Je -

1 rocks and trees, of skies and seas— His hand the won - ders wrought.
2 *rus - tling grass I hear Him pass, He speaks to me ev - ery - where.*
3 sus who died shall be sat - is - fied, And earth and heaven be one.

GOD'S HAND IN NATURE

Arranged by Richard Purvis

3 This is my Fa-ther's world, O let me ne'er for-get That though the wrong seems oft so strong, God is the rul-er yet. This is my Fa-ther's world: The bat-tle is not done; Je-sus who died shall be sat-is-fied, And earth and heaven be one.

GOD'S HAND IN NATURE

7 Great God, We Sing Your Mighty Hand

Even there shall Thy hand lead me, and Thy right hand shall hold me. — Psalm 139:10

Philip Doddridge, alt.

GERMANY
William Gardiner's *Sacred Melodies*

1 Great God, we sing Your might - y hand By which sup - port - ed
2 *By day, by night, at home, a - broad, Still are we guard - ed*
3 In scenes ex - alt - ed or de - pressed, You are our joy, and
4 *When death shall in - ter - rupt our songs And seal in si - lence*

1 still we stand; The o - pening year Your mer - cy shows,
2 *by our God, By His in - ces - sant boun - ty fed,*
3 You our rest; Your good - ness all our hopes shall raise,
4 *mor - tal tongues, In fair - er realms, O God, shall we*

1 That mer - cy crowns it 'til its close.
2 *By His un - err - ing coun - sel led.*
3 A - dored through all our chang - ing days.
4 *Your prais - es sing e - ter - nal - ly.* A - men.

8 Psalm 24

The earth is the Lord's and the fulness thereof, *the world and those who dwell therein;* for He has founded it upon the seas, *and established it upon the rivers.*

Who shall ascend the hill of the Lord? And who shall stand in His holy place? *He who has clean hands and a pure heart, who does not lift up his soul to what is false, and does not swear deceitfully.* He will receive blessings from the Lord, *and vindication from the God of his salvation.* Such is the generation of those who seek Him, *who seek the face of the God of Jacob.*

GOD'S HAND IN NATURE

Lift up your heads, O gates! and be lifted up, O ancient doors! *that the King of glory may come in.* Who is the King of glory? *The Lord, strong and mighty, the Lord, mighty in battle!* Lift up your heads, O gates! and be lifted up, O ancient doors! *that the King of glory may come in.* Who is this King of glory? *The Lord of hosts, He is the King of glory!*

—(RSV)

Teach Us What We Yet May Be

9

We then, as workers together with Him . . . — II Corinthians 6:1

Catherine C. Arnott

HYMN TO JOY
Arranged by Ludwig van Beethoven

1 God, who stretched the span-gled heav-ens In - fi - nite in time and place,
2 *We have con-quered worlds un-dreamed of Since the child-hood of our race,*
3 As Thy new ho - ri - zons beck - on, Fa - ther, give us strength to be

1 Flung the suns in burn - ing ra-diance Through the si - lent fields of space,
2 *Known the ec - sta - cy of wing-ing Through un-chart-ed realms of space,*
3 Chil - dren of cre - a - tive pur-pose, Serv - ing man and hon-oring Thee,

1 We, Thy chil - dren, in Thy like - ness, Share in - ven-tive powers with Thee—
2 *Probed the se - crets of the a - tom, Yield-ing un - im - ag-ined power—*
3 'Til our dreams are rich with mean-ing— Each en - deav-or Thy de-sign—

1 Great Cre - a - tor, still cre - a - ting, Teach us what we yet may be.
2 *Fac - ing us with life's de-struc-tion Or our most tri - um-phant hour.*
3 Great Cre - a - tor, lead us on-ward 'Til our work is one with Thine. A-men.

GOD'S HAND IN NATURE

10 Earth and All Stars

Let the sea roar, let the floods clap their hands,
let the hills be joyful together. — Psalm 98:7,8

DEXTER
David N. Johnson
Harmonized by Jan Bender

Herbert F. Brokering

Unison

1 Earth and all stars, Loud rush-ing plan-ets,
2 *Hail, wind and rain, Loud blow-ing snow-storms,*
3 Trum-pet and pipes, Loud clash-ing cym-bals,
4 *En-gines and steel, Loud pound-ing ham-mers,*
5 Knowl-edge and truth, Loud sound-ing wis-dom,

1 Sing to the Lord a new song! O vic-to-ry,
2 *Sing to the Lord a new song! Flow-ers and trees,*
3 Sing to the Lord a new song! Harp, lute and lyre,
4 *Sing to the Lord a new song! Lime-stone and beams,*
5 Sing to the Lord a new song! Daugh-ter and son,

1 Loud shout-ing ar-my, Sing to the Lord a new song!
2 *Loud rus-tling dry leaves, Sing to the Lord a new song!*
3 Loud hum-ming 'cel-los, Sing to the Lord a new song!
4 *Loud build-ing work-men, Sing to the Lord a new song!*
5 Loud prais-ing mem-bers, Sing to the Lord a new song!

GOD'S HAND IN NATURE

He has done mar - vel-ous things: I, too, will praise Him with a new song!

Psalm 104   11

O Lord, how great and all-powerful You are!
And how beautiful is the world You created for our habitation!

Even before man was brought forth from the dust,
    You prepared for him a place in which to live and grow.
    And everything man saw about him
        reflected the beauty and power of the living God.

There was clean air.
Pure water from snowcapped mountains flowed through green valleys
        and gathered together to become great lakes.
The skies shone with a million lights.
The land brought forth flowers and fruits
    to delight the eye and palate of God's creature.
And every part of the land
        and the waters that covered the land
        and the skies that looked down upon the land
        were filled with uncountable forms of life;
    and the world was vibrant and alive.

Your power and Your beauty were spread throughout the universe,
    but it was only upon the heart of man
        that You imprinted Your image.
And this creature,
    in his short stay upon this world,
    was destined to be Your son and co-worker
        in the ever-continuing process of creation.

—Leslie Brandt

GOD'S HAND IN NATURE

12 O Day of Rest and Gladness

Upon the first day of the week . . . the disciples came together, — Acts 20:7

MENDEBRAS
Traditional German Melody
Arranged by Lowell Mason

Christopher Wordsworth

1 O day of rest and glad-ness, O day of joy and light,
2 *On thee, at the cre - a - tion, The light first had its birth;*
3 To - day on wea-ry na-tions The heaven-ly man-na falls;
4 *New grac - es ev - er gain - ing From this our day of rest,*

1 O balm of care and sad-ness, Most beau - ti - ful, most bright:
2 *On thee, for our sal - va - tion, Christ rose from depths of earth;*
3 To ho - ly con-vo - ca-tions The sil - ver trump-et calls,
4 *We reach the rest re - main-ing To spir - its of the blest;*

1 On thee the high and low - ly, Through a - ges joined in tune, Sing
2 *On thee our Lord vic - to-rious The Spir - it sent from heaven; And*
3 Where gos - pel light is glow-ing With pure and ra-diant beams, And
4 *To Ho - ly Ghost be prais - es, To Fa-ther and to Son; The*

1 "Ho - ly, ho - ly, ho - ly," To the great God Tri - une.
2 *thus on thee most glo-rious A tri - ple light was given.*
3 liv - ing wa - ter flow-ing With soul-re - fresh-ing streams.
4 *Church her voice up - rais - es To Thee, blest Three in One.* A-men.

The Wonder of It All

13

For we are His workmanship created in Christ Jesus unto good works. — Ephesians 2:10

WONDER OF IT ALL
George Beverly Shea

George Beverly Shea

1 There's the won-der of sun-set at eve-ning, The won-der as
2 There's the won-der of spring-time and har-vest, The sky, the

1 sun - rise I see; But the won-der of won-ders that thrills my soul
2 stars, the sun; But the won-der of won-ders that thrills my soul

1 Is the won-der that God loves me. O, the won-der of it all! The
2 Is a won-der that's on - ly be - gun.

won-der of it all! Just to think that God loves me. O the won-der of it

all! The won-der of it all! Just to think that God loves me.

GOD'S LOVE

14   A Celebration for Family People

Leader: God has called us to live within the privilege of family life.
He has gifted us with mothers, fathers, sisters, brothers, aunts and uncles, and grandparents, and beyond this with friends who become equally precious to us.

People: PRAISE GOD FOR THE GIFT OF FAMILY LIFE!

Leader: Lord,
We thank you for older folk who link us with the past and who enrich us with their experience.
We thank you for the newborn so rich in potential greatness and goodness.
We thank you for the gifts we see emerging in our children.
We thank you for the excitement of living with those who are on the brink of adulthood, even though this is sometimes a time of struggle for all of us.

People: PRAISE GOD FOR THE GIFT OF FAMILY LIFE!

Leader: Eternal Father of us all,
Enter our homes,
not as the occupant of a guest room,
but as the senior member of each household,
that we may live out your love in the most ordinary parts of life.
Keep us human as you make us holy. Amen.

People: PRAISE GOD FOR THE GIFT OF FAMILY LIFE!
IT IS ALL YOUR DOING, LORD. IT IS WONDERFUL IN OUR EYES.

—Bryan Jeffery Leech

15   Jesus Loves the Little Children

"Suffer little children . . . to come unto Me." — Matthew 19:14

CHILDREN

Unknown

George F. Root

Je-sus loves the lit-tle chil-dren, All the chil-dren of the world. Red and yel-low, black and white, They are pre-cious in His sight — Je-sus loves the lit-tle chil-dren of the world.

Tell Me the Old, Old Story

16

Of which salvation the prophets have enquired . . . who prophesied of the grace that should come . . . . — I Peter 1:10

Katherine Hankey

EVANGEL
William H. Doane

1 Tell me the old, old story Of un-seen things a - bove, Of Je-sus
2 *Tell me the sto - ry slow - ly, That I may take it in— That won-der-*
3 Tell me the same old sto - ry When you have cause to fear, That this world's

1 and His glo - ry, Of Je-sus and His love. Tell me the sto - ry
2 *ful re - demp - tion, God's rem-e - dy for sin. Tell me the sto - ry*
3 emp - ty glo - ry Is cost-ing me too dear. Yes, and when that world's

1 sim - ply, As to a lit - tle child; For I am weak and wea - ry,
2 *of - ten, For I for - get so soon; The ear - ly dew of morn - ing*
3 glo - ry Is dawn-ing on my soul, Tell me the old, old sto - ry:

1 And help - less and de - filed.
2 *Has passed a - way at noon.* Tell me the old, old sto - ry. Tell me the
3 "Christ Je - sus makes thee whole."

old, old sto - ry. Tell me the old, old sto-ry, Of Je-sus and His love.

GOD'S LOVE

I feel like singing this morning, O Lord.
I feel like telling everyone about me
         how great You are.
If only they could know the depths of Your love
         and Your eternal concern for those who
         will follow You!
But my songs are so often off-key.
My speech is so inadequate.
I simply cannot express what I feel,
         what I know to be true about Your love
         for Your creatures upon this world.

But even the songs of the birds
         proclaim Your praises.
The heavens and the earth beneath them,
         the trees that reach toward You,
         the flowers that glow in colorful beauty,
         the green hills and soaring mountains,
         the valleys and the plains,
         the lakes and the rivers,
         the great oceans that pound our shores,
         they proclaim Your greatness, O God,
         and Your love for the sons of men.

How glorious it is to be alive, O Lord!
May every breath of my body,
         every beat of my heart,
         be dedicated to Your praise and glory.

—Leslie Brandt

18   The ℒove of God

Who shall separate us from the love of Christ?   — Romans 8:35

F. M. Lehman

F. M. Lehman
Arranged by Claudia Lehman Mays

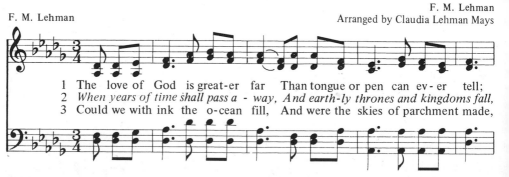

1 The love of God is great-er far   Than tongue or pen can ev-er tell;
2 *When years of time shall pass a - way, And earth-ly thrones and kingdoms fall,*
3 Could we with ink the o-cean fill,   And were the skies of parchment made,

GOD'S LOVE

1 It goes be-yond the high-est star, And reach-es to the low-est hell;
2 *When men, who here re-fuse to pray, On rocks and hills and mountains call,*
3 Were ev-ery stalk on earth a quill, And ev-ery man a scribe by trade,

1 The guilt-y pair, bowed down with care, God gave His Son to win;
2 *God's love so sure, shall still en-dure, All mea-sure-less and strong;*
3 To write the love of God a-bove Would drain the o - cean dry.

1 His err-ing child He rec-on-ciled, And par-doned from his sin.
2 *Re-deem-ing grace to A-dam's race–The saints' and an - gels' song.*
3 Nor could the scroll con-tain the whole, Though stretched from sky to sky.

O love of God, how rich and pure! How mea-sure-less and strong!

It shall for ev - er-more en-dure The saints' and an - gels' song.

GOD'S LOVE

19   John 3 : 14-21

"And as Moses lifted up the serpent in the wilderness, so must the Son of man be lifted up, that whoever believes in Him may have eternal life."

For God so loved the world that He gave His only Son, that whoever believes in Him should not perish but have eternal life. For God sent the Son into the world, not to condemn the world, but that the world might be saved through Him. He who believes in Him is not condemned; he who does not believe is condemned already, because He has not believed in the name of the only Son of God. And this is the judgment, that the light has come into the world, and men loved darkness rather than light, because their deeds were evil. For every one who does evil hates the light, and does not come to the light, lest his deeds should be exposed. But he who does what is true comes to the light, that it may be clearly seen that his deeds have been wrought in God.

                                                       −(RSV)

20   God So Loved the World

. . . He gave His only begotten Son . . . . — John 3:16

STAINER
John Stainer

John 3:16, 17

God so loved the world, God so loved the world, that He gave His on-ly be-got-ten Son, that who-so be-liev-eth, be-liev-eth in Him should not per-ish, should not per-ish but have ev-er-last-ing life. For God sent not His

GOD'S LOVE

GOD'S LOVE

21 Love Divine, All Loves Excelling

For the law of the Spirit of Life, . . . hath made us free from the law of sin and death.
— Romans 8:2 (Read Romans 7:24, 25; 8:1-5)

Charles Wesley

BEECHER
John Zundel

1 Love di-vine, all loves ex-cel-ling, Joy of heaven to earth come down,
2 *Breathe, O breathe Thy lov-ing Spir-it In - to ev-ery trou-bled breast;*
3 Come, Al-might-y to de-liv-er, Let us all Thy life re-ceive;
4 *Fin-ish then Thy new cre-a-tion, Pure and spot-less let us be;*

1 Fix in us Thy hum-ble dwell-ing, All Thy faith-ful mer-cies crown.
2 *Let us all in Thee in-her-it, Let us find Thy prom-ised rest.*
3 Sud-den-ly re-turn, and nev-er, Nev-er-more Thy tem-ples leave.
4 *Let us see Thy great sal-va-tion Per-fect-ly re-stored in Thee.*

1 Je-sus, Thou art all com-pas-sion, Pure, un-bound-ed love Thou art;
2 *Take a-way our bent to sin-ning, Al-pha and O-me-ga be;*
3 Thee we would be al-ways bless-ing, Serve Thee as Thy hosts a-bove,
4 *Changed from glo-ry in-to glo-ry, 'Til in heaven we take our place,*

1 Vis-it us with Thy sal-va-tion, En-ter ev-ery trem-bling heart.
2 *End of faith, as its be-gin-ning, Set our hearts at lib-er-ty.*
3 Pray, and praise Thee with-out ceas-ing, Glo-ry in Thy per-fect love.
4 *'Til we cast our crowns be-fore Thee, Lost in won-der, love, and praise. A-men.*

GOD'S LOVE

Arranged by Robert J. Powell

4 Fin-ish then Thy new cre-a-tion, Pure and spot-less let us be;

Let us see Thy great sal-va-tion Per-fect-ly re-stored in Thee.

Changed from glo-ry in-to glo-ry, 'Til in heaven we take our place,

'Til we cast our crowns be-fore Thee, Lost in won-der, love and praise.

GOD'S LOVE

22 One Day

When the fullness of time was come, God sent forth His son . . . . — Galatians 4:4

ONE DAY

J. Wilbur Chapman

Charles H. Marsh

1 One day when heav - en was filled with His prais - es, One day when
2 *One day they led Him up Cal - va - ry's moun-tain, One day they*
3 One day they left Him a - lone in the gar - den, One day He
4 *One day the grave could con - ceal Him no long - er, One day the*
5 One day the trum - pet will sound for His com - ing, One day the

1 sin was as black as could be, Je - sus came forth to be
2 *nailed Him to die on the tree; Suf - fer - ing an - guish, de -*
3 rest - ed, from suf - fer - ing free; An - gels came down o'er His
4 *stone rolled a - way from the door; Then He a - rose, o - ver*
5 skies with His glo - ry will shine; Won - der - ful day, my be -

1 born of a vir - gin, Dwelt a-mong men—my ex - am - ple is He!
2 *spised and re - ject - ed, Bear-ing our sins, my Re-deem-er is He!*
3 tomb to keep vig - il— Hope of the hope-less, my Sav - ior is He!
4 *death He had con-quered, Now is as - cend - ed, my Lord ev - er - more!*
5 lov - ed ones bring-ing! Glo - ri - ous Sav - ior, this Je - sus is mine!

Liv - ing, He loved me! dy - ing, He saved me! Bur - ied, He

GOD'S LOVE

car - ried my sins far a - way! Ris - ing, He jus - ti - fied

free - ly, for - ev - er! One day He's com - ing— O glo - ri - ous day!

Hosea 14 : 4b - 9

23

I will love them with all my heart,
　　for my anger has turned from them.
I will fall like dew on Israel.
　　He shall bloom like the lily,
and thrust out roots like the poplar,
　　his shoots will spread far;
he will have the beauty of the olive
　　and the fragrance of Lebanon.
They will come back to live in my shade;
　　they will grow corn that flourishes,
they will cultivate vines
　　as renowned as the wine of Helbon.
What has Ephraim to do with idols any more
　　when it is I who hear his prayer and care for him?
I am like a cypress ever green,
　　all your fruitfulness comes from me.

Let the wise men understand these words.
　　Let the intelligent man grasp their meaning.
For the ways of Jehovah are straight,
　　and virtuous men walk in them,
but sinners stumble.

—(JB)

24 O the Deep, Deep Love of Jesus

Who shall separate us from the love of Jesus? Romans 8:35

Samuel Trevor Francis

EBENEZER
Thomas J. Williams

1 O the deep, deep love of Je-sus, Vast, un-mea-sured
2 *O the deep, deep love of Je-sus— Spread His praise from*
3 O the deep, deep love of Je-sus, Love of ev-ery

1 bound-less, free! Roll-ing as a might-y o-cean In its
2 *shore to shore! How He lov-eth, ev-er lov-eth, Chang-eth*
3 love the best! 'Tis an o-cean full of bless-ing, 'Tis a

1 full-ness o-ver me! Un-der-neath me, all a-round me,
2 *nev-er, nev-er-more! How He watch-es o'er His loved ones,*
3 ha-ven giv-ing rest! O the deep, deep love of Je-sus—

1 Is the cur-rent of Thy love— Lead-ing on-ward,
2 *Died to call them all His own; How for them He*
3 'Tis a heaven of heavens to me; And it lifts me

Music copyright by Gwenlyn Evans Ltd. Used by permission.

GOD'S LOVE

1 lead-ing home-ward, To Thy glo-rious rest a-bove!
2 in - ter - ced - eth, Watch-eth o'er them from the throne!
3 up to glo - ry, For it lifts me up to Thee! A-men.

God, Thou Art Love

25

If I forget,
    Yet God remembers! If these hands of mine
Cease from their clinging, yet the hands divine
    Hold me so firmly that I cannot fall;
And if sometimes I am too tired to call
    For Him to help me, then He reads the prayer
Unspoken in my heart, and lifts my care.

I dare not fear, since certainly I know
    That I am in God's keeping, shielded so
From all that else would harm, and in the hour
    Of stern temptation strengthened by His power;
I tread no path in life to Him unknown;
    I lift no burden, bear no pain, alone:
My soul a calm, sure hiding-place has found:
    The everlasting arms my life surround.

God, Thou art love! I build my faith on that.
    I know Thee who has kept my path, and made
Light for me in the darkness, tempering sorrow
    So that it reached me like a solemn joy;
It were too strange that I should doubt Thy love.

—Robert Browning

Why Should He Love Me So?

I am not worthy of the least of Thy mercies. — Genesis 32:10

Robert Harkness

LOVE ME
Robert Harkness

1 Love sent my Sav- ior to die in my stead — Why should He love me so?
2 *Nails pierced His hands and His feet for my sin — Why should He love me so?*
3 O how He ag - o-nized there in my place — Why should He love me so?

1 Meek-ly to Cal - va-ry's cross He was led —Why should He love me so?
2 *He suf-fered sore my sal - va-tion to win—Why should He love me so?*
3 Noth-ing with-hold-ing my sin to ef-face—Why should He love me so?

Why should He love me so? Why should He love me so?

Why should my Sav-ior to Cal - va - ry go? Why should He love me so?

27 Psalm 110

God spoke to me today. He broke through my childish doubts with words of comfort and assurance. "Hang in there; sit tight; stick to My course for your life," He said, "I will not let you down."

He reminded me of how He cared for past saints, how He watched over them and kept them through their hours of suffering and uncertainty. He reviewed for me my own life, His loving concern through the days of my youth. He restated for me my commission and appointment, His trust in me as His servant in this sorry world. He reiterated His gracious promises to stand by me, to empower and support me in the conflicts that await me.

I know that God is with me today—just as surely as He was with His saints of old. I have neither to fear nor to doubt the eternal love and presence of my Lord.

—Leslie Brandt

GOD'S LOVE

Love Was When

John E. Walvoord

And the Word became flesh and dwelt among us . . . . — John 1:14

DALSEM
Don Wyrtzen

1 Love was when God be-came a man Locked in time and
  Love was God born of Jew-ish kin, Just a car-pen-
2 *Love was when God be-came a man Down where I could*
  Love was God dy-ing for my sin— And so trapped was

1 space with-out rank or place; ter with some fish-er - men. Love was when
2 *see love that reached to me; I my whole world caved in. Love was when*

1 Je-sus walked in his-to-ry— Lov-ing-ly He brought
2 *Je-sus rose to walk with me— Lov-ing-ly He brought*

1 a new life that's free; Love was God nailed to
2 *a new life that's free; Love was God— on-ly*

1 bleed and die To reach and love one such as I.
2 *He would try To reach and love one such as I.*

GOD'S LOVE

29 Wonderful Words of Life

Lord, to whom shall we go? Thou hath the words of eternal life. — John 6:68

WORDS OF LIFE

Philip P. Bliss, alt.

Philip P. Bliss

1 Sing them o-ver a-gain to me, Won-der-ful words of life;
2 *Christ, the bless-ed One, gives to all Won-der-ful words of life;*
3 Sweet-ly ech-o the gos-pel call, Won-der-ful words of life;

1 Let me more of their beau-ty see, Won-der-ful words of life.
2 *Lis-ten well to the lov-ing call, Won-der-ful words of life.*
3 Of-fer par-don and peace to all, Won-der-ful words of life.

1 Words of life and beau-ty, Teach me faith and du-ty:
2 *All the won-drous sto-ry, Show-ing us His glo-ry:*
3 Je-sus, on-ly Sav-ior, Sanc-ti-fy for-ev-er:

Beau-ti-ful words, won-der-ful words, Won-der-ful words of Life. Life.

BIBLE—WORD OF GOD

Break Thou the Bread of Life

30

Based on Matthew 14:19   *For the bread of God is He which cometh down from Heaven,*
Mary A. Lathbury, stanzas 1,2   *and giveth life unto the world.* — John 6:33
Alexander Groves, stanzas 3, 4

BREAD OF LIFE
William F. Sherwin

1 Break Thou the bread of life, Dear Lord, to me, As Thou didst
2 *Bless Thou the truth, dear Lord, To me, to me, As Thou didst*
3 Thou art the bread of life, O Lord, to me; Thy ho - ly
4 *O send Thy Spir - it, Lord, Now un - to me, That He may*

1 break the loaves Be - side the sea; Be - yond the sa - cred page
2 *bless the bread By Gal - i - lee; Then shall all bond-age cease,*
3 Word the truth That sav - eth me; Give me to eat and live
4 *touch my eyes And make me see; Show me the truth con-cealed*

1 I seek Thee, Lord; My spir - it pants for Thee, O liv - ing Word.
2 *All fet - ters fall; And I shall find my peace, My all in all.*
3 With Thee a - bove; Teach me to love Thy truth, For Thou art love.
4 *With - in Thy word, For in Thy book re-vealed I see Thee, Lord.* A-men.

Proverbs 3 : 13-26

31

Happy is the man who finds wisdom, and the man who gets understanding, for the gain from it is better than gain from silver and its profit better than gold. She is more precious than jewels, and nothing you desire can compare with her. Long life is in her right hand; in her left hand are riches and honor. Her ways are ways of pleasantness, and all her paths are peace. She is a tree of life to those who lay hold of her; those who hold her fast are called happy.

The Lord by wisdom founded the earth; by understanding He established the heavens; by His knowledge the deeps broke forth, and the clouds drop down the dew.

My son, keep sound wisdom and discretion; let them not escape from your sight, and they will be life for your soul and adornment for your neck. Then you will walk on your way securely and your foot will not stumble. If you sit down, you will not be afraid; when you lie down, your sleep will be sweet. Do not be afraid of sudden panic, or of the ruin of the wicked, when it comes; for the Lord will be your confidence and will keep your foot from being caught.

—(RSV)

BIBLE—WORD OF GOD

How Firm a Foundation

. . . And my God is the rock of my refuge. — Psalm 94:22

Based on II Timothy 2:19; Hebrews 13:5; Isaiah 43:1-2
"K" in Rippon's *Selection*, 1787

FOUNDATION
Early American Melody

1 How firm a foun - da - tion, ye saints of the Lord,
2 "Fear not, I am with thee; O be not dis - mayed,
3 "When through fier - y tri - als thy path - way shall lie,
4 "The soul that on Je - sus hath leaned for re - pose

1 Is laid for your faith in His ex - cel - lent Word!
2 For I am thy God, and will still give thee aid;
3 My grace, all suf - fi - cient, shall be thy sup - ply:
4 I will not, I will not de - sert to its foes;

1 What more can He say than to you He hath said,
2 I'll strength - en thee, help thee, and cause thee to stand,
3 The flame shall not hurt thee; I on - ly de - sign
4 That soul, though all hell should en - deav - or to shake,

1 To you who for ref - uge to Je - sus have fled?
2 Up - held by My right - eous, om - nip - o - tent hand.
3 Thy dross to con - sume and thy gold to re - fine.
4 I'll nev - er, no, nev - er, no, nev - er for - sake!"

BIBLE—WORD OF GOD

Not by Bread Alone

Man does not live by bread alone,
  but by beauty and harmony,
    truth and goodness,
      work and recreation,
        affection and friendship,
          aspiration and worship.

Man does not live by bread alone,
  but by the splendor of the starry firmament at midnight,
    the glory of the heavens at dawn,
      the gorgeous blending of colors at sunset,
        the luxuriant loveliness of magnolia trees,
          the sheer magnificence of mountains.

Man does not live by bread alone,
  but by the lyrics and sonnets of poets,
    the mature wisdom of sages,
      the holiness of saints,
        the biographies of great souls,
          the life-giving words of Holy Scripture.

Man does not live by bread alone,
  but by being faithful in prayer,
    responding to the guidance of the Holy Spirit,
      taking up the cross and following the living Christ,
        finding and doing the loving will of God now and eternally.

—Kirby Page

Holy Bible, Book Divine

Thy word is a lamp unto my feet, and a light unto my path. — Psalm 119:105

John Burton

ALETTA
William B. Bradbury

1 Ho - ly Bi - ble, book di - vine, Pre - cious treas-ure, thou art mine;
2 *Mine to chide me when I rove; Mine to show a Sav - ior's love;*
3 Mine to com-fort in dis - tress, Suf - fering in this wil - der - ness;
4 *Mine to tell of joys to come, And the reb - el sin - ner's doom;*

1 Mine to tell me whence I came; Mine to teach me which I am;
2 *Mine thou art to guide and guard; Mine to pun - ish or re - ward;*
3 Mine to show, by liv - ing faith, Man can tri-umph o - ver death;
4 *O thou ho - ly book di - vine, Pre - cious trea-sure, thou art mine.* A-men.

BIBLE—WORD OF GOD

35

Near to the Heart of God

Draw nigh to God and He will draw nigh to you. — James 4:8

McAFEE
Cleland B. McAfee   Cleland B. McAfee

1 There is a place of qui-et rest, Near to the heart of God;
2 *There is a place of com-fort sweet, Near to the heart of God;*
3 There is a place of full re-lease, Near to the heart of God;

1 A place where sin can-not mo-lest, Near to the heart of God.
2 *A place where we our Sav-ior meet, Near to the heart of God.*
3 A place where all is joy and peace, Near to the heart of God.

O Je-sus, blest Re-deem-er, Sent from the heart of God,

Hold us, who wait be-fore Thee, Near to the heart of God.

COMFORT

No One Understands Like Jesus

. . . But He knoweth the way that I take. — Job 23:10

ARIZONA
John W. Peterson

John W. Peterson

1 No one un-der-stands like Je - sus, He's a friend be-yond com-pare;
2 *No one un-der-stands like Je - sus, Ev - ery woe He sees and feels;*
3 No one un-der-stands like Je - sus, When the foes of life as - sail;
4 *No one un-der-stands like Je - sus, When you fal - ter on the way,*

1 Meet Him at the throne of mer - cy, He is wait-ing for you there.
2 *Ten - der - ly He whis-pers com-fort, And the bro-ken heart He heals.*
3 You should nev-er be dis - cour-aged, Je - sus cares and will not fail.
4 *Tho you fail Him, sad - ly fail Him, He will par-don you to - day.*

No-one un-der-stands like Je - sus, When the days are dark and grim;

No one is so near, so dear as Je - sus— Cast your ev - ery care on Him.

COMFORT

37 The Hiding Place

He shall cover thee with His feathers, and under His wings shalt thou trust...
— Psalm 91:4

HIDING PLACE
Bryan Jeffery Leech

Bryan Jeffery Leech

In a time of trou-ble, in a time for-lorn, There is a hid-ing place
In a time of dan-ger, when our faith is proved, There is a hid-ing place

where hope is born. There is a hid-ing place, a strong pro-tec-tive space,
where we are loved.

where God pro-vides the grace to per-se-vere; For noth-ing can re-move us from the

Father's love, Tho' all may change, yet nothing changes here. In a time of sor-row,
In a time of weak-ness,

in a time of grief, There is a hid-ing place to give re-lief.
in a time of fear, There is a hid-ing place where God is near. A - men.

COMFORT

The Great Physician

*Bless the Lord, O my soul . . . who forgiveth all thine iniquities
and healeth all thy diseases. — Psalm 103:1,3*

William Hunter

GREAT PHYSICIAN
John H. Stockton

1 The great Phy-si-cian now is near— The sym - pa-thiz-ing Je-sus;
2 *Your man - y sins are all for-given— O hear the voice of Je-sus;*
3 All glo - ry to the dy - ing Lamb— I now be-lieve in Je-sus;
4 *And when to that bright world a - bove We rise to be with Je-sus,*

1 He speaks the sad-dened heart to cheer— O hear the voice of Je-sus!
2 *Go on your way in peace to heaven And wear a crown with Je - sus.*
3 I love the bless-ed Sav-ior's name, I love the name of Je-sus.
4 *We'll sing a-round the throne of love His name, the name of Je-sus.*

Sweet-est note in an-gels' song! Sweet-est name on mor - tal tongue!

Sweet-est car - ol ev - er sung— Je - sus, bless - ed Je - sus!

COMFORT

39 Blessed Jesus

Sing unto the Lord, Bless His Name, ... — Psalm 96:2

Gloria Gaither

BLESSED JESUS
William J. Gaither

1 O Je - sus, You're so at the cen - ter of things,
2 *It was Your name, sweet Je - sus, our ba - by's first word,*
3 When those who have sto - len their piece of our heart,

1 Our lives are all wrapped up in You;
2 *Our old folks died prais - ing Your name;*
3 Fail, dis - ap - point - ing us so;

1 Like chil - dren we run to the arms that we know,
2 *And all in be - tween the be - gin - ning and end,*
3 You whis - per, "My child, will you too go a - way?"

1 You love us, what else could we do?
2 *Our joy, our sal - va - tion, our Friend.*
3 O Lord, to whom should we go?

COMFORT

COMFORT

40 The Lord's My Shepherd, I'll Not Want

He shall feed His flock like a shepherd.   Isaiah 40:11

Based on Psalm 23
Scottish Psalter

(FIRST TUNE)

CRIMOND
Jessie S. Irvine

1 The Lord's my shep-herd, I'll not want; He makes me down to lie
2 *My soul He doth re - store a - gain, And me to walk doth make*
3 Yea, though I walk in death's dark vale, Yet will I fear no ill,
4 *My ta - ble Thou hast fur - nish - ed In pres - ence of my foes;*
5 Good-ness and mer - cy all my life Shall sure - ly fol - low me,

1 In pas-tures green; He lead - eth me The qui - et wa - ters by.
2 *With-in the paths of right-eous-ness, E'en for His own name's sake.*
3 For Thou art with me, and Thy rod And staff me com-fort still.
4 *My head Thou dost with oil a - noint, And my cup o - ver-flows.*
5 And in God's house for - ev - er - more My dwell-ing place shall be. A-men.

41   Psalm 23

The Lord is my shepherd; I shall not want.

He maketh me to lie down in green pastures:
He leadeth me beside the still waters.

He restoreth my soul:
He leadeth me in the paths of righteousness for His name's sake.

Yea, though I walk through the valley of the shadow of death,
I will fear no evil: for Thou art with me;

Thy rod and Thy staff, they comfort me.
Thou preparest a table before me in the presence of mine enemies:

Thou annointest my head with oil;
My cup runneth over!

Surely goodness and mercy shall follow me all the days of my life:
And I will dwell in the house of the Lord forever.

                        —Psalm 23 (KJV)

COMFORT

The Lord's My Shepherd, I'll Not Want

The Lord Is My Shepherd — Psalm 23

Based on Psalm 23
Scottish Psalter

(SECOND TUNE)

BROTHER JAMES' AIR
Traditional

1 The Lord's my Shep-herd, I'll not want, He makes me down to lie
2 *My soul He doth re-store a-gain, And me to walk doth make*
3 Yea, though I walk through shad-owed vale, Yet will I fear no ill,
4 *My ta-ble Thou hast fur-nished In pres-ence of my foes.*
5 Good-ness and mer-cy all my days Shall sure-ly fol-low me,

1 In pas-tures green, He lead-eth me The si-lent wa-ters by;
2 *With-in the paths of bless-ed-ness, E'en for His own name's sake;*
3 For Thou art with me and Thy rod And staff me com-fort still;
4 *My head with oil Thou dost a-noint, And my cup o-ver-flows;*
5 And in my Fa-ther's house al-ways My dwell-ing place shall be;

1 He lead-eth me, He lead-eth me The si-lent wa-ters by.
2 *With-in the paths of bless-ed-ness E'en for His own name's sake.*
3 Thy rod and staff me com-fort still, Me com-fort still.
4 *My head with oil Thou dost a-noint, And my cup o-ver-flows.*
5 And in my heart for-ev-er-more Thy dwell-ing place shall be.

COMFORT

43 Through It All

He delivereth me . . . therefore shall I give thanks. — Psalm 18:48,49

THROUGH IT ALL
Andraé Crouch

Andraé Crouch

1 I've had man-y tears and sor-rows, I've had ques-tions for to-
2 *I've been to lots of plac-es, And I've seen a lot of*
3 I thank God for the moun-tains, And I thank Him for the

1 mor-row, There've been times I did-n't know right from wrong;
2 *fac-es, There've been times I felt so all a-lone;*
3 val-leys, I thank Him for the storms He brought me through;

1 But in ev-ery sit-u-a-tion God gave bless-ed con-so-
2 *But in my lone-ly hours, Yes, those pre-cious lone-ly*
3 For if I'd nev-er had a prob-lem I would-n't know that

1 la-tion That my tri-als come to on-ly make me strong.
2 *hours, Je-sus let me know that I was His own.*
3 He could solve them, I'd nev-er know what faith in God could do.

Through it all, Through it all, I've learned to trust in

COMFORT

Je - sus, I've learned to trust in God; Through it all,

Through it all, I've learned to de - pend up-on His Word.

Prayer for Comfort 44

Jesus, our Master, whose heart was moved with compassion toward the weak and oppressed, and who was more willing to serve than to be served; we pray for all conditions of people:

for those lacking food, shelter, or clothing;
for the sick and all who are wasting away by disease;
for the blind, deaf, and lame;
for prisoners;
for those oppressed by injustice;
for those who have lost their way in society;
for the corrupted and morally fallen;
for the lonely and depressed;
for the worried and anxious;
for all living faithfully in obscurity;
for those fighting bravely in unpopular wars or causes;
for all who are serving diligently and dependably;
for those who stand in the valley of decision;
for those who are suffering the consequences of misdeeds repented of;
for all family circles broken by death;
for those faced by tasks too great for their powers.

Let the power of Jesus' spirit be strong within us, and those for whom we pray. Amen.

—James L. Christensen

45   For Loneliness in Bereavement

Father, I am only human. I need the touch of human companionship. Sorely I miss those I love who are with Thee.

I pray, O Jesus, that Thou wilt reveal to me unseen presences. Help me to know how close my loved ones are. For if they are with Thee, and Thou art with me, I know that they cannot be far away.

Make real for me that contact of spirit with spirit that will re-establish the lost fellowship for which my heart yearns.

Give to me faith shining through my tears.

Plant peace and hope within my heart.

Point me with joy to the great reunion.

But until then, enable me to live happily and worthily of those who are with Thee. In the Name of Him who is the Lord of Life, I pray, Amen.

—Peter Marshall

46   They That Sow in Tears

Gloria Gaither
William J. Gaither

They that sow in tears shall reap in joy. — Psalm 126:5

THEY THAT SOW IN TEARS
William J. Gaither

1 Though it seems that your prayers have been in vain, Though your
2 *Though the mists of de-spair cloud the sky a - bove, Do you*
3 Does your heart fill with doubt when a - lone you pray? Does the

1 faith the world would de-stroy, Though your heart should ache 'til it
2 *pray 'til His face ap - pears? In your heart do you know that you've*
3 world your soul an - noy? Lift your sights! Look be-yond! God is

1 breaks in two, They that sow in tears shall reap in joy.
2 *touched the throne? They shall reap in joy who sow in tears.*
3 stand - ing near! They that sow in tears shall reap in joy.

COMFORT

They that sow in tears shall reap in joy, For God is on His throne, Though you've prayed 'til it seems that your heart would break, They that sow in tears shall reap in joy!

Joy at All Times

We must recognize that there is all the difference in the world between rejoicing and feeling happy. The Scripture tells us that we should always rejoice. Take the lyrical Epistle of Paul to the Philippians where he says: "Rejoice in the Lord always and again I say rejoice". He goes on saying it. To rejoice is a command, yes, but there is all the difference in the world between rejoicing and being happy. You cannot make yourself happy, but you can make yourself rejoice, in the sense that you will always rejoice in the Lord. Happiness is something within ourselves, rejoicing is "in the Lord". How important it is then, to draw the distinction between rejoicing in the Lord and feeling happy. Take the fourth chapter of the Second Epistle to the Corinthians. There you will find that the great Apostle puts it all very plainly and clearly in that series of extraordinary contrasts which he makes: "We are troubled on every side (I don't think he felt very happy at the moment) yet not distressed", "we are perplexed (he wasn't feeling happy at all at that point) but not in despair", "persecuted but not forsaken", "cast down, but not destroyed"—and so on. In other words the Apostle does not suggest a kind of happy person in a carnal sense, but he was still rejoicing. That is the difference between the two conditions.

—Martin Lloyd-Jones

COMFORT

There Is a Balm in Gilead

Go up to Gilead and take balm . . . .

Jeremiah 8:22

BALM IN GILEAD
Traditional Spiritual

There is a balm in Gil-e-ad to make the wound-ed whole;

Fine

There is a balm in Gil-e-ad to heal the sin-sick soul.

1 Some-times I feel dis-cour-aged, And think my work's in vain,
2 *If you can't preach like Pet-er, If you can't pray like Paul,*

D.C. al Fine

1 But then the Ho-ly Spir-it Re-vives my soul a-gain.
2 *Just tell the love of Je-sus, And say He died for all.*

COMFORT

I Must Tell Jesus

. . . by prayer . . . with thanksgiving let your requests be made known unto God.
— Philippians 4:6

ORWIGSBURG
Elisha A. Hoffman

Elisha A. Hoffman

1. I must tell Jesus all of my tri-als, I can-not bear these
2. *I must tell Je-sus all of my trou-bles, He is a kind, com-*
3. Tempt-ed and tried, I need a great Sav-ior, One who can help my
4. *O how the world of e-vil al-lures me! O how my heart is*

1. bur-dens a-lone; In my dis-tress He kind-ly will help me,
2. *pas-sion-ate friend; If I but ask Him, He will de-liv-er,*
3. bur-dens to bear; I must tell Je-sus, I must tell Je-sus,
4. *tempt-ed to sin! I must tell Je-sus, and He will help me*

1. He al-ways loves and cares for His own.
2. *Make of my trou-bles quick-ly an end.* I must tell Je-sus!
3. He all my cares and sor-rows will share.
4. *O-ver the world the vic-tory to win.*

I must tell Je-sus! I can-not bear my bur-dens a-lone; I must tell

Je-sus! I must tell Je-sus! Je-sus can help me, Je-sus a-lone.

COMFORT

God Is For Us

Minister: *What can we ever say to such wonderful things as these?*

People: If God is on our side, who can ever be against us?

Minister: *Since He did not spare even His own Son for us*
but gave Him up for us all,
won't He also surely give us everything else?
Who dares accuse us whom God has chosen for His own?
Will God?

People: No!
He is the one who has forgiven us
and given us right standing with Himself.

Minister: *Who then will condemn us?*
Will Christ?

People: No!
For He is the one who died for us
and came back to life again for us
and is sitting at the place of highest honor next to God,
pleading for us there in Heaven.

Minister: *Who then can ever keep Christ's love from us?*
When we have trouble or calamity,
when we are hunted down or destroyed,
is it because He doesn't love us anymore?
And if we are hungry, or penniless, or in danger, or threatened with death,
has God deserted us?

People: No,
for the Scriptures tell us that for His sake
we must be ready to face death at every moment of the day—
we are like sheep awaiting slaughter;
but despite all this,
the overwhelming victory is ours through Christ who loved us enough to die for us.

All: For I am convinced that nothing can ever separate us from His love.
Death can't, and life can't.
The angels won't, and all the powers of hell itself cannot keep God's love away!
Our fears for today,
our worries about tomorrow,
or where we are—high above the sky, or in the deepest ocean—
nothing will ever be able to separate us from the love of God
demonstrated by our Lord Jesus Christ when He died for us.

—Romans 8:28-39 (LB)

I Heard the Voice of Jesus Say 51

Come unto Me all ye who labor and are heavy laden
and I will give you rest. — Matthew 11:28

Horatius Bonar

VOX DILECTI
John B. Dykes

1 I heard the voice of Je - sus say, "Come un - to me and rest;
2 *I heard the voice of Je - sus say, "Be - hold, I free - ly give*
3 I heard the voice of Je - sus say, "I am this dark world's light;

1 Lay down, thou wea-ry one, lay down Thy head up - on my breast."
2 *The liv - ing wa - ter—thirst - y one, Stoop down, and drink, and live."*
3 Look un - to me—thy morn shall rise, And all thy day be bright."

1 I came to Je - sus as I was, Wea - ry, and worn, and sad;
2 *I came to Je - sus, and I drank Of that life - giv - ing stream;*
3 I looked to Je - sus, and I found In Him my star, my sun;

1 I found in Him a rest - ing place, And He has made me glad.
2 *My thirst was quenched, my soul re-vived, And now I live in Him.*
3 And in that light of life I'll walk, 'Til trav-eling days are done.

COMFORT

52

They that Wait upon the Lord

They that wait upon the Lord . . .
shall mount up with wings as eagles . . . . — Isaiah 40:31

Isaiah 40:31
Stuart Hamblen

TEACH ME LORD
Stuart Hamblen

They that wait up-on the Lord shall re - new their strength;

They shall mount up with wings like ea - gles;

They shall run, and not be wea - ry; They shall walk, and not faint.

Teach me, Lord, teach me, Lord, to wait.

COMFORT

Cast Thy Burden upon the Lord

53

Cast thy burden upon the Lord . . . . — Psalm 55:22

CAST THY BURDEN
From *Elijah*
Felix Mendelssohn

Based on Psalm 55:22

Cast thy bur - den up - on the Lord, and He shall sus -

tain thee; He nev - er will suf - fer the right-eous to fall:

He is at thy right hand. Thy mer - cy, Lord, is

great and far a - bove the heav'ns: Let none be made a -

sham - ed that wait up - on Thee. A - men.

COMFORT

54   There Has to Be a Song

There has to be a song —

> There are too many dark nights,
>> too many troublesome days,
>> too many wearisome miles,

There has to be a song—

> To make our burdens bearable,
> To make our hopes believable,
> To transform our successes into praise,
> To release the chains of past defeats,
> Somewhere—down deep in a forgotten corner of each man's
> heart—

There has to be a song —

> Like a cool, clear drink of water,
> Like the gentle warmth of sunshine,
> Like the tender love of a child,

There has to be a song.

—Robert Benson

55   A Prayer for Strength

O God, You have given us life through Your Son, Jesus Christ. You have given us the security of faith in a world that longs for something on which to rely. We thank You for Your gifts to us.

Teach us to stand strong for Your Kingdom: to be free in this world in order to be Christ's men and women.

Help us to know Your love and the love of each other. Set us free to become our true selves because we are loved, and to free others because we love.

Give us enough tests to make us strong;
> enough vision and endurance to follow Your way;
> enough patience to persist when the going is difficult;
> enough of reality to know our weaknesses;
> and enough humility to know these gifts come from You.

Go before us to prepare the way;
> walk behind us to be our protection;
> and walk beside us to be our companion,

through Christ our Lord, Amen.

—Richard Langford

God Will Take Care of You

... *I will never leave thee or forsake thee.* — Hebrews 13:5

56

Civilla D. Martin, alt.

GOD CARES
W. Stillman Martin

1 Be not dis-mayed what-e'er be-tide, God will take care of you;
2 *Through days of toil when your heart doth fail,* God will take care of you;
3 All you may need He will pro-vide, God will take care of you;
4 *No mat-ter what may be the test,* God will take care of you;

1 Be - neath His wings of love a - bide, God will take care of you.
2 *When dan-gers fierce your path as - sail,* God will take care of you.
3 Noth - ing you ask will be de - nied, God will take care of you.
4 *Lean, wea - ry one, up - on His breast,* God will take care of you.

God will take care of you, Through ev - ery day, o'er all the way;

He will take care of you, God will take care of you.

COMFORT

57

John 14:1-12

"Do not let your hearts be troubled.
Trust in God still, and trust in Me.

There are many rooms in my Father's house;
if there were not, I should have told you.
I am going now to prepare a place for you,
and after I have gone and prepared you a place,
I shall return to take you with Me;
so that where I am
you may be too.
You know the way to the place where I am going."

Thomas said,
"Lord, we do not know where You are going,
so how can we know the way?"

Jesus said:
"I am the Way, the Truth and the Life.
No one can come to the Father except through Me.
If you know Me,
you know my Father too.

From this moment you know Him and have seen Him."

Philip said,
"Lord, let us see the Father
and then we shall be satisfied".

"Have I been with you all this time, Philip," said Jesus to him, "and you still do not know me?"
"To have seen me is to have seen the Father,
so how can you say, 'Let us see the Father'?
Do you not believe that I am in the Father and the Father is in Me?

The words I say to you I do not speak as from Myself:
it is the Father, living in Me, who is doing this work.
You must believe Me when I say that I am in the Father and the Father is in Me;
believe it on the evidence of this work, if for no other reason.

I tell you most solemnly,
whoever believes in Me will perform the same works as I do Myself,
he will perform even greater works."

—(JB)

58

Sitting at the Feet of Jesus

. . . Mary hath chosen the good part which shall not be taken away from her. — Luke 10:42

COMFORT
Asa Hull

Author Unknown

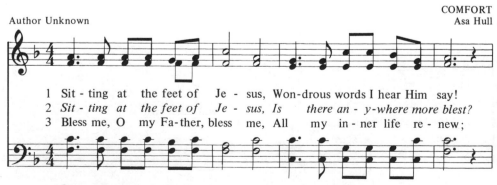

1 Sit - ting at the feet of Je - sus, Won-drous words I hear Him say!
2 *Sit - ting at the feet of Je - sus, Is there an - y-where more blest?*
3 Bless me, O my Fa - ther, bless me, All my in - ner life re - new;

COMFORT

1 Hap-py place! so near, so pre-cious! May it find me there each day.
2 *There I lay my sins and sor-rows, And when wea-ry, find His rest.*
3 Now look down in love up-on me, Let me catch a glimpse of You.

1 Sit-ting at the feet of Je-sus, I re-flect up-on the past;
2 *Sit-ting at the feet of Je-sus, There I wor-ship and I pray,*
3 Give me, Lord, the mind of Je-sus, Make me ho-ly through His Word.

1 For His love has been so gra-cious, It has won my heart at last.
2 *While I from His full-ness gath-er Grace and com-fort for to-day.*
3 May I prove I've been with Je-sus, Been with Him, my ris-en Lord.

Plans While in Prison   59

"The most important part of our task will be to tell everyone who will listen that Jesus is the only answer to the problems that are disturbing the hearts of men and nations. We shall have the right to speak because we can tell from our experience that His light is more powerful than the deepest darkness. . . How wonderful that the reality of His presence is greater than the reality of the hell about us."

—Betsie ten Boom, to her sister, Corrie

COMFORT

60 Burdens Are Lifted at Calvary

For when we were yet without strength Christ died for the ungodly. — Romans 5:6

John M. Moore

BURDENS LIFTED
John M. Moore

Slowly

1 Days are filled with sor - row and care, Hearts are lone-ly and drear;
2 *Cast your care on Je-sus to-day, Leave your wor-ry and fear;*
3 Trou-bled soul, the Sav-ior can see Ev - ery heart-ache and tear;

1 Bur-dens are lift - ed at Cal - va-ry, Je-sus is ver - ry near.
2 *Bur-dens are lift - ed at Cal - va-ry, Je-sus is ver - ry near.*
3 Bur-dens are lift - ed at Cal - va-ry, Je-sus is ver - ry near.

Bur-dens are lift - ed at Cal - va-ry, Cal - va-ry, Cal - va-ry;

Bur-dens are lift - ed at Cal - va-ry, Je-sus is ver - y near.

COMFORT

Like a Lamb Who Needs the Shepherd

61

He shall feed His flock like a shepherd; He shall gather His lambs with His arms.
— Isaiah 40:11

Ralph Carmichael

LIKE A LAMB
Ralph Carmichael

1 Where He leads me I must fol - low, With - out Him I'd
2 *Life is like a wind - ing path - way, Who can tell what*
3 Though you walk through dark - est val - leys And the sky is

1 lose my way. I will see a bright to - mor - row
2 *lies a - head? Will it lead to shad - y pas - tures,*
3 cold and gray, Though you climb the steep - est moun - tains

1 If I fol - low Him to - day. Like a lamb who
2 *Or to wild - er - ness in - stead? Like a lamb who*
3 He will nev - er let you stray. Like a lamb who

1 needs the Shep - herd, At His side I'll al - ways stay. Through the
2 *needs the Shep - herd, When in - to the night I go, Help me*
3 needs the Shep - herd, By your side He'll al - ways stay. 'Til the

1 night His strength I'll bor - row, Then I'll see an - oth - er day.
2 *find the path that's nar - row, While I trav - el here be - low.*
3 end of life's long jour - ney He will lead you all the way.

COMFORT

62

Sun of My Soul

The darkness and the light are the same to Thee. — Psalm 139:12

John Keble, alt.

HURSLEY
From *Katholisches Gesangbuch*

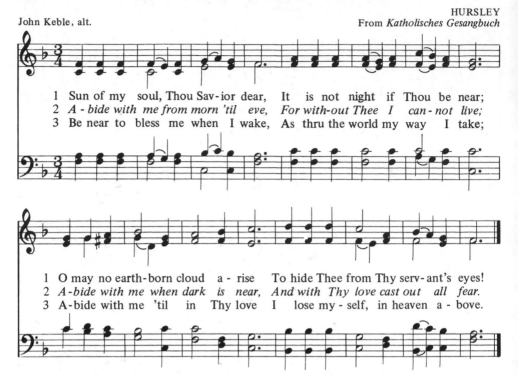

1 Sun of my soul, Thou Sav-ior dear, It is not night if Thou be near;
2 *A - bide with me from morn 'til eve, For with-out Thee I can - not live;*
3 Be near to bless me when I wake, As thru the world my way I take;

1 O may no earth-born cloud a - rise To hide Thee from Thy serv - ant's eyes!
2 *A - bide with me when dark is near, And with Thy love cast out all fear.*
3 A - bide with me 'til in Thy love I lose my - self, in heaven a - bove.

63

II Corinthians 4:6-12

For God who said, "Let light shine out of darkness," made His light shine in our hearts to give us the light of the knowledge of the glory of God in the face of Christ.

But we have this treasure in jars of clay to show that this all-surpassing power is from God and not from us. We are hard pressed on every side, but not crushed;

> perplexed, but not in despair;
>
> persecuted, but not abandoned;
>
> struck down, but not destroyed.

We always carry around in our body the death of Jesus, so that the life of Jesus may also be revealed in our body. For we who are alive are always being given over to death for Jesus' sake, so that His life may be revealed in our mortal body. So then, death is at work in us, but life is at work in you.

—(NIV)

COMFORT

Peace I Leave with You

Thou wilt keep him in perfect peace whose mind is stayed on Thee. — Isaiah 26:3

Richard Maxwell

PEACE I GIVE
William Wirges

1 Peace I leave with you; My peace I give un-to
2 *Peace I leave with you; My peace I give un-to*

1 you. Not as the world giv-eth, give I un-to you;
2 *you. Keep my com-mand-ments if you love me;*

1 Not as the world giv-eth, give I un-to you. Let not your heart be
2 *Keep my com-mand-ments, if you love Me. For I will not leave you*

1 trou-bled; Nei-ther let it be a-fraid. Peace I leave with
2 *com-fort-less; I will come un-to you. Peace I leave with*

1 you; My peace I give un-to you.
2 *you; My peace I give un-to you.* A-men.

COMFORT

65 Moment by Moment

But the Lord is faithful, who shall stablish you and keep you . . . .
— II Thessalonians 3:3

Daniel W. Whittle

WHITTLE
May W. Moody

1 Dy-ing with Je-sus, by death reck-oned mine, Liv-ing with Je-sus a
2 *Nev-er a tri-al that He is not there, Nev-er a bur-den that*
3 Nev-er a heart-ache and nev-er a groan, Nev-er a tear-drop and
4 *Nev-er a weak-ness that He doth not feel, Nev-er a sick-ness that*

1 new life di-vine, Look-ing to Je-sus 'til glo-ry doth shine,—Mo-ment by
2 *He doth not bear, Nev-er a sor-row that He doth not share,—Mo-ment by*
3 nev-er a moan; Nev-er a dan-ger, but there on the throne, Mo-ment by
4 *He can-not heal; Mo-ment by mo-ment, in woe or in weal, Je-sus, my*

1 mo-ment, O Lord, I am Thine.
2 *mo-ment, I'm un-der His care.*
3 mo-ment, He thinks of His own.
4 Sav-ior, a-bides with me still.

Mo-ment by mo-ment I'm kept in His love,

Mo-ment by mo-ment I've life from a-bove; Look-ing to Je-sus 'til

glo-ry doth shine, Mo-ment by mo-ment, O Lord, I am Thine.

ASSURANCE

My Shepherd Will Supply My Need

66

My beloved is mine and I am his; he feedeth among the lilies.
— Song of Solomon 2:16

Psalm 23, paraphrased
Isaac Watts

RESIGNATION
Traditional American Melody
Arranged by Fred Bock

1 My Shep - herd will sup - ply my need: Je - ho - vah is His
2 *When I walk through the shades of death His pres - ence is my*
3 The sure pro - vi - sions of my God At - tend me all my

1 name; In pas - tures fresh He makes me feed, Be - side the
2 *stay; One word of His sup - port - ing grace Drives all my*
3 days; O may Thy house be my a - bode, And all my

1 liv - ing stream. He brings my wan - dering spir - it back
2 *fears a - way. His hand, in sight of all my foes,*
3 work be praise. There would I find a set - tled rest,

1 When I for - sake His ways, And leads me, for His
2 *Doth still my ta - ble spread; My cup with bless - ings*
3 While oth - ers go and come; No more a strang - er,

1 mer - cy's sake, In paths of truth and grace.
2 *o - ver - flows, His oil a - noints my head.*
3 nor a guest, But like a child at home. A - men.

ASSURANCE

67 Blessed Assurance, Jesus Is Mine

. . . . Whereof He hath given assurance unto all men that He hath raised Him from the dead. — Acts 17:31

Fanny J. Crosby

ASSURANCE
Phoebe P. Knapp

1 Bless-ed as-sur-ance, Je-sus is mine! O what a fore-taste of
2 *Per-fect sub-mis-sion, per-fect de-light,* *Vi-sions of rap-ture now*
3 Per-fect sub-mis-sion, all is at rest, I in my Sav-ior am

1 glo-ry di-vine! Heir of sal-va-tion, pur-chase of God,
2 *burst on my sight;* *An-gels de-scend-ing bring from a-bove*
3 hap-py and blest; Watch-ing and wait-ing, look-ing a-bove,

1 Born of His Spir-it, washed in His blood.
2 *Ech-oes of mer-cy, whis-pers of love.* This is my sto-ry, this is my
3 Filled with His good-ness, lost in His love.

song, Prais-ing my Sav-ior all the day long; This is my sto-ry,

this is my song, Prais-ing my Sav-ior all the day long.

ASSURANCE

Arranged by Ovid Young

This is my sto - ry, this is my song, Prais - ing my

Sav - ior all the day long; This is my sto - ry, this is my

song, Prais - ing my Sav - ior, all the day long.

ll Corinthians 12:1-10   68

It is not expedient for me doubtless to glory. I will come to visions and revelations of the Lord. I knew a man in Christ above fourteen years ago, (whether in the body, I cannot tell; or whether out of the body, I cannot tell: God knoweth;) such a one caught up to the third heaven. And I knew such a man, (whether in the body, or out of the body, I cannot tell: God knoweth;) How that he was caught up into paradise, and heard unspeakable words which it is not lawful for a man to utter. Of such a one will I glory; yet of myself I will not glory, but in mine infirmities. For though I would desire to glory, I shall not be a fool; for I will say the truth: but *now* I forbear, lest any man should think of me above that which he seeth me *to be,* or *that* he heareth of me. And lest I should be exalted above measure through the abundance of the revelations, there was given to me a thorn in the flesh, the messenger of Satan to buffet me, lest I should be exalted above measure. For this thing I besought the Lord thrice, that it might depart from me. And He said unto me, My grace is sufficient for thee: for My strength is made perfect in weakness. Most gladly therefore will I rather glory in my infirmities, that the power of Christ may rest upon me. Therefore I take pleasure in infirmities, in reproaches, in necessities, in persecutions, in distresses for Christ's sake: for when I am weak, then am I strong.

—(KJV)

ASSURANCE

69 Standing on the Promises

For all the promises of God are "yes," and in him "Amen".... — II Corinthians 1:20

R. Kelso Carter

TURLOCK
Norman E. Johnson

Unison

1 Stand - ing on the prom - is - es of Christ my King,
2 *Stand - ing on the prom - is - es that can - not fail,*
3 Stand - ing on the prom - is - es of Christ the Lord,
4 *Stand - ing on the prom - is - es I can - not fall,*

1 Through e - ter - nal a - ges let His prais - es ring! Glo - ry in the
2 *When the howl-ing storms of doubt and fear as - sail; By the liv - ing*
3 Bound to Him e - ter - nal - ly by love's strong cord, O - ver-com-ing
4 *Lis - tening ev - ery mo - ment to the Spir - it's call, Rest - ing in my*

1 high - est I will shout and sing— Stand - ing on the prom-is - es of
2 *word of God I shall pre - vail— Stand - ing on the prom-is - es of*
3 dai - ly with the Spir - it's sword— Stand - ing on the prom-is - es of
4 *Sav - ior as my all in all— Stand - ing on the prom-is - es of*

1 God, Stand - ing on the prom - is - es of God!
2 *God, Stand - ing on the prom - is - es of God!*
3 God, Stand - ing on the prom - is - es of God!
4 *God, Stand - ing on the prom - is - es of God!*

ASSURANCE

Hiding in Thee

For Thou has been a shelter for me, and a strong tower from the enemy.
— Psalm 61:3

William O. Cushing

HIDING IN THEE
Ira D. Sankey

1 O safe to the Rock that is high-er than I My
2 *In the calm of the noon-tide, in sor-row's lone hour, In*
3 How oft-en in con-flict, when pressed by the foe, I have

1 soul in its con-flicts and sor-rows would fly; So sin-ful, so
2 *times when temp-ta-tion casts o'er me its power, In the tem-pests of*
3 fled to my Ref-uge and breathed out my woe; How oft-en, when

1 wea-ry—Thine, Thine would I be: Thou blest "Rock of A-ges," I'm
2 *life, on its wide, heav-ing sea, Thou blest "Rock of A-ges," I'm*
3 tri-als like sea-bil-lows roll, Have I hid-den in Thee, O Thou

1 hid-ing in Thee.
2 *hid-ing in Thee.* Hid-ing in Thee, Hid-ing in
3 Rock of my soul.

Thee, Thou blest "Rock of A-ges," I'm hid-ing in Thee.

ASSURANCE

71 Faith Is the Victory

.... for this is the victory that overcometh the world, even our faith. — I John 5:4

John H. Yates

FAITH IS THE VICTORY
Ira D. Sankey

1 En-camped a-long the hills of light, Ye Chris-tian sol-diers, rise, And
2 *His ban-ner o-ver us is love, Our sword the Word of God; We*
3 On ev-ery hand the foe we find Drawn up in dread ar-ray; Let
4 *To him that o-ver-comes the foe, White rai-ment shall be-given; Be-*

1 press the bat-tle ere the night Shall veil the glow-ing skies. A-gainst the foe in
2 *tread the road the saints a-bove With shouts of tri-umph trod. By faith they like a*
3 tents of ease be left be-hind, And on-ward to the fray. Sal-va-tion's hel-met
4 *fore the an-gels he shall know His name con-fessed in heaven. Then onward from the*

1 vales be-low Let all our strength be hurled; Faith is the vic-to-ry, we know,
2 *whirlwind's breath, Swept on o'er ev-ery field; The faith by which they conquer'd death*
3 on each head, With truth all girt a-bout, The earth shall tremble 'neath our tread,
4 *hills of light, Our hearts with love a-flame; We'll van-quish all the hosts of night,*

1 That o-ver-comes the world.
2 *Is still our shin-ing shield.*
3 And ech-o with our shout.
4 *In Je-sus' con-qu'ring name.*

Faith is the vic-to-ry! Faith is the

ASSURANCE

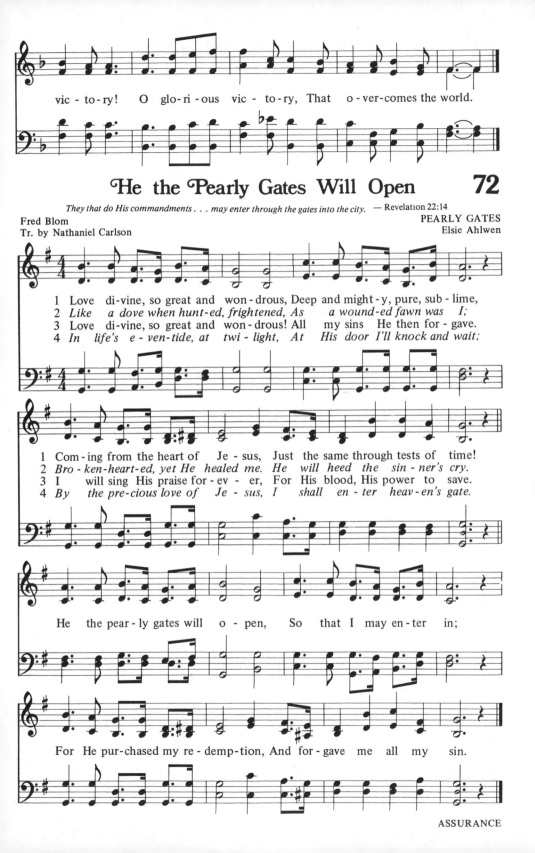

vic - to - ry! O glo - ri - ous vic - to - ry, That o - ver - comes the world.

He the Pearly Gates Will Open 72

They that do His commandments . . . may enter through the gates into the city. — Revelation 22:14

Fred Blom
Tr. by Nathaniel Carlson

PEARLY GATES
Elsie Ahlwen

1 Love di - vine, so great and won - drous, Deep and might - y, pure, sub - lime,
2 *Like a dove when hunt - ed, frightened, As a wound-ed fawn was I;*
3 Love di - vine, so great and won - drous! All my sins He then for - gave.
4 *In life's e - ven - tide, at twi - light, At His door I'll knock and wait;*

1 Com - ing from the heart of Je - sus, Just the same through tests of time!
2 *Bro - ken - heart - ed, yet He healed me. He will heed the sin - ner's cry.*
3 I will sing His praise for - ev - er, For His blood, His power to save.
4 *By the pre - cious love of Je - sus, I shall en - ter heav - en's gate.*

He the pear - ly gates will o - pen, So that I may en - ter in;

For He pur - chased my re - demp - tion, And for - gave me all my sin.

ASSURANCE

73 I Am Trusting Thee, Lord Jesus

Trust in the Lord and do good, so shall thou dwell in the land . . . . and be fed. — Psalm 37:3

BULLINGER

Frances Ridley Havergal

Ethelbert W. Bullinger

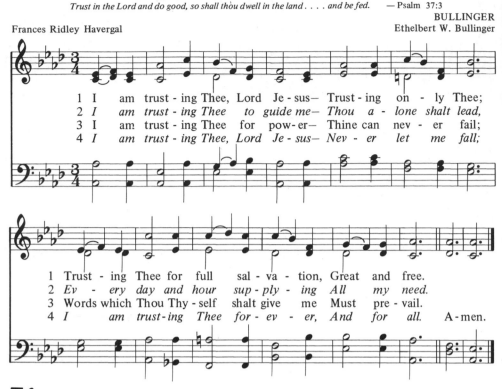

1 I am trust-ing Thee, Lord Je-sus— Trust-ing on - ly Thee;
2 *I am trust - ing Thee to guide me— Thou a - lone shalt lead,*
3 I am trust - ing Thee for pow-er— Thine can nev - er fail.
4 *I am trust - ing Thee, Lord Je - sus— Nev - er let me fall;*

1 Trust - ing Thee for full sal - va - tion, Great and free.
2 *Ev - ery day and hour sup - ply - ing All my need.*
3 Words which Thou Thy - self shalt give me Must pre - vail.
4 *I am trust-ing Thee for - ev - er, And for all.* A - men.

74

A Pledge of Trust

Father, during this coming week there may be times when I shall not be able to sense Your presence or to be aware of Your nearness.

When I am lonely and by myself
I TRUST YOU TO BE MY COMPANION.

When I am tempted to sin
I TRUST YOU TO KEEP ME FROM IT.

When I am depressed and anxious
I TRUST YOU TO LIFT MY SPIRITS.

When I am crushed by responsibility and overwhelmed by the demands of people on my time,
I TRUST YOU TO GIVE ME POISE AND A SENSE OF PURPOSE.

When I am rushed and running
I TRUST YOU TO MAKE ME STILL IN-SIDE.

When I forget You
I TRUST THAT YOU WILL NEVER FOR-GET ME.

When I forget others
I TRUST YOU TO PROMPT ME TO THINK OF THEM.

When You take something or someone from me that I want to keep; when You re-move the props I lean on for comfort in place of You; when You refuse to respond to my questions and to answer my too-selfish prayers, I will trust You even then. Amen.

—Bryan Jeffery Leech

ASSURANCE

My Faith Has Found a Resting Place

Let us labor, therefore, to enter into that rest. — Hebrews 4:11

NO OTHER PLEA
Norwegian Melody

Lidie H. Edmunds

1 My faith has found a rest-ing place, Not in a man-made creed;
2 E - nough for me that Je - sus saves, This ends my fear and doubt;
3 My soul is rest - ing on the Word, The liv - ing Word of God:
4 *The great Phy - si - cian heals the sick, The lost He came to save;*

1 I trust the ev - er liv - ing One, That He for me will plead.
2 *A sin - ful soul I come to Him, He will not cast me out.*
3 Sal - va - tion in my Sav - ior's name, Sal - va - tion through His blood.
4 *For me His pre - cious blood He shed, For me His life He gave.*

I need no oth - er ev - i - dence, I need no oth - er plea;

It is e - nough that Je - sus died And rose a - gain for me.

ASSURANCE

76 Yesterday, Today, and Tomorrow

Jack Wyrtzen

Don Wyrtzen

Jesus Christ, the same yesterday, today, and forever.
– Hebrews 13:8

YESTERDAY-TODAY-TOMORROW

Yes-ter-day He died for me, yes-ter-day, yes-ter-day,

Yes-ter-day He died for me, yes-ter-day, Yes-ter-day He

died for me, died for me— This is his-to-ry.

To-day He lives for me, to-day, to-day, To-day He

lives for me, to-day, To-day He lives for me, lives for me—

This is vic-to-ry. To-mor-row He comes for me,

He comes, He comes, To-mor-row He comes for me, He comes,

To-mor-row He comes for me, comes for me— This is mys-ter-

y. O friend, do you know Him? know Him?

know Him? O friend, do you know Him? know Him? O friend, do

you know Him? do you know Him? Je - sus Christ the Lord,

Je - sus Christ the Lord, Je - sus Christ the Lord.

ASSURANCE

77 Be Still My Soul

Be still and know that I am God. — Psalm 46:10

Katharina von Schlegel
Tr. by Jane L. Borthwick

FINLANDIA
Jean Sibelius

1 Be still, my soul! the Lord is on thy side; Bear pa-tient-ly the
2 *Be still, my soul! thy God doth un-der-take To guide the fu-ture*
3 Be still, my soul! the hour is has-tening on When we shall be for-

1 cross of grief or pain; Leave to thy God to or-der and pro-vide;
2 *as He has the past. Thy hope, thy con-fi-dence let noth-ing shake;*
3 ev-er with the Lord, When dis-ap-point-ment, grief, and fear are gone,

1 In ev-ery change He faith-ful will re-main. Be still, my soul! thy
2 *All now mys-te-rious shall be bright at last. Be still, my soul! the*
3 Sor-row for-got, love's pur-est joys re-stored. Be still, my soul! when

1 best, thy heaven-ly Friend Through thorny ways leads to a joy-ful end.
2 *waves and winds still know His voice who ruled them while He dwelt be-low.*
3 change and tears are past, All safe and bless-ed we shall meet at last.

Melody used by permission of Breitkoph & Härtel, Wiesbaden. Arrangement © Copyright 1933 by Presbyterian Board of Christian Education, renewed 1961; from "The Hymnbook": used by permission of The Westminster Press.

ASSURANCE

My Hope Is in the Lord

Christ, in you the hope of Glory. — Colossians 1:27

Norman J. Clayton

WAKEFIELD
Norman J. Clayton

1 My hope is in the Lord Who gave Him-self for me,
2 *No mer-it of my own His an-ger to sup-press,*
3 And now for me He stands Be-fore the Fa-ther's throne,
4 *His grace has planned it all, 'Tis mine but to be-lieve,*

1 And paid the price of all my sin at Cal-va-ry.
2 *My on-ly hope is found in Je-sus' right-eous-ness.*
3 And shows His wound-ed hands, and names me as His own.
4 *And rec-og-nize His work of love and Christ re-ceive.*

For me He died, For me He lives,

For me He died, For me He lives,

And ev-er-last-ing life and light He free-ly gives.

ASSURANCE

79 Trusting Jesus

Commit thy way into the Lord; trust also in Him . . . . — Psalm 37:5

Edgar P. Stites

TRUSTING JESUS
Ira D. Sankey

1 Sim - ply trust-ing ev - ery day, Trust-ing through a storm - y way;
2 *Bright - ly doth His Spir - it shine In - to this poor heart of mine;*
3 Sing - ing if my way is clear, Pray - ing if the path be drear;
4 *Trust - ing Him while life shall last, Trust - ing Him 'til earth be past;*

1 E - ven when my faith is small, Trust - ing Je - sus— that is all.
2 *While He leads I can - not fall, Trust - ing Je - sus— that is all.*
3 If in dan - ger, for Him call, Trust - ing Je - sus— that is all.
4 *'Til I hear His fi - nal call, Trust - ing Je - sus— that is all.*

Trust-ing as the mo-ments fly, Trust-ing as the days go by;

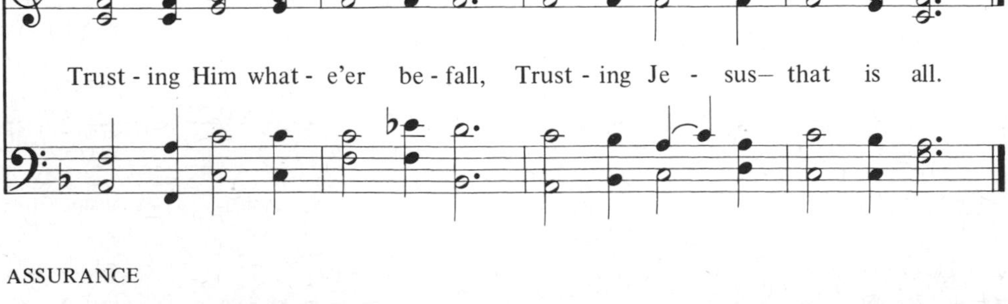

Trust-ing Him what - e'er be-fall, Trust-ing Je - sus— that is all.

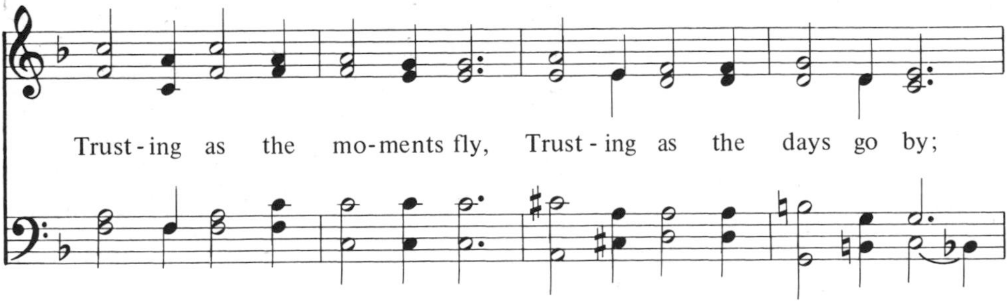

ASSURANCE

Problems

So be glad—yes, actually *be glad* that you have problems. Be grateful for them as implying that God has confidence in your ability to handle these problems with which He has entrusted you. Adopt this attitude toward problems and it will tend to syphon off the depression you may have developed from a negative reaction to them. And as you develop the habit of thinking in hopeful terms about your problems, you will find yourself doing much better with them.

This will add to your enjoyment of life too, for one of the few greatest satisfactions of this life is to handle problems efficiently and well. Morover, this successful handling tends to build up your faith that, through God's help and guidance, you have what it takes to deal with anything that may ever face you.

—Norman Vincent Peale

Let God Be God

Therefore Thou art great, O Lord God, for there is none like Thee . . . .
— II Samuel 7:22

CARLA

Bryan Jeffery Leech

Bryan Jeffery Leech

1 Let God be God, in this our pres-ent mo-ment. Let God be mas-ter hold-ing
2 *Let God be God, or we shall nev-er fin-ish   The task to which He calls us*
3 Let Christ be Lord in all His ris-en pow-er;   His gra-cious Spir-it un-sup
4 *Let this be ours as we a-wait His com-ing,   To tell the world of Him our*

1 in con-trol   All parts of life as gifts of His be-stow-ment
2 *ev-ery day;   Lest, err-ing, we in un-be-lief di-min-ish*
3 pressed and free;   Our Fa-ther, re-cre-ate us for this hour
4 *Lord and King;   O let us march to this, the dis-tant drum-ming*

CODA (after stanza 4)

1 For mak-ing men now bro-ken strong and whole.
2 *The force, the power He wish-es to dis-play.*
3 In - to the men You wish for us to be.
4 *Which in cres-cend-o soon will roar and ring. Let God be God, let Christ be King!*

ASSURANCE

82 Victory in Jesus

And this is the victory that overcometh the world, even our faith. — I John 5:4

Eugene M. Bartlett

HARTFORD
Eugene M. Bartlett

1 I heard an old, old sto - ry, how a Sav-ior came from glo - ry,
2 *I heard a - bout His heal - ing, of His cleans-ing power re - veal-ing,*
3 I heard a - bout a man-sion He has built for me in glo - ry,

1 How He gave His life on Cal - va - ry to save a wretch like me;
2 *How He made the lame to walk a - gain and caused the blind to see;*
3 And I heard a - bout the streets of gold be - yond the crys - tal sea;

1 I heard a - bout His groan - ing, of His pre - cious blood's a - ton - ing,
2 *And then I cried, "Dear Je - sus, come and heal my bro - ken spir - it,"*
3 A - bout the an - gels sing - ing and the old re - demp - tion sto - ry,

1 Then I re - pent - ed of my sins and won the vic - to - ry.
2 *And some-how Je - sus came and brought to me the vic - to - ry.*
3 And some sweet day I'll sing up there the song of vic - to - ry.

O vic - to - ry in Je - sus, my Sav - ior, for - ev - er! He sought me and

ASSURANCE

bought me with His re-deem-ing blood; He loved me ere I knew Him, and

all my love is due Him—He plunged me to vic-to-ry be-neath the cleans-ing flood.

Yesterday, Today, Forever 83

. . . A chief cornerstone, elect, precious; and he that believeth on Him shall not be confounded. — I Peter 2:6

NYACK

Albert B. Simpson

J. H. Burke

Yes-ter-day, to-day, for-ev-er, Je-sus is the same, All may change, but

Je-sus nev-er! Glo-ry to His name! Glo-ry to His name! Glo-ry

to His name! All may change, but Je-sus nev-er! Glo-ry to His name!

ASSURANCE

84 My Faith Looks Up to Thee

Then Peter said unto him, Lord . . . . Thou hast the words of eternal life. — John 6:68

OLIVET
Lowell Mason

Ray Palmer

1 My faith looks up to Thee, Thou Lamb of Cal - va - ry,
2 *May Thy rich grace im - part Strength to my faint - ing heart,*
3 While life's dark maze I tread And griefs a - round me spread,
4 *When ends life's pass - ing dream, When death's cold, threat-ening stream*

1 Sav - ior di - vine! Now hear me while I pray, Take all my
2 *My zeal in - spire; As Thou has died for me, O may my*
3 Be Thou my guide; Bid dark - ness turn to day, Wipe sor - row's
4 *Shall o'er me roll, Blest Sav - ior, then, in love, Fear and dis -*

1 guilt a - way, O let me from this day Be whol - ly Thine!
2 *love to Thee Pure, warm, and change-less be, A liv - ing fire!*
3 tears a - way, Nor let me ev - er stray From Thee a - side.
4 *trust re - move; O lift me safe a - bove, A ran-somed soul! A-men.*

85 Song of Ascent

I lift my eyes to the mountains:
    where is help to come from?
Help comes to me from Jehovah,
    who made heaven and earth.

No letting our footsteps slip!
    This guard of yours, He does not doze!
The guardian of Israel
    does not doze or sleep.

Jehovah guards you, shades you.
    With Jehovah at your right hand
sun cannot strike you down by day,
    nor moon at night.

Jehovah guards you from harm,
    He guards your lives,
He guards you leaving, coming back,
    now and for always.

—Psalm 121 (JB)

ASSURANCE

Jesus, I Am Resting, Resting

There remaineth . . . . a rest for the people of God. — Hebrews 4:9

Jean Sophia Pigott

TRANQUILITY
James Mountain

1 Je - sus, I am rest - ing, rest - ing In the joy of what Thou art;
2 *Sim - ply trust-ing Thee, Lord Je - sus, I be - hold Thee as Thou art,*
3 Ev - er lift Thy face up - on me As I work and wait for Thee;

1 I am find - ing out the great - ness Of Thy lov - ing heart.
2 *And Thy love, so pure, so change-less, Sat - is - fies my heart—*
3 Rest - ing 'neath Thy smile, Lord Je - sus, Earth's dark shad-ows flee.

1 Thou hast bid me gaze up - on Thee, And Thy beau - ty fills my soul,
2 *Sat - is - fies its deep-est long - ings, Meets, sup-plies its ev - ery need,*
3 Bright-ness of my Fa - ther's glo - ry, Sun - shine of my Fa - ther's face,

1 For by Thy trans-form - ing pow - er Thou hast made me whole.
2 *And sur-rounds me with its bless-ings: Thine is love in - deed!*
3 Keep me ev - er trust-ing, rest - ing, Fill me with Thy grace. A - men.

ASSURANCE

87 Leaning on the Everlasting Arms

The eternal God is our refuge and underneath are the everlasting arms. — Deuteronomy 33:27

SHOWALTER

Elisha A. Hoffman

Anthony J. Showalter

1 What a fel-low-ship, what a joy di-vine, Lean-ing on the ev-er-
2 *O how sweet to walk in this pil-grim way, Lean-ing on the ev-er-*
3 What have I to dread, what have I to fear, Lean-ing on the ev-er-

1 last-ing arms; What a bless-ed-ness, what a peace is mine,
2 *last-ing arms; O how bright the path grows from day to day,*
3 last-ing arms? I have bless-ed peace with my Lord so near,

1 Lean-ing on the ev-er-last-ing arms.
2 *Lean-ing on the ev-er-last-ing arms.* Lean - ing,
3 Lean-ing on the ev-er-last-ing arms. Lean-ing on Je-sus,

lean - ing, Safe and se-cure from all a-larms; Lean -
lean-ing on Je-sus,   Lean-ing on

ing, lean - ing, Lean-ing on the ev-er-last-ing arms.
Je-sus, lean-ing on Je-sus,

ASSURANCE

When We Feel Forsaken

88

Our Father, sometimes Thou dost seem so far away, as if Thou art a God in hiding, as if Thou art determined to elude all who seek Thee.

Yet we know that Thou art far more willing to be found than we are to seek. Thou hast promised "If with all your heart ye truly seek me, ye shall ever surely find me." And hast Thou not assured us that Thou art with us always?

Help us now to be as aware of Thy nearness as we are of the material things of every day. Help us to recognize Thy voice with as much assurance as we recognize the sounds of the world around us.

We would find Thee now in the privacy of our hearts, in the quiet of this moment. We would know, our Father, that Thou art near us and beside us; that Thou dost love us and art interested in all that we do, art concerned about all our affairs.

May we become aware of Thy companionship, of Him who walks beside us.

At times when we feel forsaken, may we know the presence of the Holy Spirit who brings comfort to all human hearts when we are willing to surrender ourselves.

May we be convinced that even before we reach up to Thee, Thou art reaching down to us. These blessings, together with the unexpressed longing in our hearts, we ask in the strong name of Jesus Christ, Our Lord. Amen.

—Peter Marshall

Children of the Heavenly Father

89

As a father pitieth his children, so the Lord pitieth . . . . — Psalm 103:13

Lina Sandell
Tr. by Ernst W. Olson

TRYGGARE KAN INGEN VARA
Swedish Folk Melody

1 Chil-dren of the heaven-ly Fa-ther Safe-ly in His bos-om gath-er;
2 *God His own doth tend and nour-ish, In His ho-ly courts they flour-ish;*
3 Nei-ther life nor death shall ev-er From the Lord His chil-dren sev-er;
4 *Praise the Lord in joy-ful num-bers, Your Pro-tect-or nev-er slum-bers;*
5 Though He giv-eth or He tak-eth, God His chil-dren ne'er for-sak-eth;

1 Nest-ling bird nor star in heav-en Such a ref-uge e'er was giv-en.
2 *From all e-vil things He spares them, In His might-y arms He bears them.*
3 Un-to them His grace He show-eth, And their sor-rows all He know-eth.
4 *At the will of your De-fend-er Ev-ery foe-man must sur-ren-der.*
5 His the lov-ing pur-pose sole-ly To pre-serve them pure and ho-ly.

ASSURANCE

Worship Leader: *Praise be to the God and Father of our Lord Jesus Christ, who in His great mercy gave us new birth into a living hope by the resurrection of Jesus Christ from the dead![1]*

People: Death be not proud, though some have called thee
Mighty and dreadful, for thou art not so:
For those whom thou thinkest thou dost overthrow
Die not, poor death; nor yet canst thou kill me.[2]

Worship Leader: *So be truly glad! There is wonderful joy ahead, even though the going is rough for a while down here. These trials are only to test your faith, to see whether or not it is strong and pure. It is being tested as fire tests gold and purifies it— and your faith is far more precious to God than mere gold.[3]*

People: Yet, in the maddening maze of things,
And tossed by storm and flood,
To one fixed trust my spirit clings;
I know that God is good![4]
And we know that all things work together for good to them that love God . . . [5]

Worship Leader: *You must therefore be mentally stripped for action, perfectly self-controlled. Fix your hopes on the gift of grace which is to be yours when Jesus Christ is revealed. The One who called you is holy; like Him, be holy in all your behavior, because Scripture says, "You shall be holy, for I am holy."[6]*

People: There are men who can't be bought.
There are women beyond purchase.
The fireborn are at home in fire.
The stars make no noise.
You can't hinder the wind from blowing.
Time is a great teacher.
Who can live without hope?[7]

Worship Leader: *We rejoice, then, in the hope we have of sharing God's glory! And we also rejoice in our troubles, because we know that troubles produce endurance, endurance brings God's approval, and His approval creates hope.[8]*

People: This hope does not disappoint us, because God has poured out His love into our hearts by means of His Holy Spirit, who is God's gift to us.

— Gloria Gaither

1. I Peter 1:30 (NEB)
2. John Donne from "Death Be Not Proud"
3. I Peter 1:6-7 (LB)
4. John Greenleaf Whittier from "The Eternal Goodness"
5. Romans 8:28a
6. I Peter 1:13, 15, 16 (NEB)
7. Carl Sandburg from "The People Speak"
8. Romans 5:2b-5 (TEV)

'Tis So Sweet to Trust in Jesus

. . . because we trust in the living God, who is the Savior of all men. — I Timothy 4:10

Louisa M. R. Stead

TRUST IN JESUS
William J. Kirkpatrick

1 'Tis so sweet to trust in Je - sus, Just to take Him at His word,
2 *How I love to trust in Je - sus, Just to trust His cleans-ing blood,*
3 Yes, I've learned to trust in Je - sus, And from sin and self to cease,
4 *I'm so glad I learned to trust Him, Pre - cious Je - sus, Sav-ior, Friend;*

1 Just to rest up - on His prom-ise, Just to know, "Thus saith the Lord."
2 *Just in sim - ple faith to plunge me 'Neath the heal - ing, cleans-ing flood!*
3 Now from Je - sus sim - ply tak - ing Life and rest and joy and peace.
4 *And I know that He is with me, He'll be with me to the end.*

Je - sus, Je - sus, how I trust Him! How I've proved Him o'er and o'er!

Je - sus, Je - sus, pre - cious Je - sus! O for grace to trust Him more!

ASSURANCE

92 The Solid Rock

They who trust in the Lord shall be as Mount Zion,
which cannot be moved. . . —Psalm 125:1

Edward Mote

SOLID ROCK
William B. Bradbury

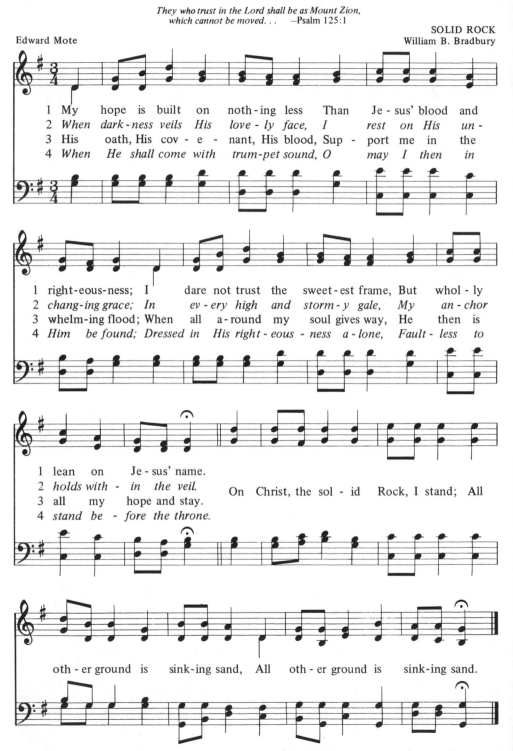

1 My hope is built on noth-ing less Than Je-sus' blood and
2 *When dark-ness veils His love-ly face, I rest on His un-*
3 His oath, His cov-e-nant, His blood, Sup-port me in the
4 *When He shall come with trum-pet sound, O may I then in*

1 right-eous-ness; I dare not trust the sweet-est frame, But whol-ly
2 *chang-ing grace; In ev-ery high and storm-y gale, My an-chor*
3 whelm-ing flood; When all a-round my soul gives way, He then is
4 *Him be found; Dressed in His right-eous-ness a-lone, Fault-less to*

1 lean on Je-sus' name.
2 *holds with-in the veil.* On Christ, the sol-id Rock, I stand; All
3 all my hope and stay.
4 *stand be-fore the throne.*

oth-er ground is sink-ing sand, All oth-er ground is sink-ing sand.

ASSURANCE

Alternate Last Verse Harmonization

Arranged by Ronn Huff

4 When He shall come with trum-pet sound, O may I then in

Him be found; Dressed in His right - eous - ness a - lone, Fault -

less to stand be - fore the throne. On Christ the sol - id Rock I stand; All

oth-er ground is sink-ing sand, All oth-er ground is sink-ing sand.

ASSURANCE

93 My God Is There Controlling

The fool hath said in his heart, there is no God. — Psalm 14:1

We search the starlit Milky Way,
A million worlds in rhythmic sway,
Yet in our blindness some will say,
"There is no God controlling!"

But as I grope from sphere to sphere,
New wonders crowd the eye, the ear,
And faith grows firmer every year:
"My God is there, controlling!"

We probe the atoms for their cause,
Explore the earth for nature's laws,
Yet seldom in our searching pause
To think of God controlling.

Each flash of fact from out the night,
Each burst of truth upon my sight
That quickens awe or adds delight,
Reveals my God controlling.

William H. Reid

94 I Am Not Skilled to Understand

But where shall wisdom be found? — Job 28:12

Dora Greenwell

EWHURST
Cecil J. Allen

1 I am not skilled to understand What God hath willed, what God hath planned; I only know at His right hand Stands One who is my Savior.

2 *I take Him at His word and deed: "Christ died to save me," this I read; And in my heart I find a need Of Him to be my Savior.*

3 That He should leave His place on high And come for sinful man to die, You count it strange? so once did I Before I knew my Savior.

4 *And O that He fulfilled may see The travail of His soul in me, And with His work contented be, As I with my dear Savior!*

5 Yes, living, dying, let me bring My strength, my solace, from this spring, That He who lives to be my King Once died to be my Savior!

Music used by permission of Cecil J. Allen.
ASSURANCE

At the Cross

*For the preaching of the cross is . . . . unto us who are saved
the power of God.* — 1 Corinthians 1:18

Isaac Watts
Refrain added by Ralph E. Hudson

HUDSON
Ralph E. Hudson

1 A - las, and did my Sav - ior bleed? And did my Sov-ereign die?
2 *Was it for crimes that I have done, He suf-fered on the tree?*
3 Well might the sun in dark - ness hide And shut his glo - ries in,
4 *But drops of grief can ne'er re - pay The debt of love I owe:*

1 Would He de - vote that sa - cred head For some - one such as I?
2 *A - maz - ing pit - y! grace un-known! And love be - yond de - gree!*
3 When Christ, the might - y Mak - er, died For man the crea - ture's sin.
4 *Here, Lord, I give my - self a - way, 'Tis all that I can do!*

At the cross, at the cross where I first saw the light, And the

bur - den of my heart rolled a - way, It was there by faith

I re - ceived my sight, And now I am hap - py all the day!

ASSURANCE

96 I Know Who Holds Tomorrow

Fear ye not . . ye are of more value than many sparrows . . . . — Matthew 10:31

I KNOW

Ira F. Stanphill

Ira F. Stanphill

1 I don't know a-bout to-mor-row, I just live
2 Ev-ery step is get-ting bright-er As the gold-
3 I don't know a-bout to-mor-row, It may bring

1 from day to day; I don't bor-row from its sun-shine,
2 en stairs I climb; Ev-ery bur-den's get-ting light-er,
3 me pov-er-ty; But the one who feeds the spar-row,

1 For its skies may turn to gray. I don't wor-ry o'er the
2 Ev-ery cloud is sil-ver-lined. There the sun is al-ways
3 Is the one who stands by me. And the path that is my

1 fu-ture, For I know what Je-sus said; And to-day
2 shin-ing, There no tear will dim the eye; At the end-
3 por-tion, May be through the flame or flood; But His pres-

1 I'll walk be-side Him, For He knows what is a-head.
2 ing of the rain-bow, Where the moun-tains touch the sky.
3 ence goes be-fore me, And I'm cov-ered with His blood.

ASSURANCE

Man - y things a - bout to - mor - row I don't
seem to un - der - stand; But I know who
holds to - mor - row, And I know who holds my hand.

Assurance 97

How easy for me to live with You, O Lord!
How easy for me to believe in You!
When my mind parts in bewilderment or falters,
then the most intelligent people see no further
than this day's end
and do not know what must be done tomorrow,
You grant me the serene certitude
that You exist and that You will take care
that not all the paths of good be closed.
Atop the ridge of earthly fame,
I look back in wonder at the path
which I alone could never have found,
a wondrous path through despair to this point
from which I, too, could transmit to mankind
a reflection of Your rays.
And as much as I must still reflect
You will give me.
But as much as I cannot take up
You will have already assigned to others.

—Aleksandr Solzhenitsyn

98 Great Is Thy Faithfulness

. . . For He is faithful that promised. — Hebrews 10:23

Based on Lamentations 3:22, 23
Thomas O. Chisholm

FAITHFULNESS
William M. Runyan

1 Great is Thy faith-ful-ness, O God my Fa-ther! There is no
2 *Sum - mer and win - ter, and spring-time and har - vest, Sun, moon, and*
3 Par - don for sin and a peace that en - dur - eth, Thine own dear

1 shad - ow of turn-ing with Thee; Thou chang-est not, Thy com-
2 *stars in their cours - es a - bove, Join with all na - ture in*
3 pres - ence to cheer and to guide, Strength for to - day and bright

1 pas-sions, they fail not: As Thou hast been Thou for - ev - er wilt be.
2 *man - i - fold wit - ness To Thy great faith-ful-ness, mer - cy, and love.*
3 hope for to - mor-row— Bless-ings all mine, with ten thou-sand be - side!

Great is Thy faith-ful-ness, Great is Thy faith-ful-ness, Morn - ing by

FAITHFULNESS

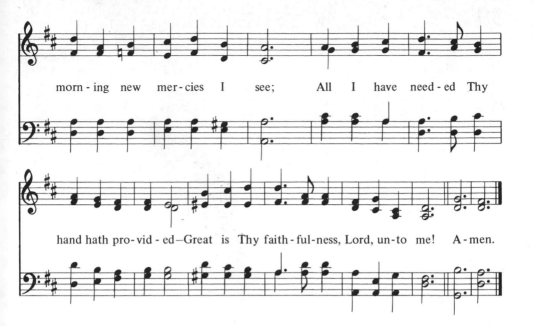

morn - ing new mer - cies I see; All I have need - ed Thy

hand hath pro - vid - ed—Great is Thy faith - ful - ness, Lord, un - to me! A - men.

Lamentations 3 : 22 - 33   99

The steadfast love of the Lord never ceases, His mercies never come to an end; they are new every morning; great is Thy faithfulness.

"The Lord is my portion," says my soul, "therefore I will hope in Him."

The Lord is good to those who wait for Him, to the soul that seeks Him. It is good that one should wait quietly for the salvation of the Lord. It is good for a man that he bear the yoke in his youth.

Let him sit alone in silence when He has laid it on him; let him put his mouth in the dust—there may yet be hope; let him give his cheek to the smiter, and be filled with insults.

For the Lord will not cast off forever, but, though He cause grief, He will have compassion according to the abundance of His steadfast love; for He does not willingly afflict or grieve the sons of men.

—(RSV)

100
Satisfied

As the heart panteth after the waterbrook so panteth my soul after Thee, O God.
— Psalm 42:1

Clara T. Williams

SATISFIED
Ralph E. Hudson

1 All my life long I had pant - ed For a drink from some cool spring
2 *Feed-ing on the food a - round me 'Til my strength was al-most gone,*
3 Well of wa - ter, ev - er spring-ing, Bread of life, so rich and free,

1 That I hoped would quench the burn-ing Of the thirst I felt with - in.
2 *Longed my soul for some-thing bet - ter, On-ly still to hun-ger on.*
3 Un - told wealth that nev - er fail - eth, My Re-deem - er is to me.

Hal - le - lu - jah! I have found Him—Whom my soul so long has craved!

Je - sus sat - is - fies my long - ings; Through His blood I now am saved.

The Haven of Rest

I will put thee in a cleft of the rock, and I will cover thee with my hand. — Exodus 33:22

GOOD SHIP

H. L. Gilmour

George D. Moore

1 My soul, in sad ex-ile, was out on life's sea. So bur-dened with
2 *I yield-ed my-self to His ten-der em-brace, And, faith tak-ing*
3 The song of my soul, since the Lord made me whole, Has been the old

1 sin and dis-tressed, 'Til I heard a sweet voice saying,"Make me your choice,"
2 *hold of the Word, My fet-ters fell off, and I an-chored my soul,*
3 sto-ry so blest Of Je-sus, who'll save who-so-ev-er will have

1 And I en-tered the ha-ven of rest.
2 *The ha-ven of rest is my Lord.* I've an-chored my soul in the
3 A home in the ha-ven of rest.

ha-ven of rest, I'll sail the wide seas no more; The tem-pest may

sweep o'er the wild, storm-y deep, In Je-sus I'm safe ev-er-more.

ASSURANCE

102

Day By Day
and With Each Passing Moment

Lina Sandell
Tr. by A. L. Skoog

As thy days so shall thy strength be. — Deuteronomy 33:25

BLOTT EN DAG
Oscar Ahnfelt

1 Day by day and with each pass-ing mo-ment, Strength I find to meet my tri-als here; Trust-ing in my Fa-ther's wise be-stow-ment, I've no cause for wor-ry or for fear. He whose heart is kind be-yond all meas-ure Gives un-to each day what He deems best— Lov-ing-ly, its part of pain and

2 *Ev-ery day the Lord Him-self is near me With a spe-cial mer-cy for each hour; All my cares He fain would bear, and cheer me, He whose name is Coun-sel-lor and Power. The pro-tec-tion of His child and treas-ure Is a charge that on Him-self He laid; "As thy days, thy strength shall be in*

3 Help me then in ev-ery trib-u-la-tion So to trust Thy prom-is-es, O Lord, That I lose not faith's sweet con-so-la-tion Of-fered me with-in Thy ho-ly word. Help me Lord, when toil and trou-ble meet-ing, E'er to take, as from a fa-ther's hand, One by one, the days, the mo-ments

ASSURANCE

1 pleas - ure,   Min - gling toil   with peace   and   rest.
2 *meas - ure,"*   *This the pledge*   *to*   *me*   *He*   *made.*
3 fleet - ing,   'Til   I   reach   the prom - ised   land.   A - men.

Morning Prayer   103

O God,
Early in the morning do I cry unto Thee.
Help me to pray,
And to think only of Thee.
I cannot pray alone.

In me there is darkness,
But with Thee there is light.
I am lonely, but Thou leavest me not.
I am feeble in heart, but Thou leavest me not.
I am restless, but with Thee there is peace.
In me there is bitterness, but with Thee there is patience;
Thy ways are past understanding, but
Thou knowest the way for me.

O heavenly Father,
I praise and thank Thee
For the peace of the night.
I praise and thank Thee for this new day.
I praise and thank Thee for all Thy goodness
and faithfulness throughout my life.
Thou hast granted me many blessings:
Now let me accept tribulation
from Thy hand.
Thou wilt not lay on me more
than I can bear.
Thou makest all things work together for good
for Thy children.

—Dietrich Bonhoeffer

104 Great God of Wonders

...And I will pardon all their iniquities .. — Jeremiah 33:8

Samuel Davies

WONDERS
John Newton

1 Great God of won - ders! all Thy ways Are match - less, God - like,
2 *In won - der lost, with trem - bling joy, We take the par - don*
3 O may this strange, this match - less grace, This God - like mir - a -

1 and di - vine; But the fair glo - ries of Thy grace More God - like
2 *of our God: Par - don for crimes of deep - est dye, A par - don*
3 cle of love, Fill the whole earth with grate - ful praise, And all th'an -

1 and un - ri - valed shine, More God - like and un - ri - valed shine.
2 *bought with Je - sus' blood, A par - don bought with Je - sus' blood.*
3 gel - ic choirs a - bove, And all th'an - gel - ic choirs a - bove.

(Use after last stanza)

Who is a par - doning God like Thee? Or who has grace so

Fine

rich and free? Or who has grace so rich and free?

GRACE, MERCY, AND FORGIVENESS

Grace Greater Than Our Sin
105

. . . But where sin abounded, grace did much more abound. — Romans 5:20

Julia H. Johnston

MOODY
Daniel B. Towner

1 Mar - vel - ous grace of our lov - ing Lord, Grace that ex - ceeds our
2 *Sin and de - spair, like the sea - waves cold, Threat - en the soul with*
3 Dark is the stain that we can - not hide, What can a - vail to
4 *Mar - vel - ous, in - fi - nite, match - less grace, Free - ly be - stowed on*

1 sin and our guilt! Yon - der on Cal - va - ry's mount out - poured—
2 *in - fi - nite loss; Grace that is great - er— yes, grace un - told—*
3 wash it a - way? Look! There is flow - ing a crim - son tide—
4 *all who be - lieve! You that are long - ing to see His face,*

1 There where the blood of the Lamb was spilt.
2 *Points to the Ref - uge, the might - y Cross.* Grace, grace,
3 Whit - er than snow you may be to - day.
4 *Will you this mo - ment His grace re - ceive?*

God's grace, Grace that will par - don and cleanse with - in; Grace,

grace, God's grace, Grace that is great - er than all our sin!

GRACE, MERCY, AND FORGIVENESS

106
We're Hungry, Lord

We're hungry for something, Lord.

We have so much rich food and cake and candy for ourselves,
*   but we're hungry.*

People around us are so stiff and tight and hard to reach.

And they make us that way.

But we're hungry for something more.

People we know keep talking about great ideas, brilliant questions,
*   and the problem of God's existence.*

But we're hungry for You, not ideas or theories.

We want You to touch us, to reach inside us and turn us on.

There are so many people who will counsel us to death.

But we're hungry for someone who really knows You and has
*   You, someone who can get so close to us that we can see You*
*   there.*

We have so many things, but we're hungry for You.

Deep, deep down inside we're hungry, even if we appear to be
*   silly, lazy, or unconcerned at times.*

We're hungry for Your kind of power and love and joy.

Feed us, Lord, feed us with Your rich food.

– Anonymous

107
Amazing Grace! How Sweet the Sound

For by grace are ye saved through faith . . . — Ephesians 2:8

AMAZING GRACE
American Melody
Carrell and Clayton's *Virginia Harmony*
Harmonized by Edwin O. Excell

John Newton
John P. Rees, stanza 5

1 A - maz-ing grace! How sweet the sound—That saved a wretch like me!
2 'Twas grace that taught my heart to fear, And grace my fears re-lieved;
3 The Lord has prom-ised good to me, His word my hope se-cures;
4 Through man-y dan-gers, toils, and snares, I have al-read-y come;
5 When we've been there ten thou-sand years, Bright shin-ing as the sun,

GRACE, MERCY, AND FORGIVENESS

1 I once was lost but now am found, Was blind but now I see.
2 *How pre-cious did that grace ap-pear The hour I first be-lieved!*
3 He will my shield and por-tion be As long as life en-dures.
4 *'Tis grace hath brought me safe thus far, And grace will lead me home.*
5 We've no less days to sing God's praise Than when we'd first be-gun.

Rock of Ages, Cleft for Me 108

. . . Hide me in the rock that is higher than I. — Psalm 61:2

Augustus M. Toplady

TOPLADY
Thomas Hastings

1 Rock of A-ges, cleft for me, Let me hide my-self in Thee;
2 *Could my tears for-ev-er flow, Could my zeal no lan-guor know,*
3 While I draw this fi-nal breath, When my eyes shall close in death,

1 Let the wa-ter and the blood, From Thy wound-ed side which flowed,
2 *These for sin could not a-tone— Thou must save, and Thou a-lone:*
3 When I rise to worlds un-known, And be-hold Thee on Thy throne,

1 Be of sin the dou-ble cure, Save from wrath and make me pure.
2 *In my hand no price I bring, Sim-ply to Thy cross I cling.*
3 Rock of A-ges, cleft for me, Let me hide my-self in Thee. A-men.

GRACE, MERCY, AND FORGIVENESS

109 Whiter Than Snow

Purge me . . . and I shall be clean;
wash me and I shall be whiter than snow. — Psalm 51:7

James Nicholson

FISCHER
William G. Fischer

1 Lord Je - sus, I long to be per - fect - ly whole; I want Thee for - ev - er to live in my soul. Break down ev - ery i - dol, cast out ev - ery foe— Now wash me and I shall be whit - er than snow.

2 *Lord Je - sus, look down from Your throne in the skies And help me to make a com - plete sac - ri - fice. I give up my - self and what - ev - er I know— Now wash me and I shall be whit - er than snow.*

3 Lord Je - sus, for this I most hum - bly en - treat; I wait, bless - ed Lord, at Thy cru - ci - fied feet. By faith, for my cleans - ing I see Your blood flow— Now wash me and I shall be whit - er than snow.

4 *Lord Je - sus, You see as I pa - tient - ly wait; Come now and with - in me a new heart cre - ate. To those who have sought You, You nev - er said, "No"— Now wash me and I shall be whit - er than snow.*

Whit - er than snow, yes, whit - er than snow— Now wash me and I shall be whit - er than snow.

GRACE, MERCY, AND FORGIVENESS

Thank God for the Promise of Spring

110

While the earth remaineth, seed time and harvest . . . shall not cease. — Genesis 8:22

Gloria Gaither
William J. Gaither

SPRINGTIME
William J. Gaither

1 Though the skies be gray a-bove me And I can't see the light of
2 *Though the earth seemed bleak and bar-ren And the seeds lay brown and*

1 day, There's a ray break-ing through the shad-ows, And His
2 *dead, Yet the prom-ise of life throbbed with-in them, And I*

1 smile can't be far a - way. Thank God for the prom-ise of
2 *knew spring was just a - head.*

spring-time, Once a - gain my heart will sing; There's a brand new

day that is dawn - ing, Thank God for the prom-ise of spring.

GRACE, MERCY, AND FORGIVENESS

111

A Certain Uncertain Future

"Wisely enough,
God does not let us skip ahead in the story of our lives,
but rather leads us page by page
to its understandable conclusion in Him.
And so, as each of us faces an uncertain future,
we can trust in God's promise as expressed by Jeremiah:
'For I know the plans I have for you,' saith the Lord,
'They are plans for good and not for evil,
to give a future and a hope.' "

—Pann Baltz

112

He Giveth More Grace

God is able to make all grace abound toward you — II Corinthians 9 :8

Annie Johnson Flint

HE GIVETH MORE GRACE
Hubert Mitchell

1 He giv-eth more grace when the burdens grow greater, He send-eth more
2 *When we have ex-haust-ed our store of en-dur-ance, When our strength has*

1 strength when the la-bors in-crease; To add-ed af-flic-tion He
2 *failed ere the day is half done, When we reach the end of our*

1 add-eth His mer-cy, To mul-ti-plied tri-als, His mul-ti-plied peace.
2 *hoard-ed re-sourc-es, Our Fa-ther's full giv-ing is on-ly be-gun.*

GRACE, MERCY, AND FORGIVENESS

His love has no lim-it, His grace has no meas-ure, His power has no bound-a-ry known un-to men; For out of His in-fi-nite rich-es in Je-sus, He giv-eth, and giv-eth, and giv-eth a-gain!

A Prayer for Our World 113

ALMIGHTY GOD: You have called us together, and by Your Holy Spirit, make us one with Your Son our Lord. We thank You for the church, for the power of Your word, and for our life together in Christ. Give us a heart to love the loveless, the lonely, the hungry, and the hurt, without pride or a calculating spirit, so that we may serve You with integrity and joy.

GOD OF GRACE: In Your world there are fields to seed and harvest. We thank You for men and women who farm the land, and for workers who prepare and distribute food. While we struggle with the problem of over-weight, millions are dying from hunger. Help us to find the wisdom and the commitment to bring hope and health to our brothers and sisters throughout the world. May no one starve because of our greed or neglect, and may we all hunger and thirst for righteousness alone; through Jesus Christ our Lord. Amen.

—Gary W. Demarest

114 Wonderful Grace of Jesus

For by grace are ye saved, through faith . . . . — Ephesians 2:8

Haldor Lillenas

WONDERFUL GRACE
Haldor Lillenas

1 Won-der-ful grace of Je - sus, Great - er than all my sin;
2 *Won-der-ful grace of Je - sus, Reach-ing to all the lost,*
3 Won-der-ful grace of Je - sus, Reach-ing the most de - filed,

1 How shall my tongue de - scribe it, Where shall its praise be - gin?
2 *By it I have been par - doned, Saved to the ut - ter - most;*
3 By its trans-form-ing pow - er Mak - ing him God's dear child,

1 Tak - ing a - way my bur - den, Set-ting my spir - it free,
2 *Chains have been torn a - sun - der, Giv - ing me lib - er - ty,*
3 Pur - chas-ing peace and heav - en For all e - ter - ni - ty—

1 For the won-der-ful grace of Je - sus reach - es me.
2 *For the won-der-ful grace of Je - sus reach - es me.*
3 And the won-der-ful grace of Je - sus reach - es me.

GRACE, MERCY, AND FORGIVENESS

Won-der-ful the matchless grace of Je - sus, Deep-er than the might-y roll - ing sea; High - er than the moun - tain, spark - ling like a foun - tain, All suf - fi - cient grace for e - ven me; Broad-er than the scope of my trans - gres - sions, Great - er far than all my sin and shame; O mag - ni - fy the pre - cious name of Je - sus, Praise His name!

GRACE, MERCY, AND FORGIVENESS

115 There's a Wideness in God's Mercy

And they sang together . . . because He is good, for His mercy endureth forever . . . . — Ezra 3:11

Frederick W. Faber

WELLESLEY
Lizzie S. Tourjée

1 There's a wide-ness in God's mer-cy Like the wide-ness of the sea;
2 *There is wel-come for the sin-ner And more grac-es for the good;*
3 For the love of God is broad-er Than the meas-ure of man's mind;
4 *If our love were but more sim-ple We should take Him at His word,*

1 There's a kind-ness in His jus-tice Which is more than lib-er-ty.
2 *There is mer-cy with the Sav-ior; There is heal-ing in His blood.*
3 And the heart of the E-ter-nal Is most won-der-ful-ly kind.
4 *And our lives would be all sun-shine In the sweet-ness of our Lord.* A-men.

116 Psalm 32

Blessed is he whose transgression is forgiven, *whose sin is covered.* Blessed is the man to whom the Lord imputes no iniquity, *and in whose spirit there is no deceit.*

When I declared not my sin, *my body wasted away through my groaning all day long.* For day and night Thy hand was heavy upon me, *my strength was dried up as by the heat of summer.*

I acknowledge my sin to Thee, and I did not hide my iniquity; *I said, "I will confess my transgressions to the Lord"; then Thou didst forgive the guilt of my sin.* Therefore let every one who is godly offer prayer to Thee; *at a time of distress, in the rush of great waters, they shall not reach Him.* Thou art a hiding place for me, Thou preservest me from trouble; *Thou dost encompass me with deliverance.*

I will instruct you and teach you the way you should go; *I will counsel you with my eye upon you.* Be not like a horse or a mule, without understanding, *which must be curbed with bit and bridle, else it will not keep with you.*

Many are the pangs of the wicked; *but steadfast love surrounds him who trusts in the Lord.* Be glad in the Lord, and rejoice, O righteous, *and shout for joy, all you upright in heart!*

—(RSV)

A Shelter in the Time of Storm 117

There is none as holy as the Lord, . . .
neither is there any rock like our God. — I Samuel 2:2

Vernon J. Charlesworth
Adapted by Ira D. Sankey

SHELTER
Ira D. Sankey

1 The Lord's our rock, in Him we hide, A shel-ter in the time of storm;
2 *A shade by day, de-fense by night, A shel-ter in the time of storm;*
3 The rag-ing storms may 'round us beat, A shel-ter in the time of storm;
4 *O Rock di-vine, O Ref-uge dear, A shel-ter in the time of storm;*

1 Se-cure what-ev-er ill be-tide, A shel-ter in the time of storm.
2 *No fears a-larm, no fears af-fright, A shel-ter in the time of storm.*
3 We'll nev-er leave our safe re-treat, A shel-ter in the time of storm.
4 *Be Thou our help-er ev-er near, A shel-ter in the time of storm.*

O Je-sus is a rock in a wea-ry land, A

wea-ry land, a wea-ry land; O, Je-sus is a

rock in a wea-ry land, A shel-ter in the time of storm.

REFUGE

118 · A Mighty Fortress Is Our God

The Lord is my rock, my fortress, and my deliverer . . . — Psalm 18:2

Based on Psalm 46
Martin Luther
Tr. by Frederick H. Hedge

EIN' FESTE BURG
Martin Luther
Descant by Mary E. Caldwell

Descant

4 That word a-bove all, a-bid - eth;

1 A might-y for-tress is our God, A bul-wark nev-er fail - ing;
2 Did we in our own strength con-fide, Our striv-ing would be los - ing,
3 And though this world with dev-ils filled, Should threat-en to un-do us,
4 That word a-bove all earth-ly powers, No thanks to them, a-bid - eth;

The gifts are ours, Who with us sid - eth.

1 Our help-er He a-mid the flood Of mor-tal ills pre-vail - ing.
2 Were not the right man on our side, The man of God's own choos - ing.
3 We will not fear, for God hath willed His truth to tri-umph through us.
4 The Spir-it and the gifts are ours Through Him who with us sid - eth.

Let goods and kin-dred go, This mor-tal life al - so— The bod-y

1 For still our an-cient foe Doth seek to work us woe— His craft and power are
2 Dost ask who that may be? Christ Je-sus, it is He— Lord Sab-a-oth His
3 The prince of dark-ness grim, We trem-ble not for him— His rage we can en-
4 Let goods and kin-dred go, This mor-tal life al-so— The bod-y they may

REFUGE

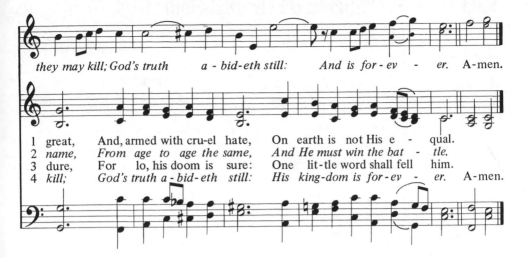

they may kill; God's truth   a - bid-eth still: And is for - ev - er. A-men.

1 great,   And, armed with cru-el hate,   On earth is not His e - qual.
2 name,   From age to age the same,   And He must win the bat - tle.
3 dure,   For lo, his doom is sure: One lit-tle word shall fell him.
4 kill;   God's truth a - bid-eth still: His king-dom is for - ev - er. A-men.

A Contemporary Te Deum   **119**

You are God: we praise You;
You are the Lord: we acclaim You;
You are the eternal Father:
All creation worships You.
To You all angels, all the powers of heaven,
Cherubim and Seraphim, sing in endless praise:
Holy, holy, holy Lord, God of power and might,
heaven and earth are full of your glory.
The glorious company of apostles praises You.
The noble fellowship of prophets praises You.
The white-robed army of martyrs praises You.
Throughout the world the holy Church acclaims You:
Father, of majesty unbounded,
Your true and only Son, worthy of all worship,
and the Holy Spirit, advocate and guide.
You, Christ, are the king of glory,
eternal Son of the Father.
When You became man to set us free
You did not disdain the Virgin's womb.
You overcame the sting of death,
and opened the kingdom of heaven to all believers.
You are seated at God's right hand in glory.
We believe that You will come, and be our judge.
Come then, Lord, sustain Your people,
bought with the price of Your own blood,
and bring us with Your saints
to everlasting glory.

He Hideth My Soul

I will put thee in a cleft of the Rock, and will cover thee with My hand. — Exodus 33:22

Fanny J. Crosby

HE HIDETH MY SOUL
William J. Kirkpatrick

1 A won - der - ful Sav - ior is Je - sus my Lord, A
2 *A won - der - ful Sav - ior is Je - sus my Lord, He*
3 With num - ber - less bless - ings each mo - ment He crowns, And,
4 *When clothed in His bright - ness trans - port - ed I rise To*

1 won - der - ful Sav - ior to me; He hid - eth my soul in the
2 *tak - eth my bur - den a - way; He hold - eth me up, and I*
3 filled with His full - ness di - vine, I sing in my rap - ture, "O
4 *meet Him in clouds of the sky, His per - fect sal - va - tion, His*

1 cleft of the rock, Where riv - ers of pleas - ure I see.
2 *shall not be moved, He giv - eth me strength for each day.*
3 glo - ry to God For such a Re - deem - er as mine!"
4 *won - der - ful love, I'll shout with the mil - lions on high.*

He hid - eth my soul in the cleft of the rock That shad - ows a

REFUGE

dry, thirst-y land; He hid - eth my life in the depths of His love,

And cov-ers me there with His hand, And cov-ers me there with His hand.

How Good Is God 121

How good is God for Israel,
for the pure of heart!

As for me, my feet had almost stumbled;
my steps had well-nigh slipped.
I was jealous of the arrogant
and envied the prosperity of the wicked.

My mind is embittered:
my thoughts, irritating.
I am so stupid, so ignorant!
I am but a dumb brute before You.

And yet I am always before You:
You keep me in Your hand.
With counsel You lead me;
You take me by the hand behind You.

I have but You in the heavens
and nothing more on earth.
My flesh and my brain may fail
but my Rock, the desire of my mind, is God evermore.

Those who avoid You will perish;
You exterminate all those who stray.
God's presence is good for me;
I make the Lord my refuge
and I will witness to His deeds.

—Psalm 73:1-3, 21-28
(Psalms in Modern Speech)

REFUGE

In the Hour of Trial

He ever liveth to make intercession for them. — Hebrews 7:25

PENITENCE
Spencer Lane

James Montgomery, alt.

1 In the hour of tri - al, Je - sus, plead for me,
2 *With for - bid - den plea - sures Would this vain world charm,*
3 Should Thy mer - cy send me Sor - row, toil, and woe,

1 Lest, by base de - ni - al, I de - part from Thee;
2 *Or its sor - did trea - sures Spread to work me harm;*
3 Or should pain at - tend me On my path be - low,

1 When Thou seest me wa - ver, With a look re - call;
2 *Bring to my re - mem - brance Sad Geth - sem - a - ne,*
3 Grant that I may nev - er Fail Thy hand to see;

1 Nor for fear or fa - vor Suf - fer me to fall.
2 *Or, in dark - er sem - blance, Rug - ged Cal - va - ry.*
3 Grant that I may ev - er Cast my care on Thee. A - men.

REFUGE

When We All Get to Heaven

123

Then we, . . . shall be caught up together with the Lord . . .
and so shall we ever be with the Lord. — I Thessalonians 4:17

HEAVEN

Eliza E. Hewitt

Emily D. Wilson

1 Sing the won-drous love of Je-sus, Sing His mer-cy and His grace;
2 *While we walk the pil-grim path-way Clouds will o - ver - spread the sky;*
3 Let us then be true and faith-ful, Trust-ing, serv - ing ev - ery day;
4 *On-ward to the prize be-fore us! Soon His beau-ty we'll be-hold;*

1 In the man-sions bright and bless-ed He'll pre-pare for us a place.
2 *But when trav-eling days are o - ver Not a shad-ow, not a sigh.*
3 Just one glimpse of Him in glo-ry Will the toils of life re-pay.
4 *Soon the pearl-y gates will o-pen— We shall tread the streets of gold.*

When we all get to heav-en, What a day of re-joic-ing that will

be! When we all see Je - sus, We'll sing and shout the vic-to-ry!

EVERLASTING LIFE

Minister: *After this I looked, and behold, a great multitude which no man could number, from every nation, from all tribes and peoples and tongues, standing before the throne and before the Lamb, clothed in white robes, with palm branches in their hands, and crying out with a loud voice,*

People: "Salvation belongs to our God who sits upon the throne and to the Lamb!"

Minister: *And all the angels stood 'round the throne and 'round the elders and the four living creatures, and they fell on their faces before the throne and worshiped God, saying,*

People: "Amen! Blessing and glory and wisdom and thanksgiving and honor and power and might be to our God for ever and ever!

Minister and People: "Amen!"

Minister: *Then one of the elders addressed me, saying,*

Women of the Congregation: "Who are these, clothed in white robes, and whence have they come?"

Minister: *I said to him, "Sir, you know." And he said to me,*

Men of the Congregation: "These are they who have come out of the great tribulation;

Women of the Congregation: they have washed their robes and made them white in the blood of the Lamb.

People (Men and Women): Therefore are they before the throne of God, and serve Him day and night within His temple; and He who sits upon the throne will shelter them with His presence.

Men of the Congregation: They shall hunger no more, neither thirst any more;

Women of the Congregation: the sun shall not strike them, nor any scorching heat.

Minister: *For the Lamb in the midst of the throne will be their shepherd,*

Women of the Congregation: and He will guide them to springs of living water;

Men of the Congregation: and God shall wipe away every tear from their eyes."

—(RSV)

EVERLASTING LIFE

Is My Name Written There?
125

And another Book was opened which is the Book of Life . . . — Revelation 20:12

Mary A. Kidder

IS MY NAME
Frank M. Davis

1 Lord, I care not for rich - es, Nei - ther sil - ver nor gold, I would
2 *Lord, my sins they are man - y, Like the sands of the sea, But Thy*
3 O that beau - ti - ful cit - y With its man-sions of light, With its

1 make sure of heav-en, I would en - ter the fold. In the book of Thy
2 *blood, O my Sav-ior, Is suf - fi-cient for me; For Thy prom-ise is*
3 glo - ri - fied be-ings In pure gar-ments of white; Where no e - vil thing

1 king-dom, With its pag-es so fair, Tell me, Je-sus, my Sav-ior, Is my
2 *writ - ten In bright let-ters that glow,"Though your sins be as scar-let, I will*
3 com-eth To de-spoil what is fair; Where the an-gels are watch-ing, Yes, my

1 name writ - ten there? Is my name writ-ten there On the page white and
2 *make them like snow." Is my name writ-ten there On the page white and*
3 name's writ-ten there. Yes, my name's writ-ten there On the page white and

1 fair? In the book of Thy king-dom, Is my name writ-ten there?
2 *fair? In the book of Thy king-dom, Is my name writ-ten there?*
3 fair! In the book of Thy king-dom, Yes, my name's writ-ten there!

EVERLASTING LIFE

I John 3:1-6

See how much the Father has loved us! His love is so great that we are called God's children—and so, in fact, we are. This is why the world does not know us: it has not known God. My dear friends, we are now God's children, but it is not yet clear what we shall become. But we know that when Christ appears, we shall become like Him, because we shall see Him as He really is. Everyone who has this hope in Christ keeps himself pure, just as Christ is pure.

Whoever sins is guilty of breaking God's law; because sin is a breaking of the law. You know that Christ appeared in order to take away men's sins, and that there is no sin in Him. So everyone who lives in Christ does not continue to sin; but whoever continues to sin has never seen Him or known Him.

—(TEV)

127 **Beyond the Sunset**

For now we see through a glass darkly; but then face to face. — I Corinthians 13:12

SUNSET

Virgil P. Brock

Blanche Kerr Brock

1 Be-yond the sun-set, O bliss-ful morn-ing, When with our
2 *Be-yond the sun-set no clouds will gath-er, No storms will*
3 Be-yond the sun-set a hand will guide me To God the
4 *Be-yond the sun-set, O glad re-un-ion, With our dear*

1 Sav-ior heaven is be-gun; Earth's toil-ing end-ed, O glo-rious
2 *threat-en, no fears an-noy; O day of glad-ness, O day un-*
3 Fa-ther, whom I a-dore; His glo-rious pres-ence, His words of
4 *loved ones who've gone be-fore; In that fair home-land we'll know no*

1 dawn-ing, Be-yond the sun-set, when day is done.
2 *end-ing, Be-yond the sun-set, e-ter-nal joy!*
3 wel-come, Will be my por-tion on that fair shore.
4 *part-ing, Be-yond the sun-set, for-ev-er-more!*

EVERLASTING LIFE

Face to Face

For now we see through a glass darkly; . . .
—I Corinthians 13:12

Carrie E. Breck

FACE TO FACE
Grant C. Tullar

1 Face to face with Christ my Sav - ior, Face to face—what will it be—
2 On - ly faint-ly now I see Him, With the dark-ened veil be - tween,
3 What re-joic-ing in His pres - ence When are ban-ished grief and pain,
4 Face to face! O bliss-ful mo - ment! Face to face— to see and know;

1 When with rap-ture I be-hold Him, Je - sus Christ who died for me?
2 But a bless-ed day is com - ing When His glo - ry shall be seen.
3 When the crook-ed ways are straight-ened And the dark things shall be plain.
4 Face to face with my Re-deem - er, Je - sus Christ who loves me so.

Face to face I shall be - hold Him, Far be-yond the star-ry sky;

Face to face in all His glo - ry, I shall see Him by and by!

EVERLASTING LIFE

129 When We See Christ

. . . We shall be like Him for we shall see Him as He is.
— I John 3:2

Esther Kerr Rusthoi

WHEN WE SEE CHRIST
Esther Kerr Rusthoi

1 Oft - times the day seems long, our tri - als hard to bear, We're
2 *Some - times the sky looks dark with not a ray of light, We're*
3 Life's day will soon be o'er, all storms for - ev - er past, We'll

1 tempt - ed to com - plain, to mur - mur and de - spair; But Christ will soon ap -
2 *tossed and driv - en on, no hu - man help in sight; But there is One in*
3 cross the great di - vide to glo - ry, safe at last. We'll share the joys of

1 pear to catch His Bride a - way, All tears for - ev - er o - ver in
2 *heaven who knows our deep - est care, Let Je - sus solve your prob - lem—just*
3 heaven— a harp, a home, a crown, The tempt - er will be ban - ished, we'll

1 God's e - ter - nal day.
2 *go to Him in prayer.* It will be worth it all when we see
3 lay our bur - den down.

Je - sus, Life's trials will seem so small when we see Christ;

EVERLASTING LIFE

One glimpse of His dear face all sor-row will e-rase,

So brave-ly run the race 'til we see Christ.

I'll Be There

130

Being justified . . . through the redemption that is in Christ Jesus.
— Romans 3:24

I'LL BE THERE

Tim Spencer

Tim Spencer

I'll be there, I'll be there, When the Sav-ior calls my name, I'll be

there; I'll be there, I'll be there, By His a - maz-ing grace and

Optional Coda

mer-cy I'll be there. By His a - maz-ing grace and mer-cy I'll be there.

EVERLASTING LIFE

131 In Heaven Above

Mine eyes have seen the King, the Lord of hosts – Isaiah 6:5

Laurentius L. Laurinus
Revised by John Åstrom
Tr. by William Maccall

HAUGE
Norwegian Folk Melody

1 In heaven a-bove, in heaven a-bove, Where God our Fa-ther
2 *In heaven a-bove, in heaven a-bove, What glo-ry deep and*
3 In heaven a-bove, in heaven a-bove, God hath a joy pre-

1 dwells, How bound-less there the bless-ed-ness! No tongue its
2 *bright! The splen-dor of the noon-day sun Grows pale be-*
3 pared Which mor-tal ear had nev-er heard Nor mor-tal

1 great-ness tells; There face to face, and full and free, For-
2 *fore its light: The heaven-ly light that ne'er goes down, A-*
3 vis-ion shared. Which nev-er en-tered mor-tal breast, By

1 ev-er, ev-er-more we see Our God, the Lord of hosts!
2 *round whose ra-diance clouds ne'er frown, Is God, the Lord of hosts!*
3 mor-tal lips was ne'er ex-pressed: 'Tis God, the Lord of hosts!

EVERLASTING LIFE

O, That Will be Glory for Me

132

But when the multitude saw it, they marvelled and glorified God – Matthew 9:8

GLORY SONG

Charles H. Gabriel

Charles H. Gabriel

1 When all my la-bors and tri-als are o'er, And I am safe on that
2 *When by the gift of His in-fi-nite grace, I am ac-cord-ed in*
3 Friends will be there I have loved long a-go; Joy like a riv-er a-

1 beau-ti-ful shore, Just to be near the dear Lord I a-dore
2 *heav-en a place, Just to be there and to look on His face*
3 round me will flow; Yet, just a smile from my Sav-ior, I know,

1 Will through the a-ges be glo-ry for me.
2 *Will through the a-ges be glo-ry for me.* O, that will be
3 Will through the a-ges be glo-ry for me. O, that will

glo-ry for me, Glo-ry for me, glo-ry for me; When by His
be glo-ry for me, Glo-ry for me, glo-ry for me;

grace I shall look on His face, That will be glo-ry, be glo-ry for me.

EVERLASTING LIFE

133 Until Then

Because Thy lovingkindness is better than life,
my lips shall praise Thee.
— Psalm 63:3

Stuart Hamblen

UNTIL THEN
Stuart Hamblen

1 My heart can sing when I pause to re-mem-ber
2 *The things of earth will dim and lose their val-ue*
3 This wea-ry world with all its toil and strug-gle

1 A heart-ache here is but a step-ping stone
2 *If we re-call they're bor-rowed for a while;*
3 May take its toll of mis-er-y and strife;

1 A-long a trail that's wind-ing al-ways up-ward,
2 *And things of earth that cause the heart to trem-ble,*
3 The soul of man is like a wait-ing fal-con;

1 This trou-bled world is not my fi-nal home.
2 *Re-mem-bered there will on-ly bring a smile.*
3 When it's re-leased, it's des-tined for the skies.

EVERLASTING LIFE

EVERLASTING LIFE

134 When I Can Read My Title Clear

"In My Father's house are many mansions." — John 14:2

PISGAH
Traditional American Melody
Kentucky Harmony

Isaac Watts

1 When I can read my ti - tle clear To man-sions in the skies,
2 *Should earth a-gainst my soul en-gage And fier - y darts be hurled,*
3 Let cares like a wild del-uge come And storms of sor-row fall!

1 I'll bid fare - well to ev - ery fear And wipe my weep-ing eyes,
2 *Then I can smile at Sa - tan's rage And face a frown-ing world;*
3 May I but safe - ly reach my home, My God, my heaven, my all;

1 And wipe my weep-ing eyes, And wipe my weep-ing eyes,
2 *And face a frown-ing world, And face a frown-ing world,*
3 My God, my heaven, my all, My God, my heaven, my all,

1 I'll bid fare - well to ev - ery fear And wipe my weep-ing eyes.
2 *Then I can smile at Sa - tan's rage And face a frown-ing world.*
3 May I but safe - ly reach my home, My God, my heaven, my all.

EVERLASTING LIFE

It Will Be Worth It All

135

Let us run with patience the race that is set before us.
— Hebrews 12:1

William J. Gaither

WORTH IT ALL
William J. Gaither

1 There's a prom-ised land made for all the free, When our race on
2 *There no sad fare-wells, there no tear-stained eyes, There no heart-ache,*

1 earth is run, Where no bro-ken dreams will mar our mem-o-
2 *grief, or woe, There no shat-tered hopes will ev-er cloud the*

1 ry; It will be worth it all when we get home. It will be worth it all just to
2 *skies; It will be worth it all when we get home.*

see His face, When He claims us for His own; Then ten mil-lion

years to sing a-maz-ing grace; It will be worth it all when we get home.

EVERLASTING LIFE

136 Praise Ye the Triune God

. . . The Father, the Word, and the Holy Spirit, and these three are one. — 1 John 5:8

Elizabeth Rundle Charles

FLEMMING
Friedrich F. Flemming

1 Praise ye the Fa-ther for His lov-ing-kind-ness; Ten-der-ly
2 *Praise ye the Sav-ior— great is His com-pas-sion; Gra-cious-ly*
3 Praise ye the Spir-it, Com-fort-er of Is-rael, Sent of the

1 cares He for His err-ing chil-dren; Praise Him, ye an-gels,
2 *cares He for His cho-sen peo-ple; Young men and maid-ens,*
3 Fa-ther and the Son to bless us; Praise ye the Fa-ther,

1 praise Him in the heav-ens, Praise ye Je-ho-vah!
2 *old-er folks and chil-dren, Praise ye the Sav-ior!*
3 Son, and Ho-ly Spir-it, Praise ye the Tri-une God! A-men.

137 The Apostles' Creed

I believe in God the Father Almighty, maker of heaven and earth:

And in Jesus Christ His only Son, our Lord; Who was conceived by the Holy Spirit, born of the Virgin Mary, suffered under Pontius Pilate, was crucified, dead, and buried; He descended into hades; the third day He rose again from the dead; He ascended into heaven, and sitteth on the right hand of God, the Father Almighty; from thence He shall come to judge the quick and the dead.

I believe in the Holy Spirit, the holy Christian church, the communion of saints, the forgiveness of sins, the resurrection of the body, and the life everlasting.

Amen.

The Nicene Creed

I believe in one God
the Father Almighty,
maker of heaven and earth,
and of all things visible and invisible:

And in one Lord Jesus Christ, the only-begotten Son of God,
begotten of His Father before all worlds,
God of God, Light of Light, very God of very God,
begotten,
not made,
being of one substance with the Father,
by whom all things were made;
Who for us men and for our salvation came down from heaven,
and was incarnate by the Holy Spirit of the Virgin Mary,
and was made man,
and crucified also for us under Pontius Pilate;

He suffered and was buried, and the third day He rose again
according to the Scriptures,
and ascended into heaven, and sitteth on the right hand of the Father;
And He shall come again with glory
to judge both the quick and the dead;
Whose kingdom shall have no end.

And I believe in the Holy Spirit, the Lord and giver of life,
who proceedeth from the Father and the Son,
who with the Father and the Son together is worshiped and glorified;
who spoke by the prophets.

And I believe in one universal and apostolic church;
I acknowledge one baptism for the remission of sins,
and I look for the resurrection of the dead, and the life of the world to come.

Amen.

139 An Affirmation

WE BELIEVE IN JESUS CHRIST THE LORD,
Who was promised to the people of Israel,
Who came in the flesh to dwell among us,
Who announced the coming of the rule of God,
Who gathered disciples and taught them,
Who died on the cross to free us from sin,
Who rose from the dead to give us life and hope,
Who reigns in heaven at the right hand of God,
Who comes to judge and bring justice to victory.

WE BELIEVE IN GOD HIS FATHER,
Who raised Him from the dead,
Who created and sustains the universe,
Who acts to deliver His people in times of need,
Who desires all men everywhere to be saved.

WE BELIEVE IN THE HOLY SPIRIT,
Who is the form of God present in the church,
Who is the guarantee of our deliverance,
Who leads us to find God's will in the Word,
Who guides us in discernment,
Who impels us to act together.

—The Mennonite Hymnal, 1967

140 Hymn to the Trinity

*There are three that bear record in heaven;
the Father, the Word, and the Holy Spirit,
and these three are one.* 1 John 5:6

Paul Sjolund

HYMN TO THE TRINITY
Paul Sjolund

Praise we the Fa-ther and the Son, and the Ho-ly Spir - it. Thanks be to

Thee whose liv-ing Word doth lead and guide us. Praise we Thy maj-es-ty,

O bless - ed Trin - i - ty! A - men, A - men.

TRINITY

We Believe in a Triune God

We believe in God, the Eternal Spirit, Father of our Lord Jesus Christ and our Father, and
to His deeds we testify:

He calls the worlds into being,
creates man in His own image,
and sets before him the ways of life and death.
He seeks in holy love to save all people from aimlessness and sin.
He judges men and nations by His righteous will declared through prophets and
apostles.
In Jesus Christ, the man of Nazareth, our crucified and risen Lord,
He has come to us and shared our common lot,
conquering sin and death,
and reconciling the world to Himself.
He bestows upon us His Holy Spirit,
creating and renewing the Church of Jesus Christ,
binding in covenant faithful people of all ages, tongues, and races.
He calls us into His Church,
to accept the cost and joy of discipleship,
to be His servants in the service of men,
to proclaim the gospel to all the world,
to resist the powers of evil,
to share in Christ's baptism and eat at His table,
to join Him in His passion and victory.
He promises to all who trust Him:
forgiveness of sins and fulness of grace,
courage in the struggle for justice and peace,
His presence in trial and rejoicing,
and eternal life in His kingdom which has no end.
Blessing and honor, glory and power be unto Him. Amen.

—Statement of Faith of the United Church of Christ,
adopted by the General Synod at Oberlin in 1959.

Gloria Patri

*And He said unto them, . . . how much more shall your
heavenly Father give the Holy Spirit . . .*   Luke 11 :13

Source unknown

GLORIA PATRI
Henry W. Greatorex

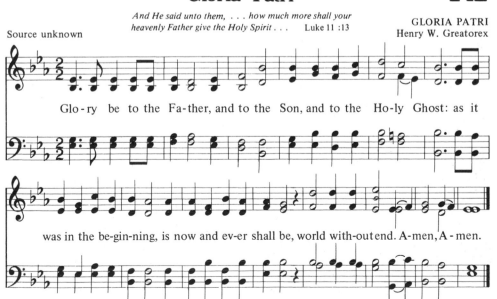

Glo - ry be to the Fa - ther, and to the Son, and to the Ho - ly Ghost: as it

was in the be - gin - ning, is now and ev - er shall be, world with - out end. A - men, A - men.

TRINITY

143 The Comforter Has Come

I will pray the Father and He will give you another Comforter. — John 14:16

COMFORTER

Frank Bottome

William J. Kirkpatrick

1 O spread the ti-dings 'round wher-ev-er man is found, Wher-
2 *The long, long night is past, the morn-ing breaks at last, And*
3 Lo, the great King of kings, with heal-ing in His wings, To
4 *O bound-less love di-vine! How shall this tongue of mine To*

1 ev - er hu-man hearts and hu-man woes a-bound; Let ev-ery Christ-ian
2 *hushed the dread-ful sound and fu - ry of the blast, As o - ver gold-en*
3 ev - ery cap-tive soul a full de-liv-erance brings; And through the va-cant
4 *won-dering mor-tals tell the match-less grace di-vine— That I, a child of*

1 tongue pro-claim the joy-ful sound: The Com-fort-er has come!
2 *hills the day ad-vanc-es fast! The Com-fort-er has come!*
3 cells the song of tri-umph rings: The Com-fort-er has come!
4 *hell, should in His im-age shine? The Com-fort-er has come!*

The Com-fort-er has come, the Com-fort-er has come! The

HOLY SPIRIT

Ho-ly Ghost from Heaven, the Fa-ther's pro-mise given; O spread the ti-dings

'round wher-ev-er man is found—The Com-fort-er has come!

Come, Holy Spirit, Heavenly Dove   144

And I saw the Spirit, descending like a dove and it abode upon Him.   John 1:32

GRÄFENBERG
Praxis Pietatis Melica
Johann Crüger

Isaac Watts

1 Come, Ho-ly Spir-it, heaven-ly Dove, With all Thy quick-ening powers;
2 *Dear Lord, and shall we ev-er live At this poor, dy-ing rate?*
3 Come, Ho-ly Spir-it, heaven-ly Dove, With all Thy quick-ening powers;

1 Kin-dle a flame of sa-cred love In these cold hearts of ours.
2 *Our love so faint, so cold to Thee, And Thine to us so great!*
3 Come, shed a-broad the Sav-ior's love, And that shall kin-dle ours. A-men.

145 Blessed Quietness

He shall give you another comforter that He may abide with you forever. — John 14:16

BLESSED QUIETNESS
W. S. Marshall
Arranged by James M. Kirk

Manie P. Ferguson

1 Joys are flow - ing like a riv - er Since the Com - fort-er has come;
2 *Bring-ing life and health and glad - ness All a - round, this heav'n-ly Guest*
3 Like the rain that falls from heav - en, Like the sun - light from the sky,
4 *See, a fruit - ful field is grow - ing, Bless - ed fruit of right-eous-ness;*
5 What a won - der - ful sal - va - tion, Where we al - ways see His face!

1 He a - bides with us for - ev - er, Makes the trust - ing heart His home.
2 *Ban-ished un - be - lief and sad - ness, Changed our wea - ri - ness to rest.*
3 So the Ho - ly Ghost is giv - en, Com - ing on us from on high.
4 *And the streams of life are flow - ing In the lone - ly wil - der - ness.*
5 What a per - fect hab - i - ta - tion, What a qui - et rest - ing place!

Bless - ed qui - et - ness, ho - ly qui - et - ness, What as - sur - ance in my soul!

On the storm - y sea He speaks peace to me, How the bil - lows cease to roll!

HOLY SPIRIT

The Holy Spirit 146

Spirit of God, Descend upon My Heart 147

And thou shalt love the Lord, thy God,
with all thy heart, and soul.... — Mark 12:30

George Croly

MORECAMBE
Frederick C. Atkinson

1 Spir - it of God, de - scend up - on my heart; Wean it from
2 *I ask no dream, no proph - et ec - sta - sies, No sud - den*
3 Hast Thou not bid us love Thee, God and King? All, all Thine
4 *Teach me to feel that Thou art al - ways nigh; Teach me the*
5 Teach me to love Thee as Thine an - gels love, One ho - ly

1 earth, through all its puls - es move; Stoop to my weak - ness, might - y
2 *rend - ing of the veil of clay, No an - gel vis - i - tant, no*
3 own - soul, heart and strength and mind! I see Thy cross—there teach my
4 *strug - gles of the soul to bear, To check the ris - ing doubt, the*
5 pas - sion fill - ing all my frame; The bap - tism of the heaven - de -

1 as Thou art, And make me love Thee as I ought to love.
2 *o - pening skies: But take the dim - ness of my soul a - way.*
3 heart to cling: O let me seek Thee, and O let me find!
4 *reb - el sigh; Teach me the pa - tience of un - an-swered prayer.*
5 scend - ed Dove: My heart an al - tar, and Thy love the flame. A-men.

HOLY SPIRIT

148 Where the Spirit of the Lord Is

Where the spirit of the Lord is there is liberty.
— II Corinthians 3:17

Stephen R. Adams

THERE IS PEACE
Stephen R. Adams

Where the Spir - it of the Lord is, there is peace;

Where the Spir - it of the Lord is, there is love.

There is com-fort in life's dark-est hour, There is light and life, there is

help and pow-er In the Spir - it, in the Spir - it of the Lord.

HOLY SPIRIT

Holy, Holy

149

They rest not day and night,
saying holy, holy, holy, Lord God almighty.
— Revelation 4:8

Jimmy Owens

HOLY, HOLY
Jimmy Owens

1 Ho - ly, ho - ly, ho - ly, ho - ly, Ho - ly, ho - ly,
2 Gra - cious Fa - ther, gra - cious Fa - ther, We're so blest to be your
3 Pre - cious Je - sus, pre - cious Je - sus, We're so glad that You've re -
4 Ho - ly Spir - it, Ho - ly Spir - it, Come and fill our hearts a -
5 Ho - ly, ho - ly, ho - ly ho - ly, Ho - ly, ho - ly,
6 Hal - le - lu - jah, hal - le - lu - jah, Hal - le - lu - jah,

1 Lord God Al - might - y; And we lift our hearts be - fore You as a
2 chil - dren, gra - cious Fa - ther; And we lift our heads be - fore You as a
3 deemed us, pre - cious Je - sus; And we lift our voice be - fore You as a
4 new, Ho - ly Spir - it; And we lift our hands be - fore You as a
5 Lord God Al - might - y; And we lift our hearts be - fore You as a
6 hal - le - lu - jah; And we lift our hearts be - fore You as a

1 to - ken of our love, Ho - ly, ho - ly, ho - ly, ho - ly.
2 to - ken of our love, Gra - cious Fa - ther, gra - cious Fa - ther.
3 to - ken of our love, Pre - cious Je - sus, pre - cious Je - sus.
4 to - ken of our love, Ho - ly Spir - it, Ho - ly Spir - it.
5 to - ken of our love, Ho - ly, ho - ly, ho - ly, ho - ly.
6 to - ken of our love, Hal - le - lu - jah, hal - le - lu - jah.

HOLY SPIRIT

150 Come, Holy Spirit

My grace is sufficient for thee; for my strength is made perfect in weakness. — II Corinthians 12:9

Gloria Gaither
William J. Gaither

COME, HOLY SPIRIT
William J. Gaither

1 Come as a wis-dom to child-ren, Come as new sight to the
2 *Come as a rest to the wea-ry,* *Come as a balm for the*
3 Come like a spring in the de-sert, Come to the with-ered of

1 blind, Come, Lord, as strength to my weak-ness, Take me: soul,
2 *sore,* *Come as a dew to my dry-ness:* *Fill me with*
3 soul; O let Your sweet heal-ing pow-er Touch me and

1 bod-y and mind.
2 *joy ev-er-more,* Come, Ho-ly Spir-it, I need You,
3 make me whole.

Come, sweet Spir-it, I pray; Come in Your strength and Your

pow-er, Come in Your own gen-tle way. A-men.

HOLY SPIRIT

Spirit, Now Live in Me

151

*. . . How much more shall your Heavenly Father give
the Holy Spirit to them that ask Him.* — Luke 11:13

LOIS

Bryan Jeffery Leech

Bryan Jeffery Leech

Unison

1 O ho-ly Dove of God de-scend-ing, You are the love that knows no end-ing,
2 *O ho-ly Wind of God now blow-ing, You are the seed that God is sow-ing,*
3 O ho-ly Rain of God now fall-ing, You make the Word of God en-thrall-ing,
4 *O ho-ly Flame of God now burn-ing, You are the power of Christ re-turn-ing,*

1 All of our shattered dreams You're mending: Spir-it, now live in me.
2 *You are the life that starts us grow-ing: Spir-it, now live in me.*
3 You are that in-ner voice now call-ing: Spir-it, now live in me.
4 *You are the an-swer to our yearn-ing: Spir-it, now live in me.* A-men.

The Day of Pentecost

152

When the day of Pentecost had come, they were all together in one place. And sudden-ly a sound came from heaven like the rush of a mighty wind, and it filled all the house where they were sitting. And there appeared to them tongues as of fire, distributed and resting on each one of them. And they were all filled with the Holy Spirit and began to speak in other tongues, as the Spirit gave them utterance.

But Peter, standing with the eleven, lifted up his voice and addressed them, "Men of Judea and all who dwell in Jerusalem, let this be known to you, and give ear to my words.

"Jesus of Nazareth, a man attested to you by God with mighty works and wonders and signs which God did through Him in your midst, as you yourselves know—this Jesus, delivered up according to the definite plan and foreknowledge of God, you crucified and killed by the hands of lawless men. But God raised Him up, having loosed the pangs of death, because it was not possible for Him to be held by it.

"Let all the house of Israel therefore know assuredly that God has made Him both Lord and Christ, this Jesus whom you crucified."

Now when they heard this they were cut to the heart, and said to Peter and the rest of the apostles, "Brethren, what shall we do?" And Peter said to them, "Repent, and be baptized every one of you in the name of Jesus Christ for the forgiveness of yours sins; and you shall receive the gift of the Holy Spirit. For the promise is to you and to your children and to all that are far off, everyone whom the Lord our God calls to Him." And he testified with many other words and exhorted them, saying, "Save yourselves from this crooked gen-eration." So those who received his word were baptized, and there were added that day about three thousand souls. And they devoted themselves to the apostles' teaching and fel-lowship, to the breaking of bread and the prayers.

—Acts 2:1-4; 14; 22b-24; 36-42. (RSV)

HOLY SPIRIT

153

Fill Me Now

Elwood R. Stokes

And to know the love of Christ, . . . that ye might be filled . . .
— Ephesians 3:19

FILL ME NOW
John R. Sweney

1 Hov - er o'er me, Ho - ly Spir - it, Bathe my trem-bling heart and brow;
2 *Thou canst fill me, gra-cious Spir - it, Though I can - not tell Thee how;*
3 I am weak-ness, full of weak-ness, At Thy sa - cred feet I bow;
4 *Cleanse and com-fort, bless and save me, Bathe, O bathe my heart and brow;*

1 Fill me with Thy hal-lowed pres-ence, Come, O come and fill me now.
2 *But I need Thee, great-ly need Thee, Come, O come and fill me now.*
3 Blest, di-vine, e - ter - nal Spir - it, Fill with power, and fill me now.
4 *Thou art com-fort - ing and sav - ing, Thou art sweet-ly fill-ing now.*

Fill me now, fill me now, Je - sus, come and fill me now;

Fill me with Thy hal-lowed pres-ence—Come, O come and fill me now.

154 The Promise Fulfilled

We want to be as full of the Holy Spirit as the sea is full of water, as the sky is full of air, as the air is full of oxygen, as the continent is full of land, and as the fire is full of flame. His purpose is to animate our spirits for the doing of God's will, to calm our souls and claim our comfort and recall Christ's promises.

The Holy Spirit is the witness of God's Presence and Power for good. He is the rush of Heaven's wind, the fire of Divine communication, and He does not rest until He has revealed Christ as the Son of God, Redeemer of believing men and inseparable Companion of the committed soul. The Holy Spirit never fails. He is imperturbable in tribulation, indomitable in spiritual action and invincible in evangelism.

—Raymond Lindquist

HOLY SPIRIT

Spirit of the Living God

155

The Holy Spirit fell on us as on them in the beginning.
— Acts 11:15

LIVING GOD
Daniel Iverson

Daniel Iverson

Spir - it of the Liv - ing God, Fall a - fresh on me,

Spir - it of the Liv - ing God, Fall a - fresh on me.

Melt me, mold me, Fill me, use me.

Spir - it of the Liv - ing God, Fall a - fresh on me.

I Corinthians 2:10-16

156

The Spirit searches all things, even the deep things of God. For who among men knows the thoughts of a man except the man's spirit within him? In the same way no one knows the thoughts of God except the Spirit of God. We have not received the spirit of the world but the Spirit who is from God, that we may understand what God has freely given us. This is what we speak, not in words taught us by human wisdom but in words taught by the Spirit, expressing spiritual truths in spiritual words. The man without the Spirit does not accept the things that come from the Spirit of God, for they are foolishness to him, and he cannot understand them, because they are spiritually discerned. The spiritual man makes judgments about all things, but he himself is not subject to any man's judgment:

"For who has known the mind of the Lord that he may instruct him?" But we have the mind of Christ.

—(NIV)

HOLY SPIRIT

157 The Spirit of Jesus Is in This Place

Gloria Gaither
William J. Gaither

SPIRIT OF JESUS
William J. Gaither

O, the Spir - it of Je - sus is in this place,

I can see the change He's mak-ing on each face;

When the power of Heaven is tapped, then, some-thing good is bound to

hap - pen, for the Spir - it of Je - sus is in this place.

O my friend, He is so near that we could touch Him,

HOLY SPIRIT

His sweet pres-ence this old world could ne'er re - place;

Won't you let His Spir - it warm you, let His might - y love trans-

form you, while the Spir - it of Je - sus is in this place.

The Outpouring of the Spirit 158

"After this I will pour out my spirit on all mankind.
Your sons and daughters shall prophesy,

> your old men shall dream dreams,

> and your young men see visions.

Even on the slaves, men and women, will I pour out my spirit in those days.
I will display portents in heaven and on earth,

> blood and fire

> and columns of smoke."

The sun will be turned into darkness, and the moon into blood,

> before the day of Jehovah dawns, that great and terrible day.

All who call on the name of Jehovah will be saved,

> for on Mount Zion there will be some who have escaped,

> as Jehovah has said,

> and in Jerusalem some survivors whom Jehovah will call.

—Joel 3:1-5 (JB)

159 Sweet, Sweet Spirit

I will not leave you comfortless; I will come to you. — John 14:18

SWEET, SWEET SPIRIT
Doris Akers

Doris Akers

1 There's a sweet, sweet Spir-it in this place, And I know that it's the
2 *There are bless-ings you can-not re-ceive* *'Til you know Him in His*
3 If you say He saved you from your sin, Now you're weak, you're bound and

1 Spir - it of the Lord; There are sweet ex - pres-sions on each
2 *full - ness and be - lieve;* *You're the one to prof - it when you*
3 can - not en - ter in; You can make it right if you will

1 face, And I know they feel the pres - ence of the Lord.
2 *say,* *"I am going to walk with Je - sus all the way."*
3 yield— You'll en - joy the Ho - ly Spir - it that we feel.

Sweet Ho - ly Spir - it, Sweet heav - en - ly Dove, Stay right here

with us, Fill - ing us with Your love; And for these

HOLY SPIRIT

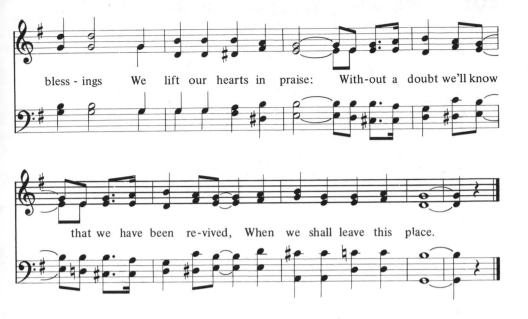

bless - ings We lift our hearts in praise: With-out a doubt we'll know

that we have been re-vived, When we shall leave this place.

Give Us Your Holy Spirit   **160**

Leader: Make us one, Lord, in our eagerness to speak good news and set all captives free.

People: *Give us Your Holy Spirit.*

Leader: Make us one, Lord, in concern for the poor, the hurt, and the downtrodden, to show them Your love.

People: *Give us Your Holy Spirit.*

Leader: Make us one, Lord, in worship, breaking bread together and singing Your praise with single voice.

People: *Give us Your Holy Spirit.*

Leader: Make us one, Lord, in faithfulness to Jesus Christ who never fails us, and who will come again in triumph.

People: *Give us Your Holy Spirit.*

Leader: Give us Your Holy Spirit, God our Father, so we may have among us the same mind that was in Christ Jesus; and proclaim Him to the world. May every knee bow down and every tongue confess Him Lord, to the glory of Your name.

People: *Amen.*

—Gary W. Demarest

161 Breathe On Me, Breath of God

Edwin Hatch

. . . that the love wherewith Thou hath loved me, may be in them, and I in them
— John 17:26

TRENTHAM
Robert Jackson

1 Breathe on me, Breath of God, Fill me with life a - new,
2 *Breathe on me, Breath of God, Un - til my heart is pure,*
3 Breathe on me, Breath of God, Till I am whol - ly Thine,
4 *Breathe on me, Breath of God, So shall I nev - er die,*

1 That I may love what Thou dost love, And do what Thou wouldst do.
2 *Un - til with Thee I will one will To do and to en - dure.*
3 Un - til this earth - ly part of me Glows with Thy fire di - vine.
4 *But live with Thee the per - fect life Of Thine e - ter - ni - ty.* A - men.

162 Holy Ghost, With Light Divine

Andrew Reed

. . . ye do well that ye heed, as unto a light
that shineth in a dark place . . . — II Peter 1:19

MERCY
Louis M. Gottschalk
Adapted by Edwin P. Parker

1 Ho - ly Ghost, with light di - vine, Shine up - on this heart of mine;
2 *Ho - ly Ghost, with power di - vine, Cleanse this guilt - y heart of mine;*
3 Ho - ly Ghost, with joy di - vine, Cheer this sad - dened heart of mine;
4 *Ho - ly Spir - it, all di - vine, Dwell with - in this heart of mine;*

1 Chase the shades of night a - way, Turn my dark - ness in - to day.
2 *Long hath sin with - out con - trol Held do - min - ion o'er my soul.*
3 Bid my man - y woes de - part, Heal my wound - ed, bleed - ing heart.
4 *Cast down ev - ery i - dol - throne, Reign su - preme and reign a - lone.* A - men.

HOLY SPIRIT

Our ascended Lord gives hope for two ages.
In the age to come, He is the judge, rejecting unrighteousness,
    isolating His enemies to hell, blessing His new creation in Christ.
In this age, His Holy Spirit is with us, calling nations to follow Christ's path,
    uniting people through Christ's love.

—"Our song of hope"—a confessional of faith.

Holy Spirit, Flow Through Me   164

Walt Mills

. . . But if ye through the Spirit do mortify the deeds of the body,
ye shall live. — Romans 8:13

MILLS
Walt Mills

1 Ho - ly Spir - it, flow through me,
2 *Ho - ly Spir - it, rest on me,*
3 Ho - ly Spir - it, flow out from me,

1 Ho - ly Spir - it, flow through me, And
2 *Ho - ly Spir - it, rest on me, And*
3 Ho - ly Spir - it, flow out through me, That

1 make my life what it ought to be,
2 *use me, Lord, win the lost to Thee,*
3 oth - ers, Lord, may see You in me,

1 Ho - ly Spir - it, flow through me.
2 *Ho - ly Spir - it, rest on me.*
3 Ho - ly Spir - it, flow out through me.

HOLY SPIRIT

Beginning

In the beginning was the Word:
the Word was with God
and the Word was God.

He was with God in the beginning.

Through Him all things came to be,
not one thing had its being but through Him.

All that came to be had life in Him
and that life was the light of men,
a light that shines in the dark,
a light that darkness could not overpower.

A man came, sent by God.

His name was John.

He came as a witness,
as a witness to speak for the light,
so that everyone might believe through him.

He was not the light,
only a witness to speak for the light.

The Word was the true light
that enlightens all men;
and He was coming into the world.

He was in the world
that had its being through Him,
and the world did not know Him.

He came to His own domain
and His own people did not accept Him.

But to all who did accept Him
He gave power to become children of God,
to all who believe in the name of Him
who was born not out of human stock
or urge of the flesh
or will of man
but of God Himself.

The Word was made flesh,
He lived among us,
and we saw His glory,
the glory that is His as the only Son of the Father,
full of grace and truth.

—John 1:1-14 (JB)

Let All Mortal Flesh Keep Silence

166

Let all mortal flesh keep silent.

— Habakkuk 2:20

Liturgy of St. James
Tr. by Gerard Moultrie

PICARDY
French Carol

Unison

1 Let all mor-tal flesh keep si - lence, And with fear and trem-bling stand;
2 *King of kings, yet born of Mar - y, As of old on earth He stood,*
3 At His feet the six-winged ser - aph; Cher - u - bim with watch-ful eye,

1 Pon-der noth-ing world - ly mind - ed, For with bless-ing in His hand
2 *Lord of lords in hu - man na - ture, In the bod - y and the blood,*
3 Veil their fac - es to His Pres - ence, As with cease-less voice they cry,

1 Christ our God to earth de-scend - eth, Our full hom-age to de - mand.
2 *He will give to all the faith - ful His own self for heaven-ly food.*
3 "Al - le - lu - ia, Al - le - lu - ia, Al - le - lu - ia, Lord most high!"

CHRISTMAS

167 The Incarnation

The Son of God became a man to enable men to become sons of God.

—C. S. Lewis

168 Come, Thou Long-Expected Jesus

HYFRYDOL

And we declare unto you glad tidings how that the promise . . . Rowland Hugh Prichard
God hath fulfilled. — Acts 13: 32,33 Descant by Paul Sjolund

Charles Wesley

Descant
f

2 Come, Lord, born to de-liv-er, Born a child, born a

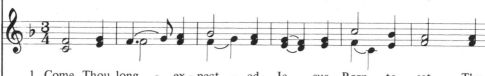

1 Come, Thou long - ex-pect-ed Je - sus, Born to set Thy
2 Born Thy peo - ple to de-liv-er, Born a child and

child and a King, born to reign, reign in us for-ev - er,

1 peo - ple free; From our fears and sins re-lease us;
2 yet a King, Born to reign in us for-ev - er,

cresc.

Now Thy gra-cious King-dom bring. By Thy Spir-it,

1 Let us find our rest in Thee. Is - rael's
2 Now Thy gra-cious King - dom bring. By Thine

CHRISTMAS

2 *Thine e - ter - nal Spir - it Rule in all our hearts a -*

1 Strength and Con - so - la - tion, Hope of all the earth Thou
2 *own e - ter - nal Spir - it Rule in all our hearts a -*

lone; Al - le - lu - ia, Al - le - lu - ia, Al - le - lu - ia,

1 art; Dear De - sire of ev - ery na - tion,
2 *lone; By Thine all - suf - fi - cient mer - it*

Al - le - lu - ia, to Thy glo - rious throne. A - men. A - men.

1 Joy of ev - ery long - ing heart.
2 *Raise us to Thy glo - rious throne. A - men.*

CHRISTMAS

169 O Come, O Come, Emmanuel

Behold, a virgin shall . . . bear a Son and shall call His name Immanuel.
— Isaiah 7:14

Latin: c. 9th Century
Tr. by John M. Neale, stanzas 1, 2, alt.
Tr. by Henry S. Coffin, stanzas 3, 4, alt.

VENI EMMANUEL
Adapted from Plainsong, Mode I
Thomas Helmore

1 O come, O come, Em-man - u-el, And ran-som cap-tive
2 *O come, Thou Day-spring, come and cheer Our spir-its by Thine*
3 O come, Thou Wis-dom from on high, And or-der all things,
4 *O come, De-sire of na - tions, bind In one the hearts of*

1 Is - ra - el, That mourns in lone-ly ex - ile here,
2 *ad - vent here; Dis-perse the gloom-y clouds of night,*
3 far and nigh; To us the path of knowl - edge show,
4 *all man - kind; Bid Thou our sad di - vi - sions cease,*

1 Un - til the Son of God ap - pear.
2 *And death's dark shad-ows put to flight.*
3 And cause us in her ways to go.
4 *And be Thy-self our King of peace.*

Re-joice! Re-joice! Em -

man - u - el Shall come to thee, O Is - ra - el! A-men.

Descant and Arrangement by Richard Purvis

CHRISTMAS

170 Thou Didst Leave Thy Throne

He came unto His own and His own received Him not.
— John 1:11

Emily E. S. Elliott

MARGARET
Timothy R. Matthews

1 Thou didst leave Thy throne and Thy king-ly crown When Thou cam-est to earth for me, But in Beth-le-hem's home there was found no room For Thy ho-ly na-tiv-i-ty. O come to my heart, Lord Je-sus: There is room in my heart for Thee!

2 *Heav-en's arch-es rang when the an-gels sang, Pro-claim-ing Thy roy-al de-gree, But in low-ly birth didst Thou come to earth And in great hu-mil-i-ty. O come to my heart, Lord Je-sus: There is room in my heart for Thee!*

3 The fox-es found rest, and the birds their nest In the shade of the for-est tree, But Thy couch was the sod, O Thou Son of God, In the des-erts of Gal-i-lee. O come to my heart, Lord Je-sus: There is room in my heart for Thee!

4 *Thou cam-est, O Lord, with the liv-ing word That should set Thy peo-ple free, But with mock-ing scorn and with crown of thorn They bore Thee to Cal-va-ry. O come to my heart, Lord Je-sus: There is room in my heart for Thee!*

5 When the heavens shall ring and the an-gels sing At Thy com-ing to vic-to-ry, Let Thy voice call me home, say-ing, "Yet there is room, There is room at my side for thee." And my heart shall re-joice, Lord Je-sus, When Thou com-est and call-est me. A-men.

Joy to the World!

171

For unto you is born this day . . . a Savior . . . .

— Luke 2:11

ANTIOCH
George Friedrich Handel
Arranged by Fred Bock
and Ralph Carmichael

Psalm 98
Adapted by Isaac Watts

1 Joy to the world! the Lord is come: Let earth re-
2 *Joy to the world! the Sav - ior reigns: Let men their*
3 No more let sins and sor - rows grow, Nor thorns in -
4 *He rules the world with truth and grace, And makes the*

1 ceive her King; Let ev - ery heart pre - pare Him
2 *songs em - ploy; While fields and floods, rocks, hills, and*
3 fest the ground; He comes to make His bless - ings
4 *na - tions prove The glo - ries of His right - eous -*

1 room, And heaven and na-ture sing, And heaven and na-ture sing, And
2 *plains Re - peat the sound-ing joy, Re - peat the sound-ing joy, Re -*
3 flow Far as the curse is found, Far as the curse is found, Far
4 *ness, And won-ders of His love, And won-ders of His love, And*

And heaven and na-ture sing,

And heaven and na-ture

1 heaven, and heaven and na - ture sing.
2 *peat, re - peat the sound - ing joy.*
3 as, far as the curse is found.
4 *won - ders, won - ders of His love. A - men.*

sing,

CHRISTMAS

172 Of the Father's Love Begotten

I am Alpha and Omega — the beginning and the end, which is, and which was, and which is to come.
— Revelation 1:8

Aurelius Clemens Prudentius
Tr. by John M. Neale, stanza 1
Tr. by Henry W. Baker, stanzas 2, 3

DIVINUM MYSTERIUM
13th Century Plainsong, Mode V

1 Of the Fa-ther's love be-got - ten, Ere the worlds be-gan to be,
2 *O ye heights of heaven a-dore Him; An - gel hosts, His prais - es sing;*
3 Christ, to Thee with God the Fa - ther And, O Ho - ly Ghost, to Thee,

1 He is Al-pha and O-me - ga, He the source, the end - ing He,
2 *Powers, do-min-ions, bow be-fore Him, And ex-tol our God and King;*
3 Hymn and chant and high thanks-giv - ing And un-wea-ried prais - es be.

1 Of the things that are, that have been, And that fu - ture
2 *Let no tongue on earth be si - lent, Ev - ery voice in*
3 Hon - or, glo - ry, and do-min - ion, And e - ter - nal

1 years shall see, Ev - er - more and ev - er - more!
2 *con - cert ring, Ev - er - more and ev - er - more!*
3 vic - to - ry, Ev - er - more and ev - er - more! A - men.

The Birth of Jesus

Now when Jesus was born in Bethlehem of Judea
in the days of Herod the king,
behold, wise men from the East came to Jerusalem, saying,
"Where is He who has been born king of the Jews?
For we have seen His star in the East,
and have come to worship Him."

When Herod the king heard this, he was troubled,
and all Jerusalem with him;
and assembling all the chief priests and scribes of the people,
he inquired of them where the Christ was to be born.

They told him, "In Bethlehem of Judea;
for so it is written by the prophet:
'And you, O Bethlehem, in the land of Judah,
are by no means least among the rulers of Judah,
for from you shall come a ruler who will govern my people Israel.' "

Then Herod summoned the wise men secretly
and ascertained from them what time the star appeared;
and he sent them to Bethlehem, saying,
"Go and search diligently for the child,
and when you have found Him bring me word,
that I too may come and worship Him."

When they had heard the king they went their way;
and lo, the star which they had seen in the East went before them,
'til it came to rest over the place where the child was.

When they saw the star, they rejoiced exceedingly with great joy;
and going into the house they saw the child with Mary His mother,
and they fell down and worshiped Him.

Then, opening their treasures, they offered Him gifts,
gold
frankincense
and myrrh.

And being warned in a dream not to return to Herod,
they departed to their own country by another way.

—Matthew 2:1-12 (RSV)

174 Lo! How a Rose E'er Blooming

I am the rose of Sharon, the lily of the valley. — Song of Solomon 2:1

German Carol
Tr. by Theodore Baker, stanzas 1,2
Tr. by Harriet Krauth Spaeth, stanza 3

ES IST EIN ROS'
Geistliche Kirchengesäng
Harmonized by Michael Praetorius

1 Lo, how a rose e'er bloom-ing From ten-der stem hath sprung!
2 *I - sa-iah 'twas fore-told it, The rose I have in mind;*
3 This flower, whose fra-grance ten-der With sweet-ness fills the air,

1 Of Jes-se's lin-eage com-ing As men of old have sung.
2 *With Mar-y we be-hold it, The vir-gin moth - er kind.*
3 Dis-pels with glo-rious splen-dor The dark-ness ev - ery-where.

1 It came, a flow - er bright, A - mid the cold of
2 *To show God's love a - right She bore to men a*
3 True man, yet ver - y God, From sin and death He

1 win - ter, When half - gone was the night.
2 *Sav - ior, When half - gone was the night.*
3 saves us And light - ens ev - ery load.

CHRISTMAS

While Shepherds Watched Their Flocks by Night

175

Fear not, for I bring you good tidings of great joy. — Luke 2:10

Nahum Tate

CHRISTMAS

Arranged from George Friedrich Handel

1 While shep-herds watched their flocks by night, All seat - ed on the
2 *"Fear not!" said he, for might-y dread Had seized their trou - bled*
3 "To you in Da - vid's town this day Is born, of Da - vid's
4 *"The heaven-ly Babe you there shall find To hu - man view dis -*
5 "All glo - ry be to God on high, And to the earth be

1 ground, The an - gel of the Lord came down, And
2 *mind; "Glad ti - dings of great joy I bring To*
3 line, The Sav - ior, who is Christ the Lord, And
4 *played, All mean - ly wrapt in swath-ing - bands And*
5 peace: Good will hence - forth from heaven to men Be -

1 glo - ry shone a - round, And glo - ry shone a - round.
2 *you and all man - kind, To you and all man - kind.*
3 this shall be the sign— And this shall be the sign:
4 *in a man - ger laid, And in a man - ger laid.*
5 gin and nev - er cease! Be - gin and nev - er cease!"

Luke 1:46b-55

176

"My soul magnifies the Lord, and my spirit rejoices in God my Savior, for He has regarded the low estate of His handmaiden. For behold, henceforth all generations will call me blessed; for He who is mighty has done great things for me, and holy is His name. And His mercy is on those who fear Him from generation to generation. He has shown strength with His arm, He has scattered the proud in the imagination of their hearts, He has put down the mighty from their thrones, and exalted those of low degree; He has filled the hungry with good things, and the rich He has sent empty away. He has helped His servant Israel, in remembrance of His mercy, as He spoke to our fathers, to Abraham and to his posterity for ever."

—(RSV)

CHRISTMAS

Good Christian Men, Rejoice

When they saw the star they rejoiced. — Matthew 2:10

Latin Carol
Tr. by John M. Neale

IN DULCI JUBILO
German Melody

1 Good Chris-tian men, re - joice   With heart and soul   and voice;
2 *Good Chris-tian men, re - joice   With heart and soul   and voice;*
3 Good Chris-tian men, re - joice   With heart and soul   and voice;

1 Give   ye heed to   what we say: News! news! Je-sus Christ is   born to-day!
2 *Now   ye hear of   end-less bliss: Joy!   joy! Je-sus Christ was   born for this!*
3 Now   ye need not   fear the grave: Peace! peace! Je-sus Christ was   born to save!

1 Ox   and ass   be - fore Him bow,   And He   is   in   the   man-ger now.
2 *He   has   o-pened heav-en's door,   And man   is   bless-ed   ev - er-more.*
3 Calls you one and   calls you all   To gain His ev - er - last-ing hall.

1 Christ   is   born   to - day!   Christ   is   born   to - day!
2 *Christ was   born   for   this!   Christ   was   born   for   this!*
3 Christ was born   to   save!   Christ   was born   to   save!

O Little Town of Bethlehem

But thou, Bethlehem, out of thee shall come He forth . . . a ruler in Israel. — Micah 5:2

ST. LOUIS
Lewis H. Redner

Phillips Brooks

1 O lit-tle town of Beth-le-hem, How still we see thee lie!
2 *For Christ is born of Ma - ry, And gath-ered all a - bove,*
3 How si - lent - ly, how si - lent - ly, The won-drous gift is given!
4 *O ho- ly Child of Beth-le-hem! De-scend to us, we pray;*

1 A - bove thy deep and dream-less sleep The si - lent stars go by;
2 *While mor-tals sleep, the an-gels keep Their watch of won-der-ing love.*
3 So God im-parts to hu-man hearts The bless-ings of His heaven.
4 *Cast out our sin and en-ter in, Be born in us to - day.*

1 Yet in thy dark streets shin - eth The ev - er-last-ing Light:
2 *O morn-ing stars, to - geth - er Pro-claim the ho-ly birth!*
3 No ear may hear His com - ing, But in this world of sin,
4 *We hear the Christ-mas an - gels The great glad ti-dings tell;*

1 The hopes and fears of all the years Are met in thee to - night.
2 *And prais-es sing to God the King, And peace to men on earth.*
3 Where meek souls will re - ceive Him still, The dear Christ en - ters in.
4 *O come to us, a - bide with us, Our Lord Em-man - u - el!* A-men.

179 The First Noel

And there were in that same country, Shepherds . . . in the field . . . .
— Luke 2:8

THE FIRST NOEL
English Melody
From Sandys' *Christmas Carols*

English Carol

1 The first no - el the an-gel did say Was to cer-tain poor
2 *They look - ed up and saw a star Shin-ing in the*
3 And by the light of that same star, Three wise men
4 *This star drew nigh to the north-west, O - ver Beth - le -*
5 Then en - tered in those wise men three, Full rev - erent-
6 *Then let us all with one ac - cord Sing prais - es*

1 shep-herds in fields as they lay— In fields where they lay keep-ing their
2 *east, be-yond them far; And to the earth it gave great*
3 came from coun - try far; To seek for a king was their in -
4 *hem it took its rest; And there it did both stop and*
5 ly up - on their knee, And of - fered there, in His
6 *to our heaven - ly Lord, That hath made heaven and earth of*

1 sheep, On a cold win-ter's night that was so deep.
2 *light, And so it con - tin-ued both day and night.*
3 tent, And to fol-low the star wher - ev - er it went.
4 *stay, Right o - ver the place where Je - sus lay.* No - el, no -
5 ence, Their gold and myrrh and frank - in-cense.
6 *naught, And with His blood man-kind hath bought.*

el! No - el, no - el! Born is the King of Is - ra - el!

Alternate Last Verse Harmonization

Descant and arrangement by Jan Sanborn

6 Then let us all with one ac-cord Sing prais-es to our heav-enly Lord, That hath made heaven and earth of naught, And with His blood man-kind hath bought. No-el, No-el! Born is the King of Is-ra-el. A-men.

CHRISTMAS

180 What Child Is This, Who, Laid to Rest?

. . . What manner of child shall this be? — Luke 1:66

William C. Dix

GREENSLEEVES
English Melody
Harmonized by John Stainer

1 What child is this, who, laid to rest, On Ma-ry's lap is sleep-ing?
2 *Why lies He in such mean es-tate Where ox and ass are feed-ing?*
3 So bring Him in-cense, gold, and myrrh, Come peas-ant, king, to own Him;

1 Whom an-gels greet with an-thems sweet, While shep-herds watch are keep-ing?
2 *Good Chris-tian, fear: for sin-ners here The si-lent Word is plead-ing.*
3 The King of kings sal-va-tion brings, Let lov-ing hearts en-throne Him.

This, this is Christ the King, Whom shep-herds guard and an-gels sing:

Haste, haste to bring Him laud, The Babe, the son of Ma-ry.

CHRISTMAS

Some Children See Him

181

Blessed are the pure in heart for they shall see God. — Matthew 5:8

SOME CHILDREN
Alfred S. Burt

Wihla Hutson

1 Some chil-dren see Him lil - y white, The ba - by Je-sus born this night,
2 *Some chil-dren see Him al-mond-eyed, This Sav-ior whom we kneel be-side,*
3 The chil-dren in each dif-ferent place Will see the ba-by Je-sus' face

1 Some chil-dren see Him lil - y white, With tress-es soft and fair.
2 *Some chil-dren see Him al-mond-eyed, With skin of yel-low hue.*
3 Like theirs, but bright with heaven-ly grace, And filled with ho-ly light.

1 Some chil-dren see Him bronzed and brown, The Lord of heaven to earth come down;
2 *Some chil-dren see Him dark as they, Sweet Ma-ry's Son, to whom we pray;*
3 O lay a-side each earth-ly thing, And with thy heart as of-fer-ing,

1 Some chil-dren see Him bronzed and brown, With dark and heav-y hair.
2 *Some chil-dren see Him dark as they, And ah! they love Him, too!*
3 Come wor-ship now the in-fant King, 'Tis love that's born to-night!

CHRISTMAS

182 How Great Our Joy!

Therefore with joy shall they draw water out of the wells of salvation.... — Isaiah 12:3

JUNGST
German Melody
Arranged by Hugo Jüngst

German Carol

1 While by the sheep we watched at night, Glad tid-ings brought an
2 *There shall be born, so he did say, In Beth-le-hem a*
3 There shall the Child lie in a stall, This Child who shall re-
4 *This gift of God we'll cher-ish well, That ev-er joy our*

1 an - gel bright. How great our joy! Great our joy!
2 *Child to - day. How great our joy! Great our joy!*
3 deem us all. How great our joy! Great our joy!
4 *hearts shall fill. How great our joy! Great our joy!*

1 Joy, joy, joy! Joy, joy, joy! Praise we the Lord in
2 *Joy, joy, joy! Joy, joy, joy! Praise we the Lord in*
3 Joy, joy, joy! Joy, joy, joy! Praise we the Lord in
4 *Joy, joy, joy! Joy, joy, joy! Praise we the Lord in*

1 heaven on high! Praise we the Lord in heaven on high!
2 *heaven on high! Praise we the Lord in heaven on high!*
3 heaven on high! Praise we the Lord in heaven on high!
4 *heaven on high! Praise we the Lord in heaven on high!*

CHRISTMAS

I Wonder As I Wander

183

As He spake by His Holy Prophets
which have been since the world began.
— Luke 1:70

Appalachian carol
Collected by John Jacob Niles

I WONDER
Appalachian Folksong
Adapted by John Jacob Niles
Arranged by Fred Bock

1 I won-der as I wan-der out un-der the sky,
2 *When Ma-ry birthed Je-sus, 'twas in a cows' stall,*
3 If Je-sus had want-ed for an-y wee thing:
4 *I won-der as I wan-der out un-der the sky,*

1 How Je-sus, the Sav-ior, did come for to die. For
2 *With wise-men and far-mers and shep-herds and all. But*
3 A star in the sky, or a bird on the wing; Or
4 *How Je-sus, the Sav-ior did come for to die. For*

1 poor, or-nery peo-ple like you and like I— I
2 *high from God's heav-en a star's light did fall, And the*
3 all of God's an-gels in heav-en to sing, He
4 *poor, or-nery peo-ple like you and like I— I*

1 won-der as I wan-der, Out un-der the sky.
2 *prom-ise of a-ges It then did re-call.*
3 sure-ly could have had it, 'Cause He was the King!
4 *won-der as I wan-der, Out un-der the sky.*

CHRISTMAS

184 Hark! the Herald Angels Sing

And suddenly there was with the Angel a multitude of the Heavenly Host praising God. . . .
— Luke 2:13

MENDELSSOHN
Felix Mendelssohn
Descant by Paul Liljestrand

Charles Wesley

Descant

3 All hail the Sun of Right - eous - ness!

1 Hark! the her - ald an - gels sing, "Glo - ry to the new-born King:
2 *Christ, by high - est heaven a - dored; Christ, the ev - er - last - ing Lord!*
3 Hail the heaven-born Prince of Peace! Hail the Sun of Right - eous - ness!

He is risen with heal - ing

1 Peace on earth, and mer - cy mild, God and sin - ners
2 *Late in time be - hold Him come, Off - spring of the*
3 Light and life to all He brings, Risen with heal - ing

1 rec - on - ciled!" Joy - ful, all ye na - tions, rise, Join the tri - umph
2 *Vir - gin's womb. Veiled in flesh the God-head see;* *Hail th'in - car - nate*
3 in His wings. Mild He lays His glo - ry by, Born that man no

in His wings. His glo - ry by, No

CHRISTMAS

more may die; Born to raise the

1 of the skies; With the an - gel - ic host pro - claim,
2 De - i - ty, Pleased as man with men to dwell,
3 more may die; Born to raise the sons of earth,

sons of earth to sec - ond birth.

1 "Christ is born in Beth - le - hem!" Hark! the her - ald
2 Je - sus, our Em - man - u - el. Hark! the her - ald
3 Born to give them sec - ond birth. Hark! the her - ald

Hark! the her - ald an - gels sing to the new - born King. A - men.

1 an - gels sing, "Glo - ry to the new - born King."
2 an - gels sing, "Glo - ry to the new - born King."
3 an - gels sing, "Glo - ry to the new - born King." A - men.

CHRISTMAS

185

Away in a Manger

Source unknown, stanzas 1, 2
John Thomas McFarland, stanza 3

. . . there was no room for them in the inn.
— Luke 2:7

AWAY IN A MANGER
James R. Murray

Unison (FIRST TUNE)

1 A - way   in a   man-ger, no crib for a   bed, The lit - tle Lord
2 *The cat - tle are low-ing, the ba - by a - wakes, The lit - tle Lord*
3 Be near me, Lord Je - sus! I   ask Thee to stay Close by me for -

1 Je - sus laid down His sweet head. The stars in the sky all looked
2 *Je - sus, no   cry - ing He makes. I   love Thee, Lord Je - sus! Look*
3 ev - er, and love me, I   pray. Bless all   the dear chil - dren in

1 down where He lay, The lit - tle Lord Je - sus, a - sleep on the hay.
2 *down from the sky, And stay by my   side un - til morn-ing is nigh.*
3 Thy ten - der care, And fit us for heav - en, to live with Thee there.

186   Luke 2 : 1-12

At that time Emperor Augustus sent out an order for all the citizens of the Empire to register themselves for the census. When this first census took place, Quirinius was the governor of Syria. Everyone went to register himself, each to his own town.

Joseph went from the town of Nazareth, in Galilee, to Judea, to the town named Bethlehem, where King David was born. Joseph went there because he was a descendant of David. He went to register himself with Mary, who was promised in marriage to him. She was pregnant, and while they were in Bethlehem, the time came for her to have her baby. She gave birth to her first son, wrapped Him in cloths and laid Him in a manger—there was no room for them to stay in the inn.

There were some shepherds in that part of the country who were spending the night in the fields, taking care of their flocks. An angel of the Lord appeared to them, and the glory of the Lord shone over them. They were terribly afraid, but the angel said to them, "Don't be afraid! I am here with good news for you, which will bring great joy to all the people. This very day in David's town your Savior was born—Christ the Lord! What will prove it to you is this: you will find a baby wrapped in cloths and lying in a manger."

— (TEV)

CHRISTMAS

Away in a Manger 187

"Ye shall find the babe... lying in a manger." — Luke 2:12

Source unknown, stanzas 1, 2
John Thomas McFarland, stanza 3

(SECOND TUNE)

CRADLE SONG
William J. Kirkpatrick

Unison

1 A - way in a man-ger, no crib for a bed, The lit - tle Lord
2 *The cat - tle are low-ing, the ba - by a - wakes, But lit - tle Lord*
3 Be near me, Lord Je - sus! I ask Thee to stay Close by me for -

1 Je - sus laid down His sweet head. The stars in the bright sky looked
2 *Je - sus, no cry - ing He makes. I love Thee, Lord Je - sus! Look*
3 ev - er, and love me, I pray. Bless all the dear chil - dren in

1 down where He lay, The lit - tle Lord Je-sus, a - sleep on the hay.
2 *down from the sky, And stay by my side un - til morn - ing is nigh.*
3 Thy ten - der care, And fit us for heav - en, to live with Thee there.

Christmas 188

We yearn, our Father, for the simple beauty of Christmas—for all the old familiar melodies and words that remind us of that great miracle when He who had made all things was one night to come as a Babe, to lie in the crook of a woman's arm.

Before such mystery we kneel, as we follow the Shepherds and Wise Men to bring Thee the gift of our love—a love we confess that has not always been as warm or sincere or real as it should have been. But now, on this Christmas Day, that love would find its Beloved, and from Thee receive the grace to make it pure again, warm and real.

We bring Thee our gratitude for every token of Thy love.

—*Peter Marshall*

ᛒHow ᛒProper ᛒIt ᛒIs

How proper it is that Christmas should follow Advent.
—For him who looks toward the future, the Manger is situated on Golgotha,
and the Cross has already been raised in Bethlehem.

—Dag Hammarskjöld

190 ᛒAngels from the ᛒRealms of Glory

. . . We have come to worship Him. — Matthew 2:2

REGENT SQUARE
Henry T. Smart

James Montgomery

1 An - gels, from the realms of glo - ry, Wing your flight o'er all the earth;
2 *Shep-herds, in the fields a - bid - ing, Watch-ing o'er your flocks by night,*
3 Wise men, leave your con - tem - pla - tion, Bright - er vi - sions beam a - far;
4 *Saints be - fore the al - tar bend-ing, Watch-ing long in hope and fear,*

1 Ye who sang cre - a - tion's sto - ry, Now pro-claim Mes - si - ah's birth:
2 *God with man is now re - sid - ing, Yon - der shines the in - fant light:*
3 Seek the great De - sire of na-tions, Ye have seen His na - tal star:
4 *Sud - den - ly the Lord, de-scend-ing, In His tem - ple shall ap - pear:*

Come and wor-ship, come and wor-ship, Wor-ship Christ, the new-born King. A-men.

Alternate Last Verse Harmonization

Arranged by Fred Bock

4 Saints be-fore the al - tar bend-ing, Watch-ing long in hope and fear,

Sud-den-ly the Lord, de-scend-ing, In His tem-ple shall ap-pear:

Come and wor-ship, come and wor-ship, Wor-ship Christ, the new-born King. A-men.

Luke 1: 68-79

191

"Blessed be the Lord God of Israel, for He has visited and redeemed His people, and has raised up a horn of salvation for us in the house of His servant David, as He spoke by the mouth of His holy prophets from of old, that we should be saved from our enemies, and from the hand of all who hate us; to perform the mercy promised to our fathers, and to remember His holy covenant, the oath which He swore to our father Abraham, to grant us that we, being delivered from the hand of our enemies, might serve Him without fear, in holiness and righteousness before Him all the days of our life. And you, child, will be called the prophet of the Most High; for You will go before the Lord to prepare His ways, to give knowledge of salvation to His people in the forgiveness of their sins, through the tender mercy of our God, when the day shall dawn upon us from on high to give light to those who sit in darkness and in the shadow of death, to guide our feet into the way of peace."

—(RSV)

192 Angels We Have Heard On High

. . . Glory to God in the highest. — Luke 2:14

GLORIA
French Carol

French Carol

1 An - gels we have heard on high Sweet - ly sing - ing o'er the plains,
2 *Shep - herds, why this ju - bi - lee? Why your joy - ous strains pro - long?*
3 Come to Beth - le - hem and see Him whose birth the an - gels sing;

1 And the moun - tains in re - ply Ech - o back their joy - ous strains.
2 *Say what may the ti - dings be, Which in - spire your heaven - ly song?*
3 Come a - dore, on bend - ed knee, Christ, the Lord, the new - born King.

Glo - - - - - - - ri - a

in ex - cel - sis De - o, Glo - - - -

- - - - ri - a in ex - cel - sis De - o.

CHRISTMAS

O Come, All Ye Faithful

193

Let us go even unto Bethlehem. — Luke 2:15

ADESTE FIDELES
John F. Wade's *Cantus Diversi*
Descant by Fred Bock

Latin: John F. Wade
Tr. by Frederick Oakeley

1 O come, all ye faith-ful, joy-ful and tri-um-phant, O come ye, O
2 *Sing, choirs of an-gels, sing in ex-ul-ta-tion, O sing, all ye*
3 Yea, Lord, we greet Thee, born this hap-py morn-ing, O Je-sus, to

1 come ye to Beth-le-hem; Come and behold Him, born the King of an-gels;
2 *cit-i-zens of heaven a-bove; Glo-ry to God, all glo-ry in the high-est;*
3 Thee be all glo-ry given; Word of the Fa-ther, now in flesh ap-pear-ing;

Descant

O come, O come,

O come, let us a-dore Him, O come, let us a-dore Him,

O come, let us a-dore Him, Christ, the Lord. A-men.

O come, let us a-dore Him, Christ, the Lord. A-men.

CHRISTMAS

194 Infant Holy, Infant Lowly

For He is Lord of lords, and King of kings . . .
and they that are with Him are called, chosen, and faithful.
— Revelation 17:14

Paraphrase by Edith M. G. Reed

W ZLOBIE LEZY
Polish Carol

1 In - fant ho - ly, in-fant low - ly, for His bed a cat-tle stall;
2 *Flocks were sleep-ing: shep-herds keep-ing vig - il till the morn-ing new*

1 Ox - en low - ing, lit - tle know-ing Christ, the babe, is Lord of all.
2 *Saw the glo - ry, heard the sto - ry, ti - dings of a gos-pel true.*

1 Swift are wing - ing an - gels sing - ing, no - els ring - ing,
2 *Thus re - joic - ing, free from sor - row, Prais-es voic - ing*

1 tid - ings bring - ing: Christ the babe is Lord of all.
2 *greet the mor - row: Christ the babe was born for you.*

Taken with permission from the "Kingsway Carol Book". Published by Evans Brothers, London.

CHRISTMAS

Silent Night, Holy Night

Joseph Mohr
Tr. by John F. Young

195
STILLE NACHT
Franz Gruber

And they . . . found Mary and Joseph, and the baby . . . .
— Luke 2:16

1 Si - lent night, ho - ly night, All is calm, all is bright
2 *Si - lent night, ho - ly night, Shep-herds quake at the sight.*
3 Si - lent night, ho - ly night, Son of God, love's pure light

1 Round yon vir - gin moth-er and child. Ho - ly in-fant so ten-der and mild,
2 *Glo - ries stream from heav-en a - far, Heaven-ly hosts sing al - le - lu - ia;*
3 Ra - diant beams from Thy ho - ly face, With the dawn of re - deem - ing grace,

1 Sleep in heav - en - ly peace, Sleep in heav - en - ly peace.
2 *Christ the Sav - ior, is born! Christ, the Sav - ior, is born!*
3 Je - sus, Lord, at Thy birth, Je - sus, Lord, at Thy birth.

For Unto Us

196

For unto us a Child is born, unto us a Son is given:
and the government shall be upon His shoulder:
and His name shall be called Wonderful, Counsellor, The mighty God,
The everlasting Father, The Prince of Peace.
Of the increase of His government and peace there shall be no end, upon the throne of David, and upon His kingdom, to order it, and to establish it with judgment and with justice from henceforth even for ever.
With righteousness shall He judge the poor,
and reprove with equity for the meek of the earth:
and He shall smite the earth with the rod of His mouth, and with the breath of His lips shall He slay the wicked.

—Isaiah 9:6-7; 11:4 (KJV)

CHRISTMAS

197 It Came upon the Midnight Clear

Through the tender mercies of our God . . . the dayspring from on high hath visited us. — Luke 1:78

Edmund H. Sears

CAROL
Richard S. Willis

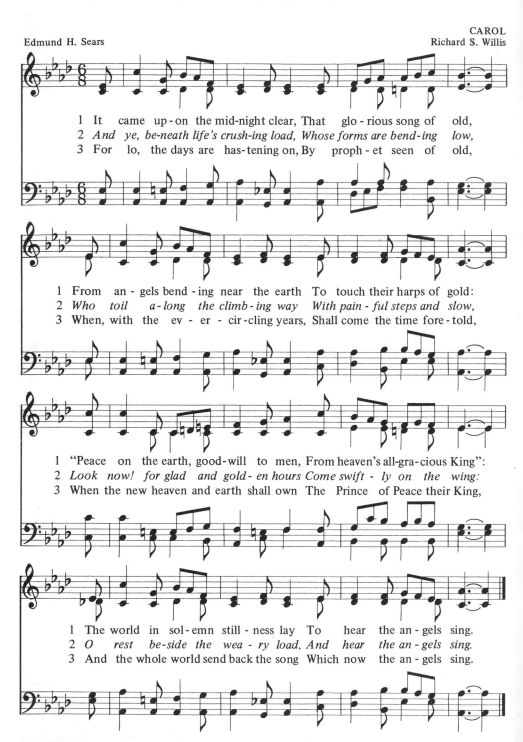

1 It came up-on the mid-night clear, That glo-rious song of old,
2 *And ye, be-neath life's crush-ing load, Whose forms are bend-ing low,*
3 For lo, the days are has-tening on, By proph-et seen of old,

1 From an-gels bend-ing near the earth To touch their harps of gold:
2 *Who toil a-long the climb-ing way With pain-ful steps and slow,*
3 When, with the ev-er-cir-cling years, Shall come the time fore-told,

1 "Peace on the earth, good-will to men, From heaven's all-gra-cious King":
2 *Look now! for glad and gold-en hours Come swift-ly on the wing:*
3 When the new heaven and earth shall own The Prince of Peace their King,

1 The world in sol-emn still-ness lay To hear the an-gels sing.
2 *O rest be-side the wea-ry load, And hear the an-gels sing.*
3 And the whole world send back the song Which now the an-gels sing.

CHRISTMAS

Child in the Manger

198

And this shall be a sign unto you; you shall find the child . . . lying in a manger. — Luke 2:12

Mary MacDonald
Fred Bock

BUNESSAN
Traditional Gaelic Melody
Arranged by Fred Bock

1 Child in the man - ger, In - fant of Ma - ry,
2 Pro - phets fore - told Him, In - fant of won - der,

1 Came as a stran - ger born in the stall;
2 An - gels be - hold Him there on His throne;

1 Sweet lit - tle Je - sus sent down from heav - en,
2 Wor - thy the Sav - ior of all our prais - es,

1 God's gift of new life of - fered to all.
2 Hap - py and ev - er blest are His own. A - men.

CHRISTMAS

199 Redeeming Love

Surely He hath borne our griefs and carried our sorrows. — Isaiah 53:4

REDEEMING LOVE
William J. Gaither
Adapted by Ronn Huff

Gloria Gaither

1 From God's heav-en to a man-ger, From great rich-es to the
2 *From a lov-ing heaven-ly Fa-ther, To a world that knew Him*

1 poor, Came the ho-ly Son of God, a lit-tle Child;
2 *not, Came a man of sor-rows, Je-sus Christ, the Lord;*

1 From the a-zure halls of heav-en To a low-ly man-ger stall,
2 *In my wan-dering Je-sus found me, Touched my life with His great love,*

1 Je-sus came, and here He gave His life for all.
2 *And this Babe has grown to be my sov-ereign Lord.*

Re-deem-ing love, a love that knows no lim-it; Re-deem-ing

CHRISTMAS

love, a love that nev-er dies; My soul shall sing through-out the end-less

a - ges The ad-o - ra-tion of this great love on high.

His Love......Reaching 200

Right from the beginning God's love has reached, and from the beginning man has refused to understand. But love went on reaching, offering itself. Love offered the eternal . . . we wanted the immediate. Love offered deep joy . . . we wanted thrills. Love offered freedom . . . we wanted license. Love offered communion with God Himself . . . we wanted to worship at the shrine of our own minds. Love offered peace . . . we wanted approval for our wars. Even yet, love went on reaching. And still today, after two thousand years, patiently, lovingly, Christ is reaching out to us today. Right through the chaos of our world, through the confusion of our minds. He is reaching . . . longing to share with us . . . the very being of God.

His love still is longing, His love still is reaching, right past the shackles of my mind. And the Word of the Father became Mary's little Son. And His love reached all the way to where I was.

—Gloria Gaither

201 The Star Carol

When they saw the star, they rejoiced . . . — Matthew 2:10

Wihla Hutson

STAR CAROL
Alfred S. Burt

1 Long years a - go on a deep win - ter night,
2 *Je - sus, the Lord, was that Ba - by so small,*
3 Dear Ba - by Je - sus, How ti - ny Thou art,

1 High in the heavens a star shone bright,
2 *Laid down to sleep in a hum - ble stall;*
3 I'll make a place for Thee in my heart,

1 While in a man - ger a wee Ba - by lay,
2 *Then came the star and it stood o - ver - head,*
3 And when the stars in the heav - ens I see,

1 Sweet - ly a - sleep on a bed of hay.
2 *Shed - ding its light 'round His lit - tle bed.*
3 Ev - er and al - ways I think of Thee.

CHRISTMAS

As with Gladness Men of Old

202

And they sang praises with gladness and bowed their heads and worshipped.
— II Chronicles 29:30

DIX

William C. Dix

Conrad Kocher

1 As with glad - ness men of old Did the guid - ing
2 *As with joy - ful steps they sped To that low - ly*
3 As they of - fered gifts most rare At that man - ger
4 *Ho - ly Je - sus, ev - ery day Keep us in the*

1 star be - hold, As with joy they hailed its light,
2 *man - ger bed, There to bend the knee be - fore*
3 rude and bare, So may we with ho - ly joy,
4 *nar - row way; And when earth - ly things are past,*

1 Lead - ing on - ward, beam - ing bright, So, most gra - cious
2 *Him whom heaven and earth a - dore, So, may we with*
3 Pure and free from sin's al - loy, All our cost - liest
4 *Bring our ran - somed souls at last Where they need no*

1 Lord, may we Ev - er - more be led to Thee.
2 *will - ing feet Ev - er seek the mer - cy seat.*
3 treas - ures bring, Christ, to Thee, our heaven - ly King.
4 *star to guide, Where no clouds Thy glo - ry hide.* A - men.

CHRISTMAS

203 All My Heart Today Rejoices

When they saw the star they rejoiced with exceeding great joy. — Matthew 2:10

Paul Gerhardt
Tr. by Catherine Winkworth

WARUM SOLLT ICH
Johann G. Ebeling

1 All my heart to-day re-joic-es As I hear, Far and near,
2 *Hark! a voice from yon-der man - ger, Soft and sweet, Doth en-treat:*
3 Come, then, let us has-ten yon - der! Here let all, Great and small,

1 Sweet-est an-gel voic - es. "Christ is born," their choirs are sing - ing,
2 *"Flee from woe and dan - ger! Breth-ren, come! from all that grieves you,*
3 Kneel in awe and won - der! Love Him who with love is yearn - ing!

1 'Til the air Ev - ery-where Now with joy is ring - ing.
2 *You are freed— All you need I will sure - ly give you."*
3 Hail the star That from far Bright with hope is burn - ing!

204 Peace on Earth

This is God's Christmas greeting.

In the beautiful story of Jesus' birth,

it was sung by a chorus of angelic voices.

Heard at first only by Judean shepherds outside the town of Bethlehem,

nevertheless, it is a message that the whole world should hear.

On each Christmas Day,

God repeats His greeting.

—Anonymous

Go, Tell It on the Mountains

They made known abroad the saying . . . concerning this child.
— Luke 2:17

GO TELL IT ON THE MOUNTAINS
American Folk Song

Traditional

Unison

Go, tell it on the moun-tains, O-ver the hills and ev-ery-where;

Fine

Go, tell it on the moun-tains That Je-sus Christ is born!

Harmony

1 While shep-herds kept their watch-ing O'er si-lent flocks by night, Be-
2 *The shep-herds feared and trem-bled When lo! A-bove the earth Rang*
3 Down in a low-ly man-ger The hum-ble Christ was born, And

D.C.

1 hold through-out the heav-ens There shone a ho-ly light.
2 *out the an-gel cho-rus That hailed our Sav-ior's birth.*
3 brought us God's sal-va-tion That bless-ed Christ-mas morn.

CHRISTMAS

206 We Three Kings of Orient Are

Now when Jesus was born in Bethlehem
. . . there came wise men from the East . . . . — Matthew 2:1

KINGS OF ORIENT
John H. Hopkins, Jr.

John H. Hopkins, Jr.

1 We three kings of O - ri - ent are, Bear - ing gifts we trav - erse a - far
2 *Born a King on Beth-le-hem's plain, Gold I bring to crown Him a - gain,*
3 Frank - in - cense to of - fer have I, In - cense owns a De - i - ty nigh;
4 *Myrrh is mine, its bit - ter per - fume Breathes a life of gath - er - ing gloom:*
5 Glo - rious now be - hold Him a - rise, King and God and Sac - ri - fice;

1 Field and foun - tain, moor and moun - tain, Fol - low - ing yon - der star.
2 *King for - ev - er, ceas - ing nev - er O - ver us all to reign.*
3 Prayer and prais - ing all men rais - ing, Wor - ship Him, God on high.
4 *Sor - row - ing, sigh - ing, bleed - ing, dy - ing, Sealed in the stone-cold tomb.*
5 Al - le - lu - ia, Al - le - lu - ia! Sounds thru the earth and skies.

O star of won - der, star of night, Star with roy - al beau - ty bright,

West - ward lead - ing, still pro - ceed - ing, Guide us to Thy per - fect light. A - men.

CHRISTMAS

Break Forth, O Beauteous Heavenly Light 207

Johann Rist
Tr. by John Troutbeck, stanza 1
Norman E. Johnson, stanza 2

For He is our peace who hath . . .
broken down the middle wall
of partition between us. — Ephesians 2:14

ERMUNTRE DICH
Johann Schop
Harmonized by J. S. Bach

1 Break forth, O beau-teous heaven-ly light, And ush-er in the
2 *Break forth, O beau-teous heaven-ly light, To her-ald our sal-*

1 morn - ing; Ye shep-herds, shrink not with af-fright, But
2 *va - tion; He stoops to earth— the God of might, Our*

1 hear the an-gel's warn - ing. This Child, now weak in in - fan-cy, Our
2 *hope and ex-pec - ta - tion. He comes in hu-man flesh to dwell, Our*

1 con - fi-dence and joy shall be, The power of Sa - tan
2 *God with us, Im-man-u - el, The night of dark - ness*

1 break - ing, Our peace e-ter - nal mak - ing.
2 *end - ing, Our fall - en race be-friend - ing.*

CHRISTMAS

208

O Sing a Song

To this end was I born, and for this cause came I into the world. — John 18:37

KINGSFOLD
Melody collected by Lucy Broadman
Arranged by Ralph Vaughan Williams

Louis F. Benson

1 O sing a song of Beth-le-hem, Of shep-herds watch-ing there,
2 O sing a song of Naz-a-reth, Of sun-ny days of joy,
3 O sing a song of Gal-i-lee, Of lake and woods and hill,
4 O sing a song of Cal-va-ry, Its glo-ry and dis-may,

1 And of the news that came to them From an-gels in the air:
2 O sing of fra-grant flow-ers' breath, And of the sin-less Boy:
3 Of Him who walked up-on the sea And bade the waves be still:
4 Of Him who hung up-on the tree, And took our sins a-way:

1 The light that shone on Beth-le-hem Fills all the world to-day;
2 For now the flowers of Naz-a-reth In ev-ery heart may grow;
3 For though like waves on Gal-i-lee, Dark seas of trou-ble roll,
4 For He who died on Cal-va-ry Is ris-en from the grave,

1 Of Je-sus' birth and peace on earth The an-gels sing al-way.
2 Now spreads the fame of His dear name On all the winds that blow.
3 When faith has heard the Mas-ter's word, Falls peace up-on the soul.
4 And Christ, our Lord, by heaven a-dored, Is might-y now to save. A-men.

Music from "The English Hymnal", by permission of Oxford University Press.

THE LIFE AND MINISTRY OF JESUS CHRIST

If you have any encouragement
from being united with Christ,
if any comfort from His love,
if any fellowship with the Spirit,
if any tenderness and compassion,
then make my joy complete
by being like-minded,
having the same love,
being one in spirit and purpose.

Do nothing out of selfish ambition or vain conceit,
but in humility
consider others better than yourselves.

Each of you should look not only to your own interests,
but also to the interests of others.

Your attitude should be the same as that of Christ Jesus:

Who, being in very nature God,
did not consider equality with God
something to be grasped,
but made Himself nothing, taking the very
nature of a servant,
being made in human likeness.
And being found in appearance as a man, He
humbled Himself
and became obedient to death—
even death on a cross!
Therefore God exalted Him to the highest place
and gave Him the name that is above every name,
that at the name of Jesus every knee should bow,
in heaven and on earth and under the earth,
and every tongue confess that Jesus Christ is Lord,
to the glory of God the Father.

—Philippians 2:1-11 (NIV)

210 I Cannot Tell

The righteous shall be glad in the Lord, and shall trust in Him . . . — Psalm 64:10

W. Y. Fullerton

LONDONDERRY AIR
Traditional Irish Melody

1 I can-not tell why He, whom an-gels wor - ship Should set His
2 *I can-not tell how si-lent-ly He suf - fered As with His*
3 I can-not tell how He will win the na - tions, How He will
4 *I can-not tell how all the lands shall wor - ship When at His*

1 love up - on the sons of men, Or why, as Shep-herd, He should seek the
2 *peace He graced this place of tears, Or how His heart up - on the cross was*
3 claim His earth-ly her - i - tage, Or sat-is - fy the needs and as - pir -
4 *bidd - ing ev - ery storm is stilled, Or who can say how great the ju - bi -*

1 wan-der-ers To bring them back, they know not how or when.
2 *bro - ken, The crown of pain to three and thir-ty years.*
3 a - tions Of east and west, of sin - ner and of sage.
4 *la - tion When all the hearts of men with love are filled.*

1 But this I know, that He was born of Ma - ry When Beth-lehem's
2 *But this I know, He heals the bro-ken heart - ed And stays our*
3 But this I know, all flesh shall see His glo - ry, And He shall
4 *But this I know, the skies will thrill with rap - ture, And count-less*

THE LIFE AND MINISTRY OF JESUS CHRIST

1 man - ger was His on - ly home, And that He lived at
2 sin and calms our lurk-ing fear, And lifts the bur - den
3 reap the har - vest He has sown, And some glad day His
4 voic - es then will join to sing, And earth to heaven, and

1 Naz - a-reth and la-bored, And so the Sav-ior, Sav-ior of the world, is come.
2 from the heav - y la - den, For yet the Sav-ior, Sav-ior of the world, is here.
3 sun will shine in splen - dor When He the Sav-ior, Sav-ior of the world, is known.
4 heaven to earth will an-swer: "At last the Sav-ior, Sav-ior of the world, is King!"

Jesus and the Children   211

Leader: *And they brought young children to Him, that He should touch them: and His disciples rebuked those that brought them.*

People: But when Jesus saw it, He was much displeased, and said unto them, Suffer the little children to come unto Me, and forbid them not: for of such is the kingdom of God.

Leader: *Verily I say unto you, Whosoever shall not receive the kingdom of God as a little child, he shall not enter therein.*

People: And He took them up in His arms, put His hands upon them, and blessed them.[1]

Leader: *And He took a child, and set him in the midst of them: and when He had taken him in His arms, He said unto them, Whosoever shall receive one of such children in My name, receiveth Me: and whosoever shall receive Me, receiveth not Me, but Him that sent Me.[2]*

People: Verily I say unto you, Except ye be converted, and become as little children, ye shall not enter the kingdom of heaven.

Leader: *Whosoever therefore shall humble himself as this little child, the same is greatest in the kingdom of heaven.*

People: And whoso shall receive one such little child in My name, receiveth Me.[3]

1. Mark 10:14-16
2. Mark 9:35-37
3. Matthew 18:3-6 (KJV)

212   Tell Me the Stories of Jesus

. . . I count all things but loss for the excellency of the knowledge of Christ Jesus . . . . —Philippians 3:8

William H. Parker

STORIES OF JESUS
Frederic A. Challinor

Unison or duet

1 Tell me the sto - ries of Je - sus I love to hear;
2 *First let me hear how the chil - dren Stood 'round His knee,*
3 In - to the cit - y I'd fol - low The chil - dren's band,

1 Things I would ask Him to tell me If He were here:
2 *I shall im - ag - ine His bless - ing Rest - ing on me;*
3 Wav - ing a branch of the palm - tree High in my hand;

1 Scenes by the way - side, Tales of the sea,
2 *Words full of kind - ness, Deeds full of grace,*
3 One of His her - alds, Yes, I would sing

1 Sto - ries of Je - sus, Tell them to me.
2 *All in the bright - ness Of Je - sus' face.*
3 Loud - est ho - san - nas, "Je - sus is King!"

THE LIFE AND MINISTRY OF JESUS CHRIST

I Think, When I Read That Sweet Story 213

Then were there brought little children, that He should put His hands on them . . .

— Matthew 19:13

Based on Mark 10:13-15
Jemima T. Luke

SWEET STORY
Greek Melody
Adapted by William B. Bradbury

1 I think, when I read that sweet sto - ry of old, When
2 *I wish that His hands had been placed on my head, That His*
3 Yet still to His foot - stool in prayer I may go And

1 Je - sus was here a - mong men, How He called lit - tle chil - dren as
2 *arms had been thrown a-round me, And that I might have seen His kind*
3 ask for a share in His love; And if I thus ear - nest - ly

1 lambs to His fold— I should like to have been with Him then.
2 *look when He said, "Let the lit - tle ones come un - to Me."*
3 seek Him be - low, I shall see Him and hear Him a - bove.

I Timothy 3: 16b 214

He appeared in a body,
was vindicated by the Spirit,
was seen by angels,
was preached among the nations,
was believed on in the world,
was taken up in glory.

—(NIV)

THE LIFE AND MINISTRY OF JESUS CHRIST

215
Tell Me the Story of Jesus

Did not our hearts burn within us when He talked to us?
— Luke 24:32

Fanny J. Crosby

STORY OF JESUS
John R. Sweney

1 Tell me the sto - ry of Je - sus, Write on my heart ev - ery word;
2 *Fast - ing a - lone in the des - ert, Tell of the days that are past,*
3 Tell of the cross where they nailed Him, Writh - ing in an - guish and pain;

Refrain: Tell me the sto - ry of Je - sus, Write on my heart ev - ery word;

Fine

1 Tell me the sto - ry most pre - cious, Sweet - est that ev - er was heard.
2 *How for our sins He was tempt - ed, Yet was tri - um - phant at last.*
3 Tell of the grave where they laid Him, Tell how He liv - eth a - gain.

Refrain: Tell me the sto - ry most pre - cious, Sweet - est that ev - er was heard.

1 Tell how the an - gels in cho - rus Sang as they wel - comed His birth,
2 *Tell of the years of His la - bor, Tell of the sor - row He bore,*
3 Love in that sto - ry so ten - der Clear - er than ev - er I see:

D.C. for Refrain

1 "Glo - ry to God in the high - est! Peace and good ti - dings to earth."
2 *He was de - spised and af - flict - ed, Home - less, re - ject - ed and poor.*
3 Lord, may I al - ways re - mem - ber Love paid the ran - som for me.

THE LIFE AND MINISTRY OF JESUS CHRIST

Strong, Righteous Man of Galilee

216

All things are delivered to Me of My Father.

— Luke 10:22

MELITA

Harry Webb Farrington

John Bacchus Dykes

1 Strong, right-eous Man of Gal-i-lee, With bor-rowed peace we
2 *Firm, peace-ful Man of Gal-i-lee, With bor-rowed strength we*
3 Calm, suf-fering Man of Gal-i-lee, With bor-rowed grace we
4 *God's peace-ful Man of Gal-i-lee, Love's tri-umph, we shall*

1 fol-low Thee: In tem-ple court Thy cleans-ing rod, On
2 *fol-low Thee: Not to re-venge but heal and pray, To*
3 fol-low Thee: Love at the well, share Mar-tha's loss, For-
4 *fol-low Thee: To crum-ble ev-ery boun-dary wall, Build*

1 Phar-i-sees the scorn of God. With bor-rowed peace we
2 *turn the cheek and trib-ute pay. With bor-rowed strength we*
3 give the nails and take the cross. With bor-rowed grace we
4 *high-ways to the hearts of all. Love's tri-umph, we shall*

1 fol-low Thee, Strong, right-eous Man of Gal-i-lee.
2 *fol-low Thee, Firm, peace-ful Man of Gal-i-lee.*
3 fol-low Thee, Calm, suf-fering Man of Gal-i-lee.
4 *fol-low Thee, God's peace-ful Man of Gal-i-lee.* A-men.

THE LIFE AND MINISTRY OF JESUS CHRIST

217 Jesus Walked This Lonesome Valley

He was in all points tempted as we are, yet without sin. — Hebrews 4:15

Traditional
Erna Moorman, 2nd stanza

LONESOME VALLEY
Traditional Spiritual

1 Je - sus walked this lone-some val - ley, He had to
2 As we walk our lone-some val - ley, We do not

1 walk it by Him - self; O no-bod-y else could walk it
2 walk it by our - selves; For God sent His Son to walk it

1 for Him, He had to walk it by Him - self.
2 with us, We do not walk it by our - selves.

218 The Humanity of Jesus

May our prayer, O Christ, awaken all Thy human reminiscences, that we may feel in our hearts the sympathizing Jesus.

Thou hast walked this earthly vale and hast not forgotten what it is to be tired, what it is to know aching muscles, as Thou didst work long hours at the carpenter's bench.

Thou hast not forgotten what it is to feel the sharp stabs of pain, or hunger, or thirst.

Thou knowest what it is to be forgotten, to be lonely.

Thou dost remember the feel of hot and scalding tears running down Thy cheeks. O we thank Thee that Thou wert willing to come to earth and share with us the weakness of the flesh, for now we know that Thou dost understand all that we are ever called upon to bear.

We know that Thou, our God, art still able to do more than we ask or expect. So bless us, each one, not according to our deserving, but according to the riches in glory of Christ Jesus, our Lord. Amen.

—Peter Marshall

Jesus Is the Friend of Sinners

219

They that are whole need not a physician, but they that are sick.
— Matthew 9:12

John W. Peterson

FRIEND OF SINNERS
John W. Peterson

1 Je - sus is the friend of sin - ners, Friend of sin - ners,
2 *If you trust Him, He will save you, He will save you,*
3 He will walk a - long be - side you, Walk be - side you,

1 friend of sin - ners; Je - sus is the Friend of sin - ners;
2 *He will save you; If you trust Him, He will save you,*
3 Walk be - side you; He will walk a - long be - side you,

1-2   **3**

1 He can set you free.
2 *give you life a - new.*
3 guide you day by day.

4 *He will lead you*

4 *on to glo - ry, On to glo - ry, on to glo - ry;*

4 *He will lead you on to glo - ry, Home for - ev - er - more!*

JESUS CHRIST—FRIEND

220 I've Found a Friend, O Such a Friend

A friend loveth at all times. — Proverbs 17:17

James G. Small

FRIEND
George C. Stebbins

1 I've found a Friend, O such a Friend! He loved me ere I knew Him;
2 *I've found a Friend, O such a Friend! He bled, He died to save me:*
3 I've found a Friend, O such a Friend! So kind, and true, and ten-der,

1 He drew me with the cords of love, And thus He bound me to Him.
2 *And not a-lone the gift of life, But His own self He gave me.*
3 So wise a Coun-se-lor and Guide, So might-y a De-fend-er!

1 And 'round my heart still close-ly twine Those ties which can't be sev-ered.
2 *Naught that I have my own I call, I hold it for the giv-er;*
3 From Him who loves me now so well, What power my soul can sev-er?

1 For I am His, and He is mine, For-ev-er and for-ev-er.
2 *My heart, my strength, my life, my all Are His, and His for-ev-er.*
3 Shall life or death, shall earth or hell? No! I am His for-ev-er.

JESUS CHRIST—FRIEND

No, Not One!

There is a friend that sticketh closer than a brother. — Proverbs 18:24

NO, NOT ONE

Johnson Oatman, Jr.

George C. Hugg

1 There's not a friend like the low-ly Je-sus, No, not one! no, not one!
2 *No friend like Him is so high and ho-ly,* *No, not one! no, not one!*
3 There's not an hour that He is not near us, No, not one! no, not one!
4 *Did ev-er saint find this friend for-sake him?* *No, not one! no, not one!*
5 Was e'er a gift like the Sav-ior giv-en? No, not one! no, not one!

1 None else could heal all our soul's dis-eas-es, No, not one! no, not one!
2 *And yet no friend is so meek and low-ly,* *No, not one! no, not one!*
3 No night so dark but His love can cheer us, No, not one! no, not one!
4 *Or sin-ner find that He would not take him?* *No, not one! no, not one!*
5 Will He re-fuse us a home in heav-en? No, not one! no, not one!

Je-sus knows all a-bout our strug-gles, He will guide 'til the day is done;

There's not a friend like the low-ly Je-sus, No, not one! no, not one!

JESUS CHRIST—FRIEND

222

Jesus, Lover of My Soul

For Thou hath been a shelter for me and a strong tower....

—Psalm 61:3

Charles Wesley

ABERYSTWYTH
Joseph Parry

1 Je - sus, lov - er of my soul, Let me to Thy bos - om fly,
2 *Oth - er ref - uge have I none, Hangs my help - less soul on Thee;*
3 Plen-teous grace with Thee is found, Grace to cov - er all my sin;

1 While the near - er wa - ters roll, While the tem - pest still is high.
2 *Leave, O leave me not a - lone, Still sup - port and com-fort me.*
3 Let the heal - ing streams a - bound, Make and keep me pure with - in.

1 Hide me, O my Sav - ior, hide, 'Til the storm of life is past;
2 *All my trust on Thee is stayed, All my help from Thee I bring;*
3 Thou of life the foun-tain art, Free - ly let me take of Thee;

1 Safe in - to the ha-ven guide, O re - ceive my soul at last!
2 *Cov - er my de-fense-less head With the shad - ow of Thy wing.*
3 Spring Thou up with-in my heart, Rise to all e - ter-ni - ty. A-men.

JESUS CHRIST—HIS LOVE

I Stand Amazed

223

God, who is rich in mercy, for His great love wherewith He loved us . . .

— Ephesians 2:4

MY SAVIOR'S LOVE

Charles H. Gabriel

Charles H. Gabriel

1 I stand a-mazed in the pres-ence Of Je-sus the Naz-a-rene,
2 *For me it was in the gar-den He prayed,"Not my will, but Thine;"*
3 In pit-y an-gels be-held Him, And came from the world of light
4 *He took my sins and my sor-rows, He made them His ver-y own;*
5 When with the ran-somed in glo-ry His face I at last shall see,

1 And won-der how He could love me, A sin-ner, con-demned, un-clean.
2 *He had no tears for His own griefs, But sweat drops of blood for mine.*
3 To com-fort Him in the sor-rows He bore for my soul that night.
4 *He bore the bur-den to Cal-vary, And suf-fered and died a-lone.*
5 'Twill be my joy through the a-ges To sing of His love for me.

How mar-vel-ous! how won-der-ful! And my song shall ev-er be:

How mar-vel-ous! how won-der-ful Is my Sav-ior's love for me!

JESUS CHRIST—HIS LOVE

224

If That Isn't Love

So Christ was once offered to bear the sins of many.... Hebrews 9:28

Dottie Rambo

LOVE
Dottie Rambo

1 He left the splen-dor of heav-en, Know-ing His des-ti-
2 E - ven in death He re - mem-bered The thief hang-ing by His

1 ny Was the lone - ly hill of Gol-goth-a, There to lay down His
2 side; ___ He spoke with love and com-pas-sion Then He took him to

1 life for me. If that is-n't love the o-cean is
2 Par - a - dise.

dry, There's no star in the sky and the spar-row can't

fly! If that is-n't love then heav-en's a myth,

There's no feel-ing like this, if that is-n't love.

JESUS CHRIST—HIS LOVE

Jesus Loves Even Me

Christ came into the world to save sinners of whom I am chief.
— I Timothy 1:15

Philip P. Bliss

GLADNESS
Philip P. Bliss

1 I am so glad that my Fa - ther in heaven Tells of His love in the Book He has given; Won - der - ful things in the Bi - ble I see— This is the dear - est, that Je - sus loves me.

2 Though I for - get Him and wan - der a - way, Still Je - sus loves me wher - ev - er I stray; Back to His dear lov - ing arms I would flee, When I re - mem - ber that Je - sus loves me.

3 O if there's on - ly one song I can sing, When in His beau - ty I see the great King, This shall my song in e - ter - ni - ty be: O, what a won - der that Je - sus loves me!"

I am so glad that Je-sus loves me, Je - sus loves me, Je - sus loves me;
I am so glad that Je-sus loves me, Je - sus loves e - ven me.

JESUS CHRIST—HIS LOVE

226 Jesus Loves Me, This I Know

I love them that love Me, and those who seek Me early shall find Me.

— Proverbs 8:17

Anna B. Warner

JESUS LOVES ME
William B. Bradbury

1 Je - sus loves me! this I know, For the Bi - ble tells me so;
2 *Je - sus loves me! He who died Heav-en's gate to o - pen wide;*
3 Je - sus, take this heart of mine, Make it pure and whol - ly Thine;

1 Lit - tle ones to Him be - long, They are weak but He is strong.
2 *He will wash a - way my sin, Let His lit - tle child come in.*
3 On the cross You died for me, I will try to live for Thee.

Yes, Je - sus loves me! Yes, Je - sus loves me!

Yes, Je - sus loves me! The Bi - ble tells me so.

JESUS CHRIST—HIS LOVE

There's Something About That Name 227

The Spirit and the bride say, Come. And let him that heareth say, Come . . . . and
whosoever will let him take of the water of life freely . . . . — Revelation 22:17

Gloria Gaither
William J. Gaither

THAT NAME
William J. Gaither

Je - sus, Je - sus, Je - sus! There's just some-thing a - bout that

name! Mas - ter, Sav - ior, Je - sus! Like the fra - grance

af - ter the rain; Je - sus, Je - sus, Je - sus! Let all

Heav - en and earth pro - claim: Kings and king-doms will

all pass a - way, But there's some-thing a - bout that name!

JESUS CHRIST—HIS NAME

228 I Will Sing of My Redeemer

For I know that my Redeemer liveth . . . — Job 19:25

MY REDEEMER

Philip P. Bliss

James McGranahan

*1 I will sing of my Re-deem-er And His won-drous love to me;
2 I will tell the won-drous sto-ry, How my lost es-tate to save,
3 I will praise my dear Re-deem-er, His tri-um-phant power I'll tell,
4 I will sing of my Re-deem-er, And His heaven-ly love to me;

1 On the cru-el cross He suf-fered From the curse to set me free.
2 In His bound-less love and mer-cy, He the ran-som free-ly gave.
3 How the vic-to-ry He giv-eth O-ver sin and death and hell.
4 He from death to life hath brought me, Son of God, with Him to be.

Sing, O sing of my Re-deem-er, With His
sing of my Re-deem-er, Sing, O sing of my Re-deem-er,

blood He pur-chased me; On the
He pur-chased me, He pur-chased me,

*These words may also be sung to the hymn-tune HYFRYDOL.

JESUS CHRIST—HIS NAME

cross He sealed my par - don, Paid the

He sealed my par - don, On the cross He sealed my par - don,

debt and made me free.

and made me free, and made me free.

How Sweet the Name of Jesus Sounds 229

. . . He that loveth Me shall be loved of My Father, and I will love Him . . . — John 14:21

ST. PETER
Alexander R. Reinagle

John Newton

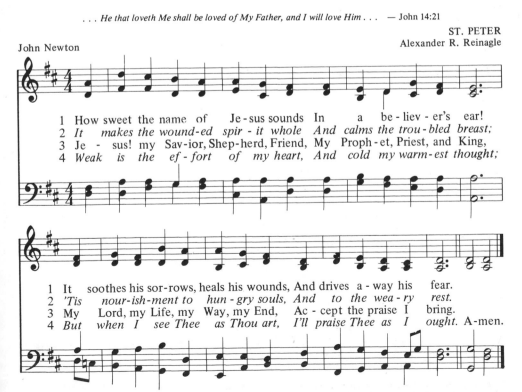

1 How sweet the name of Je-sus sounds In a be-liev-er's ear!
2 *It makes the wound-ed spir-it whole And calms the trou-bled breast;*
3 Je - sus! my Sav-ior, Shep-herd, Friend, My Proph-et, Priest, and King,
4 *Weak is the ef-fort of my heart, And cold my warm-est thought;*

1 It soothes his sor-rows, heals his wounds, And drives a - way his fear.
2 *'Tis nour-ish-ment to hun-gry souls, And to the wea-ry rest.*
3 My Lord, my Life, my Way, my End, Ac-cept the praise I bring.
4 *But when I see Thee as Thou art, I'll praise Thee as I ought.* A-men.

JESUS CHRIST—HIS NAME

230 His Name Is Wonderful

. . . Which is, and which was, and which is to come, the Almighty.

— Revelation 1:8

Audrey Mieir

MIEIR
Audrey Mieir

His name is Won-der-ful, His name is Won-der-ful, His name is Won-der-ful, Je-sus, my Lord; He is the might-y King, Mas-ter of ev-ery-thing, His name is Won-der-ful, Je-sus, my Lord. He's the great Shep-herd, the Rock of all a - ges, Al-might-y God is He; Bow down be-fore Him, Love and a-

JESUS CHRIST—HIS NAME

dore Him, His name is Won-der-ful, Je - sus, my Lord.

Take the Name of Jesus with You 231

Neither is there salvation in any other . . . . — Acts 4:12

PRECIOUS NAME
William H. Doane

Lydia Baxter

1 Take the name of Je - sus with you, Child of sor-row and of woe.
2 *Take the name of Je - sus ev - er As pro - tec-tion ev - ery - where;*
3 At the name of Je - sus bow-ing, When in heav - en we shall meet,

1 It will joy and com-fort give you, Take it then wher-e'er you go.
2 *If temp-ta-tions 'round you gath - er, Breathe that ho - ly name in prayer.*
3 King of kings, we'll glad-ly crown Him When our jour - ney is com - plete.

Pre - cious name, O how sweet! Hope of earth and joy of heaven,

Pre - cious name, O how sweet— Hope of earth and joy of heaven.

232 Join All the Glorious Names

Wonderful, Counselor, The Almighty God, Everlasting Father, Prince of Peace....

— Isaiah 9:6

DARWALL'S 148th
John Darwall

Isaac Watts

1 Join all the glo-rious names Of wis-dom, love, and power,
2 *Great Proph-et of my God, My life would bless Thy name;*
3 Di - vine, al - might - y Lord, My Con-queror and my King,
4 *Now let my soul a - rise And tread the tempt-er down;*

1 That ev - er mor-tals knew, That an-gels ev - er bore:
2 *By Thee the joy - ful news Of our sal - va - tion came:*
3 Thy scep-ter and Thy sword, Thy reign-ing grace I sing:
4 *My cap-tain leads me forth To con-quest and a crown:*

1 All are too poor to speak His worth,
2 *The joy - ful news of sins for - given,*
3 Thine is the power! Be - hold I sit
4 A fee - ble saint shall win the day,

1 Too poor to set my Sav - ior forth.
2 *Of hell sub - dued, and peace with heaven.*
3 And to Your lord - ly power sub - mit.
4 *Though death and hell ob - struct the way.*

JESUS CHRIST—HIS NAME

He is the image of the invisible God, the firstborn over all creation. For by Him all things were created: things in heaven and on earth, visible and invisible, whether thrones or powers or rulers or authorities; all things were created by Him and for Him. He is before all things, and in Him all things hold together. And He is the head of the body, the church; He is the beginning and the firstborn from among the dead, so that in everything He might have the supremacy. For God was pleased to have all His fullness dwell in Him, and through Him to reconcile to Himself all things, whether things on earth or things in heaven, by making peace through His blood, shed on the cross.

Once you were alienated from God and were enemies in your minds because of your evil behavior. But now He has reconciled you by Christ's physical body through death to present you holy in His sight, without blemish and free from accusation—if you continue in your faith, established and firm, not moved from the hope held out in the gospel. This is the gospel that you heard and that has been proclaimed to every creature under heaven, and of which I, Paul, have become a servant.

—Colossians 1:15-23 (NIV)

He Is Lord   **234**

And that every tongue should confess that Jesus Christ is Lord. — Philippians 2:11

Based on Philippians 2:11

HE IS LORD
Traditional

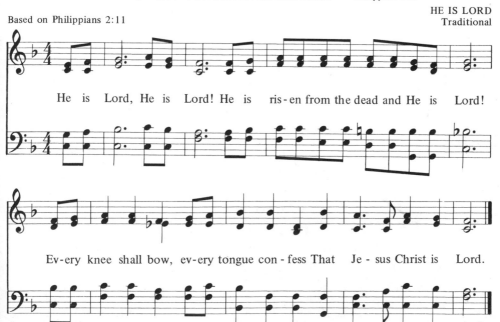

He is Lord, He is Lord! He is ris-en from the dead and He is Lord!

Ev-ery knee shall bow, ev-ery tongue con-fess That Je-sus Christ is Lord.

235 Jesus Is Lord of All

No man can serve two masters; . . . he will hold to one . . . . — Matthew 6:24

Gloria Gaither
William J. Gaither

LORD OF ALL
William J. Gaither

1 All my to-mor-rows, all my past, Je-sus is Lord of
2 *All of my con-flicts, all my thoughts, Je-sus is Lord of*
3 All of my long-ings, all my dreams, Je-sus is Lord of

1 all. I've quit my strug-gles, con-tent-ment at last,
2 *all. His love wins the bat-tles I could not have fought,*
3 all. All of my fail-ures His pow-er re-deems,

1 Je-sus is Lord of all.
2 *Je-sus is Lord of all.* King of kings, Lord of lords,
3 Je-sus is Lord of all.

Je-sus is Lord of all; All my pos-sess-ions and

all my life, Je-sus is Lord of all.

JESUS CHRIST—LORDSHIP

The Unveiled Christ

236

And Jesus . . . gave up the ghost.
And the veil of the temple was rent from the top to the bottom.
— Mark 15:37, 38

N. B. Herrell

UNVEILED CHRIST
N. B. Herrell

1 Once our bless-ed Christ of beau - ty Was veiled off from hu-man view;
2 *Yes, He is with God, the Fa - ther, In - ter-ced-ing there for you;*
3 Ho - ly an - gels bow be-fore Him, Men of earth give prais-es due;

1 But through suf-fering, death, and sor - row He has rent the veil in two.
2 *For He is the Well-be - lov - ed Since He rent the veil in two.*
3 For He is the might-y Con-queror Since He rent the veil in two.

O be-hold the Man of Sor - rows! O be-hold Him in plain view!

Lo! He is the might-y Con-queror Since He rent the veil in two;

Lo! He is the might-y Con-queror Since He rent the veil in two.

JESUS CHRIST—LORDSHIP

Revelation 15:3b-4

Great and wonderful are Thy deeds,
O Lord God the Almighty!
Just and true are Thy ways,
O, King of the ages!
Who shall not fear and glorify Thy name, O Lord?
For Thou alone art holy.
All nations shall come and worship Thee,
For Thy judgments have been revealed.

—(RSV)

238 Jesus Shall Reign Where'er the Sun

Based on Psalm 72
Isaac Watts

His kingdom is an everlasting kingdom,
and His dominion from generation to generation. — Daniel 4:3

DUKE STREET
John Hatton

1 Je - sus shall reign wher - e'er the sun Does His suc - ces - sive
2 *To Him shall end - less prayer be made, And end - less prais - es*
3 Peo - ple and realms of ev - ery tongue Dwell on His love with
4 *Let ev - ery crea - ture rise and bring His grate - ful hon - ors*

1 jour - neys run, His king - dom spread from shore to shore,
2 *crown His head; His name like sweet per - fume shall rise*
3 sweet - est song; And in - fant voic - es shall pro - claim
4 *to our King; An - gels de - scend with songs a - gain,*

|1, 2, 4 **||3**

1 'Til moons shall wax and wane no more.
2 *With ev - ery morn - ing sac - ri - fice.*
3 Their ear - ly bless - ings on His name. (name.)
4 *And earth re - peat the loud "A - men!"*

JESUS CHRIST—LORDSHIP

Alternate Last Verse Harmonization

Arranged by Steven R. Quesnel

4 Let ev - ery crea - ture rise and bring

His grate - ful hon - ors to our King:

An - gels de - scend with songs a - gain,

And earth re - peat the loud "A - men!"

JESUS CHRIST—LORDSHIP

239

Lift Up Your Heads, Ye Mighty Gates

Give unto the Lord the glory due His name.

—— I Chronicles 16:29

Based on Psalm 24:7
Georg Weissel
Tr. by Catherine Winkworth

TRURO
Psalmodia Evangelica

1. Lift up your heads, ye might-y gates: Be - hold, the King of glo - ry waits! The King of kings is draw - ing near, The Sav - ior of the world is here.

2. O blest the land, the cit - y blest, Where Christ the rul - er is con - fessed! O hap - py hearts and hap - py homes To whom this King of tri - umph comes!

3. Fling wide the por - tals of your heart: Make it a tem - ple, set a - part From earth - ly use for heaven's em - ploy, A - dorned with prayer and love and joy.

4. Re - deem - er, come! I o - pen wide My heart to Thee: here, Lord, a - bide! Let me Thy in - ner pres - ence feel: Thy grace and love in me re - veal.

5. So come, my Sov - ereign, en - ter in! Let new and no - bler life be - gin! Thy Ho - ly Spir - it guide us on, Un - til the glo - rious crown be won. A - men.

Fairest Lord Jesus

240

Thou art fairer than the children of men.
— Psalm 45:2

From *Münster Gesangbuch*

CRUSADERS' HYMN
Silesian Folk Melody

1 Fair - est Lord Je - sus, Rul - er of all na - ture,
2 *Fair are the mead - ows, Fair - er still the wood - lands,*
3 Fair is the sun - shine, Fair - er still the moon - light,
4 *Beau - ti - ful Sav - ior! Lord of the na - tions!*

1 O Thou of God and man the Son: Thee will I cher - ish,
2 *Robed in the bloom-ing garb of spring: Je - sus is fair - er,*
3 And all the twin - kling star - ry host: Je - sus shines bright - er,
4 *Son of God and Son of Man! Glo - ry and hon - or,*

1 Thee will I hon - or, Thou my soul's glo-ry, joy, and crown.
2 *Je - sus is pur - er, Who makes the woe-ful heart to sing.*
3 Je - sus shines pur - er Than all the an-gels heaven can boast.
4 *Praise, ad - o - ra - tion, Now and for-ev - er-more be Thine!* A-men.

No Distant Lord

241

No distant Lord have I,
    Loving afar to be,
Made flesh for me He cannot rest
    Until He rests in me.

I need not journey far
    This dearest friend to see,
Companionship is always mine,
    He makes His home with me.

I envy not the twelve,
    Nearer to me is He,
The life He once lived here on earth
    He lives again in me.

Ascended now to God
    My witness there to be,
His witness here am I because
    His Spirit dwells in me.

O glorious Son of God,
    Incarnate Deity,
I shall forever be with Thee
    Because Thou art with me.

—Maltbie D. Babcock

JESUS CHRIST—LORDSHIP

242 He's Still the King of Kings

Gloria Gaither
William J. Gaither
Ronn Huff

. . . And of His kingdom there shall be no end.
— Luke 1:33

KING OF KINGS
William J. Gaither

1 Hear the voice of your ser - vant, a man sent of God
2 *He is light that is come to a world that is dark,*

1 To bear wit - ness of hope for the na - tions;
2 *He is love and a - round Him is ha - tred;*

1 "There will be One come af - ter, Whose mes - sage to us
2 *E - ven few of His own ev - er saw Him as truth,*

1 Will bring life from the Fa - ther in Heav - en."
2 *But He comes e - ven now to for - give them.*

Ho - san - na! Ho - san - na! The whole world is sing - ing! The hope of all

JESUS CHRIST—LORDSHIP

a - ges is come; Sing His praise, sing His great-ness, Let

ev - ery-one know He's still the King of kings, and Lord of lords.

Who Is This Man? 243

Worship Leader:	*Jesus asked His disciples, "Who do men say that I the Son of man am?"*
Choir:	And they said, "Some say that Thou art John the Baptist; some, Elias; and others Jeremias, or one of the prophets."
Worship Leader:	*Who do men say that I am?*
Men:	I have looked far and wide, inside and outside my own head and heart, and I have found nothing other than this Man and His words which offer any answers to the dilemmas of this tragic, troubled time. If His light has gone out, then, as far as I am concerned, there is no light.[1]
Worship Leader:	*Who do men say that I am?*
Women:	He is the one Person in this world who is always present to me. When others only half-listen, He hears. When others are preoccupied with problems of their own, He is tuned in to my pain or joy. Yet it is this very presence in my life that strangely turns my attentions to the needs of others.
Worship Leader:	*Who do men say that I am?*
Choir:	Some say Jesus was an impressive personality, a strong leader and a great teacher. The world needs such men.
Worship Leader:	*Who do men say that I am?*
Youth (ages 12-25):	There are those who say, "Every person needs to believe in *something* or *someone*. Christ was a good person, a good pattern for our lives."
Worship Leader:	*He said to them, "But, who do* **you** *say that I am?"*
All:	You are the Christ, the Son of the Living God![2]

–Compiled by Gloria Gaither

1. Malcolm Muggeridge
2. Matthew 16:13b-16 (KJV)

JESUS CHRIST–LORDSHIP

244 Jesus! What a Friend for Sinners

Behold, . . . a friend of publicans and sinners.
— Luke 7:34

HYFRYDOL
Rowland H. Prichard
Arranged by Robert Harkness

J. Wilbur Chapman

1 Je - sus! what a friend for sin-ners! Je - sus! lov-er of my soul!
2 *Je - sus! what a strength in weak-ness! Let me hide my-self in Him;*
3 Je - sus! what a help in sor-row! While the bil-lows o'er me roll!
4 *Je - sus! what a guide and keep-er! While the tem-pest still is high;*
5 Je - sus! I do now re-ceive Him, More than all in Him I find;

1 Friends may fail me, foes as-sail me, He, my Sav - ior, makes me whole.
2 *Tempt-ed, tried, and some-times fail - ing, He, my strength, my vic - tory wins.*
3 E - ven when my heart is break-ing, He, my com-fort, helps my soul.
4 *Storms a-bout me, night o'er-takes me, He, my pi - lot, hears my cry.*
5 He hath grant - ed me for - give-ness, I am His, and He is mine.

Hal - le - lu - jah! what a Sav - ior! Hal - le - lu - jah! what a friend!

Sav - ing, help - ing, keep - ing, lov - ing, He is with me to the end.

JESUS CHRIST—SAVIOR

Christ Is Crucified Anew

Not only once, and long ago,
There on Golgotha's side,
Has Christ, the Lord, been crucified
Because He loved a lost world so.
But hourly souls, sin-satisfied,
Mock His great love, flout His commands.
And I drive nails deep in His hands,
You thrust the spear within His side.

—John Richard Moreland

"Man of Sorrows," What a Name!

Who hath believed our report? And to whom is the arm of the Lord revealed? — Isaiah 53:1

HALLELUJAH! WHAT A SAVIOR
Philip P. Bliss

Philip P. Bliss

1 "Man of sor - rows!" what a name For the Son of God who came
2 Bear - ing shame and scoff - ing rude, In my place con - demned He stood,
3 Guilt - y, vile, and help - less we, Spot - less Lamb of God was He;
4 Lift - ed up was He to die, "It is fin - ished," was His cry;
5 When He comes, our glo - rious King, All His ran-somed home to bring,

1 Ru - ined sin - ners to re-claim! Hal - le - lu - jah, what a Sav - ior!
2 Sealed my par - don with His blood; Hal - le - lu - jah, what a Sav - ior!
3 Full a - tone-ment! Can it be? Hal - le - lu - jah, what a Sav - ior!
4 Now in heaven ex - alt - ed high, Hal - le - lu - jah, what a Sav - ior!
5 Then a - new this song we'll sing, Hal - le - lu - jah, what a Sav - ior!

JESUS CHRIST—SAVIOR

247 He's the Savior of My Soul

. . . My soul shall be joyful in my God . . .

— Isaiah 61:10

SAVIOR OF MY SOUL
Spanish Melody

Adapted

He's the Sav - ior of my soul, My Je - sus, My Je - sus, He's the Sav - ior of my soul, He's the Sav - ior of my soul. Je - sus, Je - sus, Je - sus, Je - sus. He's the Sav - ior of my soul, He's the Sav - ior of my soul.

JESUS CHRIST—SAVIOR

Hosanna, Loud Hosanna

248

Blessed is He that cometh in the name of the Lord; Hosanna in the highest.

— Matthew 21:9

Based on Matthew 21:15, 16
Jennette Threlfall
Jeff Redd, stanza 2

ELLACOMBE
Gesangbuch der Herzogl, Wirtemberg

1 Ho - san - na, loud ho - san - na, The lit - tle chil - dren sang;
2 *From Ol - i - vet they fol - lowed, A hap - py, joy-ous crowd,*
3 "Ho - san - na in the high - est!" That an - cient song we sing,

1 Through pil-lared court and tem - ple The love - ly an - them rang:
2 *Their large palm branch-es wav - ing, And sing-ing clear and loud;*
3 For Christ is our Re - deem - er, The Lord of heaven our King;

1 To Je - sus, who had blessed them Close fold - ed to His breast,
2 *The Lord of men and an - gels Rode on in sim-ple joy,*
3 O may we ev - er praise Him With heart and life and voice,

1 The chil-dren sang their prais - es, The sim - plest and the best.
2 *And wel-comed all the chil - dren: Each lit - tle girl and boy.*
3 And in His ho - ly pres - ence E - ter - nal - ly re - joice!

THE TRIUMPHAL ENTRY OF JESUS CHRIST

249 All Glory, Laud and Honor

. . . Hosanna; Blessed is the King of Israel that cometh in the name of the Lord.
— John 12 :13

Theodulph of Orleans
Tr. by John M. Neale

ST. THEODULPH
Melchior Teschner

1 All glo-ry, laud, and hon - or To Thee, Re-deem-er, King,
2 *The com-pa-ny of an - gels Are prais-ing Thee on high,*
3 To Thee, be-fore Thy pas - sion, They sang their hymns of praise;

1 To whom the lips of chil - dren Made sweet ho-san-nas ring:
2 *And mor-tal men and all things Cre - at - ed make re - ply:*
3 To Thee, now high ex - alt - ed, Our mel - o - dy we raise:

1 Thou art the King of Is - ra - el, Thou Da - vid's roy-al Son,
2 *The peo - ple of the He - brews With palms be-fore Thee went;*
3 Thou didst ac - cept their prais - es— Ac - cept the praise we bring,

1 Who in the Lord's name com - est, The King and bless-ed one!
2 *Our praise and prayer and an - thems Be - fore Thee we pre - sent.*
3 Who in all good de - light - est, Thou good and gra-cious King! A-men.

THE TRIUMPHAL ENTRY OF JESUS CHRIST

Descant and arranged by A. Royce Eckhardt

Descant

3 Be - fore Thy pas - sion they sang their hymns of praise;
Now high ex - alt - ed, our mel - o - dy we raise.

3 Ac-cept their prais - es; ac - cept the praise we bring,

3 Who in all good de - light - est, Thou good and gra-cious King. A - men.

THE TRIUMPHAL ENTRY OF JESUS CHRIST

250 Calvary Covers It All

And that He might reconcile unto God . . . by the cross . . .
– Ephesians 2:16

Mrs. Walter G. Taylor

CALVARY COVERS IT
Mrs. Walter G. Taylor

1 Far dear-er than all that the world can im-part Was the mes-sage that
2 *The stripes that He bore and the thorns that He wore Told His mer-cy and*
3 How match-less the grace, when I looked in the face Of this Je-sus, my
4 *How bless-ed the thought, that my soul by Him bought, Shall be His in the*

1 came to my heart; How that Je-sus a-lone for my
2 *love ev-er-more; And my heart bowed in shame as I*
3 cru-ci-fied Lord; My re-demp-tion com-plete I then
4 *glo-ry on high, Where with glad-ness and song I'll be*

1 sin did a-tone, And Cal-va-ry cov-ers it all.
2 *called on His name, And Cal-va-ry cov-ers it all.*
3 found at His feet, And Cal-va-ry cov-ers it all.
4 *one of the throng, And Cal-va-ry cov-ers it all.*

Cal-va-ry cov-ers it all, My past with its sin and stain; My

guilt and de-spair Je-sus took on Him there, and Cal-va-ry cov-ers it all.

THE CROSS OF JESUS CHRIST

In the Cross of Christ I Glory

God forbid that I should glory, save in the Cross....

— Galatians 6:14

John Bowring

RATHBUN
Ithamar Conkey

1 In the cross of Christ I glo - ry, Tower - ing o'er the wrecks of time; All the light of sa - cred sto - ry Gath - ers round its head sub - lime.

2 *When the woes of life o'er - take me, Hopes de - ceive, and fears an - noy, Nev - er shall the cross for - sake me: Lo! it glows with peace and joy.*

3 When the sun of bliss is beam - ing Light and love up - on my way, From the cross the ra - diance stream - ing Adds more lus - ter to the day.

4 *Bane and bless - ing, pain and pleas - ure, By the cross are sanc - ti - fied; Peace is there that knows no meas - ure, Joys that through all time a - bide.* A - men.

---

1 Corinthians 2:1-5

252

When I came to you, brothers, I did not come with eloquence or superior wisdom as I proclaimed to you the testimony about God. For I resolved to know nothing while I was with you except Jesus Christ and Him crucified. I came to you in weakness and fear, and with much trembling. My message and my preaching were not with wise and persuasive words, but with a demonstration of the Spirit's power, so that your faith might not rest on men's wisdom, but on God's power.

—(NIV)

Beneath the Cross of Jesus

Now there stood by the cross of Jesus. . . .
— John 19:25

Elizabeth C. Clephane

ST. CHRISTOPHER
Frederick C. Maker

1 Be - neath the cross of Je - sus I glad - ly take my stand:
2 *Up - on that cross of Je - sus My eyes at times can see*
3 I take, O cross, thy shad - ow For my a - bid - ing place;

1 The shad - ow of a might - y rock With - in a wea - ry land,
2 *The ver - y dy - ing form of One Who suf - fered there for me;*
3 I ask no oth - er sun - shine than The sun - shine of His face,

1 A home with - in the wil - der - ness, A rest up - on the way,
2 *And from my smit - ten heart, with tears, Two won - ders I con - fess—*
3 Con - tent to let the world go by, To know no gain or loss,

1 From the burn - ing of the noon - tide heat And the bur - den of the day.
2 *The won - ders of His glo - rious love And my un - wor - thi - ness.*
3 My sin - ful self my on - ly shame, My glo - ry all the cross.

THE CROSS OF JESUS CHRIST

Near the Cross

I will open rivers in high places, and fountains . . .

– Isaiah 41:18

NEAR THE CROSS
William H. Doane

Fanny J. Crosby

1 Je - sus, keep me near the cross— There a pre - cious foun - tain,
2 *At the cross I stood one day. Love and mer - cy found me;*
3 Near the cross! O Lamb of God, Bring its scenes be - fore me;
4 *Near the cross I'll watch and wait, Hop - ing, trust - ing ev - er,*

1 Free to all, a heal - ing stream, Flows from Cal - vary's moun - tain.
2 *There the bright and morn - ing star Shed its beams a - round me.*
3 Help me walk from day to day With its shad - ow o'er me.
4 *'Til I reach the gold - en strand Just be - yond the riv - er.*

In the cross, in the cross, Be my glo - ry ev - er,

'Til my rap - tured soul shall find Rest be - yond the riv - er. A - men.

THE CROSS OF JESUS CHRIST

255 Down at the Cross

I am crucified with Christ; Nevertheless I live . . .

— Galatians 2:20

Elisha A. Hoffman

GLORY TO HIS NAME

John H. Stockton

1 Down at the cross where my Sav-ior died, Down where for cleans-ing from
2 *I am so won-drous-ly saved from sin, Je - sus so sweet-ly a-*
3 O, pre-cious foun-tain that saves from sin, I am so glad I have
4 *Come to this foun-tain so rich and sweet; Cast your poor soul at the*

1 sin I cried, There to my heart was the blood ap-plied;
2 *bides with - in; There at the cross where He took me in;*
3 en - tered in; There Je - sus saves me and keeps me clean;
4 *Sav - ior's feet; Plunge in to - day, and be made com-plete;*

Glo-ry to His name. Glo-ry to His name, Glo-ry to His name!

There to my heart was the blood ap-plied; Glo-ry to His name.

THE CROSS OF JESUS CHRIST

The Old Rugged Cross

256

Who for the joy that was set before Him endured the cross....
— Hebrews 12:2

George Bennard

RUGGED CROSS
George Bennard

1 On a hill far a-way stood an old rug-ged cross, The em-blem of
2 O that old rug-ged cross, so de-spised by the world, Has a won-drous at-
3 In the old rug-ged cross, stained with blood so di-vine, A won - drous
4 To the old rug-ged cross I will ev - er be true, Its shame and re-

1 suf-fering and shame; And I love that old cross where the dear-est and best
2 trac - tion for me; For the dear Lamb of God left His glo - ry a-bove
3 beau - ty I see; For 'twas on that old cross Je-sus suf-fered and died
4 proach glad-ly bear; Then He'll call me some day to my home far a-way,

1 For a world of lost sin-ners was slain.
2 To bear it to dark Cal-va - ry.   So I'll cher-ish the old rug-ged
3 To par-don and sanc-ti-fy me.
4 Where His glo - ry for-ev - er I'll share.

cross, 'Til my tro-phies at last I lay down; I will cling to the

old rug-ged cross, And ex-change it some day for a crown.

THE CROSS OF JESUS CHRIST

257 Good Friday

We acknowledge, O Lord, that there is so little in us that is lovable. So often we are not lovely in our thoughts, in our words, or in our deeds. And yet Thou dost love us still, with a love that neither ebbs nor flows, a love that does not grow weary, but is constant—year after year, age after age.

O God, may our hearts be opened to that love today. With bright skies above us, the fields and woods and gardens bursting with new life and beauty, how can we fail to respond? With the clear notes of bird songs challenging us to praise, with every lowly shrub and blooming tree catching new life and beauty, our hearts indeed would proclaim Thee Lord, and we would invite Thee to reign over us and make us truly Thine own. May Thy healing love invade our inmost hearts, healing sorrow, pain, frustration, defeat, and despair.

May this day create within us a love for Thee of stronger stuff than vague sentimentality—a love which seeks to know Thy will and do it. So grant that this day of hallowed remembrance may be the beginning of a new way of life for each of us, a new kind of living that shall be the best answer to the confusion and to the challenge of evil in our day. This we ask in Jesus' name. Amen.

—Peter Marshall

258 When I Survey the Wondrous Cross

HAMBURG

What things were gain to me, those I counted loss for Christ.
— Philippians 3:7

Isaac Watts

Based on Gregorian Chant
Arr. by Lowell Mason

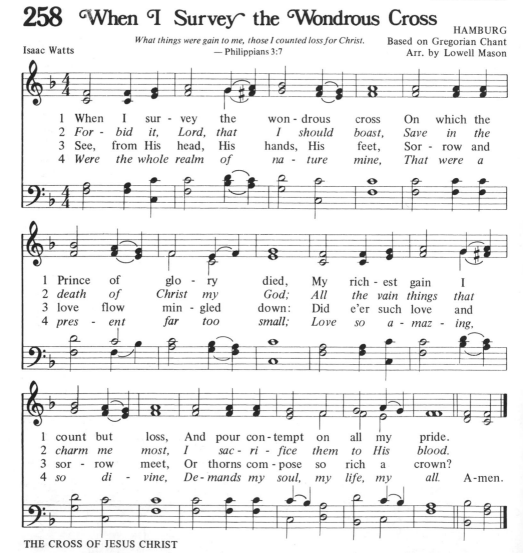

1 When I sur-vey the won-drous cross On which the
2 For-bid it, Lord, that I should boast, Save in the
3 See, from His head, His hands, His feet, Sor-row and
4 Were the whole realm of na-ture mine, That were a

1 Prince of glo-ry died, My rich-est gain I
2 death of Christ my God; All the vain things that
3 love flow min-gled down: Did e'er such love and
4 pres-ent far too small; Love so a-maz-ing,

1 count but loss, And pour con-tempt on all my pride.
2 charm me most, I sac-ri-fice them to His blood.
3 sor-row meet, Or thorns com-pose so rich a crown?
4 so di-vine, De-mands my soul, my life, my all. A-men.

THE CROSS OF JESUS CHRIST

Are You Washed in the Blood?

But if we walk in the light . . . the blood of Jesus Christ cleanses us . . .

— I John 1:7

Elisha A. Hoffman

WASHED IN THE BLOOD
Elisha A. Hoffman

1 Have you been to Je-sus for the cleans-ing power? Are you
2 *Are you walk-ing dai-ly by the Sav-ior's side? Are you*
3 When the Bride-groom com-eth, will your robes be white, Pure and
4 *Lay a-side the gar-ments that are stained with sin And be*

1 washed in the blood of the Lamb? Are you ful-ly trust-ing in His
2 *washed in the blood of the Lamb? Do you rest each mo-ment in the*
3 white in the blood of the Lamb? Will your souls be read-y for the
4 *washed in the blood of the Lamb? There's a foun-tain flow-ing for the*

1 grace this hour? Are you washed in the blood of the Lamb?
2 *Cru - ci - fied? Are you washed in the blood of the Lamb?*
3 man - sions bright And be washed in the blood of the Lamb?
4 *soul un - clean; O be washed in the blood of the Lamb?*

Are you

washed in the blood, In the soul-cleans-ing blood of the Lamb? Are your

garments spotless? Are they white as snow? Are you washed in the blood of the Lamb?

THE BLOOD OF JESUS CHRIST

260 And Can It Be That I Should Gain?

For God hath not appointed us to wrath, but . . . salvation, by our Lord Jesus Christ.

— I Thessalonians 5:9

Charles Wesley

SAGINA
Thomas Campbell

1 And can it be that I should gain An in - terest
2 *He left His Fa - ther's throne a - bove, So free, so*
3 Long my im - pris - oned spir - it lay Fast bound in
4 *No con - dem - na - tion now I dread: Je - sus, and*

1 in the Sav - ior's blood? Died He for me, who caused His pain?
2 *in - fi - nite His grace! Emp - tied Him - self of all but love,*
3 sin and na - ture's night. Thine eye dif - fused a quick - ening ray;
4 *all in Him, is mine! A - live in Him, my liv - ing Head,*

1 For me, who Him to death pur - sued? A - maz - ing love! how
2 *And bled for A - dam's help - less race! 'Tis mer - cy all, im -*
3 I woke— the dun - geon flamed with light! My chains fell off, my
4 *And clothed in right - eous - ness di - vine, Bold I ap - proach th'e -*

1 can it be That Thou, my God, shouldst die for me?
2 *mense and free, For, O my God, it found out me.*
3 heart was free, I rose, went forth, and fol - lowed Thee.
4 *ter - nal throne, And claim the crown, through Christ my own.*

THE BLOOD OF JESUS CHRIST

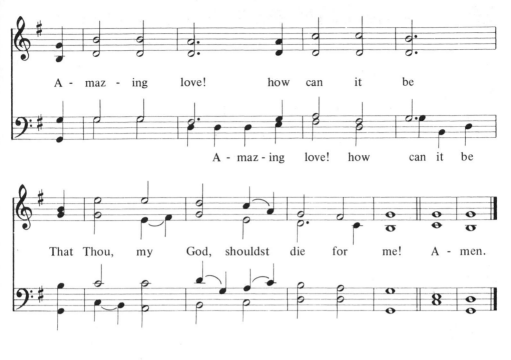

A - maz - ing love! how can it be

A - maz - ing love! how can it be

That Thou, my God, shouldst die for me! A - men.

ℓLuke 4 : 14 -22

261

And Jesus returned in the power of the Spirit into Galilee: and there went out a fame of Him through all the region round about. And He taught in their synagogues, being glorified of all.

And He came to Nazareth, where He had been brought up: and, as His custom was, He went into the synagogue on the sabbath day, and stood up for to read. And there was delivered unto Him the book of the prophet Esaias. And when He had opened the book, He found the place where it was written, The Spirit of the Lord is upon me, because He hath annointed me to preach the gospel to the poor; He hath sent me to heal the brokenhearted, to preach deliverance to the captives, and recovering of sight to the blind, to set at liberty them that are bruised, to preach the acceptable year of the Lord. And He closed the book, and He gave it again to the minister, and sat down. And the eyes of all them that were in the synagogue were fastened on Him. And He began to say unto them, This day is this Scripture fulfilled in your ears. And all bare Him witness, and wondered at the gracious words which proceeded out of His mouth.

—(KJV)

THE BLOOD OF JESUS CHRIST

262 The Blood Will Never Lose Its Power

Now the God of peace . . . through the everlasting covenant, make you perfect . . . .

— Hebrews 13:20, 21

Andraé Crouch

THE BLOOD
Andraé Crouch

1 The blood that Je - sus shed for me, Way back on
2 *It soothes my doubts and calms my fears, And it dries*

1 Cal - va - ry, The blood that gives me strength from day to
2 *all my tears; The blood that gives me strength from day to*

1 day, It will nev - er lose its power.
2 *day, It will nev - er lose its power.*

It reach-es to the high - est moun-tain. It flows to the

low - est val - ley The blood that gives me strength from

THE BLOOD OF JESUS CHRIST

day to day, It will nev - er lose its power.

There Is a Fountain Filled with Blood 263

BELMONT

For in Thee is the fountain of life: in Thy light shall we see light – Psalm 36:9

William Cowper

William Gardiner

1 There is a foun - tain filled with blood Drawn from Em-
2 *The dy - ing thief re - joiced to see That foun - tain*
3 Dear dy - ing Lamb, Thy pre - cious blood Shall nev - er
4 *And since, by faith, I saw the stream Thy flow - ing*

1 man - uel's veins; And sin - ners, plunged be - neath that
2 *in his day; And there may I, though sin - ful,*
3 lose its power, 'Til all the ran - somed Church of
4 *wounds sup - ply, Re - deem - ing love has been my*

1 flood, Lose all their guilt - y stains.
2 *too, Wash all my sins a - way,*
3 God Be saved, to sin no more,
4 *theme, And shall be 'til I die. A - men.*

THE BLOOD OF JESUS CHRIST

264   I Peter 1:18-21

You know that you were ransomed from the futile ways inherited from your fathers,
not with perishable things,
such as silver or gold,
but with the precious blood of Christ,
like that of a lamb without spot or blemish.
Through Him you have confidence in God who raised Him from the dead
and gave Him glory, so that your faith and hope are in God.

—(RSV)

265   I Know a Fount

In that day there shall be a fountain opened . . . for sin and for uncleanness.   I KNOW A FOUNT
— Zechariah 13:1

O. Cooke   O. Cooke

I know a fount where sins are washed a - way,

I know a place where night is turned to day;

Bur - dens are lift - ed, blind eyes made to see; There's a

won - der work - ing power in the blood of Cal - va - ry.

THE BLOOD OF JESUS CHRIST

Nothing but the Blood

266

*Christ died for us, much more then,
being now justified by His blood, we shall be saved.*

— Romans 5:8, 9

PLAINFIELD
Robert Lowry

Robert Lowry

1 What can wash a - way my sin? Noth-ing but the blood of Je - sus;
2 *For my par - don this I see— Noth-ing but the blood of Je - sus;*
3 Noth-ing can for sin a-tone— Noth-ing but the blood of Je - sus;
4 *This is all my hope and peace— Noth-ing but the blood of Je - sus;*

1 What can make me whole a - gain? Noth-ing but the blood of Je - sus.
2 *For my cleans-ing this my plea— Noth-ing but the blood of Je - sus.*
3 Naught of good that I have done— Noth-ing but the blood of Je - sus.
4 *This is all my right- eous-ness— Noth-ing but the blood of Je - sus.*

O! pre - cious is the flow That makes me white as snow;

No oth - er fount I know, Noth-ing but the blood of Je - sus.

THE BLOOD OF JESUS CHRIST

267

I John 1:6-9

So if we say we are His friends,
but go on living in spiritual darkness and sin,
we are lying.
But if we are living in the light of God's presence,
just as Christ does,
then we have wonderful fellowship and joy with each other,
and the blood of Jesus, His Son, cleanses us from every sin.
If we say that we have no sin,
we are only fooling ourselves,
and refusing to accept the truth.
But if we confess our sins to Him, He can be depended on to forgive us
and to cleanse us from every wrong.
– (LB)

268

Jesus, Thy Blood and Righteousness

. . . our Lord Jesus Christ, by whom we have now received the atonement.

Nicolaus L. von Zinzendorf
Tr. by John Wesley

— Romans 5:11

GERMANY
William Gardiner's *Sacred Melodies*

1 Je - sus, Thy blood and right - eous - ness My beau - ty
2 *Bold shall I stand in that great day, For who aught*
3 Lord, I be - lieve Thy pre - cious blood, Which, at the
4 *Lord, I be - lieve were sin - ners more Than sands up -*

1 are, my glo - rious dress; 'Midst flam - ing worlds, in these ar -
2 *to my charge shall lay? Ful - ly ab - solved through these I*
3 mer - cy seat of God, For - ev - er doth for sin - ners
4 *on the o - cean shore, Thou hast for all a ran - som*

1 rayed, With joy shall I lift up my head.
2 *am, From sin and fear, from guilt and shame.*
3 plead, For me, e'en for my soul was shed.
4 *paid, For all a full a - tone - ment made.* A - men.

THE BLOOD OF JESUS CHRIST

Jesus, the Son of God

Believe me that I am in the Father, and the Father in me. — John 14:11

SWEET WONDER
G. T. Haywood

G. T. Haywood

1 Do you know Je-sus, Our Lord, our Sav-ior, Je-sus, the
2 *God gave Him, a ran-som, Our souls to re-cov-er;* Je-sus, the
3 O who would re-ject Him, De-spise, or for-sake Him, Je-sus, the
4 *If you will ac-cept Him And trust and be-lieve Him,* Je-sus, the
5 Then some-day from heav-en, On clouds of bright glo-ry, Je-sus, the

1 Son of God? Have you ev-er seen Him, Or shared of His fa-vor?
2 *Son of God; His blood made us wor-thy His Spir-it to hov-er:*
3 Son of God? O who ev-er sought Him, And He would not take him?
4 *Son of God. Your soul will ex-alt Him, And nev-er will leave Him;*
5 Son of God, Will come for His jew-els, Most pre-cious and ho-ly,

Je-sus, the Son of God. O sweet Won-der! O sweet Won-der!

Je-sus, the Son of God; How I a-dore Thee!

O how I love Thee! Je-sus, the Son of God.

THE ATONEMENT, CRUCIFIXION AND DEATH OF JESUS CHRIST

270 I Believe in a Hill Called Mount Calvary

And when they came to the place called Calvary, they crucified Him – Luke 23:33

Dale Oldham
Gloria Gaither
William J. Gaither

MOUNT CALVARY
William J. Gaither

1 There are things as we trav - el this earth's shift - ing sands
2 *I be - lieve that the Christ who was slain on that cross*
3 I be - lieve that this life with its great mys - ter - ies

1 That trans - cend all the rea - son of man;
2 *Has the pow - er to change lives to - day;*
3 Sure - ly some - day will come to an end;

1 But the things that mat - ter the most in this world,
2 *For He changed me com - plete - ly, a new life is mine,*
3 But faith will con - quer the dark - ness and death

1 They can nev - er be held in our hand.
2 *That is why by the cross I will stay.*
3 And will lead me at last to my friend.

I be - lieve in a hill called Mount Cal-vary— I'll be - lieve what-

THE ATONEMENT, CRUCIFIXION AND DEATH OF JESUS CHRIST

ev - er   the   cost;   And when time   has sur - ren - dered   and

earth   is   no more,   I'll still   cling   to that   old   rug - ged   cross.

The Good Shepherd   **271**

I am the good shepherd;

I know my own

and my own know me,

just as the Father knows me

and I know the Father;

and I lay down my life for my sheep.

And there are other sheep I have

that are not of this fold,

and these I have to lead as well.

They too will listen to my voice,

and there will be only one flock,

and one shepherd.

The Father loves me,

because I lay down my life

in order to take it up again.

No one takes it from me;

I lay it down of my own free will,

And as it is in my power to lay it down,

so it is in my power to take it up again;

and this is the command I have been given by my Father.

—John 10:14-18 (JB)

THE ATONEMENT, CRUCIFIXION AND DEATH OF JESUS CHRIST

See, My Servant shall prosper; He shall be highly exalted. Yet many shall be amazed when they see Him—yes, even far-off foreign nations and their kings; they shall stand dumbfounded, speechless in His presence. For they shall see and understand what they had not been told before. They shall see My Servant beaten and bloodied, so disfigured one would scarcely know it was a person standing there. So shall He cleanse many nations.

But, oh, how few believe it! Who will listen? To whom will God reveal His saving power? In God's eyes He was like a tender green shoot, sprouting from a root in dry and sterile ground. But in our eyes there was no attractiveness at all, nothing to make us want Him. We despised Him and rejected Him—a man of sorrows, acquainted with bitterest grief. We turned our backs on Him and looked the other way when He went by. He was despised and we didn't care.

Yet it was *our* grief He bore, *our* sorrows that weighed Him down. And we thought His troubles were a punishment from God, for His *own* sins! But He was wounded and bruised for *our* sins. He was chastised that we might have peace; He was lashed—and we were healed! *We* are the ones who strayed away like sheep! *We,* who left God's paths to follow our own. Yet God laid on *Him* the guilt and sins of every one of us!

He was oppressed and He was afflicted, yet He never said a word. He was brought as a lamb to the slaughter; and as a sheep before her shearers is dumb, so He stood silent before the ones condemning Him. From prison and trial they led Him away to His death. But who among the people of that day realized it was their sins that He was dying for—that He was suffering their punishment? He was buried like a criminal in a rich man's grave; but He had done no wrong, and had never spoken an evil word.

Yet it was the Lord's good plan to bruise Him and fill Him with grief. But when His soul has been made an offering for sin, then He shall have a multitude of children, many heirs. He shall live again and God's program shall prosper in His hands. And when He sees all that is accomplished by the anguish of His soul, He shall be satisfied; and because of what He had experienced, My righteous Servant shall make many to be counted righteous before God, for He shall bear all their sins. Therefore I will give Him the honors of one who is mighty and great, because He has poured out His soul unto death. He was counted as a sinner, and He bore the sins of many, and He pled with God for sinners.

—Isaiah 52:13-53:12 (LB)

THE ATONEMENT, CRUCIFIXION AND DEATH OF JESUS CHRIST

Jesus Paid It All

273

Ye are bought with a price; be ye not servants of men.
— I Corinthians 7: 23

Elvina M. Hall

ALL TO CHRIST
John T. Grape

1 I hear the Sav-ior say, "Thy strength in-deed is small!
2 For noth-ing good have I Where-by Thy grace to claim—
3 And when be-fore the throne I stand in Him com-plete,

1 Child of weak-ness watch and pray, Find in me thine all in all."
2 I will wash my gar-ments white In the blood of Cal-vary's Lamb.
3 "Je-sus died my soul to save," My lips shall still re-peat.

Je - sus paid it all, All to Him I owe;

Sin had left a crim-son stain— He washed it white as snow.

THE ATONEMENT, CRUCIFIXION AND DEATH OF JESUS CHRIST

274

Alas! and Did My Savior Bleed

He was bruised for our iniquities. — Isaiah 53:5

Isaac Watts

MARTYRDOM
Hugh Wilson

1 A - las! and did my Sav - ior bleed And
2 *Was it for sins that I have done He*
3 Well might the sun in dark - ness hide And
4 *Thus might I hide my blush - ing face While*
5 But drops of grief can ne'er re - pay The

1 did my sov - ereign die? Would He de - vote that
2 *suf - fered on the tree? A - maz - ing pit - y!*
3 shut his glo - ries in, When Christ, the great Re -
4 *His dear cross ap - pears, Dis - solve my heart in*
5 debt of love I owe: Here, Lord, I give my

1 sa - cred Head For sin - ners such as I?
2 *grace un - known! And love be - yond de - gree!*
3 deem - er, died For man the crea - ture's sin.
4 *thank - ful - ness, And melt mine eyes to tears.*
5 self a - way— 'Tis all that I can do. A - men.

THE ATONEMENT, CRUCIFIXION AND DEATH OF JESUS CHRIST

Blessed Redeemer

275

Avis B. Christiansen

And the Redeemed shall come to Zion,
and unto them that turn from transgression . . . — Isaiah 59:20

REDEEMER
Harry Dixon Loes

1 Up Cal-vary's moun-tain, one dread-ful morn, Walked Christ my Sav-ior,
2 "Fa-ther, for-give them!" thus did He pray, E'en while His life-blood
3 O how I love Him, Sav-ior and Friend! How can my prais-es

1 wea-ry and worn; Fac-ing for sin-ners death on the cross,
2 flowed fast a-way; Pray-ing for sin-ners while in such woe—
3 ev-er find end! Thru years un-num-bered on heav-en's shore,

1 That He might save them from end-less loss.
2 No one but Je-sus ev-er loved so.
3 My tongue shall praise Him for-ev-er-more.

Bless-ed Re-deem-er, pre-cious Re-

deem-er! Seems now I see Him on Cal-va-ry's tree Wound-ed and

bleed-ing, for sin-ners plead-ing—Blind and un-heed-ing—dy-ing for me!

THE ATONEMENT, CRUCIFIXION AND DEATH OF JESUS CHRIST

276 Come to Calvary's Holy Mountain

And this voice . . . we heard when we were . . . in the holy mount.
— II Peter 1:18

James Montgomery

HOLY MOUNTAIN
Ludwig M. Lindeman

1 Come to Cal-vary's ho-ly moun-tain, Sin-ners ru-ined
2 *Come in pov-er-ty and mean-ness, Come de-filed, with-*
3 Come in sor-row and con-tri-tion, Wound-ed, im-po-
4 *He that drinks shall live for-ev-er— 'Tis a soul-re-*

1 by the fall; Here a pure and heal-ing foun-tain
2 *out, with-in; From in-fec-tion and un-clean-ness,*
3 tent, and blind; Here the guilt-y free re-mis-sion,
4 *new-ing flood; God is faith-ful, God will nev-er*

1 Flows to you, to me, to all, In a full, per-
2 *From the lep-ro-sy of sin, Wash your robes and*
3 Here the trou-bled peace may find: Health this foun-tain
4 *Break His cov-e-nant of blood, Signed when our Re-*

1 pet-ual tide, O-pened when our Sav-ior died.
2 *make them white: Ye shall walk with God in light.*
3 will re-store; He that drinks shall thirst no more.
4 *deem-er died, Sealed when He was glo-ri-fied.*

THE ATONEMENT, CRUCIFIXION AND DEATH OF JESUS CHRIST

Jesus, Priceless Treasure

277

Like a merchantman, . . . who, when he had found a pearl of great price,
went and . . . bought it. — Matthew 13:45, 46

Johann Franck
Tr. by Catherine Winkworth

JESU, MEINE FREUDE
German Melody
Adapted by Johann Crüger

1 Je - sus, price - less treas - ure, Source of pur - est pleas - ure,
2 *In Thy strength I rest me; Foes who would mo - lest me*
3 Ban - ished is our sad - ness! For the Lord of glad - ness,

1 Tru - est friend to me: Long my heart hath pant - ed, 'Til it well-nigh
2 *Can - not reach me here. Though the earth be shak - ing, Ev - ery heart be*
3 Je - sus, en - ters in. Those who love the Fa - ther, Though the storms may

1 faint - ed, Thirst-ing aft - er Thee. Thine I am, O spot-less Lamb,
2 *quak - ing, God dis-pels our fear. Sin and hell in con-flict fell*
3 gath - er, Still have peace with - in. Yea, what-e'er we here must bear,

1 I will suf-fer nought to hide Thee, Ask for naught be-side Thee.
2 *With their heav-iest storms as-sail us: Je - sus will not fail us.*
3 Still in Thee lies pur-est pleas - ure, Je - sus, price-less treas-ure! A-men.

THE ATONEMENT, CRUCIFIXION AND DEATH OF JESUS CHRIST

278 There Is a Green Hill Far Away

Wherefore . . . Jesus also suffered outside the gate . . .
– Hebrews 13:12

GREEN HILL
George C. Stebbins
Arranged by A. Royce Eckhardt

Cecil Frances Alexander

1 There is a green hill far a-way, Out - side a cit - y wall,
2 *We may not know, we can - not tell What pains He had to bear,*
3 He died that we might be for-given, He died to make us good,
4 *There was no oth - er good e-nough To pay the price of sin;*

1 Where the dear Lord was cru - ci-fied, Who died to save us all.
2 *But we be - lieve it was for us He hung and suf - fered there.*
3 That we might go at last to heaven, Saved by His pre - cious blood.
4 *He on - ly could un - lock the gate Of heaven and let us in.*

O dear - ly, dear-ly has He loved, And we must love Him too,

And trust in His re - deem-ing blood, And try His works to do.

THE ATONEMENT, CRUCIFIXION AND DEATH OF JESUS CHRIST

Savior, Thy Dying Love

279

It was the third hour and they crucified Him

– Mark 15:25

S. Dryden Phelps, alt.

SOMETHING FOR JESUS
Robert Lowry

1 Sav - ior, Thy dy - ing love -Thou gav - est me,
2 *Give me a faith - ful heart,* *Guid - ed by Thee,*
3 All that I am and have, Thy gifts so free,

1 Noth - ing should I with-hold, Dear Lord, from Thee;
2 *That each de - part - ing day* *Hence - forth may see*
3 Ev - er in joy or grief, My Lord, for Thee;

1 In love my soul would bow, My heart ful - fill its vow,
2 *Some work of love be - gun,* *Some deed of kind - ness done,*
3 And when Thy face I see, My ran-somed soul shall be,

1 Some of - fering bring Thee now, Some - thing for Thee.
2 *Some wan-derer sought and won,* *Some - thing for Thee.*
3 Through all e - ter - ni - ty, Some - thing for Thee. A-men.

THE ATONEMENT, CRUCIFIXION AND DEATH OF JESUS CHRIST

280 Justified by Faith

Therefore, since we are justified by faith,
we have peace with God through our Lord Jesus Christ.
Through Him
we have obtained access to this grace in which we stand,
and we rejoice in our hope of sharing the glory of God.

More than that, we rejoice in our sufferings,
knowing that suffering produces endurance,
and endurance produces character,
and character produces hope,
and hope does not disappoint us,
because God's love has been poured into our hearts
through the Holy Spirit which has been given to us.

While we were still weak,
at the right time Christ died for the ungodly.
Why, one will hardly die for a righteous man—
though perhaps for a good man one will dare even to die.

But God shows His love for us in that while we were yet sinners
Christ died for us.

Since, therefore, we are now justified by His blood,
much more shall we be saved by Him from the wrath of God.

For if while we were enemies we were reconciled to God by the death of His Son,
much more, now that we are reconciled,
shall we be saved by His life.
Not only so, but we also rejoice in God through our Lord Jesus Christ,
through whom we have now received our reconciliation.

—Romans 5:1-11 (RSV)

281 Go to Dark Gethsemane

That I might know Him, . . ., and the fellowship of His suffering.
— Philippians 3:10

James Montgomery

REDHEAD No. 76
Richard Redhead

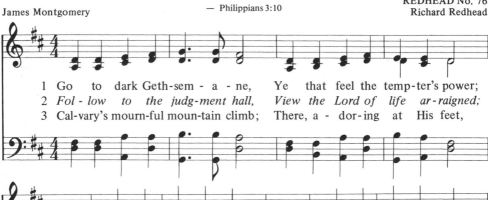

1 Go to dark Geth-sem - a - ne, Ye that feel the temp-ter's power;
2 *Fol - low to the judg-ment hall,* *View the Lord of life ar-raigned;*
3 Cal-vary's mourn-ful moun-tain climb; There, a - dor-ing at His feet,

1 Your Re-deem-er's con - flict see, Watch with Him one bit - ter hour:
2 *O the worm-wood and the gall!* *O the pangs His soul sus - tained!*
3 Mark the mir - a - cle of time, God's own sac - ri - fice com - plete:

THE ATONEMENT, CRUCIFIXION AND DEATH OF JESUS CHRIST

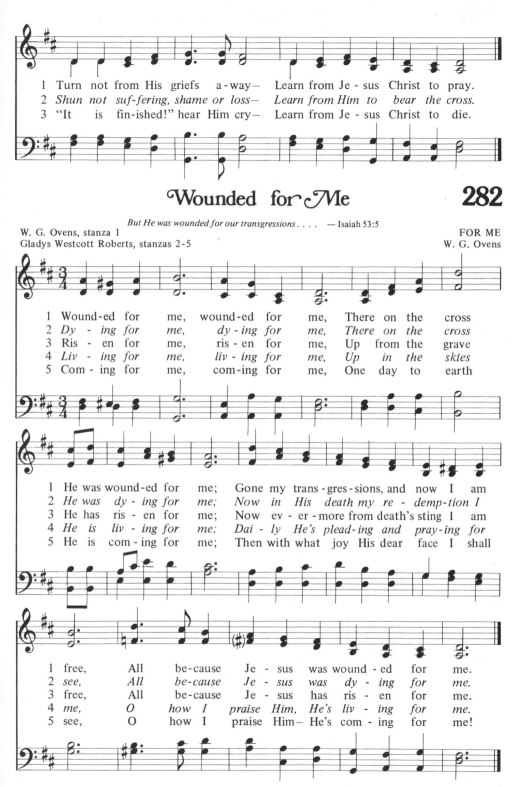

1 Turn not from His griefs a-way— Learn from Je-sus Christ to pray.
2 *Shun not suf-fering, shame or loss— Learn from Him to bear the cross.*
3 "It is fin-ished!" hear Him cry— Learn from Je-sus Christ to die.

Wounded for Me

282

But He was wounded for our transgressions.... — Isaiah 53:5

W. G. Ovens, stanza 1
Gladys Westcott Roberts, stanzas 2-5

FOR ME
W. G. Ovens

1 Wound-ed for me, wound-ed for me, There on the cross
2 *Dy-ing for me, dy-ing for me, There on the cross*
3 Ris-en for me, ris-en for me, Up from the grave
4 *Liv-ing for me, liv-ing for me, Up in the skies*
5 Com-ing for me, com-ing for me, One day to earth

1 He was wound-ed for me; Gone my trans-gres-sions, and now I am
2 *He was dy-ing for me; Now in His death my re-demp-tion I*
3 He has ris-en for me; Now ev-er-more from death's sting I am
4 *He is liv-ing for me; Dai-ly He's plead-ing and pray-ing for*
5 He is com-ing for me; Then with what joy His dear face I shall

1 free, All be-cause Je-sus was wound-ed for me.
2 *see, All be-cause Je-sus was dy-ing for me.*
3 free, All be-cause Je-sus has ris-en for me.
4 *me, O how I praise Him, He's liv-ing for me.*
5 see, O how I praise Him— He's com-ing for me!

THE ATONEMENT, CRUCIFIXION AND DEATH OF JESUS CHRIST

283

What Wondrous Love Is This?

We all like sheep have gone astray . . .
and the Lord hath laid on Him the iniquity of us all

— Isaiah 53:6

American Folk Hymn

WONDROUS LOVE
Southern Harmony

1 What won-drous love is this, O my soul, O my soul, What
2 *To God and to the Lamb I will sing, I will sing, To*
3 And when from death I'm free, I'll sing on, I'll sing on, And

1 won-drous love is this, O my soul! What won-drous love is
2 *God and to the Lamb I will sing; To God and to the*
3 when from death I'm free, I'll sing on; And when from death I'm

1 this that caused the Lord of bliss To bear the dread-ful curse for my
2 *Lamb, who is the great "I Am," While mil-lions join the theme, I will*
3 free, I'll sing and joy-ful be, And through e - ter - ni - ty I'll sing

1 soul, for my soul, To bear the dread-ful curse for my soul!
2 *sing, I will sing, While mil-lions join the theme, I will sing!*
3 on, I'll sing on, And through e - ter - ni - ty I'll sing on!

THE ATONEMENT, CRUCIFIXION AND DEATH OF JESUS CHRIST

O Sacred Head, Now Wounded 284

When they had platted a crown of thorns they put it upon His head.
— Matthew 27:29

Latin: 12th Century
German: Paul Gerhardt
Tr. by James W. Alexander, alt.

PASSION CHORALE
Hans Leo Hassler
Harmonized by J. S. Bach

1 O   sa-cred Head, now wound-ed, With grief and shame weighed down,
2 *What Thou, my Lord, hast suf-fered Was all for sin-ners' gain;*
3 What lan-guage shall I   bor-row To   thank Thee, dear-est   friend,

1 Now scorn-ful-ly sur-round-ed With thorns, Thy on-ly crown,
2 *Mine, mine was the trans-gres-sion, But Thine the dead-ly pain.*
3 For   this Thy dy-ing sor-row, Thy pit-y with-out   end?

1 How art Thou pale with an-guish, With sore a-buse and   scorn!
2 *Lo, here I fall, my Sav-ior! 'Tis I de-serve Thy place;*
3 O   make me Thine for-ev-er; And, should I faint-ing   be,

1 How does that vis-age lan-guish Which once was bright as morn!
2 *Look on me with Thy fa-vor, Vouch-safe to me Thy grace.*
3 Lord, let me nev-er, nev-er Out-live my love for Thee! A-men.

THE ATONEMENT, CRUCIFIXION AND DEATH OF JESUS CHRIST

285 Worthy the Lamb

Gloria Gaither
William J. Gaither

Thou art worthy, O Lord, to receive glory, and honor, and power....
— Revelation 4:11

WORTHY
William J. Gaither

1 Hear the cries of the shack-led from the on-set of
2 *Then the cry-ing is stilled as the cho-rus rings*
3 Then all the arch - an-gels, the saints of all

1 time— For the chains of de - feat there's no key; See the
2 *out— The shack-led re - leased from their chains; And*
3 time, Hold-ing their crowns in their hands,

1 tears of the bro - ken, the cries of the slaves— "Is there
2 *thou - sands of voic - es are swell-ing the song—*
3 Fall down be - fore Him, join - ing the song—

1 no one worth - y to set us free?"
2 *"Worth-y the Lamb that was slain."* Worth-y,
3 "Worth-y, worth-y the Lamb."

worth - y, Worth-y the Lamb that was slain; slain.

THE ATONEMENT, CRUCIFIXION AND DEATH OF JESUS CHRIST

Minister:	*If we had been Jews, would we have spoken out for Him*
	    when the Sanhedrin accused Him of blasphemy?
	If we had been Gentiles, would we have defended Him
	    when the Romans condemned Him to death?
	If we had been disciples, would we have stayed with Him
	    when the crowd became a crucifying mob?
	Or would we have been like Peter—
	    who followed Him and loved Him
	    and denied Him three times before the dawn?

Choir *(sings)*:	**Were you there when they crucified my Lord?** **O! Sometimes it causes me to tremble, tremble, tremble.**

Minister:	*And the Christ who was crucified there, once said:*
	    "As you have done it to the least of these, My brothers,
	    you have done it unto Me."
	As nations rise in war
	As governments oppress the poor
	As passive people turn and look aside
	In silence
	We crucify.
	Again—
	We crucify.

People:	As indifference forms the pattern of our lives, As hungry children cry for food, As widows mourn alone in empty rooms, In apathy— We crucify. Again— We crucify.
Choir *(sings)*:	**Were you there when they nailed Him to the tree?** **O! Sometimes it causes me to tremble, tremble, tremble.**

Minister:	*I think of the nails that crucified my Lord.*
	They were made of iron; but more—
	They were made of hatred, prejudice and greed.
	And I wonder—
	What part of myself is found in the shadow of that mob
	    that stretches down through history?
	What part of myself creates nails in other forms
	    that wound my brother—and my Lord?

People:	You know how many times I have betrayed You, Lord. You know the times I have chosen evil over good. Guilt lies upon me like an iron cloak. My soul is heavy—my burden hard.
Choir *(sings)*:	**Were you there when He rose up from the grave?** **O! Sometimes it causes me to tremble, tremble, tremble.**
Minister:	*In the act of death He absorbs our sins.* *In love, He forgives our failures.* *In the act of resurrection He gives the promise of acceptance,* *the assurance of forgiveness, the affirmation of eternal life.* *"Your sins are forgiven you", He said, "Go and sin no more."*
People:	Through Your love, I am made whole, Through Your death, I have found new life. You are my shield, my redeemer and my hope. My sins are forgiven—Hallelujah!

—Marilee Zdenek

THE ATONEMENT, CRUCIFIXION AND DEATH OF JESUS CHRIST

287

Were You There?

He is . . . a man of sorrows and acquainted with grief;
and we hid as it were our faces from Him. — Isaiah 53:3

American Folk Hymn

WERE YOU THERE
American Folk Melody

1 Were you there when they cru-ci-fied my Lord? Were you
2 *Were you there when they nailed Him to the tree?* Were you
3 Were you there when they laid Him in the tomb? Were you
4 *Were you there when He rose up from the grave?* Were you

1 there when they cru-ci-fied my Lord?
2 *there when they nailed Him to the tree?*
3 there when they laid Him in the tomb? O! - - -
4 *there when He rose up from the grave?*

Some-times it caus-es me to trem-ble, trem-ble, trem-ble.

1 Were you there when they cru-ci-fied my Lord?
2 *Were you there when they nailed Him to the tree?*
3 Were you there when they laid Him in the tomb?
4 *Were you there when He rose up from the grave?*

EASTER

Jesus Lives, and So Shall I

288

Now is Christ risen to become the firstfruits of them that slept.
— I Corinthians 15:20

Christian F. Gellert
Tr. by Philip Schaff

JESU, MEINE ZUVERSICHT
Johann Crüger

1 Je-sus lives, and so shall I: Death, thy sting is gone for-
2 *Je-sus lives and reigns su-preme: And, His king-dom still re-*
3 Je-sus lives— and by His grace, Vic-tory o'er my pas-sions
4 *Je-sus lives— I know full well Naught from Him my heart can*
5 Je-sus lives— and death is now But my en-trance in-to

1 ev - er! He for me hath deigned to die,
2 *main - ing, I shall al - so be with Him,*
3 giv - ing, I will cleanse my heart and ways,
4 *sev - er, Life nor death nor powers of hell,*
5 glo - ry; Cour - age, then, my soul, for thou

1 Lives the bands of death to sev - er. He shall raise me
2 *Ev - er liv - ing, ev - er reign - ing. God has prom-ised—*
3 Ev - er to His glo - ry liv - ing. Me He rais - es
4 *Joy nor grief, hence-forth for - ev - er. None of all His*
5 Hast a crown of life be - fore thee. Thou shalt find thy

1 from the dust: Je - sus is my hope and trust.
2 *be it must: Je - sus is my hope and trust.*
3 from the dust: Je - sus is my hope and trust.
4 *saints is lost: Je - sus is my hope and trust.*
5 hopes were just: Je - sus is my hope and trust. A-men.

EASTER

289 Christ the Lord Is Risen Today

Ye seek Jesus of Nazareth who was crucified; He is risen . . .

— Mark 16:6

Charles Wesley

EASTER HYMN
"Lyra Davidica"
Descant by Paul Sjolund

Descant

3, 4 Ah_____ Al - le - lu - ia! Ah_

1 Christ the Lord is risen to-day,
2 *Lives a - gain our glo-rious King,*
3 Love's re-deem-ing work is done,
*4 Sing we to our God a-bove,

Al - le - lu - ia!

_____ Al - le - lu - ia! Ah

1 Sons of men and an - gels say:
2 *Where, O death, is now thy sting?*
3 Fought the fight, the bat - tle won,
4 Praise e - ter - nal as His love;

Al - le - lu - ia!

_____ Al - le-lu - ia! Al -

1 Raise your joys and tri - umphs high,
2 *Dy - ing once, He all doth save,*
3 Death in vain for - bids Him rise,
4 *Praise Him, all ye heaven-ly host,*

Al - le - lu - ia!

1 Sing, ye heavens, and earth re - ply:
2 *Where thy vic - to - ry, O grave?*
3 Christ has o - pened par - a - dise,
4 *Fa - ther, Son, and Ho - ly Ghost.*

- - le - lu -ia! Al - le-lu -ia! A - men.

Al - le - lu - ia! A - men.

CHRIST THE LORD IS RISEN TODAY

Descant by Paul Sjolund

TPT. I
PART I: play on stanzas 1, 4.

TPT. II
PART II: play on stanzas 2, 4.

"Amen" after stanza 4.

(A - men.)

EASTER

Now if Christ is preached as raised from the dead,
how can some of you say that there is no resurrection of the dead?
But if there is no resurrection of the dead,
then Christ has not been raised;
if Christ has not been raised,
then our preaching is in vain and your faith is in vain.

We are even found to be misrepresenting God,
because we testified of God that He raised Christ,
whom He did not raise if it is true that the dead are not raised.
For if the dead are not raised,
then Christ has not been raised.

If Christ has not been raised,
your faith is futile and you are still in your sins.

Then those also who have fallen asleep in Christ have perished.

If in this life only we have hoped in Christ,
we are of all men most to be pitied.

But, in fact, Christ has been raised from the dead,
the first fruits of those who have fallen asleep.

For as by a man came death,
by a man has come also the resurrection of the dead.
For as in Adam all die,
so also in Christ shall all be made alive.

But each in his own order:
Christ the first fruits, then at His coming those who belong to Christ.

Then comes the end,
when He delivers the kingdom to God the Father
after destroying every rule and every authority and power.

For He must reign until He has put all His enemies under His feet.

The last enemy to be destroyed is death.

"For God has put all things in subjection under His feet."

But when it says, "All things are put in subjection under Him,"
it is plain that He is excepted who put all things under Him.

When all things are subjected to Him,
then the Son Himself will also be subjected to Him who put all things under Him,
that God may be everything to everyone.

—(RSV)

EASTER

Thine Is the Glory

For Thine is the Kingdom, and the power, and the glory, forever.
— Matthew 6:13

291

Edmond L. Budry
Tr. by R. Birch Hoyle

JUDAS MACCABEUS
George Friedrich Handel

1 Thine is the glo - ry, Ris - en, con-quering Son; End-less is the
2 *Lo! Je - sus meets us, Ris - en from the tomb; Lov-ing - ly He*
3 No more we doubt Thee, Glo-rious Prince of life! Life is naught with-

1 vic - tory Thou o'er death hast won. An - gels in bright rai - ment
2 *greets us, Scat - ters fear and gloom. Let His church with glad - ness*
3 out Thee: Aid us in our strife. Make us more than con-querors,

1 Rolled the stone a - way, Kept the fold - ed grave - clothes
2 *Hymns of tri - umph sing, For her Lord now liv - eth:*
3 Through Thy death - less love: Bring us safe through Jor - dan

1 Where Thy bod - y lay.
2 *Death hath lost its sting.* Thine is the glo - ry, Ris - en, con-quering Son;
3 To Thy home a - bove.

End - less is the vic - tory Thou o'er death hast won. A - men.

Words from "Cantate Domino." © Copyright by World Student Christian Federation. Used by permission.

EASTER

292 Because He Lives

Because I live, ye shall live also. — John 14:19

Gloria Gaither
William J. Gaither

RESURRECTION
William J. Gaither
Final chorus arranged by Ronn Huff

1 God sent His Son, they called Him Je - sus, He came to love,
2 *How sweet to hold a new-born ba - by, And feel the pride,*
3 And then one day I'll cross the riv - er, I'll fight life's fi -

1 heal, and for - give; He lived and died to buy my
2 *and joy He gives; But great - er still the calm as -*
3 nal war with pain; And then as death gives way to

1 par-don, An emp - ty grave is there to prove my Sav - ior lives.
2 *sur-ance, This child can face un - cer-tain days be-cause He lives.*
3 vic-tory, I'll see the lights of glo - ry and I'll know He lives.

Be-cause He lives I can face to - mor-row, Be-cause He lives

all fear is gone; Be-cause I know He holds the

EASTER

fu-ture. And life is worth the liv-ing just be-cause He lives.

Congregation sing melody in unison; accompaniment play as written.

3 lives.   (Be-cause He   lives   I can face to-

mor - row;   Be-cause He   lives   all fear is

gone;   Be - cause I   know   He holds the fu - ture,

And life is worth the liv-ing just be-cause He lives!)

EASTER

293 Christ Whose Glory Fills the Skies

The sun of righteousness shall rise with healing in His wings. — Malachi 4:2

Charles Wesley

LUX PRIMA
Charles Gounod

1 Christ, whose glo-ry fills the skies, Christ, the true, the on-ly Light,
2 *Dark and cheer-less is the morn Un-ac-com-pa-nied by Thee;*
3 Vis-it, then, this soul of mine; Pierce the gloom of sin and grief;

1 Sun of Right-eous-ness, a-rise, Tri-umph o'er the shades of night;
2 *Joy-less is the day's re-turn Till Thy mer-cy's beams I see;*
3 Fill me, Ra-dian-cy Di-vine; Scat-ter all my un-be-lief;

1 Day-spring from on high, be near; Day-star, in my heart ap-pear.
2 *Till they in-ward light im-part, Cheer my eyes and warm my heart.*
3 More and more Thy-self dis-play, Shin-ing to the per-fect day. A-men.

294 Easter

We thank Thee for the beauty of this day, for the glorious message that all nature proclaims:

the Easter lilies with their waxen throats eloquently singing the good news;

the birds, so early this morning, impatient to begin their song;

every flowering tree, shrub, and flaming bush, a living proclamation from Thee.

O pen our hearts that we may hear it too!

Lead us, we pray Thee, to the grave that is empty, into the garden of the Resurrection where we may meet our risen Lord. May we never again live as if Thou were dead!

In Thy presence restore our faith, our hope, our joy.

Grant to our spirits refreshment, rest, and peace.

Maintain within our hearts an unruffled calm, an unbroken serenity that no storms of life shall ever be able to take from us.

From this moment, O living Christ, we ask Thee to go with us wherever we go; be our Companion in all that we do. And for this greatest of all gifts, we offer Thee our sacrifices of thanksgiving. Amen.

—Peter Marshall

EASTER

I Know That My Redeemer Lives

295

For I know that my Redeemer liveth . . . — Job 19:25

Samuel Medley

DUKE STREET
John Hatton

1 I know that my Re - deem - er lives: What joy the blest as -
2 *He lives, to bless me with His love; He lives to plead for*
3 He lives, and grants me dai - ly breath; He lives, and I shall
4 *He lives, all glo - ry to His Name; He lives, my Sav - ior,*

1 sur - ance gives! He lives, He lives, who once was dead;
2 *me a - bove; He lives, my hun - gry soul to feed;*
3 con - quer death; He lives, my fu - ture to pre - pare;
4 *still the same; What joy the blest as - sur - ance gives:*

1 He lives, my ev - er - last - ing Head!
2 *He lives, to help in time of need.*
3 He lives, to bring me safe - ly there.
4 *I know that my Re - deem - er lives!* A - men.

1 Corinthians 15: 51-58

296

Lo! I tell you a mystery. We shall not all sleep, but we shall all be changed, in a moment, in the twinkling of an eye, at the last trumpet. For the trumpet will sound, and the dead will be raised imperishable, and we shall be changed. For this perishable nature must put on the imperishable, and this mortal nature must put on immortality. When the perishable puts on the imperishable, and the mortal puts on immortality, then shall come to pass the saying that is written: "Death is swallowed up in victory." "O death, where is thy victory? O death, where is thy sting?" The sting of death is sin, and the power of sin is the law. But thanks be to God, who gives us the victory through our Lord Jesus Christ.

Therefore, my beloved brethren, be steadfast, immovable, always abounding in the work of the Lord, knowing that in the Lord your labor is not in vain.

—(RSV)
EASTER

297 Jesus Christ Is Risen Today

Praise ye the Lord, Sing unto the Lord a new song.

— Psalm 149:1

Latin: 14th Century
English translation, *New Version*
Charles Wesley, stanza 4

LLANFAIR
Robert Williams
Harmonized by John Roberts

1 Je - sus Christ is risen to - day,
2 *Hymns of praise then let us sing,*
3 But the pains which He en - dured,
4 *Sing we to our God a - bove,*

Al - le - lu - ia!

1 Our tri - um - phant ho - ly day,
2 *Un - to Christ, our heaven-ly King,*
3 Our sal - va - tion have pro - cured;
4 *Praise e - ter - nal as His love;*

Al - le - lu - ia!

1 Who did once up - on the cross,
2 *Who en - dured the cross and grave,*
3 Now a - bove the sky He's King,
4 *Praise Him, all ye heaven - ly host,*

Al - le - lu - ia!

1 Suf - fer to re - deem our loss.
2 *Sin - ners to re - deem and save.*
3 Where the an - gels ev - er sing.
4 *Fa - ther, Son and Ho - ly Ghost.*

Al - le - lu - ia!

A - men.

EASTER

Christ Arose

Thou hast led captivity captive . . .

CHRIST AROSE
Robert Lowry

298

Robert Lowry

1 Low in the grave He lay, Je - sus, my Sav - ior! Wait - ing the
2 *Vain - ly they watched His bed,* Je - sus, my Sav - ior! *Vain - ly they*
3 Death could not keep his prey, Je - sus, my Sav - ior! He tore the

1 com-ing day, Je - sus, my Lord!
2 *sealed the dead,* Je - sus, my Lord! Up from the grave He a - rose,
3 bars a - way, Je - sus, my Lord! He a-rose,

With a might-y tri - umph o'er His foes; He a - rose a vic-tor from the
He a-rose;

dark do-main, And He lives for - ev - er with His saints to reign; He a -

rose! He a - rose! Hal - le - lu - jah! Christ a - rose!
He a-rose! He a - rose!

EASTER

299

He Lives

Alfred H. Ackley

Go quickly and tell . . . His disciples that He is risen from the dead.
— Matthew 28:7

ACKLEY
Alfred H. Ackley

1 I serve a ris-en Sav-ior, He's in the world to-day;
2 *In all the world a-round me I see His lov-ing care,*
3 Re-joice, re-joice, O Chris-tian, lift up your voice and sing

1 I know that He is liv-ing, what-ev-er men may say;
2 *And though my heart grows wea-ry I nev-er will de-spair;*
3 E-ter-nal hal-le-lu-jahs to Je-sus Christ the King!

1 I see His hand of mer-cy, I hear His voice of cheer,
2 *I know that He is lead-ing through all the storm-y blast,*
3 The Hope of all who seek Him, the Help of all who find,

1 And just the time I need Him He's al-ways near.
2 *The day of His ap-pear-ing will come at last.*
3 None oth-er is so lov-ing, so good and kind.

He lives, He lives, Christ Je-sus lives to-day!
He lives, He lives,

EASTER

He walks with me and talks with me a - long life's nar - row way.

He lives, He lives, sal - va - tion to im - part!
He lives, He lives,

You ask me how I know He lives? He lives with - in my heart.

Easter 300

Some years ago a newspaper editor telephoned and asked me to tell in a few words what Easter means to me. My testimony was this: Easter means Christ to me. It means Christ in His kingly splendor, Christ in His serene glory, Christ in His gracious condescension. This is because Easter is the return of Christ from inflicted violence, from induced death, from imprisonment in a tomb. Easter is Christ triumphant over all that sin and death and man could do to Him. Easter means Christ.

And where Christ goes, drama goes. For it is impossible to look anywhere in the Gospels and fail to find something powerful happening. This is because Christ is Himself the Gospel and He is life, abundant life, and His life means action, pilgrimage, arrival.

Easter means life. Christ defeated death in order that life in Him might always live. And it is life that we want, life in Christ. Whether we put it in words or not, our constant thought is "Life, more life, always more and more life." We want life in ourselves, in our loved ones, in our friends, the kind of life that cannot be diminished, the kind of life that always expands. Easter is Christ's victory over all that would restrict, deny and strangle life. "For to me to live is Christ." That is Easter.

—Raymond Lindquist

301 The Easter Song

He is not here, but is risen . . .
— Luke 24:6

Anne Herring

EASTER SONG
Anne Herring

1 Hear the bells ring-ing, they're sing-ing that we can be
2 *Hear the bells ring-ing, they're sing-ing, "Christ is ris - en*

1 born a - gain!
2 *from the dead!"*

The an - gel up - on the tomb-stone said, "He is

ris - en just as He said. Quick - ly now go tell His dis-

ci - ples that Je - sus Christ is no long - er dead!"

EASTER

Joy to the world, He is ris - en, Al -

le - lu - ia! He's ris - en, Al - le - lu - ia! He's

ris - en, Al - le - lu - ia!

He Is Risen! 302

"Why do you look
for the living
among
the
dead?

He is not here:
He has been raised!

Remember what He said to you,
while He was still in Galilee—

that the Son of Man must be betrayed into the hands of sinful men,
and must be crucified,
and must rise again on the third day."

—Luke 24:5b-7 (PHILLIPS)

303 Christ Is Coming!

. . . Surely I come quickly; even so, come, Lord Jesus. — Revelation 22:20

BRYN CALFARIA
William Owen
Harmonized by Carlton R. Young

John R. MacDuff

1 Christ is com-ing! let cre - a-tion From her groans and trav-ail cease;
2 *Earth can now but tell the sto - ry Of Thy bit - ter cross and pain;*
3 With that bless-ed hope be-fore us, Let no harp re - main un-strung;

1 Let the glo-rious proc - la - ma-tion Hope re-store and faith in-crease:
2 *She shall yet be-hold Thy glo - ry When Thou com-est back to reign:*
3 Let the might-y ad-vent cho-rus On-ward roll from tongue to tongue:

1 Christ is com - ing, Christ is com - ing, Christ is com - ing—
2 *Christ is com - ing, Christ is com - ing, Christ is com - ing—*
3 Christ is com - ing, Christ is com - ing, Christ is com - ing—

broaden   a tempo

1 Come, Thou bless-ed Prince of Peace! Come, Thou bless-ed Prince of Peace!
2 *Let each heart re-peat the strain! Let each heart re - peat the strain!*
3 Come, Lord Je-sus, quick-ly come! Come, Lord Je-sus, quick-ly come! A-men.

THE SECOND COMING OF JESUS CHRIST

Christ Returneth!

. . . be ye also ready; for in such an hour as ye think not the Son of man cometh.

— Matthew 24:44

CHRIST RETURNETH

H. L. Turner

James McGranahan

1 It may be at morn, when the day is a wak-ing, When
2 *It may be at mid - day, it may be at twi - light, It*
3 While hosts cry "Ho - san - na," from heav - en de - scend-ing, With
4 *O joy! O de - light! Should we go with - out dy - ing, No*

1 sun-light through dark-ness and shad-ow is break-ing, That Je - sus will
2 *may be, per - chance, that the black - ness of mid-night Will burst in - to*
3 glo - ri - fied saints and the an - gels at - tend - ing, With grace on His
4 *sick-ness, no sad - ness, no dread and no cry - ing, Caught up through the*

1 come in the full - ness of glo - ry, To re - ceive from the world His own.
2 *light in the blaze of His glo - ry, When Je - sus re - ceives His own.*
3 brow, like a ha - lo of glo - ry, Will Je - sus re - ceive His own.
4 *clouds with our Lord in - to glo - ry, When Je - sus re - ceives His own.*

O, Lord Je-sus, how long, how long 'Til we shout the glad song Christ re-

turn-eth! Hal - le - lu-jah! hal - le - lu-jah! A - men, Hal - le - lu-jah! A - men.

THE SECOND COMING OF JESUS CHRIST

305 Jesus Is Coming Again

Watch, therefore, for ye know neither the day nor the hour . . . . — Matthew 25:13

COMING AGAIN

John W. Peterson

John W. Peterson

1 Mar - vel - ous mes - sage we bring, Glo - ri - ous car - ol we
2 *For - est and flow - er ex - claim, Moun - tain and mead - ow the*
3 Stand - ing be - fore Him at last, Tri - al and trou - ble all

1 sing, Won - der - ful word of the King: Je - sus is
2 *same, All earth and heav - en pro - claim: Je - sus is*
3 past, Crowns at His feet we will cast: Je - sus is

1 com - ing a - gain!
2 *com - ing a - gain!* Com - ing a - gain, com - ing a -
3 com - ing a - gain!

gain; May-be morn-ing, may - be noon, may-be eve-ning and may-be soon!

Com - ing a - gain, com - ing a - gain; O, what a

THE SECOND COMING OF JESUS CHRIST

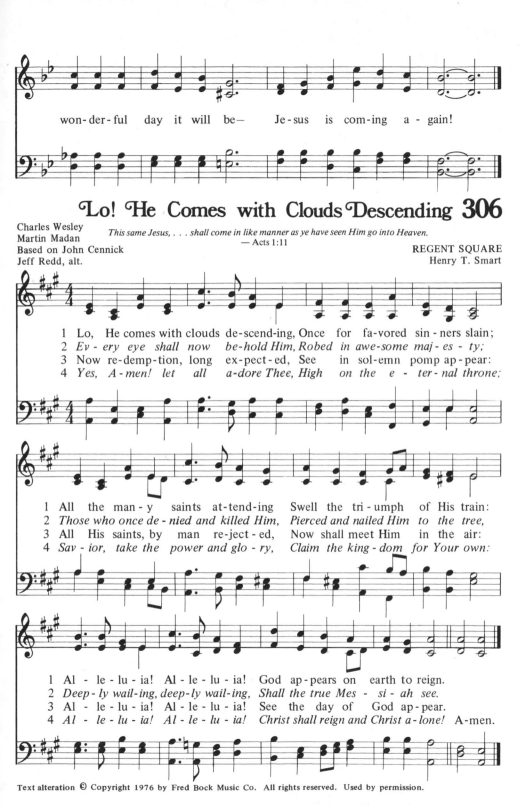

Lo! He Comes with Clouds Descending 306

Charles Wesley
Martin Madan
Based on John Cennick
Jeff Redd, alt.

This same Jesus, . . . shall come in like manner as ye have seen Him go into Heaven.
— Acts 1:11

REGENT SQUARE
Henry T. Smart

won-der-ful day it will be— Je-sus is com-ing a - gain!

1 Lo, He comes with clouds de-scend-ing, Once for fa-vored sin - ners slain;
2 *Ev - ery eye shall now be-hold Him, Robed in awe-some maj - es - ty;*
3 Now re-demp-tion, long ex-pect-ed, See in sol-emn pomp ap-pear:
4 *Yes, A - men! let all a-dore Thee, High on the e - ter - nal throne;*

1 All the man - y saints at-tend-ing Swell the tri - umph of His train:
2 *Those who once de - nied and killed Him, Pierced and nailed Him to the tree,*
3 All His saints, by man re-ject-ed, Now shall meet Him in the air:
4 *Sav - ior, take the power and glo - ry, Claim the king - dom for Your own:*

1 Al - le-lu - ia! Al - le - lu - ia! God ap-pears on earth to reign.
2 *Deep-ly wail-ing, deep-ly wail-ing, Shall the true Mes - si - ah see.*
3 Al - le - lu - ia! Al - le - lu - ia! See the day of God ap-pear.
4 *Al - le-lu - ia! Al - le - lu - ia! Christ shall reign and Christ a-lone!* A-men.

THE SECOND COMING OF JESUS CHRIST

307 This Could Be the Dawning of that Day

. . . Ye do well that ye take heed as unto a light, . . . in a dark place, until the day dawn . . . .
— II Peter 1:19

Gloria Gaither
William Gaither

DAWNING
William J. Gaither

1 A par - ade be - gan at Cal - vary,
2 *Noth - ing here holds their al - le - giance,*
3 All the saints are get - ting rest - less,

1 And the saints of all the a - ges fill its ranks;
2 *They're not bound by shack - les forged of earth - ly gold;*
3 O what glo - rious ex - pec - ta - tion fills each face!

1 O'er the sands of time they're march - ing to their King's great cor - o -
2 *Since that day they knelt at Cal - vary, they've been pil - grims ev - er*
3 Dreams and hopes of all the a - ges are a - wait - ing His re -

1 na - tion, And this could be the dawn - ing of that day!
2 *wan - dering, Just look - ing for a place to rest their souls.*
3 turn - ing, And this could be the dawn - ing of that day!

THE SECOND COMING OF JESUS CHRIST

O this could be the dawn - ing of that grand and glo - rious day, When the face of Je - sus we be - hold! Dreams and hopes of all the a - ges Are a - wait - ing His re - turn - ing, And this could be the dawn - ing of that day!

THE SECOND COMING OF JESUS CHRIST

308   The Son of Man in His Glory

"When the Son of man comes in His glory, and all the angels with Him, then He will sit on His glorious throne. Before Him will be gathered all the nations, and He will separate them one from another as a shepherd separates the sheep from the goats, and He will place the sheep at His right hand, but the goats at the left.

"Then the King will say to those at His right hand, 'Come, O blessed of My Father, inherit the kingdom prepared for you from the foundation of the world; for I was hungry and you gave Me food, I was thirsty and you gave Me drink, I was a stranger and you welcomed Me, I was naked and you clothed Me, I was sick and you visited Me, I was in prison and you came to Me.' Then the righteous will answer Him, 'Lord, when did we see Thee hungry and feed Thee, or thirsty and give Thee drink? And when did we see Thee a stranger and welcome Thee, or naked and clothe Thee? And when did we see Thee sick or in prison and visit Thee?' And the King will answer them, 'Truly, I say to you, as you did it to one of the least of these My brethren, you did it to Me.'

"Then He will say to those at His left hand, 'Depart from Me, you cursed, into the eternal fire prepared for the devil and his angels; for I was hungry and you gave Me no food, I was thirsty and you gave Me no drink, I was a stranger and you did not welcome Me, naked and you did not clothe Me, sick and in prison and you did not visit Me.' Then they also will answer, 'Lord, when did we see Thee hungry or thirsty or a stranger or naked or sick or in prison, and did not minister to Thee?" Then He will answer them, 'Truly, I say to you, as you did it not to one of the least of these, you did it not to Me.' And they will go away into eternal punishment, but the righteous into eternal life."

—Matthew 25:31-46 (RSV)

309   When He Shall Come

Almeda J. Pearce

And if I go to prepare a place for you, I will come again,
. . . that where I am there ye may be also.   John 14:3

PEARCE
Almeda J. Pearce

1 When He shall come, re-splen-dent in His glo-ry, To take His
2 *When I shall stand with-in the court of heav-en Where white-robed*
3 When He shall call, from earth's re-mot-est cor-ners, All who have

1 own from out this vale of night, O may I know the
2 *pil-grims pass be-fore my sight— Earth's mar-tyred saints and*
3 stood tri-um-phant in His might, O to be wor-thy

1 joy at His ap-pear-ing—On-ly at morn to walk with Him in white!
2 *blood-washed o-ver-com-ers— These then are they who walk with Him in white!*
3 then to stand be-side them, And in that morn to walk with Him in white!

THE SECOND COMING OF JESUS CHRIST

Is It the Crowning Day?

Looking for and hasting unto the coming of the Day of God.

George Walker Whitcomb

— I John 3:12

310

GLAD DAY
Charles H. Marsh

1 Je - sus may come to - day, Glad day! Glad day! And I would
2 *I may go home to - day, Glad day! Glad day! Seems like I*
3 Faith - ful I'll be to - day, Glad day! Glad day! And I will

1 see my Friend; Dan - gers and trou - bles would end If
2 *hear their song; Hail to the ra - di - ant throng! If*
3 free - ly tell Why I should love Him so well, For

1 Je - sus should come to - day.
2 *I should go home to - day.* Glad day! Glad day! Is it the crown - ing
3 He is my all to - day.

day? I'll live for to - day, nor anx - ious be, Je - sus, my Lord, I

soon shall see; Glad day! Glad day! Is it the crown - ing day?

THE SECOND COMING OF JESUS CHRIST

311 What If It Were Today?

"Jesus has gone away to Heaven, and some day, just as He went, He will return." — Acts 1:11b

WHAT IF IT WERE TODAY?

Lelia N. Morris

Lelia N. Morris

1 Je - sus is com-ing to earth a-gain, What if it were to - day?
2 Sa - tan's do-min-ion will then be o'er, O that it were to - day!
3 Faith-ful and true would He find us here If He should come to-day?

1 Com - ing in pow-er and love to reign, What if it were to - day?
2 Sor - row and sigh-ing shall be no more, O that it were to - day!
3 Watch-ing in glad-ness and not in fear, If He should come to-day?

1 Com - ing to claim His cho-sen Bride, All the re-deemed and pu - ri -fied,
2 Then shall the dead in Christ a-rise, Caught up to meet Him in the skies,
3 Signs of His com - ing mul-ti-ply, Morning light breaks in east-ern sky,

1 O - ver this whole earth scat-tered wide, What if it were to - day?
2 When shall these glo - ries meet our eyes? What if it were to - day?
3 Watch, for the time is draw - ing nigh, What if it were to - day?

Glo - ry, glo - ry! Joy to my heart 'twill bring; Glo - ry,

THE SECOND COMING OF JESUS CHRIST

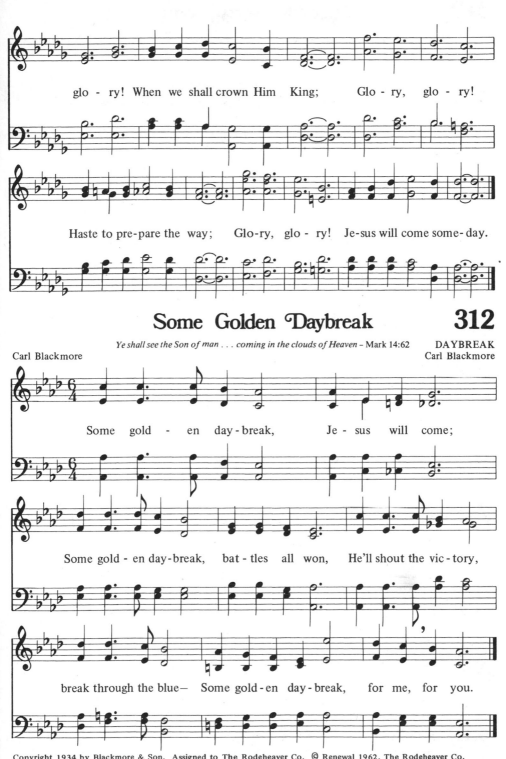

glo - ry! When we shall crown Him King; Glo - ry, glo - ry!

Haste to pre-pare the way; Glo-ry, glo - ry! Je-sus will come some-day.

Some Golden Daybreak

312

Ye shall see the Son of man . . . coming in the clouds of Heaven – Mark 14:62

Carl Blackmore

DAYBREAK
Carl Blackmore

Some gold - en day - break, Je - sus will come;

Some gold - en day-break, bat - tles all won, He'll shout the vic - tory,

break through the blue— Some gold - en day - break, for me, for you.

THE SECOND COMING OF JESUS CHRIST

313

The King Is Coming

Gloria Gaither, stanzas 1, 2, 3
William J. Gaither, stanzas 1, 2, 3
Charles Millhuff, stanza 3

Behold, the Lord cometh
with ten thousands of His saints.
— Jude 1:14

KING IS COMING
William J. Gaither
Final chorus arranged by Ronn Huff

1 The mar-ket place is emp-ty, No more traf-fic in the streets, All the
2 *Hap-py fac-es line the hall-ways, Those whose lives have been redeemed, Broken*
3 I can hear the char-iots rum-ble, I can see the march-ing throng, The

1 build-ers' tools are si-lent, No more time to har-vest wheat; Bus-y house-wives
2 *homes that He has mend-ed, Those from pris-on He has freed; Lit-tle chil-dren*
3 flur-ry of God's trum-pets Spells the end of sin and wrong; Re-gal robes are

1 cease their la-bors, In the court room no de-bate, Work on earth is all sus-
2 *and the a-ged Hand in hand stand all a-glow, Who were crippled, broken,*
3 now un-fold-ing, Heav-en's grandstands all in place, Heav-en's choir is now as-

1 pend-ed As the King comes thru the gate.
2 *ru-ined, Clad in gar-ments white as snow.* O the King is com-ing, the
3 sem-bled, Start to sing "A-maz-ing Grace!"

King is com-ing! I just heard the trumpets sounding, And now His face I see;

THE SECOND COMING OF JESUS CHRIST

Congregation sing melody in unison; accompanist play as written.

O the King is com-ing, the King is com-ing! Praise God, He's

com-ing for me! me! O the King is coming, the

King is com-ing! I just heard the trumpet sounding, And now His face I

see; O the King is coming, the King is

com-ing! Praise God! He's com-ing for me!

THE SECOND COMING OF JESUS CHRIST

314 What a Day That Will Be

And the Lord will wipe all tears from their eyes;
. . . for the former things are passed away. — Revelation 21:4

Jim Hill

WHAT A DAY
Jim Hill

1 There is com - ing a day when no heart-aches shall come,
2 *There'll be no sor-row there, no more bur-dens to bear,*

1 No more clouds in the sky, no more tears to dim the eye; All is
2 *No more sick-ness, no pain, no more part-ing o-ver there; And for-*

1 peace for ev - er-more on that hap-py gold-en shore—What a day,
2 *ev - er I will be with the One who died for me— What a day,*

1 glo - ri-ous day, that will be.
2 *glo - ri-ous day, that will be.*

What a day that will be when my

Je - sus I shall see, And I look up - on His face—the One who

THE SECOND COMING OF JESUS CHRIST

saved me by His grace; When He takes me by the hand, and leads me

through the Prom-ised Land, What a day, glo - ri - ous day, that will be.

For God So Loved the World 315

Based on John 3:16
Frances Townsend

While we were yet sinners, Christ died for us.
— Romans 5:8

GOD LOVED THE WORLD
Alfred B. Smith

Unison

For God so loved the world He gave His on-ly Son To

die on Cal-vary's tree, From sin to set me free; Some day He's com-ing

back, What glo - ry that will be! Won-der-ful His love to me.

THE SECOND COMING OF JESUS CHRIST

316 My Lord, What a Morning!

They shall see the Son of man coming in the clouds of heaven . . . .
— Matthew 24:30

Traditional

STARS FALL
Traditional Spiritual

My Lord, what a morn-ing! My Lord, what a morn-ing! O

my Lord, what a morn-ing, When the stars be-gin to fall.

Fine

1 You'll hear   a sin-ner mourn, To wake the   na-tions un-der-ground!
2 *You'll hear   a sin-ner pray, To wake the   na-tions un-der-ground!*
3 You'll hear   a Chris-tian shout, To wake the   na-tions un-der-ground!
4 *You'll hear   a Chris-tian sing, To wake the   na-tions un-der-ground!*

D.C.

Look-ing to my God's right hand, When the stars be-gin to fall!

THE SECOND COMING OF JESUS CHRIST

Our
Love for God

317 Let's Just Praise the Lord

The Lord Jehovah is my strength and my song . . .

— Isaiah 12:2

Gloria Gaither
William J. Gaither

LET'S JUST PRAISE THE LORD
William J. Gaither

Let's just praise the Lord! Praise the Lord! Let's just lift our hearts* to heav - en and praise the Lord; Let's just praise the Lord! Praise the Lord! Let's just lift our hearts* to heav - en and praise the Lord!

Fine

*Alternate lyrics, "voices", "hands".

WORSHIP AND ADORATION

D.C.

1 O we thank You for Your kind - ness, we thank You for Your
2 *Just the pre - cious name of Je - sus is worth - y of our*

1 love, We have been in heaven-ly plac - es, felt bless-ings from a -
2 *praise, Let us bow our knees be - fore Him, our hands to heav - en*

1 bove; We've been shar - ing all the good things, the fam - ily can af -
2 *raise; When He comes in clouds of glo - ry, with Him to ev - er*

1 ford, Let's just turn our praise toward heav - en and praise the Lord.
2 *reign, Let's just lift our hap - py voic - es, and praise His name.*

318 Come, Thou Fount of Every Blessing

In that day shall a fountain be opened . . . for sin and uncleaness.

— Zechariah 13:1

Robert Robinson
Jeff Redd, 2nd stanza, alt.

NETTLETON
John Wyeth

1 Come, Thou Fount of ev-ery bless-ing, Tune my heart to sing Thy grace;
2 *This my glad com-mem-o-ra-tion That 'til now I've safe-ly come;*
3 O to grace how great a debt-or Dai-ly I'm con-strained to be!

1 Streams of mer-cy, nev-er ceas-ing, Call for songs of loud-est praise.
2 *And I hope, by Thy good pleas-ure, Safe-ly to ar-rive at home.*
3 Let Thy good-ness, like a fet-ter, Bind my wan-dering heart to Thee:

1 Teach me some me-lo-dious son-net, Sung by flaming tongues a-bove; Praise the
2 *Je-sus sought me when a strang-er, Wan-dering from the fold of God; He, to*
3 Prone to wan-der, Lord, I feel it, Prone to leave the God I love: Here's my

*Alternate ending for
2nd stanza into har-
monization.*

1 mount! I'm fixed up-on it, Mount of Thy redeeming love.
2 *res-cue me from dan-ger, Interposed His pre-cious blood.* blood.
3 heart, O take and seal it, Seal it for Thy courts a-bove. A-men.

WORSHIP AND ADORATION

Arranged by Richard Bolks

3 O to grace how great a debt-or Dai-ly I'm con-strained to be! Let Thy

good-ness like a fet-ter, Bind my wan-dering heart to Thee. Prone to wan - der,

Lord, I feel it, Prone to leave the God I love: Here's my heart, O take and

seal it, Seal it for Thy courts a - bove. A - men.

WORSHIP AND ADORATION

319 Immortal, Invisible, God Only Wise

He that keepeth thee shall not slumber . . . or sleep.

— Psalm 121: 3,4

Walter Chalmers Smith

ST. DENIO
Welsh Melody

1 Im - mor - tal, in - vis - i - ble, God on - ly wise,
2 *Un - rest - ing, un - hast - ing, and si - lent as light,*
3 To all, life Thou giv - est, to both great and small;
4 *Great Fa - ther of glo - ry, pure Fa - ther of light,*

1 In light in - ac - ces - si - ble hid from our eyes,
2 *Nor want - ing, nor wast - ing, Thou rul - est in might;*
3 In all life Thou liv - est, the true life of all;
4 *Thine an - gels a - dore Thee, all veil - ing their sight;*

1 Most bless - ed, most glo - rious, the An - cient of Days,
2 *Thy jus - tice like moun - tains high soar - ing a - bove*
3 We blos - som and flour - ish as leaves on the tree,
4 *All praise we would ren - der: O help us to see*

1 Al - might - y, vic - to - rious, Thy great name we praise.
2 *Thy clouds, which are foun - tains of good - ness and love.*
3 And with - er and per - ish—but naught chang - eth Thee.
4 *'Tis on - ly the splen - dor of light hid - eth Thee.* A - men.

Arranged by Mary E. Caldwell

4 Great Fa - ther of glo - ry, pure Fa - ther of

light, Thine an - gels a - dore Thee, all

veil - ing their sight; All praise we would ren - der: O

help us to see 'Tis on - ly the splen-dor of

light hid - eth Thee. A - men.

WORSHIP AND ADORATION

320 Let Us Celebrate the Glories of Our God

Now unto God and our Father be glory forever and ever. — Philippians 4:20

BELLAMY
Jean Joseph Mouret
Arranged by Fred Bock

Bryan Jeffery Leech

1 Let us cel-e-brate the glo-ries of our Lord, And let us look for His swift re-
2 (Let us) cel-e-brate the glo-ries of our Lord, And let us tell Him how good and
3 (Let us) cel-e-brate the glo-ries of our Lord, And let us men-tion His great a-

1 turn - ing; What a glo - rious hope we have in the dark-est hour To
2 great He is; Let's re - hearse the songs we'll sing when He comes to reign, And
3 chieve - ments; For we can - not tell too much how He went to die And

1 know He's com-ing soon with power. 1 As we look for His ap - pear - ing,
2 take His right-ful place a - gain. 2 Je - sus Christ is now the vic - tor,
3 how our God has raised Him high.

1 We must share the good news with ev-ery man on earth. As we see this mo-ment
2 Know-ing that He's with us, what cause is there to fear? There's a sound of dis-tant

1 near - ing, We must live to serve Him for all that we are worth! 2 Let us
2 drum-ming, For His prom-ised com - ing is ver - y, ver - y near! 3 Let us

WORSHIP AND ADORATION

Brethren, We Have Met to Worship

321

Jesus sayeth . . ., No man cometh unto the Father but by Me. — John 14:6

George Atkins
Alt. Bryan Jeffery Leech

HOLY MANNA
William Moore
in *Columbian Harmony*

1 Breth-ren, we have met to wor-ship To a-dore the Lord and God;
2 *Let us love our God su-preme-ly, Let us love our broth-ers too;*

1 Will you pray with ex-pec-ta-tion As we preach the liv-ing Word?
2 *Let us pray and care for peo-ple 'Til God makes their lives a-new.*

1 All is vain un-less the Spir-it Of the Ho-ly One comes down;
2 *When at last we're called to heav-en, In His pre-sence we'll sit down;*

1 Breth-ren, pray, and God's great bless-ing Will be show-ered all a-round.
2 *And the Lord will then re-ward us Giv-ing us a heaven-ly crown.*

WORSHIP AND ADORATION

322 When Morning Gilds the Skies

Unto Him be glory in the church by Jesus Christ throughout all ages world without end.

— Ephesians 3:21

From the German
Tr. by Edward Caswall

LAUDES DOMINI
Joseph Barnby

1 When morn - ing gilds the skies, My heart a - wak - ing cries, May Je - sus Christ be praised! A - like at work and prayer To Je - sus I re - pair, May Je - sus Christ be praised!

2 *Does sad - ness fill my mind? A sol - ace here I find, May Je - sus Christ be praised! Or fades my earth - ly bliss? My com - fort still is this, May Je - sus Christ be praised!*

3 The night be - comes as day When from the heart we say, May Je - sus Christ be praised! The powers of dark - ness fear When this sweet chant they hear, May Je - sus Christ be praised!

4 *Ye na - tions of man - kind In this your one - ness find, May Je - sus Christ be praised! Let all the earth a - round Ring joy - ous with the sound, May Je - sus Christ be praised!*

5 Be this, while life is mine, My can - ti - cle di - vine, May Je - sus Christ be praised! Be this th'e - ter - nal song Through all the a - ges long, May Je - sus Christ be praised! A - men.

Alternate Last Verse Harmonization

Arranged by Fred Bock

5 Be this, while life is mine, My can-ti-cle di-vine, May Je-sus Christ be praised: Be this th'e-ter-nal song, Through all the a-ges long, May Je-sus Christ be praised! A-men.

WORSHIP AND ADORATION

323 Holy! Holy! Holy! Lord God Almighty

Holy, holy, holy, Lord God Almighty; who was, and is, and is to come. — Revelation 4:8

NICAEA
John B. Dykes
Descant by David McK. Williams

Reginald Heber

Descant

4 Ho - - - - - - - - ly,

Ho - - - - - - - - ly,

Ho - - - - - . - - - ly,

1 Ho - ly, ho - ly, ho - ly! Lord God Al - might - y!
2 *Ho - ly, ho - ly, ho - ly! all the saints a - dore Thee,*
3 Ho - ly, ho - ly, ho - ly! though the dark - ness hide Thee,
4 *Ho - ly, ho - ly, ho - ly! Lord God Al - might - y!*

1 Ear - ly in the morn - ing our song shall rise to Thee;
2 *Cast - ing down their gold - en crowns a - round the glass - y sea;*
3 Though the eye of sin - ful man Thy glo - ry may not see;
4 *All Thy works shall praise Thy name in earth and sky and sea;*

1 Ho - ly, ho - ly, ho - ly! mer - ci - ful and might - y!
2 *Cher - u - bim and ser - a - phim fall - ing down be - fore Thee,*
3 On - ly Thou art ho - ly— there is none be - side Thee
4 *Ho - ly, ho - ly, ho - ly! mer - ci - ful and might - y!*

WORSHIP AND ADORATION

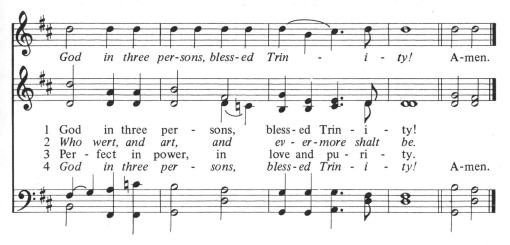

God in three per-sons, bless-ed Trin - i - ty! A-men.

1 God in three per - sons, bless-ed Trin - i - ty!
2 Who wert, and art, and ev - er-more shalt be.
3 Per - fect in power, in love and pu - ri - ty.
4 God in three per - sons, bless-ed Trin - i - ty! A-men.

Te Deum

324

We praise Thee, O God:
We acknowledge Thee to be the Lord.
All the earth doth worship Thee, the Father everlasting.
To Thee all angels cry aloud; the heavens and all the powers therein.
To Thee cherubim and seraphim continually do cry:
Holy, Holy, Holy, Lord God of Sabaoth.
Heaven and earth are full of the majesty of Thy glory.
The glorious company of the apostles praise Thee.
The goodly fellowship of the prophets praise Thee.
The noble army of martyrs praise Thee.
The holy Church, throughout all the world, doth acknowledge Thee,
The Father of an infinite majesty;
Thine adorable, true, and only Son;
Also the Holy Spirit, the Comforter.
Thou art the King of glory, O Christ.
Thou art the everlasting Son of the Father.
When Thou tookest upon Thee to deliver man,
Thou didst humble Thyself to be born of a virgin.
When Thou hadst overcome the sharpness of death,
Thou didst open the kingdom of heaven to all believers.
Thou sittest at the right hand of God, in the glory of the Father.
We believe that Thou shalt come to be our Judge.
We therefore pray Thee, help Thy servants,
Whom Thou hast redeemed with Thy precious blood.
Make them to be numbered with Thy saints in glory everlasting.
O Lord, save Thy people, and bless Thy heritage.
Govern them, and lift them up forever.
Day by day we magnify Thee;
And we worship Thy name ever, world without end.
Vouchsafe, O Lord, to keep us this day without sin.
O Lord, have mercy upon us, have mercy upon us.
O Lord, let Thy mercy be upon us, as our trust is in Thee.
O Lord, in Thee have I trusted;
Let me never be confounded.

Amen.

325 All Hail the Power of Jesus' Name

Great is the Lord and greatly to be praised. — Psalm 145:3

(FIRST TUNE)

Edward Perronet
John Rippon, alt.

CORONATION
Oliver Holden

1 All hail the power of Je - sus' name! Let an - gels pros - trate
2 *Ye cho - sen seed of Is - rael's race, Ye ran-somed from the*
3 Let ev - ery kin - dred, ev - ery tribe, On this ter - res - trial
4 *O that with yon - der sa - cred throng We at His feet may*

1 fall; Bring forth the roy - al di - a - dem, And crown Him
2 *fall, Hail Him who saves you by His grace, And crown Him*
3 ball, To Him all maj - es - ty as - cribe, And crown Him
4 *fall! We'll join the ev - er - last - ing song, And crown Him*

1 Lord of all; Bring forth the roy - al di - a - dem, And
2 *Lord of all; Hail Him who saves you by His grace, And*
3 Lord of all; To Him all maj - es - ty as - cribe, And
4 *Lord of all; We'll join the ev - er - last - ing song, And*

1 crown Him Lord of all!
2 *crown Him Lord of all!*
3 crown Him Lord of all!
4 *crown Him Lord of all!* A - men.

WORSHIP AND ADORATION

Alternate Last Verse Harmonization

Arranged by Fred Bock

4 O that with yon-der sa-cred throng We at His feet may fall! We'll join the ev-er-last-ing song, And crown Him Lord of all. We'll join the ev-er-last-ing song, And crown Him Lord of all! A-men.

WORSHIP AND ADORATION

326 All Hail the Power of Jesus' Name

Thou art worthy, O Lord, to receive glory, and honor, and power: — Revelation 4:11

Edward Perronet
John Rippon, alt.

(SECOND TUNE)

DIADEM
James Ellor

1 All hail the power of Je - sus' name! Let an - gels
2 *Ye cho - sen seed of Is - rael's race, Ye ran - somed*
3 Let ev - ery kin - dred, ev - ery tribe, On this ter -
4 *O that with yon - der sa - cred throng We at His*

1 pros - trate fall, Let an - gels pros - trate fall; Bring forth the
2 *from the fall, Ye ran - somed from the fall; Hail Him who*
3 res - trial ball, On this ter - res - trial ball, To Him all
4 *feet may fall, We at His feet may fall! We'll join the*

1 roy - al di - a - dem,
2 *saves you by His grace,* And crown
3 maj - es - ty as - cribe,
4 *ev - er - last - ing song,* And crown Him, crown Him,

Him, crown Him, crown Him,
crown Him, crown Him, crown Him, crown Him,

crown

crown Him, And crown Him Lord of all. A - men.

Him,

All Hail the Power of Jesus' Name 327

We made known unto you the power, and coming of our Lord Jesus Christ;
. . . were eyewitness of His majesty. — II Peter 1:16

Edward Perronet
John Rippon, alt.

(THIRD TUNE)

MILES LANE
William Shrubsole

1 All hail the power of Je - sus' name! Let an - gels pros - trate fall;
2 *Ye cho-sen seed of Is - rael's race, Ye ran-somed from the fall,*
3 Let ev - ery kin - dred, ev - ery tribe, On this ter - res - trial ball,
4 *O that with yon-der sa - cred throng We at His feet may fall!*

1 Bring forth the roy - al di - a - dem,
2 *Hail Him who saves you by His grace,* And crown Him, crown Him,
3 To Him all maj - es - ty as - cribe,
4 *We'll join the ev - er - last - ing song,*

crown Him, Crown Him Lord of all! A - men.

WORSHIP AND ADORATION

328 Begin, My Tongue, Some Heavenly Theme

. . . Every hill shall be brought low, and the crooked shall be made straight,
and the rough ways shall be made smooth.
— Luke 3:5

Isaac Watts

MANOAH
Henry W. Greatorex's *Collection*

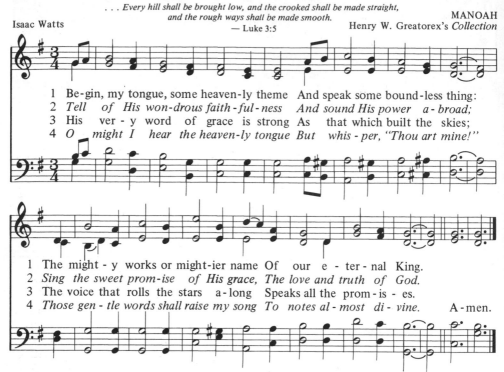

1 Be-gin, my tongue, some heaven-ly theme And speak some bound-less thing:
2 *Tell of His won-drous faith-ful-ness And sound His power a-broad;*
3 His ver-y word of grace is strong As that which built the skies;
4 *O might I hear the heaven-ly tongue But whis-per, "Thou art mine!"*

1 The might-y works or might-ier name Of our e-ter-nal King.
2 *Sing the sweet prom-ise of His grace, The love and truth of God.*
3 The voice that rolls the stars a-long Speaks all the prom-is-es.
4 *Those gen-tle words shall raise my song To notes al-most di-vine.* A-men.

329 Worship

Minister: It would make a tremendous difference if this congregation would do certain things.

People: *When we come to church, we ought to come prepared.*

Minister: There are so very few people who make any preparation for worship at all. They have to hurry to get ready; they have to hurry down the road; they take their places almost at the last moment; and there is no preparation at all.

If every person who comes to church would, before he comes, or even on the road there, think of God for just a moment or two, and say a prayer for himself and for the preacher and the people who will meet in worship, it would make a whole world of difference.

People: *We should come seeking.*

Minister: To come to the services of the church should never be simply a matter of habit, a burden of duty, a hallmark of respectability, the satisfying of a convention. It should be a deliberate attempt to come out of the world and to find contact with God.

One of the great secrets of success in any of the business of life is to know what we want, when we are doing a thing; and when we come to church we should want God.

People: *We should come determined to give all of ourselves.*

Minister: He who comes to church only to get will, in the end, get nothing. We should come determined to give our interest, our prayer, our devotion, our sympathy. The success of any gathering, the happiness of any party, is always dependent on the people who are prepared to give themselves to the fellowship of the occasion.

—William Barclay

It Is Good to Sing Thy Praises

Rejoice in the Lord, O Ye righteous, for praise is comely for the upright.

— Psalm 33:1

From Psalm 92
The Psalter

ELLESDIE
Wolfgang A. Mozart

1 It is good to sing Thy prais-es And to thank Thee, O Most High,
2 *Thou hast filled my heart with gladness Thro the works Thy hands have wrought;*
3 But the good shall live be - fore Thee, Plant - ed in Thy dwell-ing place,

1 Show-ing forth Thy lov - ing-kind-ness When the morn-ing lights the sky.
2 *Thou hast made my life vic - to-rious, Great Thy works and deep Thy thought.*
3 Fruit- ful trees and ev - er ver-dant, Nour-ished by Thy bound-less grace.

1 It is good when night is fall - ing Of Thy faith-ful - ness to tell,
2 *Thou, O Lord, on high ex - alt - ed, Reign-est ev - er - more in might;*
3 In His good-ness to the right-eous God His right-eous - ness dis-plays;

1 While with sweet, me-lo-dious prais-es Songs of ad - o - ra-tion swell.
2 *All Thy en - e - mies shall per - ish, Sin be ban-ished from Thy sight.*
3 God my rock, my strength, my ref-uge, Just and true are all His ways. A-men.

WORSHIP AND ADORATION

331 Sometimes "Alleluia"

Blessed is His glorious name forever; let the whole earth be filled with His glory.

— Psalm 72:19

SOMETIMES ALLELUIA
Chuck Girard

Chuck Girard

Some-times "Al - le - lu - ia," Some-times "Praise the Lord;" Some-times gent - ly sing - ing, Our hearts in one ac-cord.

1 O let us lift our
2 *O let our joy be*
3 O let us feel His
4 *O let the Spir - it*

1 voic - es, Look toward the sky and start to sing;
2 *un - con-fined, Let us sing with free-dom un - re - strained;*
3 pres - ence, Let the sound of prais - es fill the air;
4 *o - ver-flow, As we are filled from head to toe;*

WORSHIP AND ADORATION

1 O, let us now re-turn His love—
2 *Let's take this feel-ing that we're feel-ing now*
3 O, let us sing the song of Je-sus' love
4 *We love You Fa-ther, Son and Ho-ly Ghost,*

Just let our
Out-side these
To peo-ple
And we want

1, 2, 3   D.C. 4

1 voic - es ring.
2 *walls and let it rain.*
3 ev - ery - where.
4 *this world to know.*

Some-times "Al - le - lu - ia," Some-times "Praise the Lord;"

Some-times gent - ly sing - ing, Our hearts in one ac - cord.

332 The God of Abraham Praise!

The eternal God is thy refuge, and underneath are the everlasting arms.
— Deuteronomy 33:27

Revised version of the *Yigdal*
Daniel ben Judah
Tr. by Newton Mann
and Max Landsberg

LEONI
Hebrew Melody
Adapted by Meyer Lyon

1 The God of A-braham praise, All prais - ed be His name,
2 *His spir - it flow - eth free, High surg - ing where it will;*
3 He hath e - ter - nal life Im - plant - ed in the soul;

1 Who was, and is, and is to be, Al - ways the same!
2 *In proph - et's word He spoke of old, He speak - eth still.*
3 His love shall be our strength-en - ing While a - ges roll.

1 The one e - ter - nal God, Whose time - less - ness is clear;
2 *Es - tab - lished is His law, And change-less it shall stand,*
3 Praise to the liv - ing God! All prais - ed be His name,

1 The First, the Last: be - yond all thought, Through-out the years!
2 *Now writ - ten deep up - on the heart, On sea or land.*
3 Who was, and is, and is to be, Al - ways the same! A-men.

Worship is the highest and noblest act that any person can do. When men worship, God is satisfied! "The Father seeketh such to worship Him." Amazing, isn't it? And when you worship, you are fulfilled! Think about this: why did Jesus Christ come? He came to make worshipers out of rebels. We who were once self-centered have to be completely changed so that we can shift our attention outside of ourselves and become able to worship Him.

—Raymond C. Ortlund

We Praise Thee, O God, Our Redeemer 334

KREMSER

As for our Redeemer, the Lord of hosts is His name. — Isaiah 47:4

Netherlands Folk Song

Julia C. Cory

Arranged by Edward Kremser

1 We praise Thee, O God, our Re-deem-er, Cre-a-tor,
2 *We wor-ship Thee, God of our fa-thers, we bless Thee;*
3 With voic-es u-ni-ted our prais-es we of-fer,

1 In grate-ful de-vo-tion our trib-ute we bring.
2 *Through life's storm and tem-pest our guide hast Thou been.*
3 And glad-ly our songs of true wor-ship we raise.

1 We lay it be-fore Thee, we kneel and a-dore Thee,
2 *When per-ils o'er-take us, Thou wilt not for-sake us,*
3 Thy strong arm will guide us, our God is be-side us,

1 We bless Thy ho-ly name, glad prais-es we sing.
2 *And with Thy help, O Lord, life's bat-tles we win.*
3 To Thee, our great Re-deem-er, for-ev-er be praise. A-men.

335 Praise the Lord! Ye Heavens Adore Him

Praise ye Him sun and moon; praise Him all ye stars. — Psalm 148:3

From Psalm 148
Foundling Hospital Collection, Stanzas 1, 2
Edward Osler, Stanza 3

FABEN
John H. Willcox

1 Praise the Lord! ye heavens, a-dore Him, Praise Him, an - gels in the height;
2 *Praise the Lord! for He is glo - rious, Nev - er shall His prom-ise fail;*
3 Wor - ship, hon - or, glo - ry, bless - ing, Lord, we of - fer un - to Thee;

1 Sun and moon, re -joice be - fore Him, Praise Him, all ye stars of light.
2 *God hath made His saints vic - to-rious, Sin and death shall not pre - vail.*
3 Young and old, Thy praise ex - press-ing, In glad hom - age bend the knee.

1 Praise the Lord! for He hath spo - ken, Worlds His might - y voice o - beyed:
2 *Praise the God of our sal - va - tion, Hosts on high, His power pro - claim;*
3 All the saints in heaven a - dore Thee, We would bow be-fore Thy throne:

1 Laws which nev - er shall be bro - ken For their guid-ance He hath made.
2 *Heaven and earth and all cre - a - tion Laud and mag-ni - fy His name.*
3 As Thine an - gels serve be - fore Thee, So on earth Thy will be done. A-men.

Arranged by Ovid Young

3 Wor-ship, hon- or, glo - ry, bless - ing, Lord, we of - fer un-to Thee; Young and

old, Thy praise ex - press-ing, In glad hom - age bend the knee. All the

saints in heav'n a - dore Thee; We would bow be-fore Thy throne: As Thine

an - gels serve be - fore Thee, So on earth Thy will be done. A - men.

WORSHIP AND ADORATION

336 O Worship the King

The true worshipper shall worship the Father in spirit and in truth. — John 4:23

LYONS
Robert Grant
Adapted from Johann Michael Haydn

1 O wor-ship the King all glo-rious a-bove, And
2 *O tell of His might and sing of His grace, Whose*
3 Thy boun-ti-ful care what tongue can re-cite? It
4 *Frail chil-dren of dust, and fee-ble as frail, In*

1 grate-ful-ly sing His won-der-ful love; Our Shield and De-
2 *robe is the light, whose can-o-py space; His char-iots of*
3 breathes in the air, it shines in the light, It streams from the
4 *Thee do we trust, nor find Thee to fail; Thy mer-cies how*

1 fend-er, the An-cient of Days, Pa-vil-ioned in
2 *wrath the deep thun-der-clouds form, And dark is His*
3 hills, it de-scends to the plain, And sweet-ly dis-
4 *ten-der, how firm to the end, Our Mak-er, De-*

Alternate ending for 3rd stanza into harmonization

1 splen-dor and gird-ed with praise.
2 *path on the wings of the storm.*
3 tills in the dew and the rain.
4 *fend-er, Re-deem-er and Friend.* A-men.

rain.

WORSHIP AND ADORATION

Arranged by Fred Bock

Frail chil - dren of dust, and fee - ble as frail, In

Thee do we trust, nor find Thee to fail; Thy

mer - cies how ten - der; how firm to the end! Our Mak - er, De -

fend - er, Re - deem - er and Friend! A - men.

WORSHIP AND ADORATION

337 Praise to the Lord, the Almighty

For then shalt thou have delight in the Almighty.
— Job 22:26

Joachim Neander
Tr. by Catherine Winkworth

LOBE DEN HERREN
"Stralsund Gesangbuch"

1 Praise to the Lord, the Al - might-y, the King of cre - a - tion!
2 *Praise to the Lord, who o'er all things so won-drous-ly reign - eth,*
3 Praise to the Lord, who doth pros-per thy work and de - fend thee;
4 *Praise to the Lord! O let all that is in me a - dore Him!*

1 O my soul, praise Him, for He is thy health and sal - va - tion!
2 *Shel-ters thee un - der His wings, yes, so gen - tly sus - tain - eth!*
3 Sure - ly His good-ness and mer - cy here dai - ly at - tend thee.
4 *All that hath life and breath, come now with prais-es be - fore Him.*

1 All ye who hear, Now to His tem - ple draw near;
2 *Hast thou not seen How all thy long - ings have been*
3 Pon - der a - new What the Al - might - y can do,
4 *Let the A - men Sound from His peo - ple a - gain:*

1 Join me in glad ad - o - ra - tion!
2 *Grant-ed in what He or - dain - eth?*
3 If with His love He be - friend thee.
4 *Glad - ly for aye we a - dore Him. A - men.*

WORSHIP AND ADORATION

We Sing the Greatness of Our God

Great is our Lord, and of great power; His understanding is infinite.

— Psalm 147:5

Isaac Watts
Jeff Redd, alt.

ELLACOMBE
"Gesangbuch der Herzogl," Wirtemberg

1 We sing the great-ness of our God That made the moun-tains rise,
2 *We sing the good-ness of the Lord That filled the earth with food;*
3 There's not a plant or flower be-low But makes Thy glo-ries known;

1 That spread the flow-ing seas a-broad And built the loft-y skies.
2 *He formed the crea-tures with His word And then pro-nounced them good.*
3 And clouds a-rise and tem-pests blow By or-der from Thy throne,

1 We sing the wis-dom that or-dained The sun to rule the day;
2 *Lord, how Thy won-ders are dis-played Wher-e'er we turn our eyes:*
3 While all that bor-rows life from Thee Is ev-er in Thy care,

1 The moon shines full at His com-mand, And all the stars o-bey.
2 *In ev-ery sea-son of the year, And through the changing skies.*
3 And ev-ery-where that man can be, Thou, God, art pres-ent there. A-men.

WORSHIP AND ADORATION

339 Praise My Soul, the King of Heaven

'Til we all come to the unity and knowledge of the Son of God. — Ephesians 4:13

LAUDA ANIMA
Mark Andrews
Handbell descant by Bob Burroughs

Henry F. Lyte

Two-octave handbells descant, 4th stanza

Unison

1 Praise, my soul, the King of heav-en, To His feet thy
2 *Praise Him for His grace and fa-vor To our fa-thers*
3 Frail as sum-mer's flower we flour-ish, Blows the wind and
4 *An-gels in the height, a-dore Him; Ye be-hold Him*

1 trib-ute bring; Ran-somed, healed, re-stored, for-giv-en,
2 *in dis-tress; Praise Him, still the same as ev-er,*
3 it is gone; But, while mor-tals rise and per-ish,
4 *face to face; Saints tri-um-phant, bow be-fore Him,*

1 Ev-er-more His prais-es sing; Al-le-lu-ia!
2 *Slow to chide and swift to bless; Al-le-lu-ia!*
3 God en-dures un-chang-ing on: Al-le-lu-ia!
4 *Gath-ered in from ev-ery race; Al-le-lu-ia!*

WORSHIP AND ADORATION

1 Al - le - lu - ia! Praise the ev - er - last - ing King.
2 *Al - le - lu - ia! Glo - rious in His faith - ful - ness.*
3 Al - le - lu - ia! Praise the high e - ter - nal one.
4 *Al - le - lu - ia! Praise with us the God of grace.* A - men.

A Call to Worship

340

Minister: Let all who love Him come rejoicing.
People: *God is in His heaven.*
Minister: To the Almighty praises voicing!
People: *God is in His heaven!*
Minister: All nature does to Him belong,
Yet we, His children, own the song
That age to age has made us strong.
People: *God is in His heaven.*

Minister: There dawns no day but by His blessing.
People: *God is in His heaven!*
Minister: No night without the stars confessing.
People: *God is in His heaven!*
Minister: Within His hand He does contain
All pow'r of sun, moon, wind and rain,
And watchful to His vast domain:
People: *God is in His heaven.*

Minister: Through all the years that are before us:
People: *God is in His heaven!*
Minister: His love forever reigning o'er us:
People: *God is in His heaven!*
Minister: Each season in its turn shall be
A glimpse of His eternity,
As God has been, so God shall be!
People: *God is in His heaven!*

—Jacqueline Hanna McNair

341 Come, Thou Almighty King

Until the Ancient of Days came . . . and . . . the saints possessed the Kingdom.
— Daniel 7:22

Anonymous

ITALIAN HYMN
Felice de Giardini

1 Come, Thou Al - might - y King, Help us Thy
2 *Come, Thou In - car - nate Word, Gird on Thy*
3 Come, Ho - ly Com - fort - er, Thy sa - cred
4 *To Thee, great One in Three, The high - est*

1 name to sing, Help us to praise: Fa - ther, all -
2 *might - y sword, Our prayer at - tend: Come, and Thy*
3 wit - ness bear In this glad hour: Thou who al -
4 *prais - es be, Hence ev - er - more! Thy sov - ereign*

1 glo - ri - ous, O'er all vic - to - ri - ous, Come, and reign
2 *peo - ple bless, And give Thy word suc - cess; Spir - it of*
3 might - y art, Now rule in ev - ery heart, Nev - er from
4 *maj - es - ty May we in glo - ry see, And to e -*

1 o - ver us, An - cient of Days.
2 *ho - li - ness, On us de - scend.*
3 us de - part, Spir - it of power.
4 *ter - ni - ty Love and a - dore.* A - men.

WORSHIP AND ADORATION

Alternate Last Verse Harmonization   Arranged by Van Denman Thompson and Fred Bock

4 To Thee, great One in Three, The high - est prais - es be, Hence-ev - er more! Thy sov-ereign maj - es - ty May we in glo - ry see, And to e - ter - ni - ty Love and a - dore. A - men.

WORSHIP AND ADORATION

342 Come, Christians, Join to Sing

For . . . we have a building of God, a house not made with hands, eternal in the heavens.
— II Corinthians 5:1

Christian Henry Bateman

MADRID
Traditional

1 Come, Chris - tians, join to sing   Al - le - lu - ia! A - men!
2 *Come, lift your hearts on high;*   *Al - le - lu - ia! A - men!*
3 Praise yet our Christ a - gain;   Al - le - lu - ia! A - men!

1 Loud praise to Christ our King;   Al - le - lu - ia! A - men!
2 *Let prais - es fill the sky;*   *Al - le - lu - ia! A - men!*
3 Life shall not end the strain;   Al - le - lu - ia! A - men!

1 Let all, with heart and voice, Be - fore His throne re - joice; Praise is His
2 *He is our Guide and Friend; To us He'll con - de - scend; His love shall*
3 On heav-en's bliss - ful shore His good - ness we'll a - dore, Sing - ing for -

Alternate ending for 2nd stanza into harmonization

1 gra - cious choice: Al - le - lu - ia! A - men!
2 *nev - er end: Al - le - lu - ia! A - men! A - men!*
3 ev - er-more, "Al - le - lu - ia! A - men!" A-men.

WORSHIP AND ADORATION

Alternate Last Verse Harmonization

Arranged by Fred Bock

3 Praise yet our Christ a-gain; Al - le - lu - ia! A - men!

Life shall not end the strain; Al-le - lu - ia! A - men! On heav-en's

bliss-ful shore His good-ness we'll a-dore, Sing - ing for -

ev - er-more, "Al-le-lu-ia! A - men!" A - men!

WORSHIP AND ADORATION

343 Sing Praise to God Who Reigns Above

The Lord reigneth; let the earth rejoice.
— Psalm 97:1

Johann J. Schütz
Tr. by Frances E. Cox

MIT FREUDEN ZART
Bohemian Brethren's "Kirchengesänge"

1 Sing praise to God who reigns a - bove, The God of all cre - a - tion, The God of pow'r, the God of love, The God of our sal - va - tion; With heal-ing balm my soul He fills, And ev - er - y faith-less mur - mer stills: To God all praise and glo - ry.

2 *What God's al - might-y power hath made His gra - cious mer - cy keep-eth; By morn-ing glow or eve-ning shade His watch-ful eye ne'er sleep - eth; With - in the king-dom of His might, Lo! all is just and all is right: To God all praise and glo - ry.*

3 The Lord is nev - er far a - way, But, through all grief dis - tress-ing, An ev - er - pres-ent help and stay, Our peace, and joy, and bless - ing; As with a moth-er's ten - der hand, He leads His own, His cho - sen band: To God all praise and glo - ry.

4 *Thus, all my glad-some way a - long, I sing a - loud His prais - es, That men may hear the grate-ful song My voice un-wea - ried rais - es, Be joy - ful in the Lord, my heart, Both soul and bod - y bear your part: To God all praise and glo - ry.* A - men.

WORSHIP AND ADORATION

O Could I Speak the Matchless Worth
344

This is the Lord's doing, and it is marvelous in our eyes.
— Psalm 118:23

ARIEL
Wolfgang A. Mozart
Adapted by Lowell Mason

Samuel Medley

1 O could I speak the match-less worth, O could I sound the
2 *I'd sing the pre-cious blood He spilt, My ran-som from the*
3 *I'd sing the char-ac-ter He bears, And all the forms of*
4 *Soon the de-light-ful day will come When my dear Lord will*

1 glo-ries forth Which in my Sav-ior shine! I'd sing His
2 *dread-ful guilt Of sin, and wrath di-vine; I'd sing His*
3 love He wears, Ex-alt-ed on His throne; In loft-iest
4 *bring me home, And I shall see His face; Then with my*

1 per-fect right-eous-ness, And mag-ni-fy the won-drous grace
2 *glo-rious ho-li-ness, In which all-per-fect, heaven-ly dress*
3 songs of sweet-est praise, I would to ev-er-last-ing days
4 *Sav-ior, broth-er, friend, A blest e-ter-ni-ty I'll spend,*

1 Which made sal-va-tion mine, Which made sal-va-tion mine.
2 *My soul shall ev-er shine, My soul shall ev-er shine.*
3 Make all His glo-ries known, Make all His glo-ries known.
4 *Tri-um-phant in His grace, Tri-um-phant in His grace.*

WORSHIP AND ADORATION

345 Crown Him with Many Crowns

And on His head were many crowns.
— Revelation 19:12

Matthew Bridges
Godfrey Thring

DIADEMATA
George J. Elvey
Descant by Paul Sjolund

Descant: 5 Crown Him, crown Him the Lord of years: The

1 Crown Him with man-y crowns, The Lamb up-on His
2 Crown Him the Lord of love: Be - hold His hands and
3 Crown Him the Lord of life: Who tri-umphed o'er the
4 Crown Him the Lord of heaven: One with the Fa - ther
5 Crown Him the Lord of years: The po - ten-tate of

Descant: Lord of time, Cre - a - tor of the roll - ing spheres,

1 throne: Hark! how the heaven-ly an - them drowns All
2 side, Rich wounds, yet vis - i - ble a - bove, In
3 grave, Who rose vic - to - rious to the strife For
4 known, One with the Spir - it through Him given From
5 time, Cre - a - tor of the roll - ing spheres, In -

Descant: In - ef - fa - bly sub - lime. All hail, Re-deem-er

1 mu - sic but its own! A - wake, my soul, and sing Of
2 beau - ty glo - ri - fied; No an - gel in the sky Can
3 those He came to save; His glo - ries now we sing, Who
4 yon - der glo - rious throne. To Thee be end - less praise, For
5 ef - fa - bly sub - lime. All hail, Re - deem - er, hail! For

WORSHIP AND ADORATION

hail!   For Thou all   praise,   glo - ry

1 Him who died for thee;   And   hail Him as   thy
2 *ful - ly bear that sight,*   *But   down - ward bends His*
3 died and rose on high,   Who   died e - ter - nal
4 *Thou for us hast died;*   *Be   Thou, O Lord, through*
5 Thou hast died for me;   Thy   praise and glo - ry

shall not fail Through - out e - ter - ni - ty.   A - men.

1 match - less King Through all e - ter - ni - ty.
2 *won - dering eye At mys - ter - ies so bright.*
3 life to bring, And lives that death may die.
4 *end - less days A - dored and mag - ni - fied.*
5 shall not fail Through - out e - ter - ni - ty.   A - men.

Who Shall Ascend?   346

		He
Lord?	place?	who
the	holy	has
of	His	clean
hill	in	hands
the	stand	and
ascend	shall	a
shall	who	pure
Who	and	heart.

—from Psalm 24
styled by Bruce Leafblad

347 All Creatures of Our God and King

Francis of Assisi
Tr. by William H. Draper
Bryan Jeffery Leech, stanza 5

Sing unto the Lord a new song, and praise Him in the congregation.
— Psalm 149:1

LASST UNS ERFREUEN
Geistliche Kirchengesäng

1 All crea-tures of our God and King, Lift up your voice and with us
2 *Thou rush-ing wind that art so strong,* Ye clouds that sail in heaven a-
3 Thou flow-ing wa-ter, pure and clear, Make mu-sic for thy Lord to
4 *Let all things their Cre-a-tor bless,* And wor-ship Him in hum-ble-
(optional) 5 Lift up your voic-es once a-gain, And then be-fore the last "A-

1 sing, Al-le-lu-ia! Al-le-lu-ia! Thou burn-ing sun with
2 *long,* O praise Him! Al-le-lu-ia! *Thou ris-ing morn, in*
3 hear, Al-le-lu-ia! Al-le-lu-ia! Thou fire so mas-ter-
4 *ness.* O praise Him! Al-le-lu-ia! *Praise, praise the Fa-ther,*
5 men!" Lis-ten to the or-gan play-ing: [- - - - -

1 gold-en beam, Thou sil-ver moon with soft-er gleam, O praise Him!
2 *praise re-joice,* Ye lights of eve-ning, find a voice! O praise Him!
3 ful and bright, That giv-est man both warmth and light, O praise Him!
4 *praise the Son,* And praise the Spir-it, Three in One! O praise Him!
5 - - - - - - - - - - - - - - - - -] O praise Him!

O praise Him! Al-le-lu-ia! Al-le-lu-ia! Al-le-lu-ia!

WORSHIP AND ADORATION

Bryan Jeffery Leech, stanza 5   **Alternate Last Verse Harmonization**   Arranged by Fred Bock

5 Lift up your voic-es once a-gain, And then be-fore the last "A-

men!" Lis-ten to the or-gan play - ing: [- - -

Full organ

Ped.

- - - -]

Choir: Sing Al - le - lu - ia! Al - le -

Congregation:
O praise Him! O praise Him! Al - le - lu - ia! Al - le -

lu - ia! Sing Al - le-lu - ia! A - men.

lu - ia! Al - le - lu - ia!

WORSHIP AND ADORATION

348

Praise to God

Leader: We lift up our hearts,
and bring You our worship and praise!

People: We lift up our voices
and sing You our worship and praise!

Leader and People: Praise and honor, glory and might,
to Him who sits on the throne,
and to the Lamb for ever and ever! Amen!!

349

O for a Thousand Tongues to Sing

My tongue shall speak . . . praise all the day long. — Psalm 35:28

AZMON
Carl G. Gläser
Descant by Eugene Butler

Charles Wesley

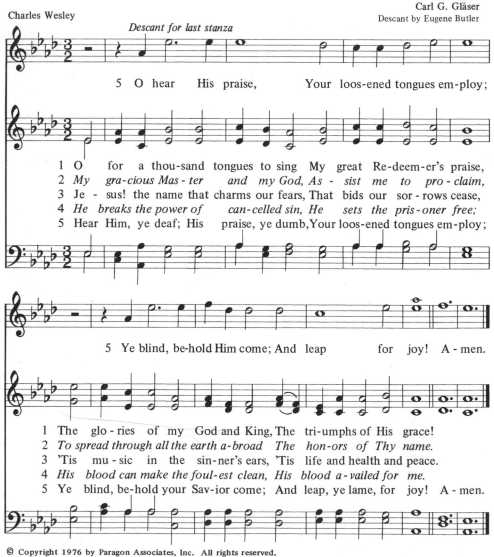

Descant for last stanza

5 O hear His praise, Your loos-ened tongues em-ploy;

1 O for a thou-sand tongues to sing My great Re-deem-er's praise,
2 *My gra-cious Mas-ter and my God, As-sist me to pro-claim,*
3 Je-sus! the name that charms our fears, That bids our sor-rows cease,
4 *He breaks the power of can-celled sin, He sets the pris-oner free;*
5 Hear Him, ye deaf; His praise, ye dumb, Your loos-ened tongues em-ploy;

5 Ye blind, be-hold Him come; And leap for joy! A-men.

1 The glo-ries of my God and King, The tri-umphs of His grace!
2 *To spread through all the earth a-broad The hon-ors of Thy name.*
3 'Tis mu-sic in the sin-ner's ears, 'Tis life and health and peace.
4 *His blood can make the foul-est clean, His blood a-vailed for me.*
5 Ye blind, be-hold your Sav-ior come; And leap, ye lame, for joy! A-men.

WORSHIP AND ADORATION

The Joy of His Presence

(A CALL TO WORSHIP)

Minister: *I was glad when they said unto me, let us go into the house of the Lord.*

Women: Calm my spirit, Lord. Stop the churning inside of me caused by the rush of getting everyone fed and here on time. Quiet my confusion, Lord. In all the tension of getting here, I know I made the effort because I really do need You. Lord, speak to me in the quietness.

Minister: *Enter His gates with thanksgiving and into His courts with praise; be thankful unto Him and bless His name. For the Lord is good.*

Men: I am thankful, Lord for what we have. But this week has been so hectic, and it seems that no matter how hard I work and how well I plan, there is always something I didn't plan on, and there isn't enough time to go around. Forgive me, Lord, for letting worry get in the way of my gratitude. You are good to us, Lord. We do have so much to praise You for.

Minister: *Make a joyful noise unto the Lord, all lands. Serve the Lord with gladness; come before His presence with singing.*

Youth (12-18): It's hard to sing so early in the morning. And it's hard to come here with gladness too sometimes. It was not so easy serving You this week at school—and especially hard to keep the joy. This world is not very fair and it seems like I can't do much to change things. But I know that it's just because the problems are so close to me that I can't seem to see the answers. But I do know that You're the answer—and for that I will sing to You with my whole heart.

Minister: *The Lord is my shepherd, I shall not want. He makes me to lie down in green pastures. He restores my soul.*

All: Restore my soul, O Lord, and renew a right spirit within me. Make me to hear joy and gladness; that the bones which You have broken may rejoice. Cast me not away from Your presence; and take not Your Holy Spirit from me. Restore to me the joy of Your salvation and uphold me with Your free spirit.

— Compiled by Gloria Gaither

351 At the Name of Jesus

Blessed be His glorious name forever; let the whole earth be filled with His glory.
— Psalm 72:19

Based on Philippians 2:5-11
Caroline M. Noel

KING'S WESTON
Ralph Vaughan Williams

1 At the name of Je - sus Ev - ery knee shall bow,
2 *At His voice cre - a - tion Sprang at once to sight,*
3 Hum-bled for a sea - son, To re - ceive a name
4 *In your hearts en - throne Him: There let Him sub - due*
5 Broth-ers, this Lord Je - sus Shall re - turn a - gain,

1 Ev - ery tongue con - fess Him King of glo - ry now;
2 *All the an - gel fac - es, All the hosts of light,*
3 From the lips of sin - ners, Un - to whom He came;
4 *All that is not ho - ly, All that is not true;*
5 With His Fa - ther's glo - ry, With His an - gel train;

1 'Tis the Fa - ther's pleas - ure We should call Him Lord,
2 *Thrones and dom-i - na - tions, Stars up - on their way,*
3 He is God the Sav - ior, He is Christ the Lord,
4 *Crown Him as your cap - tain In temp-ta - tion's hour,*
5 For all wreaths of em - pire Meet up - on His brow,

1 Who from the be - gin-ning Was the might - y Word.
2 *All the heaven-ly or - ders In their great ar - ray.*
3 Ev - er to be wor-shipped, Trust-ed and a - dored.
4 *Let His will en - fold you In its light and power.*
5 And our hearts con - fess Him King of glo - ry now. A - men.

Music from "Enlarged Songs of Praise" by permission of Oxford University Press.

WORSHIP AND ADORATION

Blessed Be the Name

For He must reign until He hath put all enemies under His feet.
— I Corinthians 15: 25

W. H. Clark
Refrain added by Ralph E. Hudson

BLESSED BE THE NAME
Ralph E. Hudson
Harmonized by William J. Kirkpatrick

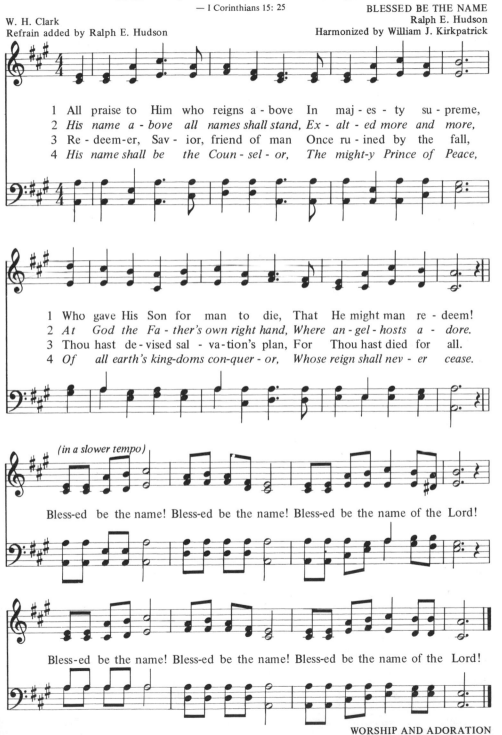

1 All praise to Him who reigns a-bove In maj-es-ty su-preme,
2 *His name a-bove all names shall stand, Ex-alt-ed more and more,*
3 Re-deem-er, Sav-ior, friend of man Once ru-ined by the fall,
4 *His name shall be the Coun-sel-or, The might-y Prince of Peace,*

1 Who gave His Son for man to die, That He might man re-deem!
2 *At God the Fa-ther's own right hand, Where an-gel-hosts a-dore.*
3 Thou hast de-vised sal-va-tion's plan, For Thou hast died for all.
4 *Of all earth's king-doms con-quer-or, Whose reign shall nev-er cease.*

(in a slower tempo)

Bless-ed be the name! Bless-ed be the name! Bless-ed be the name of the Lord!

Bless-ed be the name! Bless-ed be the name! Bless-ed be the name of the Lord!

WORSHIP AND ADORATION

353
God the Omnipotent

All power is given unto me in heaven and in earth.
— Matthew 28:18

Henry F. Chorley, stanzas 1, 2, alt.
John Ellerton, stanzas 3, 4, alt.

RUSSIAN HYMN
Alexis F. Lvov
Descant by Paul Sjolund

Descant

4 God: all the earth by Thy chas - tening

1 God the Om - nip - o - tent, King who or - dain - est
2 *God the All - mer - ci - ful, earth hath for - sak - en*
3 God the All - right - eous One, man hath de - fied Thee,
4 *God the All - prov - i - dent, earth by Thy chas - tening*

Yet shall to free-dom and truth be re - stored. O

1 Thun - der Thy clar - ion, the light - ning Thy sword,
2 *Thy ways all - ho - ly, and slight - ed Thy word;*
3 Yet to e - ter - ni - ty stand - eth Thy word;
4 *Yet shall to free - dom and truth be re - stored;*

God, through the dark-ness, O bring now Thy king - dom, Lord

1 Show forth Thy pit - y on high where Thou reign - est:
2 *Bid not Thy wrath in its ter - rors a - wak - en:*
3 False-hood and wrong shall not tar - ry be - side Thee:
4 *Through the thick dark - ness Thy king - dom is has - tening:*

WORSHIP AND ADORATION

God: Thou wilt give us peace with - in Thy time, O Lord. A-men.

1 Give to us peace in our time, O Lord.
2 *Give to us peace in our time, O Lord.*
3 Give to us peace in our time, O Lord.
4 *Thou wilt give peace in Thy time, O Lord. A-men.*

The Joy of the Lord   354

And those things write we unto you that your joy may be full.   THE JOY OF THE LORD

Based on Nehemiah 8:10   — John 1:4   Alliene G. Vale

Unison

1 The joy of the Lord is my strength, The
2 *If you want joy you must praise for it, If*
3 He giv - eth liv - ing wa - ter and I thirst no more, He
4 *He heals the bro - ken heart-ed and they cry no more, He*

1 joy of the Lord is my strength, The joy of the
2 *you want joy you must praise for it, If you want*
3 giv - eth liv - ing wa - ter and I thirst no more, He giv - eth liv - ing
4 *heals the bro - ken heart-ed and they cry no more, He heals the bro - ken*

1 Lord is my strength, The joy of the Lord is my strength.
2 *joy you must praise for it — The joy of the Lord is my strength.*
3 wa - ter and I thirst no more — The joy of the Lord is my strength.
4 *heart - ed and they cry no more — The joy of the Lord is my strength.*

WORSHIP AND ADORATION

355 We Praise You, Father

We praise You, Father, that You have met us along the way
with mercy and love and new life in Christ.

With praise and dedication we offer ourselves.

We thank You for our responsible calling,
to be stewards of life in Your kingdom.

Help us to be good stewards of all You have placed in our care.

We thank You, Lord, for the ability to learn
and to do countless creative tasks.

*Motivate us to develop our skills
and to use them in accord with the teaching of Jesus.*

We thank You for all the rich resources
with which the world has been supplied.

*Make us determined so to use the soil, the air, the water—
all of nature's bounty—
that future generations are not robbed by our irresponsibility.*

We thank You, Father, for the family we have.

Teach us to live mindful of each other's need and each other's worth.

We thank You, Father, for the human family,
for the rich gift of each nationality and every culture.

*Grant us the spirit of Christ, to be brothers and sisters of all persons,
to be ever mindful of the needs of others,
and to be instruments of peace.*

We thank You for our wealth, great or small,
and for opportunities money brings.

*May all our earning and spending,
our saving and giving,
be acceptable in Your sight, Lord;
and grant us the resolve to fulfil our pledge of giving,
to the glory of Your name, in the ministry of Christ.
Amen.*

—James E. Dahlgren

The Love of Christ 356

Here is love,
that God sent His Son,

His Son that never offended,
His Son that was always His delight.

Herein is love, that He sent Him to save sinners;
to save them by bearing their sins,
by bearing their curse, by dying their death, and by carrying their sorrows.

Here is love, in that while we were yet enemies, Christ died for us;
yes, here is love,
in that while we were yet without strength, Christ died for the ungodly.

—John Bunyan

O for a Heart to Praise My God 357

God forbid that I glory, save in the cross of our Lord Jesus Christ. . . .
— Galatians 6:14

Charles Wesley

RICHMOND
Thomas Haweis

1 O for a heart to praise my God, A heart from
2 A humble, lowly, contrite heart, Believing,
3 A heart in every thought renewed, And full of
4 Thy nature, gracious Lord, impart— Come quickly

1 sin set free, A heart that always feels Thy
2 true and clean, Which neither life nor death can
3 love divine; Perfect and right and pure and
4 from above; Write Thy new name upon my

1 blood So freely shed for me!
2 part From Him that dwells within.
3 good, A copy, Lord, of Thine!
4 heart, Thy new best name of Love. A-men.

WORSHIP AND ADORATION

358 Christ, We Do All Adore Thee

Thou art worthy, O Lord, to receive glory and honor, and power....

— Revelation 4:11

Adoramus Te
English version by Theodore Baker

ADORE THEE
From "The Seven Last Words of Christ"
Theodore Dubois

Christ, we do all a - dore Thee, and we do praise Thee for - ev - er;

Christ, we do all a - dore Thee, and we do praise Thee for - ev - er,

For on the ho - ly cross hast Thou the world from sin re - deem - ed.

Christ, we do all a - dore Thee, and we do praise Thee for - ev - er.

*Organ

Christ, we do all a - dore Thee!

*May be omitted
WORSHIP AND ADORATION

I Will Praise Him!

359

And they overcame Him by the blood of the Lamb.

— Revelation 12:11

Margaret J. Harris

I WILL PRAISE HIM
Margaret J. Harris

1 When I saw the cleans-ing foun-tain,   O - pen wide for all my   sin,
2 *Tho the way seems straight and nar-row,*   *All I claimed was swept a - way;*
3 Bless - ed be the name of Je - sus!   I'm so glad He took me in;
4 *Glo - ry, glo - ry to the Fa-ther!*   *Glo - ry, glo - ry to the Son!*

1 I   o-beyed the Spir - it's call - ing   When He said, "Wilt thou be clean?"
2 *My am - bi - tions, plans and wish-es*   *At my feet in dis - ar - ray.*
3 He's for-giv - en my trans-gres-sions,   He has cleansed my heart from sin.
4 *Glo - ry, glo - ry to the Spir - it!*   *Glo - ry to the Three in One!*

I will praise Him!   I will praise Him!   Praise the Lamb for sin-ners slain;

Give Him glo-ry, all ye peo-ple,   For His blood can wash a-way each stain.

WORSHIP AND ADORATION

360

You Servants of God, Your Master Proclaim

God hath fulfilled the same unto us . . . in that He hath raised up Jesus again.

— Acts 13:33

Charles Wesley

HANOVER
William Croft

1 You serv-ants of God, your Mas-ter pro-claim,
2 *God rul-eth on high, al-might-y to save,*
3 "Sal-va-tion to God, who sits on the throne!"
4 *Then let us a-dore and give Him His right—*

1 And pub-lish a-broad His won-der-ful name;
2 *And still He is nigh, His pres-ence we have;*
3 Let all cry a-loud and hon-or the Son;
4 *All glo-ry and power, all wis-dom and might,*

1 The name, all vic-to-rious, of Je-sus ex-tol:
2 *The great con-gre-ga-tion His tri-umph shall sing,*
3 The prais-es of Je-sus the an-gels pro-claim,
4 *All hon-or and bless-ing, with an-gels a-bove,*

1 His king-dom is glo-rious, He rules o-ver all.
2 *As-crib-ing sal-va-tion to Je-sus, our King.*
3 Fall down on their fac-es and wor-ship the Lamb.
4 *And thanks nev-er-ceas-ing, and in-fi-nite love.*

WORSHIP AND ADORATION

Alleluia

361

And I heard as it were the voices of a great multitude . . .
saying Alleluia for the Lord God omnipotent reigneth. — Revelation 19:6

Traditional text

ALLELUIA
Traditional melody

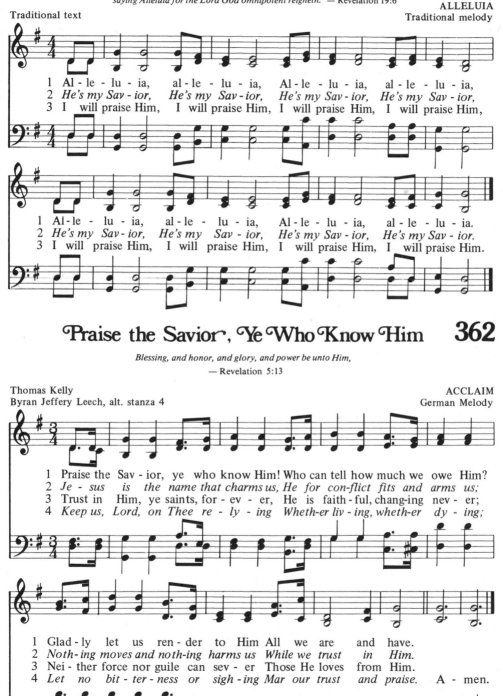

1 Al - le - lu - ia, al - le - lu - ia, Al - le - lu - ia, al - le - lu - ia,
2 *He's my Sav - ior, He's my Sav - ior, He's my Sav - ior, He's my Sav - ior,*
3 I will praise Him, I will praise Him, I will praise Him, I will praise Him,

1 Al - le - lu - ia, al - le - lu - ia, Al - le - lu - ia, al - le - lu - ia.
2 *He's my Sav - ior, He's my Sav - ior, He's my Sav - ior, He's my Sav - ior.*
3 I will praise Him, I will praise Him, I will praise Him, I will praise Him.

Praise the Savior, Ye Who Know Him

362

Blessing, and honor, and glory, and power be unto Him,
— Revelation 5:13

Thomas Kelly
Byran Jeffery Leech, alt. stanza 4

ACCLAIM
German Melody

1 Praise the Sav - ior, ye who know Him! Who can tell how much we owe Him?
2 *Je - sus is the name that charms us, He for con-flict fits and arms us;*
3 Trust in Him, ye saints, for - ev - er, He is faith - ful, chang-ing nev - er;
4 *Keep us, Lord, on Thee re - ly - ing Wheth-er liv-ing, wheth-er dy - ing;*

1 Glad - ly let us ren - der to Him All we are and have.
2 *Noth - ing moves and noth-ing harms us While we trust in Him.*
3 Nei - ther force nor guile can sev - er Those He loves from Him.
4 *Let no bit - ter - ness or sigh - ing Mar our trust and praise.* A - men.

WORSHIP AND ADORATION

363 To God Be the Glory

That ye may with one mind and one mouth glorify God . . . .
— Romans 15:6

TO GOD BE THE GLORY

Fanny J. Crosby

William H. Doane

1 To God be the glo - ry—great things He hath done! So loved He the
2 *O per - fect re - demp - tion, the pur - chase of blood, To ev - ery be -*
3 Great things He hath taught us, great things He hath done, And great our re -

1 world that He gave us His Son, Who yield - ed His life an a -
2 *liev - er the prom - ise of God; The vil - est of - fen - der who*
3 joic - ing through Je - sus the Son; But pur - er, and high - er, and

1 tone - ment for sin, And o - pened the life - gate that all may go in.
2 *tru - ly be - lieves, That mo - ment from Je - sus a par - don re - ceives.*
3 great - er will be Our won - der, our trans - port, when Je - sus we see.

Praise the Lord, praise the Lord, Let the earth hear His voice! Praise the

Lord, praise the Lord, Let the peo - ple re - joice! O come to the Fa - ther thru

WORSHIP AND ADORATION

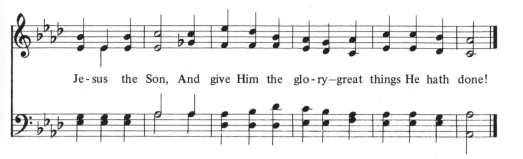

Je-sus the Son, And give Him the glo-ry—great things He hath done!

The Chief End of Man   364

"The chief end of man
is to glorify God
and to enjoy Him forever."

It would be scripturally false to leave out the second phrase—
"and to enjoy Him forever."

The men who formulated this showed
great wisdom and insight in saying,
"and to enjoy Him forever."

Nevertheless, the first phrase is the first phrase:
"The chief end of man
is to glorify God."
And in Christianity we have a non-determined God
who did not need to create
because there was love and communication within the Trinity,
and yet having been created, we as men can glorify God.

But we must feel the force of both sides of the issue.
If we fail to emphasize that we can glorify God,
we raise the whole question of whether men are significant at all.
We begin to lose our humanity as soon as we begin to lose the emphasis
that what we do makes a difference.
We can glorify God, and both the Old and New Testament say
that we can even make God sad.

That is tremendous.

—Francis A. Schaeffer

365

My Tribute

Not unto us, O Lord, but unto Thy name give glory. — Psalm 115:1

Andraé Crouch

MY TRIBUTE
Andraé Crouch

How can I say thanks for the things You have done for me?

Things so un-de-served, Yet You gave to prove Your love for me; The

voic-es of a mil-lion an-gels could not ex-press my gra-ti-tude.

All that I am, and ev-er hope to be; I owe it all to Thee.

To God be the glo-ry, To God be the glo-ry,

WORSHIP AND ADORATION

To God be the glo - ry For the things He has done.

With His blood He has saved me; With His power He has raised me;

Fine

To God be the glo - ry for the things He has done.

Just let me live my life —— Let it be pleas-ing, Lord, to Thee;

D.S. al Fine

And if I gain an-y praise, Let it go to Cal - va - ry. With His

366 Praise Be to Jesus

Ho, everyone that thirsteth, come ye to the waters. . . .— Isaiah 55:1

Gloria Gaither

PRAISE TO JESUS
William J. Gaither

1 Let him who is thirst-y come to clear wa - ter,
2 *The hills and the moun-tains break forth in - to sing-ing,*
3 Then shall the light break forth in - to morn-ing,

1 Let him who is hun-gry come by and eat;
2 *The tall state-ly trees and fields clap their hands;*
3 Bring-ing beau - ty for ash - es, strength for the days;

1 For mon-ey can't buy this cool liv - ing wa - ter,
2 *In place of the thorn there shall grow a tall fir tree,*
3 And hearts that were heav - y shall stand in His pres-ence,

1 Or this milk and hon - ey so sweet.
2 *A ten - der plant sprouts from the sand.*
3 Wrapped in the gar - ment of praise.

WORSHIP AND ADORATION

Praise be to Je-sus, the sweet Rose of Sha-ron, Praise to the Christ, the Re-
deem - er of men; Praise to the King who is reign-ing for-
ev - er, The Hope of the a - ges, my Mas-ter and Friend.

Lord, We Praise You

367

Sing unto Him, sing unto him;
talk ye of all His wondrous works. . . . — Psalm 105:2

Otis Skillings

LORD, WE PRAISE YOU
Otis Skillings

1 Lord, we praise You, Lord, we praise You,
2 *Lord, we thank You, Lord, we thank You,*
3 Lord, we love You, Lord, we love You,

1 Lord, we praise You, We praise You, Lord!
2 *Lord, we thank You, We thank You, Lord!*
3 Lord, we love You, We love You, Lord!

WORSHIP AND ADORATION

368 My Wonderful Lord

His name shall be called wonderful . . . — Isaiah 9:6

Haldor Lillenas

WONDERFUL LORD
Haldor Lillenas

1 I have found a deep peace that I nev-er had known, And a joy this world
2 *I de-sire that my life shall be or-dered by Thee, That my will be in*
3 All the tal-ents I have I have laid at Thy feet, Thy ap-prov-al shall
4 *Thou art fair-er to me than the fair-est of earth, Thou om-nip-o-tent,*

1 could not af-ford; Since I yield-ed con-trol of my bod-y and soul
2 *per-fect ac-cord With Thine own sov-ereign will, Thy de-sires to ful-fill,*
3 be my re-ward; Be my store great or small, I sur-ren-der it all
4 *life-giv-ing Word; O Thou An-cient of Days, Thou art wor-thy all praise,*

1 To my won-der-ful, won-der-ful Lord.
2 *My won-der-ful, won-der-ful Lord.*
3 To my won-der-ful, won-der-ful Lord.
4 *My won-der-ful, won-der-ful Lord.*

My won-der-ful Lord, my

won-der-ful Lord, By an-gels and ser-aphs in heav-en a-dored! I

bow at Thy shrine, my Sav-ior di-vine, My won-der-ful, won-der-ful Lord.

WORSHIP AND ADORATION

Psalm 90

369

Lord, Thou hast been our dwelling place in all generations.

> *Before the mountains were brought forth, or ever Thou hadst formed the earth and the world, from everlasting to everlasting Thou art God.*

Thou turnest man back to the dust, and sayest, "Turn back, O children of men!"

> *For a thousand years in Thy sight are but as yesterday when it is past, or as a watch in the night.*

Thou dost sweep men away; they are like a dream, like grass which is renewed in the morning:

> *In the morning it flourishes and is renewed; in the evening it fades and withers.*

For we are consumed by Thy anger; by Thy wrath we are overwhelmed.

> *Thou hast set our iniquities before Thee, our secret sins in the light of Thy countenance.*

For all our days pass away under Thy wrath, our years come to an end like a sigh.

> *The years of our life are threescore and ten, or even by reason of strength fourscore; yet their span is but toil and trouble; they are soon gone, and we fly away.*

Who considers the power of Thy anger, and Thy wrath according to the fear of Thee?

> *So teach us to number our days that we may get a heart of wisdom.*

—Psalm 90:1-12 (RSV)

O God, Our Help in Ages Past   **370**

Our soul waiteth for the Lord; He is our help . . . . — Psalm 33:20

Psalm 90
Isaac Watts

ST. ANNE
William Croft

1 O God, our help in a - ges past, Our hope for years to come,
2 *Un - der the shad - ow of Thy throne Still may we dwell se - cure;*
3 Be - fore the hills in or - der stood, Or earth re - ceived her frame,
4 *A thou-sand a - ges in Thy sight Are like an eve - ning gone;*
5 O God, our help in a - ges past, Our hope for years to come,

1 Our shel - ter from the storm - y blast, And our e - ter - nal home!
2 *Suf - fi - cient is Thine arm a - lone, And our de - fense is sure.*
3 From ev - er - last - ing Thou art God, To end - less years the same.
4 *Short as the watch that ends the night, Be - fore the ris - ing sun.*
5 Be Thou our guide while life shall last, And our e - ter - nal home! A-men.

WORSHIP AND ADORATION

371 Free from the Guilted Cage

Lord Jesus Christ, today I want to live my life as an expression of your love rather than as an effort to earn or deserve your love. Like Paul, I have tried about everything to prove my worth. Nothing satisfies. I am weary of doing the right thing because of guilt and not grace. Thank you for the limitless power of your love which sets me free from a guilted cage to fly and soar to new heights of joyous praise today. Amen.

—Lloyd John Ogilvie

372 What a Wonderful Savior

. . . by the righteousness of One the free Gift came upon all men unto justification of life.
— Romans 5:18

Elisha A. Hoffman

BENTON HARBOR
Elisha A. Hoffman

1 Christ has for sin a-tone-ment made— What a won-der-ful Sav-ior!
2 *I praise Him for the cleans-ing blood—What a won-der-ful Sav-ior!*
3 He cleansed my heart from all its sin— What a won-der-ful Sav-ior!
4 *He gives me o-ver-com-ing power— What a won-der-ful Sav-ior!*

1 We are re-deemed, the price is paid—What a won-der-ful Sav-ior!
2 *That rec-on-ciled my soul to God—What a won-der-ful Sav-ior!*
3 And now He reigns and rules there-in— What a won-der-ful Sav-ior!
4 *And tri-umph in each try-ing hour—What a won-der-ful Sav-ior!*

What a won-der-ful Sav-ior is Je-sus, my Je-sus!

What a won-der-ful Sav-ior is Je-sus, my Lord!

WORSHIP AND ADORATION

Praise the Lord, His Glories Show

373

Great is the Lord and greatly to be praised.
— Psalm 145:3

Based on Psalm 150
Henry Francis Lyte

LLANFAIR
Robert Williams
Harmonized by John Roberts

1 Praise the Lord, His glo - ries show, Al - le - lu - ia!
2 *Earth to heaven and heaven to earth,* Al - le - lu - ia!
3 Praise the Lord, His mer - cies trace, Al - le - lu - ia!

1 Saints with - in His courts be - low, Al - le - lu - ia!
2 *Tell His won - ders, sing His worth,* Al - le - lu - ia!
3 Praise His prov - i - dence and grace, Al - le - lu - ia!

1 An - gels 'round His throne a - bove, A - le - lu - ia!
2 *Age to age and shore to shore,* A - le - lu - ia!
3 All that He for man hath done, A - le - lu - ia!

1 All that see and share His love. A - le - lu - ia!
2 *Praise Him, praise Him ev - er - more!* A - le - lu - ia!
3 All He sends us through His Son. A - le - lu - ia!

WORSHIP AND ADORATION

374 Rejoice, the Lord Is King!

Rejoice in the Lord always; and again I say, Rejoice.

— Philippians 4:4

Based on Philippians 4:4
Charles Wesley

DARWALL'S 148th
John Darwall
Handbell descant by Bob Burroughs

Two-octave handbell descant for stanza 4

1 Re - joice, the Lord is King! Your Lord and King a - dore!
2 *The Lord, our Sav - ior, reigns, The God of truth and love;*
3 His king - dom can - not fail, He rules o'er earth and heaven;
4 *Re - joice in glo - rious hope! Our Lord the judge shall come*

1 Re - joice, give thanks, and sing, And tri - umph ev - er - er -
2 *When He had purged our stains, He took His seat a -*
3 The keys of death and hell Are to our Je - sus
4 *And take His serv - ants up To their e - ter - nal*

1 more:
2 *bove:*
3 given:
4 *home:*

Lift up your heart, lift up your voice! Re -

WORSHIP AND ADORATION

joice, a-gain I say, re - joice! A - men.

Praises to the Lord 375

Praise the Lord! Praise God in His sanctuary;

praise Him in His mighty firmament!

Praise Him for His mighty deeds;

praise Him according to His exceeding greatness!

Praise Him with trumpet sound;
praise Him with lute and harp!

Praise Him with timbrel and dance;
praise Him with strings and pipe!

Praise Him with sounding cymbals;

praise Him with loud clashing cymbals!

Let everything that breathes praise the Lord!

Praise the Lord!*

Make a joyful noise to the Lord, all the lands!

Serve the Lord with gladness! Come into His presence with singing!

Know that the Lord is God!

It is He that made us, and we are His; we are His people, and the sheep of His pasture.

Enter His gates with thanksgiving, and His courts with praise!

Give thanks to Him, bless His name!

For the Lord is good;

His steadfast love endures for ever, and His faithfulness to all generations.†

—*Psalm 150 (RSV)
—†Psalm 100 (RSV)

376 Glorious Things of Thee Are Spoken

Glorious things of Thee are spoken, O City of God. — Psalm 87:3

Based on Psalm 87:3; Isaiah 33:20, 21
John Newton

AUSTRIAN HYMN
Franz Joseph Haydn

1 Glo - rious things of thee are spo - ken, Zi - on, cit - y of our God;
2 *See, the streams of liv - ing wa - ters, Spring-ing from e - ter - nal Love,*
3 Round each hab - i - ta-tion hov-ering, See the cloud and fire ap - pear

1 He whose word can-not be bro - ken Formed thee for His own a - bode.
2 *Well sup-ply thy sons and daugh-ters, And all fear of want re - move.*
3 For a glo - ry and a cov-ering, Show - ing that the Lord is near!

1 On the Rock of A - ges found - ed, What can shake thy sure re - pose?
2 *Who can faint while such a riv - er Ev - er flows their thirst to assuage?*
3 Thus de - riv - ing from their ban - ner Light by night and shade by day,

1 With sal - va-tion's walls sur-round-ed, Thou mayest smile at all thy foes.
2 *Grace which, like the Lord, the Giv - er, Nev - er fails from age to age!*
3 Safe they feed up - on the man - na Which He gives them when they pray. A - men.

Arranged by Gordon Young

3 Round each hab-i - ta-tion hov-ering, See the cloud and fire ap-pear

For a glo-ry and a cov-ering, Show-ing that the Lord is near:

Thus de-riv - ing from their ban-ner Light by night and shade by day,

Safe they feed up - on the man-na Which He gives them when they pray. A - men.

WORSHIP AND ADORATION

377 Joyful, Joyful, We Adore Thee

But unto you . . . the sun of righteousness shall arise with healing in His wings. — Malachi 4:2

HYMN TO JOY
Ludwig van Beethoven
Adapted by Edward Hodges

Henry van Dyke

1 Joy - ful, joy - ful, we a - dore Thee, God of glo - ry, Lord of love;
2 *All Thy works with joy sur - round Thee, Earth and heaven re - flect Thy rays,*
3 Thou art giv - ing and for - giv - ing, Ev - er bless - ing, ev - er blest,
4 *Mor - tals, join the hap - py cho - rus With the morn - ing stars be - gan;*

1 Hearts un - fold like flowers be - fore Thee, Open - ing to the sun a - bove.
2 *Stars and an - gels sing a - round Thee, Cen - ter of un - bro - ken praise.*
3 Well - spring of the joy of liv - ing, O - cean depth of hap - py rest!
4 *Fa - ther love is reign - ing o'er us, Broth - er love binds man to man.*

1 Melt the clouds of sin and sad - ness, Drive the dark of doubt a - way;
2 *Field and for - est, vale and moun - tain, Flow - ery mead - ow, flash - ing sea,*
3 Thou our Fa - ther, Christ our Broth - er— All who live in love are Thine;
4 *Ev - er sing - ing, march we on - ward, Vic - tors in the midst of strife,*

1 Giv - er of im - mor - tal glad - ness, Fill us with the light of day.
2 *Chant - ing bird and flow - ing foun - tain, Call us to re - joice in Thee.*
3 Teach us how to love each oth - er, Lift us to the joy di - vine.
4 *Joy - ful mu - sic leads us sun - ward In the tri - umph song of life.* A - men.

WORSHIP AND ADORATION

Bless the Lord, O my soul;
and all that is within me, bless His holy name!
Bless the Lord, O my soul, and forget not all His benefits,
Who forgives all your iniquity,
Who heals all your diseases,
Who redeems your life from the Pit,
Who crowns you with steadfast love and mercy,
Who satisfies you with good as long as you live so that your youth is renewed like the eagle's.

The Lord has established His throne in the heavens,
and His kingdom rules over all.
Bless the Lord, O you His angels,
You mighty ones who do His word, hearkening to the voice of His word!
Bless the Lord, all His hosts,
His ministers that do His will!
Bless the Lord, all His works, in all places of His dominion.
Bless the Lord, O my soul!

—Psalm 103:1-5, 19-22 (RSV)

Bless His Holy Name

379

O Bless our God, ye people, and make the voice of His praise to be heard. — Psalm 66:8

Psalm 103
Andraé Crouch

BLESS THE LORD
Andraé Crouch

Bless the Lord, O my soul, and all that is with-in me, Bless His

Fine

ho - ly Name. He has done great things, He has done great

D.C. al Fine

things, He has done great things, Bless His ho - ly Name.

WORSHIP AND ADORATION

380 God Is Light

Minister: God is light, and in Him there is no darkness.

PEOPLE: GREAT IS THE LORD, AND GREATLY TO BE PRAISED.

Minister: God is love, and in Him we can all be fulfilled.

PEOPLE: GREAT IS THE LORD, AND GREATLY TO BE PRAISED.

Minister: God is truth, and in His Son we see something of what He is like and something of what we can become.

PEOPLE: GREAT IS THE LORD, AND GREATLY TO BE PRAISED.

Minister: God is holy, and through His generosity we can please Him with a borrowed goodness.

PEOPLE: GREAT IS THE LORD, AND GREATLY TO BE PRAISED.

Minister: Here is the wonder, that we are recipients of grace, and grace is God giving us for free that which none of us can afford.

PEOPLE: GREAT IS THE LORD, AND GREATLY TO BE PRAISED.

—Bryan Jeffery Leech
based on I John 1:5-7

381 All People That on Earth Do Dwell

Let all the people praise thee, O God . . . — Psalm 67:3

Based on Psalm 100
Attr. to William Kethe

OLD 100th
Genevan Psalter
Attributed to Louis Bourgeois

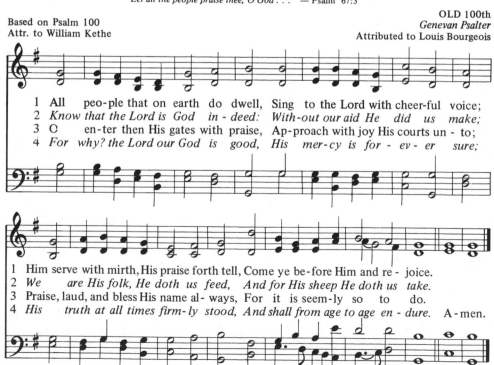

1 All people that on earth do dwell, Sing to the Lord with cheer-ful voice;
2 *Know that the Lord is God in - deed: With-out our aid He did us make;*
3 O en-ter then His gates with praise, Ap-proach with joy His courts un - to;
4 *For why? the Lord our God is good, His mer-cy is for - ev - er sure;*

1 Him serve with mirth, His praise forth tell, Come ye be-fore Him and re - joice.
2 *We are His folk, He doth us feed, And for His sheep He doth us take.*
3 Praise, laud, and bless His name al-ways, For it is seem-ly so to do.
4 *His truth at all times firm-ly stood, And shall from age to age en - dure. A - men.*

WORSHIP AND ADORATION

Praise God, from Whom All Blessings Flow 382

. . . Who hath blessed us with all spiritual blessings. — Ephesians 1:3

OLD 100th
Attributed to Louis Bourgeois
Genevan Psalter

Thomas Ken

FIRST VERSION

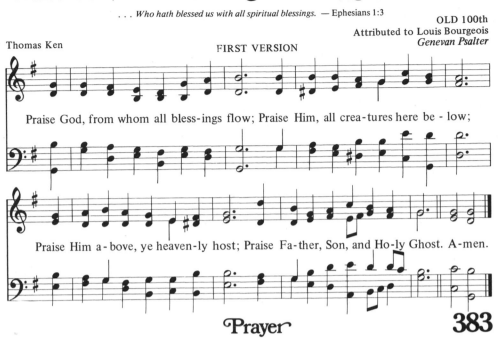

Praise God, from whom all bless-ings flow; Praise Him, all crea-tures here be - low;

Praise Him a - bove, ye heaven-ly host; Praise Fa-ther, Son, and Ho-ly Ghost. A-men.

Prayer 383

To be there before You, Lord, that's all.
To shut the eyes of my body,
To shut the eyes of my soul,
And be still and silent,
To expose myself to You who are there, exposed to me.
To be there before You, the eternal Presence.

—Michel Quoist

Doxology 384

I will greatly praise the Lord with my mouth; yea, I will praise Him
among the multitudes. — Psalm 109:30

OLD 100th (original)
Attributed to Louis Bourgeois
Genevan Psalter

Thomas Ken

SECOND VERSION

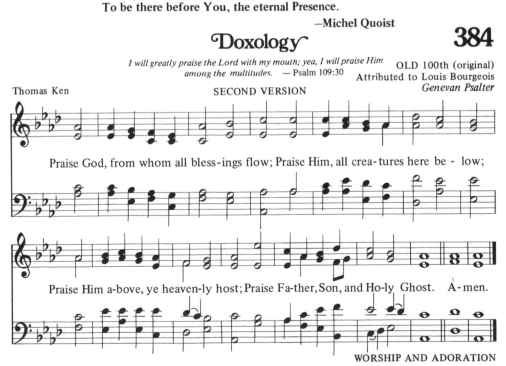

Praise God, from whom all bless-ings flow; Praise Him, all crea-tures here be - low;

Praise Him a-bove, ye heaven-ly host; Praise Fa-ther, Son, and Ho-ly Ghost. A-men.

WORSHIP AND ADORATION

385 Holy God, We Praise Thy Name

I dwell in the high and holy place with him that is of a humble spirit. —Isaiah 57:15

Attr. to Ignaz Franz
Tr. by Clarence A. Walworth

GROSSER GOTT
"Allgemeines Katholisches Gesangbuch"

1 Ho - ly God, we praise Thy name; Lord of all, we
2 *Hark, the glad ce - les - tial hymn An - gel choirs a -*
3 Ho - ly Fa - ther, ho - ly Son, Ho - ly Spir - it:

1 bow be - fore Thee; All on earth Thy scep - ter claim,
2 *bove are rais - ing; Cher - u - bim and ser - a - phim,*
3 three we name Thee, Though in es - sence on - ly one;

1 All in heaven a - bove a - dore Thee: In - fi - nite Thy
2 *In un - ceas - ing cho - rus prais - ing; Fill the heavens with*
3 Un - di - vid - ed God we claim Thee, And a - dor - ing,

1 vast do - main, Ev - er - last - ing is Thy reign.
2 *sweet ac - cord: Ho - ly, ho - ly, ho - ly Lord.*
3 bend the knee, While we own the mys - ter - y. A - men.

WORSHIP AND ADORATION

Thanks to God for My Redeemer

Thanks be to God for His unspeakable gift. — II Corinthians 9:15

August Ludwig Storm
Tr. by Carl E. Backstrom

TACK O GUD
J. A. Hultman

1 Thanks to God for my Re - deem - er, Thanks for all Thou dost pro-vide!
2 *Thanks for prayers that Thou hast answered, Thanks for what Thou dost de - ny!*
3 Thanks for ros - es by the way - side, Thanks for thorns their stems contain!

1 Thanks for times now but a mem-ory, Thanks for Je - sus by my side!
2 *Thanks for storms that I have weath-ered, Thanks for all Thou dost sup-ply!*
3 Thanks for home and thanks for fire - side, Thanks for hope, that sweet re-frain!

1 Thanks for pleas - ant, balm - y spring-time, Thanks for dark and drear-y fall!
2 *Thanks for pain and thanks for pleas - ure, Thanks for com-fort in de - spair!*
3 Thanks for joy and thanks for sor - row, Thanks for heav'n-ly peace with Thee!

1 Thanks for tears by now for- got- ten, Thanks for peace within my soul!
2 *Thanks for grace that none can measure, Thanks for love beyond compare!*
3 Thanks for hope in the to - mor-row, Thanks thru all e - ter - ni - ty! A- men.

THANKSGIVING

387 We Gather Together

If God be for us who can be against us? — Romans 8:31

KREMSER
Netherlands Folk Song
Harmonized by Edward Kremser
Descant by Tom Fettke

Netherlands Folk Song
Tr. by Theodore Baker

3 We all do ex-tol Thee, Thou lead-er tri-um-phant, And

1 We gath-er to-geth-er to ask the Lord's bless-ing— He
2 *Be-side us to guide us, our God with us join-ing, Or-*
3 We all do ex-tol Thee, Thou lead-er tri-um-phant, And

1 chas-tens and has-tens His will to make known; The
2 *dain-ing, main-tain-ing His king-dom di-vine; So*
3 pray that Thou still our de-fend-er wilt be; Let

1 wick-ed op-press-ing now cease from dis-tress-ing: Sing
2 *from the be-gin-ning the fight we were win-ning: Thou,*
3 Thy con-gre-ga-tion es-cape trib-u-la-tion: Thy

Let Thy con-gre-ga-tion es-cape trib-u-la-tion.

pray that Thou still our de-fend-er wilt be;

THANKSGIVING

Thy name be ev-er praised! O Lord, make us free! A - men.

1 prais - es to His name— He for - gets not His own.
2 *Lord, wast at our side— all glo - ry be Thine.*
3 name be ev-er praised! O Lord, make us free! A - men.

His Love Is Everlasting

388

Leader:	Give thanks to the Lord, for He is good,
People:	HIS LOVE IS EVERLASTING!
Leader:	Give thanks to the God of gods,
People:	HIS LOVE IS EVERLASTING!
Leader:	Give thanks to the Lord of lords,
People:	HIS LOVE IS EVERLASTING!
Leader:	He alone performs great marvels,
People:	HIS LOVE IS EVERLASTING!
Leader:	His wisdom made the heavens,
People:	HIS LOVE IS EVERLASTING!
Leader:	He set the earth on the waters,
People:	HIS LOVE IS EVERLASTING!
Leader:	He made the great lights,
People:	HIS LOVE IS EVERLASTING!
Leader:	The sun to govern the day,
People:	HIS LOVE IS EVERLASTING!
Leader:	Moon and stars to govern the night,
People:	HIS LOVE IS EVERLASTING!
Leader:	He led His people through the wilderness,
People:	HIS LOVE IS EVERLASTING!
Leader:	He remembered us when we were down,
People:	HIS LOVE IS EVERLASTING!
Leader:	And snatched us from our oppressors,
People:	HIS LOVE IS EVERLASTING!
Leader:	He provides for all living creatures,
People:	HIS LOVE IS EVERLASTING!
Leader:	Give thanks to the God of Heaven,
People:	HIS LOVE IS EVERLASTING!

—Psalm 126:1-9; 16-18 (JB)

389 Let All Things Now Living

Sing unto the Lord, all the earth, show forth from day to day His salvation.

—I Chronicles 16:23

Katherine K. Davis
Previously attributed to
John Cowley

ASH GROVE
Traditional Welsh Melody
Descant by Katherine K. Davis

Descant

2 Ah_____ O sun, in Thy

1 Let all things now liv-ing A song of thanks-giv-ing To God the Cre-
2 *His law He en-forc-es: the stars in their cours-es, The sun in His*

or-bit, o-be-dient-ly shine. Ah_____

1 a-tor tri-um-phant-ly raise, Who fash-ioned and made us, pro-
2 *or-bit, o-be-dient-ly shine; The hills and the moun-tains, The*

_____ The deeps of the o-cean pro-claim Him di-

1 tect-ed and stayed us, Who guid-eth us on to the end of our
2 *riv-ers and foun-tains, The deeps of the o-cean pro-claim Him di-*

THANKSGIVING

vine. Re - joice,_____ re - joice! With glad ad - o -

1 days. His ban-ners are o'er us, His light goes be - fore us, A pil-lar of
2 vine. We too, should be voic-ing our love and re - joic-ing, With glad ad - o -

ra-tion a song let us raise. Ah,_____

1 fire shin-ing forth in the night, 'Til shad-ows have van - ished And dark-ness is
2 ra - tion a song let us raise, 'Til all things now liv - ing u - nite in thanks-

_____ To God in the high - est, ho - san-na and praise. A - men.

1 ban-ished, As for-ward we trav - el from light in-to light.
2 giv - ing To God in the high-est, ho - san-na and praise! A - men.

390
O Let Your Soul Now Be Filled with Gladness

Therefore God hath anointed thee with the oil of gladness. . . .
— Hebrews 1:9

Peter Jönsson Aschan
Tr. by Karl A. Olsson

RANSOMED SOUL
Swedish Folk Melody
Harmonized by A. Royce Eckhardt

1 O let your soul now be filled with glad-ness, Your heart re-deemed, re-
2 *If you seem emp-ty of an-y feel-ing, Re-joice—you are His*
3 It is a good, ev-ery good tran-scend-ing, That Christ has died for

1 joice in-deed! O may the thought ban-ish all your sad-ness That
2 *ran-somed bride! If those you cher-ish seem not to love you, And*
3 you and me! It is a glad-ness that has no end-ing There-

1 in His blood you have been freed, That God's un-fail-ing love is yours,
2 *dark as-sails from ev-ery side, Still yours the prom-ise, come what may,*
3 in God's won-drous love to see! Praise be to Him, the spot-less Lamb,

1 That you the on - ly Son were giv-en, That by His
2 *In loss and tri-umph, in laugh-ter, cry-ing, In want and*
3 Who through the des-ert my soul is lead-ing To that fair

THANKSGIVING

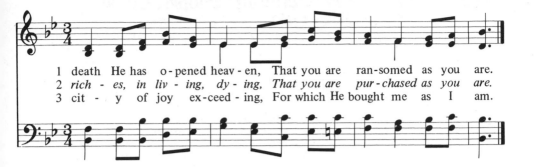

1 death He has o-pened heav-en, That you are ran-somed as you are.
2 rich - es, in liv - ing, dy - ing, That you are pur-chased as you are.
3 cit - y of joy ex-ceed - ing, For which He bought me as I am.

Thanksgiving Day   391

Father, we around this table thank Thee:

for Thy great gift of life,

that Thy love for us is not dependent upon any unworthiness of ours,

for good health,

that we know neither hunger nor want,

for warm clothes to wear,

for those who love us best,

for friends whose words of encouragement have often chased away dark clouds,

for the zest of living,

for many an answered prayer,

for kindly providences that have preserved us from danger and harm.

We thank Thee that still we live in a land bountifully able to supply all our needs, a land which still by Thy Providence knows peace, whose skies are not darkened by the machines of the enemy, whose fields and woodlands are still unblasted by the flames of war, a land with peaceful valleys and smiling meadows still serene.

O help us to appreciate all that we have, to be content with it, to be grateful for it, to be proud of it—not in an arrogant pride that boasts, but in a grateful pride that strives to be more worthy.

In Thy name, to whose bounty we owe these blessings spread before us, to Thee we give our gratitude. Amen.

—Peter Marshall

392 Come, Ye Thankful People, Come

Then shall the righteous shine forth as the sun in the Kingdom . . .

— Matthew 13:43

ST. GEORGE'S WINDSOR

Henry Alford

George J. Elvey

1 Come, ye thank-ful peo - ple, come, Raise the song of har - vest - home;
2 *All the world is God's own field, Fruit un - to His praise to yield;*
3 For the Lord our God shall come And shall take His har - vest - home;
4 *E - ven so, Lord, quick-ly come To Thy fi - nal har - vest - home;*

1 All is safe - ly gath - ered in, Ere the win - ter storms be - gin:
2 *Wheat and tares to - geth - er sown, Un - to joy or sor - rows grown:*
3 From His field shall in that day All of - fens - es purge a - way,
4 *Gath - er Thou Thy peo - ple in, Free from sor - row, free from sin:*

1 God, our Mak - er, doth pro - vide For our wants to be sup - plied;
2 *First the blade, and then the ear, Then the full corn shall ap - pear;*
3 Give His an - gels charge at last In the fire the tares to cast,
4 *There for - ev - er pu - ri - fied, In Thy pres - ence to a - bide;*

1 Come to God's own tem - ple, come, Raise the song of har - vest - home.
2 *Lord of har - vest, grant that we Whole-some grain and pure may be.*
3 But the fruit-ful ears to store In His gar - ner ev - er - more.
4 *Come, with all Thine an - gels, come, Raise the glo - rious har - vest - home.* A - men.

THANKSGIVING

Arranged by John Ness Beck

4 E - ven so, Lord, quick - ly come To Thy fi - nal
har - vest - home; Gath - er Thou Thy peo - ple in,
Free from sor - row, free from sin: There for - ev - er pur - i - fied,
In Thy pres - ence to a - bide: Come, with all Thine
an - gels, come, Raise the glo - rious har - vest - home.

THANKSGIVING

393   Thanksgiving and Praise

Thanksgiving and praise are to be the major elements in our singing. It is possible to give thanks and praise God individually but if any congregation took time to let everyone do that, it would take all day.... Singing is something we can do together. So through the ages the believers in God both of the Old and New Testament have sung their praises and thanksgiving. . . . It is the reason we should be careful not to sing in a desultory manner. There is nothing more conducive to dullness in a service than half-hearted singing. So the exhortation here is most appropriate. "O, come, let us sing to the Lord: let us make a joyful noise to the rock of our salvation."

—Ray Stedman

394   Rejoice, Ye Pure in Heart

We will rejoice in Thy salvation and in the name of our God. . . . — Psalm 20:5

Edward H. Plumptre

MARION
Arthur H. Messiter

1 Re - joice, ye pure in heart, Re - joice, give thanks and sing;
2 *Go on through life's long path, Still chant-ing as ye go;*
3 Then on, ye pure in heart, Re - joice, give thanks and sing;

1 Your fes - tive ban - ner wave on high, The cross of Christ your King:
2 *From youth to age, by night and day, In glad-ness and in woe:*
3 Your glo - rious ban - ner wave on high, The cross of Christ your King:

Re - joice, re - joice, Re - joice, give thanks and sing. A - men.
Re - joice, re - joice,

Alternate Last Verse Harmonization

Arranged by Fred Bock

3 Then on, ye pure in heart, Re - joice, give thanks and sing; Your glo - rious ban - ner wave on high, The cross of Christ your King: Re - joice, re - joice, Re - joice, give thanks and sing! A - men.

THANKSGIVING

395

We Plow the Fields and Scatter the Good Seed

The field is the world; the good seed are the children of the Kingdom.
— Matthew 13:38

Mathias Claudius
Tr. by Jane M. Campbell

WIR PFLÜGEN
Johann A. P. Schulz

1 We plow the fields and scat - ter The good seed on the land,
2 *He on - ly is the mak - er Of all things near and far,*
3 We thank Thee, then, O Fa - ther, For all things bright and good—

1 But it is fed and wa - tered By God's al-might - y hand;
2 *He paints the way - side flow - er, He lights the eve - ning star;*
3 The seed - time and the har - vest, Our life, our health, our food;

1 He sends the snow in win - ter, The warmth to swell the grain,
2 *The winds and waves o - bey Him, By Him the birds are fed:*
3 Ac - cept the gifts we of - fer For all Thy love im - parts,

1 The breez - es and the sun - shine, And soft, re - fresh - ing rain.
2 *Much more, to us His chil - dren, He gives our dai - ly bread.*
3 And, what Thou most de - sir - est, Our hum - ble, thank - ful hearts.

All good gifts a - round us Are sent from heaven a - bove:

Then thank the Lord, O thank the Lord For all His love. A-men.

A General Thanksgiving 396

Almighty God, Father of all mercies,
we your unworthy servants give you humble thanks
for all Your goodness and loving-kindness to us
and to all men.

We bless You for our creation, preservation,
and all the blessings of this life;
but above all for Your incomparable love
in the redemption of the world by our Lord Jesus Christ;
for the means of grace, and for the hope of glory.

And, we pray, give us such an awareness of Your mercies,
that with truly thankful hearts
we may make known Your praise,
not only with our lips, but in our lives,
by giving up ourselves to Your service,
and by walking before You in holiness and righteousness all our days;
through Jesus Christ our Lord,
to whom, with You and the Holy Spirit,
be all honor and glory throughout all ages.

Amen.

—Standard Book of Common Prayer

397

I Will Serve Thee

If any man serve Me let him follow Me....
— John 12:26

Gloria Gaither
William J. Gaither

SERVING
William J. Gaither

I will serve Thee be-cause I love Thee, You have giv-en life to me; I was noth-ing be-fore You found me, You have giv-en life to me. Heart-aches, bro-ken piec-es, Ru-ined lives are why You died on Cal-vary; Your touch was what I longed for, You have giv-en life to me.

COMMITMENT AND SUBMISSION

Rise Up, O Men of God

398

. . . love the Lord, your God and serve Him . . .
— Deuteronomy 11:13

William P. Merrill

FESTAL SONG
William H. Walter

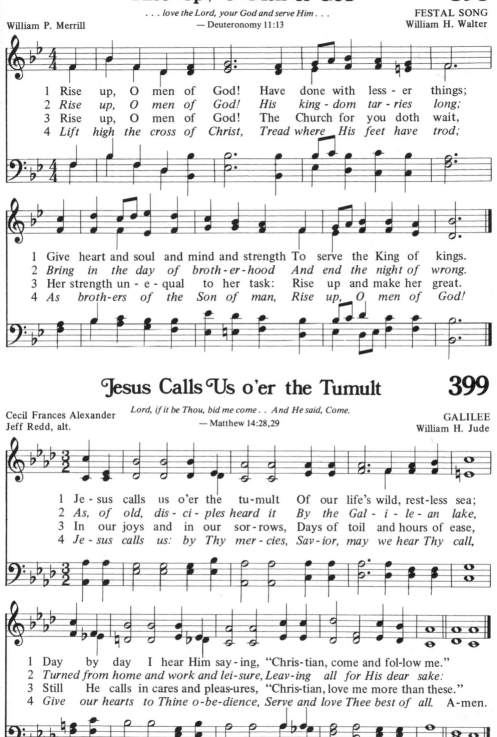

1 Rise up, O men of God! Have done with less-er things;
2 *Rise up, O men of God! His king-dom tar-ries long;*
3 Rise up, O men of God! The Church for you doth wait,
4 *Lift high the cross of Christ, Tread where His feet have trod;*

1 Give heart and soul and mind and strength To serve the King of kings.
2 *Bring in the day of broth-er-hood And end the night of wrong.*
3 Her strength un-e-qual to her task: Rise up and make her great.
4 *As broth-ers of the Son of man, Rise up, O men of God!*

Jesus Calls Us o'er the Tumult

399

Cecil Frances Alexander
Jeff Redd, alt.

Lord, if it be Thou, bid me come . . And He said, Come.
— Matthew 14:28,29

GALILEE
William H. Jude

1 Je-sus calls us o'er the tu-mult Of our life's wild, rest-less sea;
2 *As, of old, dis-ci-ples heard it By the Gal-i-le-an lake,*
3 In our joys and in our sor-rows, Days of toil and hours of ease,
4 *Je-sus calls us: by Thy mer-cies, Sav-ior, may we hear Thy call,*

1 Day by day I hear Him say-ing, "Chris-tian, come and fol-low me."
2 *Turned from home and work and lei-sure, Leav-ing all for His dear sake:*
3 Still He calls in cares and pleas-ures, "Chris-tian, love me more than these."
4 *Give our hearts to Thine o-be-dience, Serve and love Thee best of all.* A-men.

COMMITMENT AND SUBMISSION

400 Have Thine Own Way, Lord!

Give me understanding and I shall keep thy Law . . . I shall observe it with all my heart.

— Psalm 119:34

Adelaide A. Pollard

ADELAIDE
George C. Stebbins

1 Have Thine own way, Lord! Have Thine own way!
2 *Have Thine own way, Lord! Have Thine own way!*
3 Have Thine own way, Lord! Have Thine own way!
4 *Have Thine own way, Lord! Have Thine own way!*

1 Thou art the pot - ter, I am the clay!
2 *Search me and try me, Mas - ter, to - day!*
3 Wound - ed and wea - ry, Help me, I pray!
4 *Hold o'er my be - ing Ab - so - lute sway!*

1 Mold me and make me Aft - er Thy will,
2 *Whit - er than snow, Lord, Wash me just now,*
3 Pow - er— all pow - er— Sure - ly is Thine!
4 *Fill with Thy Spir - it 'Til all shall see*

1 While I am wait - ing, Yield - ed and still.
2 *As in Thy pres - ence Hum - bly I bow.*
3 Touch me and heal me, Sav - ior di - vine!
4 *Christ on - ly, al - ways, Liv - ing in me!* A - men.

COMMITMENT AND SUBMISSION

Jesus, I Come

401

The Lord . . . hath sent me to bind the broken hearted . . . .
— Isaiah 61:1

William T. Sleeper
Jeff Redd, alt.

JESUS, I COME
George C. Stebbins

1 Out of my bond-age, sor-row and night, Je-sus, I come, Je-sus, I come;
2 *Out of my shame-ful fail-ure and loss, Je-sus, I come, Je-sus, I come;*
3 Out of un-rest and ar-ro-gant pride, Je-sus, I come, Je-sus, I come;
4 *Out of the fear and dread of the tomb, Je-sus, I come, Je-sus, I come;*

1 In-to Thy free-dom, glad-ness and light, Je-sus, I come to Thee.
2 *In-to the glo-rious gain of Thy cross, Je-sus, I come to Thee.*
3 In-to Thy bless-ed will to a-bide, Je-sus, I come to Thee.
4 *In-to the joy and light of Thy home, Je-sus, I come to Thee.*

1 Out of my sick-ness in-to Thy health, Out of my need and in-to Thy wealth,
2 *Out of earth's sor-rows in-to Thy balm, Out of life's storms and in-to Thy calm,*
3 Out of my-self to dwell in Thy love, Out of de-spair to rap-tures a-bove,
4 *Out of the depths of ru-in un-told, In-to Thy peace-ful, shel-ter-ing fold,*

1 Out of my sin and in-to Thy-self, Je-sus, I come to Thee.
2 *Out of dis-tress to ju-bi-lant psalm, Je-sus, I come to Thee.*
3 Up-ward I rise on wings like a dove, Je-sus, I come to Thee.
4 *Ev-er Thy glo-rious face to be-hold, Je-sus, I come to Thee.*

COMMITMENT AND SUBMISSION

402

O Jesus, I Have Promised

He died for all that they . . . should not henceforth live unto themselves.

— II Corinthians 5:15

John E. Bode

ANGEL'S STORY
Arthur H. Mann

1 O Je-sus, I have prom-ised To serve Thee to the end; Be Thou for-ev-er
2 *O let me feel Thee near me, The world is ev-er near; I see the sights that*
3 O Je-sus, Thou hast prom-ised To all who fol-low Thee That where Thou art in

1 near me, My Mas-ter and my Friend; I shall not fear the bat-tle If Thou art
2 *daz-zle, The tempt-ing sounds I hear; My foes are ev-er near me, A-round me*
3 glo-ry There shall Thy ser-vant be; And, Je-sus, I have prom-ised To serve Thee

1 by my side, Nor wan-der from the path-way If Thou wilt be my Guide.
2 *and with-in; But, Je-sus, draw Thou near-er, And shield my soul from sin.*
3 to the end; O give me grace to fol-low My Mas-ter and my Friend.

403

A Confession of Faith

I believe in God, who is for me spirit, love, the principle of all things.

I believe that God is in me, as I am in Him.

I believe that the true welfare of man consists in fulfilling the will of God.

I believe that from the fulfillment of the will of God there can follow nothing but that

which is good for me and for all men.   *(more on next page)*

COMMITMENT AND SUBMISSION

I believe that the will of God is that every man should love his fellow men, and should act
    toward others as he desires that they should act toward him.
I believe that the reason of life is for each of us simply to grow in love.
I believe that this growth in love will contribute more than any other force to establish the
    Kingdom of God on earth.

—Leo Tolstoy

O Love That Will Not Let Me Go 404

The Lord shall be unto thee an everlasting light....
— Isaiah 60:19

George Matheson

ST. MARGARET
Albert L. Peace

1 O Love that will not let me go, I rest my
2 O Light that fol-lowest all my way, I yield my
3 O Joy that seek-est me through pain, I can - not
4 O Cross that lift-est up my head, I dare not

1 wea - ry soul in Thee; I give Thee back the life I owe,
2 flick-ering torch to Thee; My heart re-stores its bor-rowed ray,
3 close my heart to Thee; I trace the rain-bow through the rain,
4 ask to fly from Thee; I lay in dust life's glo - ry dead,

1 That in Thine o-cean depths its flow May rich - er, full - er be.
2 That in Thy sun-shine's blaze its day May bright-er, fair - er be.
3 And feel the prom-ise is not vain That morn shall tear-less be.
4 And from the ground there blos-soms red, Life that shall end - less be. A-men.

COMMITMENT AND SUBMISSION

405 Close to Thee

He that sayeth he abideth in Him ought himself also to walk even as He walked. — I John 2:6

Fanny J. Crosby

CLOSE TO THEE
Silas J. Vail

1 Thou, my ev - er-last-ing por - tion, More than friend or life to me,
2 *Not for ease or world-ly pleas-ure Nor for fame my prayer shall be;*
3 Lead me through the vale of shad-ows, Bear me o'er life's fit - ful sea;

1 All a - long my pil-grim jour - ney, Sav - ior, let me walk with Thee.
2 *Glad-ly will I toil and suf - fer, On - ly let me walk with Thee.*
3 Then the gate of life e - ter - nal May I en - ter, Lord, with Thee.

1 Close to Thee, close to Thee, Close to Thee, close to Thee; All a -
2 *Close to Thee, close to Thee, Close to Thee, close to Thee; Glad - ly*
3 Close to Thee, close to Thee, Close to Thee, close to Thee; Then the

1 long my pil - grim jour-ney, Sav - ior, let me walk with Thee.
2 *will I toil and suf-fer, On - ly let me walk with Thee.*
3 gate of life e - ter - nal May I en - ter, Lord, with Thee. A - men.

COMMITMENT AND SUBMISSION

Lord, I'm Coming Home

406

None of his sins which he hath committed shall be mentioned unto him.

— Ezekiel 33:16

COMING HOME

William J. Kirkpatrick

William J. Kirkpatrick

1 I've wan-dered far a - way from God, Now I'm com-ing home;
2 I've wast - ed man - y pre - cious years, Now I'm com-ing home;
3 I've tired of sin and stray - ing, Lord, Now I'm com-ing home;
4 *My soul is sick, my heart is sore, Now I'm com-ing home;*

1 The paths of sin too long I've trod, Lord, I'm com-ing home.
2 *I now re-pent with bit - ter tears, Lord, I'm com-ing home.*
3 I'll trust Thy love, be - lieve Thy word, Lord, I'm com-ing home.
4 *My strength re-new, my hope re-store, Lord, I'm com-ing home.*

Com-ing home, com - ing home, Nev - er - more to roam,

O - pen wide Thine arms of love, Lord, I'm com-ing home.

COMMITMENT AND SUBMISSION

407 Lead Me to Calvary

And they came to a place which was called Gethsemane. . . .

— Mark 14:32

Jennie Evelyn Hussey

LEAD ME TO CALVARY
William J. Kirkpatrick

1 King of my life I crown Thee now— Thine shall the glo - ry be;
2 *Show me the tomb where Thou wast laid, Ten - der - ly mourned and wept,*
3 Let me like Ma - ry, through the gloom, Come with a gift to Thee;
4 *May I be will - ing, Lord, to bear Dai - ly my cross for Thee;*

1 Lest I for-get Thy thorn-crowned brow, Lead me to Cal - va - ry.
2 *An - gels in robes of light ar - rayed Guard-ed Thee whilst Thou slept.*
3 Show to me now the emp - ty tomb— Lead me to Cal - va - ry.
4 *E - ven Thy cup of grief to share— Thou hast borne all for me.*

Lest I for-get Geth - sem - a - ne, Lest I for-get Thine ag - o - ny,

Lest I for-get Thy love for me, Lead me to Cal-va - ry. A-men.

COMMITMENT AND SUBMISSION

I Surrender All

He that loveth his life shall lose it; He that hateth his life in this world shall keep it unto life eternal.
— John 12:25

SURRENDER

Judson W. Van de Venter

Winfield S. Weeden

1 All to Je-sus I sur-ren-der, All to Him I free-ly give;
2 *All to Je-sus I sur-ren-der, Hum-bly at His feet I bow,*
3 All to Je-sus I sur-ren-der, Make me, Sav-ior, whol-ly Thine.
4 *All to Je-sus I sur-ren-der, Lord, I give my-self to Thee;*

1 I will ev-er love and trust Him, In His pres-ence dai-ly live.
2 *World-ly plea-sures all for-sak-en; Take me, Je-sus, take me now.*
3 Let me feel the Ho-ly Spir-it, Tru-ly know that Thou art mine.
4 *Fill me with Thy love and pow-er, Let Thy bless-ing fall on me.*

I sur-ren-der all, I sur-ren-der all,
I sur-ren-der all, I sur-ren-der all,

All to Thee, my bless-ed Sav-ior, I sur-ren-der all.

COMMITMENT AND SUBMISSION

409

Who Is on the Lord's Side?

Who is on the Lord's side?
— Exodus 32:26

Frances R. Havergal

ARMAGEDDON
C. Luise Reichardt

1 Who is on the Lord's side? Who will serve the King? Who will
2 *Not for weight of glo - ry, Nor for crown and palm, En - ter*
3 Je - sus, Thou hast bought us, Not with gold or gem, But with
4 *Fierce may be the con - flict, Strong may be the foe, But the*

1 be His help - ers, Oth - er lives to bring? Who will leave the
2 *we the ar - my, Raise the war - rior - psalm; But for Love that*
3 Thine own life - blood, For Thy di - a - dem; With Thy bless - ing
4 *King's own ar - my None can o - ver - throw; 'Round His stan - dard*

1 world's side? Who will face the foe? Who is on the
2 *claim - eth Lives for whom He died: He whom Je - sus*
3 fill - ing Each who comes to Thee, Thou hast made us
4 *rang - ing, Vic - tory is se - cure, For His truth un -*

1 Lord's side? Who for Him will go? By Thy call of mer - cy,
2 *nam - eth Must be on His side. By Thy love con - strain - ing,*
3 will - ing, Thou hast made us free. By Thy grand re - demp - tion,
4 *chang - ing Makes the tri - umph sure. Joy - ful - ly en - list - ing,*

By Thy grace di - vine, We are on the Lord's side—Sav - ior, we are Thine!

COMMITMENT AND SUBMISSION

God is not a personage who orders us to a prostrate ourselves before Him
— a radically false position—
but one who says:
"Stand up,
here is my task for you;
take it and get on with it."

God does not require incense from us;
what He does require
is that we should *listen* and *take action*—
the true response of love.

God did not stop speaking two thousand years ago.
He speaks to you personally today
every time an inward voice asks you to do a kind or generous deed
or to suffer for the sake of someone else.

It is to you personally that God speaks at this moment,
and it is *through you* that He speaks when He inspires you to do some service.
Be brave enough to listen at first hand to what God says to you.

—John W. Harvey and Christina Yates

Am I a Soldier of the Cross?   **411**

No soldier that wareth entangleth himself with the affairs of this life.... — II Timothy 2:4

Isaac Watts

ARLINGTON
Thomas A. Arne

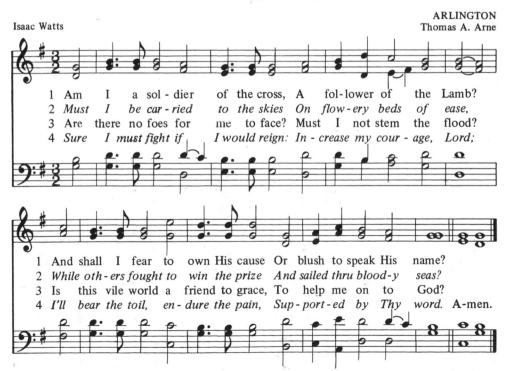

1 Am I a sol-dier of the cross, A fol-lower of the Lamb?
2 Must I be car-ried to the skies On flow-ery beds of ease,
3 Are there no foes for me to face? Must I not stem the flood?
4 Sure I must fight if I would reign: In-crease my cour-age, Lord;

1 And shall I fear to own His cause Or blush to speak His name?
2 While oth-ers fought to win the prize And sailed thru blood-y seas?
3 Is this vile world a friend to grace, To help me on to God?
4 I'll bear the toil, en-dure the pain, Sup-port-ed by Thy word. A-men.

412 Under His Wings

Hide me under the shadow of Thy Wing.
— Psalm 17:8

William O. Cushing

HINGHAM
Ira D. Sankey

1 Un - der His wings I am safe - ly a - bid - ing, Though the night
2 *Un - der His wings, what a ref - uge in sor - row! How the heart*
3 Un - der His wings, O what pre - cious en - joy - ment! There will I

1 deep - ens and tem - pests are wild; Still I can trust Him— I
2 *yearn - ing - ly turns to His rest! Oft - en when earth has no*
3 hide 'til life's tri - als are o'er; Shel - tered, pro - tect - ed, no

1 know He will keep me, He has re - deemed me and I am His child.
2 *balm for my heal - ing, There I find com - fort and there I am blest.*
3 e - vil can harm me, Rest - ing in Je - sus I'm safe ev - er - more.

Un - der His wings, un - der His wings, Who from His love can sev - er?

Un - der His wings my soul shall a - bide, Safe - ly a - bide for - ev - er.

COMMITMENT AND SUBMISSION

The Good News of God's Forgiveness

413

Left Side:
Those who let go of self
and hold on to Christ are forgiven.

Do you believe it?

Right Side:
With all our hearts!
Forgiveness is God's free gift
to be accepted by faith alone in Christ.

Do you believe it?

Left Side:
We do! With all our hearts!

Right Side:
Then your new name is "Set Free."

Left Side:
And yours is "Forgiven."

All:
If God no longer accuses us,
we will stop accusing ourselves.
We will celebrate His love and sing His praises!
Amen.

—Howard Childers

Father, I Adore You

414

God is a Spirit; and they that worship Him must worship him in spirit and in truth. — John 4:24

MARANATHA
Terrye Coelho

Terrye Coelho

1 Fa - ther, I a - dore You, Lay my life be -
2 *Je - sus, I a - dore You, Lay my life be -*
3 Spir - it, I a - dore You, Lay my life be -

1 fore You, How I love You.
2 *fore You, How I love You.*
3 fore You, How I love You.

COMMITMENT AND SUBMISSION

415
At Calvary

And when they were come to . . . Calvary they crucified Him . . .
— Luke 23:33

William R. Newell

CALVARY
Daniel B. Towner

1 Years I spent in van-i-ty and pride, Car-ing not my Lord was
2 *By God's Word at last my sin I learned; Then I trem-bled at the*
3 Now I've given to Je-sus ev-ery-thing; Now I glad-ly own Him
4 *O the love that drew sal-va-tion's plan! O the grace that brought it*

1 cru-ci-fied, Know-ing not it was for me He died On Cal-va-ry.
2 *law I'd spurned, 'Til my guilt-y soul im-plor-ing turned To Cal-va-ry.*
3 as my King; Now my rap-tured soul can on-ly sing Of Cal-va-ry.
4 *down to man! O the might-y gulf that God did span At Cal-va-ry.*

Mer-cy there was great and grace was free, Par-don there was mul-ti-

plied to me, There my bur-dened soul found lib-er-ty —At Cal-va-ry.

CONFESSION AND REPENTANCE

Pass Me Not, O Gentle Savior

And he sought to see Jesus . . . for He was to pass that way.

— Luke 19: 3-4

Fanny J. Crosby

PASS ME NOT
William H. Doane

1 Pass me not, O gen-tle Sav-ior— Hear my hum-ble cry!
2 *Let me at a throne of mer-cy Find a sweet re-lief;*
3 Trust-ing on-ly in Thy mer-it, Would I seek Thy face;
4 *Thou the spring of all my com-fort, More than life to me!*

1 While on oth-ers Thou art call-ing, Do not pass me by.
2 *Kneel-ing there in deep con-tri-tion, Help my un-be-lief.*
3 Heal my wound-ed, bro-ken spir-it, Save me by Thy grace.
4 *Whom have I on earth be-side Thee? Whom in heaven but Thee?*

Sav-ior, Sav-ior, Hear my hum-ble cry!

While on oth-ers Thou art call-ing, Do not pass me by. A-men.

CONFESSION AND REPENTANCE

417   Just As I Am, Without One Plea

Ho, everyone who is athirst, come . . . without money . . . and without price.

— Isaiah 55:1

Charlotte Elliott

WOODWORTH
William B. Bradbury

1 Just as I am, with - out one plea, But
2 *Just as I am, and wait - ing not To*
3 Just as I am, Thou wilt re - ceive, Wilt
4 *Just as I am, Thy love un - known Hath*

1 that Thy blood was shed for me, And that Thou biddest me
2 *rid my soul of one dark blot; To Thee, whose blood can*
3 wel - come, par - don, cleanse, re - lieve; Be - cause Thy prom - ise
4 *bro - ken ev - ery bar - rier down; Now, to be Thine, yes,*

1 come to Thee— O Lamb of God, I come, I come!
2 *cleanse each spot, O Lamb of God, I come, I come!*
3 I be - lieve, O Lamb of God, I come, I come!
4 *Thine a - lone, O Lamb of God, I come, I come!* A-men.

418   The General Confession

(All in unison)

Almighty and most merciful Father, we have erred, and strayed from Thy ways like lost sheep. We have offended against Thy holy laws. We have left undone those things which we ought to have done, and we have done those things which we ought not to have done; and there is no health in us.

O Lord, have mercy upon us, miserable offenders. Spare them, O Lord, which confess their faults. Restore them that are penitent, according to Thy promises declared unto mankind in Christ Jesus our Lord. And grant, O most merciful Father, for His sake, that we may hereafter live a godly, righteous, and sober life—to the glory of Thy holy name. Amen.

Kind and Merciful God

419

That . . . He might show the exceeding riches of His grace in His kindness . . .
— Ephesians 2:7

Bryan Jeffery Leech

ELFAKER
Swedish Melody
Adapted by Bryan Jeffery Leech

1 Kind and mer - ci - ful God, we have sinned in Your sight,
2 *Kind and mer - ci - ful God, we've ne - glect - ed Your Word*
3 Kind and mer - ci - ful God, we have brok - en Your laws
4 *Kind and mer - ci - ful God, in Christ's death on the cross*
5 Kind and mer - ci - ful God, bid us lift up our heads

1 We have all wan - dered far from Your way;
2 *And the truth that would guide us a - right;*
3 And in con - duct have veered from the norm;
4 *You pro - vid - ed a cleans - ing from sin;*
5 And com - mand us to rise from our knees;

1 We have fol - lowed de - sire, We have failed to as - pire
2 *We have lived in the shade Of the dark we have made,*
3 We have dreamed of the good, But the good that we could
4 *Speak the words that for - give That hence - forth we may live*
5 May our hearts now be changed And no long - er es - tranged,

1 To the vir - tue we ought to dis - play.
2 *When you willed us to walk in the light.*
3 We have fre - quent - ly failed to per - form.
4 *By the might of Your Spir - it with - in.*
5 Through the power of Your par - don and peace. A - men.

CONFESSION AND REPENTANCE

The Ten Commandments

Then God spoke all these words.
He said, "I am Jehovah your God
who brought you out of the land of Egypt, out of the house of slavery.

"You shall have no gods except Me.

"You shall not make yourself a carved image of any likeness of anything
in heaven or on earth beneath or in the waters under the earth;
you shall not bow down to them or serve them.
For I, Jehovah your God, am a jealous God
and I punish the father's fault in the sons,
the grandsons, and the great-grandsons of those who hate Me;
but I show kindness to thousands of those who love Me and keep My commandments.

"You shall not utter the name of Jehovah your God to misuse it,
for Jehovah will not leave unpunished the man who utters His name to misuse it.

"Remember the sabbath day and keep it holy.
For six days you shall labor and do all your work,
but the seventh day is a sabbath for Jehovah your God.
You shall do no work that day,
neither you nor your son nor your daughter nor your servants,
men or women,
nor your animals nor the stranger who lives with you.
For in six days Jehovah made the heavens and the earth and the sea and all that these hold,
but on the seventh day He rested;
that is why Jehovah has blessed the sabbath day and made it sacred.

"Honor your father and your mother
so that you may have a long life in the land that Jehovah your God has given to you.

"You shall not kill.

"You shall not commit adultery.

"You shall not steal.

"You shall not bear false witness against your neighbor.

"You shall not covet your neighbor's house.
You shall not covet your neighbor's wife,
or his servant, man or woman, or his ox, or his donkey, or anything that is his."

—Exodus 20:1-17 (JB)

CONFESSION AND REPENTANCE

Lord, I Want to Be a Christian

And be renewed in the spirit of your mind. — Ephesians 4:23

I WANT TO BE A CHRISTIAN
American Folk Melody

American Folk Hymn

1 Lord, I want to be a Chris-tian in my heart, in my
2 *Lord, I want to be more lov-ing in my heart, in my*
3 Lord, I want to be more ho-ly in my heart, in my
4 *Lord, I want to be like Je-sus in my heart, in my*

1 heart; Lord, I want to be a Chris-tian in my
2 *heart; Lord, I want to be more lov-ing in my*
3 heart; Lord, I want to be more ho-ly in my
4 *heart; Lord, I want to be like Je-sus in my*

1 heart.   In my heart,   in my heart,
2 *heart.   In my heart,   in my heart,*
3 heart.   In my heart,   in my heart,
4 *heart.   In my heart,   in my heart,*

1 Lord, I want to be a Chris-tian in my heart.
2 *Lord, I want to be more lov-ing in my heart.*
3 Lord, I want to be more ho-ly in my heart.
4 *Lord, I want to be like Je-sus in my heart.*

CONFESSION AND REPENTANCE

Dear Lord and Father of Mankind

And after the earthquake, a fire; . . . And after the fire a still small voice.

REST

John Greenleaf Whittier — I Kings 19:12 Frederick C. Maker

1 Dear Lord and Fa - ther of man-kind, For - give our fool - ish ways!
2 *In sim - ple trust like theirs who heard, Be - side the Syr - ian sea,*
3 O sab - bath rest by Gal - i - lee! O calm of hills a - bove!
4 *Drop Thy still dews of qui - et - ness 'Til all our striv - ings cease;*
5 Breathe through the heat of our de - sire Thy cool - ness and Thy balm;

1 Re - clothe us in our right - ful mind; In pur - er lives Thy
2 *The gra - cious call - ing of the Lord, Let us, like them, with -*
3 Where Je - sus knelt to share with Thee The si - lence of e -
4 *Take from our souls the strain and stress, And let our or - dered*
5 Let sense be dumb, let flesh re - tire; Speak through the earth-quake,

1 serv - ice find, In deep - er rev - erence, praise.
2 *out a word, Rise up and fol - low Thee.*
3 ter - ni - ty, In - ter - pret - ed by love.
4 *lives con - fess The beau - ty of Thy peace.*
5 wind, and fire, O still, small voice of calm. A - men.

423 Prayers of Confession

(All in unison)

O Lord, that we dare confess anything at all to You before our brothers and sisters here in this church today is proof that we believe that You already know us as we are; that we believe that You are able to do something about it; and that we are willing to step from our worlds of pretense, fantasy and illusion into a kind of "facing-up-to-things-as-they-are" where You can touch us, and forgive us, and love us, and accept us and make us new. This is hard, Lord, but here we are. Amen.

(Silent, personal confession)

"And now, Lord, I confess specifically to . . ." *(Pray individually and silently)*

Minister only: Amen.

— Howard Childers,

Minister: This statement is completely reliable and should be universally accepted: Christ Jesus entered the world to rescue sinners.

He personally bore our sins in His body on the cross, so that we might be dead to sin and be alive to all that is good.

God's mercy never ends. I tell you, in the name of Jesus Christ, we are forgiven.

People: Amen.

—Kenneth Working

Cleanse Me

425

He is faithful and just . . . to cleanse us from all unrighteousness. — I John 1:9

Edwin Orr

MAORI
Maori Melody

1 Search me, O God, and know my heart to-day; Try me, O
2 *I praise Thee, Lord, for cleans-ing me from sin;* Ful-fill Thy
3 Lord, take my life, and make it whol-ly Thine; Fill my poor
4 *O Ho-ly Ghost, re-viv-al comes from Thee;* Send a re-

1 Sav-ior, know my thoughts, I pray. See if there be some wick-ed
2 *Word and make me pure with-in.* Fill me with fire, where once I
3 heart with Thy great love di-vine. Take all my will, my pas-sion,
4 *viv-al, start the work in me.* Thy Word de-clares Thou wilt sup-

1 way in me; Cleanse me from ev-ery sin, and set me free.
2 *burned with shame; Grant my de-sire to mag-ni-fy Thy name.*
3 self and pride; I now sur-ren-der, Lord—in me a-bide.
4 *ply our need; For bless-ing now, O Lord, I hum-bly plead.*

CONFESSION AND REPENTANCE

O God, may the measure of Your eternal love
          be the measure of Your mercy.
And may the measure of Your mercy
          be sufficient to blot out my great sins
          and cancel out the guilt of my wrongdoing.

I have failed, O Lord, and my failures weigh
          heavily upon my heart.
I cannot share them all with my brother lest
          they weigh too heavily upon him
          and may even threaten my relationship with him.
But You know what they are, O God,
          and how far I have fallen short of Your
          standards and expectations.

I am only human, Lord.
It was not by my choice that I was propelled
          into this fractured world.
The weaknesses that plague me are not all
          of my doing,
          nor can I handle them by my strength alone.

I know that nothing can be hidden from You.
I can only acknowledge my indictment
          and accept Your loving forgiveness.
Purge me of my guilt, O Lord;
          heal the hurts of those
          who have been afflicted by my failures.

Revive my flagging spirit, O God.
Restore to me the joy and assurance of a right
          relationship with You.
Reinstate me in Your purposes, and help me to
          avoid the snares and pitfalls along the way.

It is only then that my tongue will be set free
          to sing Your praises
          and my hands to perform the tasks You have
          set before me.
It is only then that I can relate deeply
          and meaningfully to my brother
          and communicate to him the message
          of reconciling love.

I bring You no oblation or sacrifice, my God,
          only a foolish and self-centered heart.
I do come to You with a sincere desire to be
          Your servant,
          to walk in Your course for my life,
          to receive Your love, and to channel such love
          to my fellowmen about me.

I thank You, God, that this is acceptable to You
          and that I will remain Your child forever.

                                          —Leslie Brandt

I Lay My Sins on Jesus

Behold the Lamb of God that taketh away the sins of the world.
— John 1:29

CRUCIFIX
Greek Melody

Horatius Bonar

1 I lay my sins on Je - sus, The spot - less Lamb of God;
2 *I lay my wants on Je - sus— All full - ness dwells in Him;*
3 I long to be like Je - sus— Pure, lov - ing, low - ly, mild;

1 He bears them all, and frees us From ev - ery guilt - y load.
2 *He heals all my dis - eas - es, He doth my soul re - deem.*
3 I long to be like Je - sus— The Fa - ther's ho - ly child.

1 I bring my guilt to Je - sus, To wash my crim - son stains
2 *I lay my griefs on Je - sus, My bur - dens and my cares;*
3 I long to be with Je - sus, A - mid the heaven - ly throng,

1 White in His blood most pre - cious, 'Til not a spot re - mains.
2 *He from them all re - leas - es, He all my sor - row shares.*
3 To sing with saints His prais - es, To learn the an - gels' song.

CONFESSION AND REPENTANCE

428 Come, Ye Sinners, Poor and Needy

He that cometh unto Me I will in no wise cast out. — John 6:37

BEACH SPRING
"The Sacred Harp"
Harmonized by A. Royce Eckhardt

Joseph Hart

1 Come, ye sin - ners, poor and need - y, Bruised and bro-ken by the fall;
2 *Let not con-science make you lin - ger, Nor of fit - ness fond-ly dream;*
3 Lo! th'in - car - nate God, as - cend - ed, Pleads the mer - it of His blood;

1 Je - sus read - y stands to save you, Full of par - doning love for all.
2 *All that He re - quires of sin - ners Is to turn and trust in Him.*
3 Ven-ture on Him, ven - ture whol - ly Let no oth - er trust in - trude;

1 He is a - ble, He is a - ble, He is will - ing, doubt no more;
2 *He will save you, He will save you, 'Tis the gos - pel's con-stant theme.*
3 None but Je - sus, none but Je - sus Can do help-less sin - ners good.

1 He is a - ble, He is a - ble, He is will - ing, doubt no more.
2 *He will save you, He will save you, 'Tis the gos - pel's con-stant theme.*
3 None but Je - sus, none but Je - sus Can do help - less sin -ners good.

INVITATION

Even So, Lord Jesus, Come

429

He which testifieth these things saith, Surely, I come quickly . . .

— Revelation 22:20

Gloria Gaither
William J. Gaither

LORD JESUS, COME
William J. Gaither

1 In a world of fear and tur-moil, In a race that seems so
2 *When my eyes shall span the riv-er, When I gaze in-to the*

1 hard to run; Lord, I need Thy rich in-fill-ing,
2 *vast un-known; May I say with calm as-sur-ance,*

1 E-ven so, Lord Je-sus, come. E-ven so, Lord Je-sus,
2 *"E-ven now, Lord Je-sus, come."*

come— My heart doth long for Thee; Though I've failed and be-

trayed Thy trust, E-ven so, Lord Je-sus, come.

INVITATION

430 Reach Out to Jesus

When she had heard of Jesus, came . . . and touched his garment.
— Mark 5:27

Ralph Carmichael

REACH OUT TO JESUS
Ralph Carmichael

1 Is your bur - den heav - y as you bear it all a - lone?
2 *Is the life you're liv - ing filled with sor - row and de - spair?*

1 Does the road you trav - el har - bor dan - ger yet un - known?
2 *Does the fu - ture press you with its wor - ry and its care?*

1 Are you grow-ing wea - ry in the strug - gle of it all? Je - sus will
2 *Are you tired and friend-less, have you al - most lost your way? Je - sus will*

1 help you when on His name you call.
2 *help you, just come to Him to - day.* He is al - ways there,

hear - ing ev - ery prayer, faith - ful and true; Walk - ing by our side,

INVITATION

in His love we hide all the day through. When you get dis-cour-aged just re-mem - ber what to do— Reach out to Je-sus, He's reach-ing out to you.

Prayer of Acceptance   **431**

Minister:

Here is a simple prayer
for those who have decided to receive Jesus:—

People:

Dear Father,
I believe that Jesus Christ is Your only begotten Son,
and that He became a human being,
shed His blood and died on the Cross
to clean away my sin that was separating me from You.
I believe that He rose from the dead,
physically,
to give me new life.

Lord Jesus, I invite You to come into my heart.
I accept You as my Savior and Lord.
I confess my sins, and ask You to wash them away.
I believe that You have come and are living in me right now.
Thank you, Jesus!
Amen.

—Dennis and Rita Bennett

432 Softly and Tenderly

Come unto Me, all ye who labor and are heavy laden . . . .
— Matthew 11:28

Will L. Thompson

THOMPSON
Will L. Thompson

1 Soft - ly and ten - der - ly Je - sus is call - ing, Call - ing for
2 *Why should we lin - ger when Je - sus is plead - ing, Plead-ing for*
3 O for the won - der - ful love He has prom - ised, Prom-ised for

1 you and for me; Pa - tient and lov - ing, He's wait - ing and watch-ing,
2 *you and for me? Why should we wait, then, and heed not His mer - cies?*
3 you and for me; Tho' we have sinned He has mer - cy and par - don,

1 Watch-ing for you and for me. Come home, come home,
2 *Mer - cies for you and for me?* Come home come home,
3 Par - don for you and for me.

Ye who are wea - ry, come home; Ear - nest - ly,

ten - der - ly, Je - sus is call - ing— Call - ing, "O sin - ner, come home!"

INVITATION

Let Jesus Come Into Your Heart

433

Behold, now is the accepted time . . . now is the day of salvation.
—II Corinthians 6:2

McCONNELSVILLE
Lelia N. Morris

Lelia N. Morris

1 If you are tired of the load of your sin, Let Je - sus come
2 If 'tis for pu - ri - ty now that you sigh, Let Je - sus come
3 If there's a tem - pest your voice can - not still, Let Je - sus come
4 If you would join the glad songs of the blest, Let Je - sus come

1 in - to your heart; If you de - sire a new life to be - gin,
2 in - to your heart; Foun-tains for cleans-ing are flow-ing near by,
3 in - to your heart; If there's a void this world nev - er can fill,
4 in - to your heart; If you would en - ter the man-sions of rest,

Let Je - sus come in - to your heart. Just now, your

doubt-ings give o'er; Just now, re - ject Him no more; Just now, throw

o - pen the door; Let Je - sus come in - to your heart.

INVITATION

434 Jesus Is Calling

Be of good comfort; He calleth thee.
—Matthew 10:49

John 11:28
Fanny J. Crosby

CALLING TODAY
George C. Stebbins

1 Je - sus is ten - der - ly call - ing you home— Call - ing to - day,
2 *Je - sus is call - ing the wea - ry to rest—* *Call - ing to - day,*
3 Je - sus is wait - ing, O come to Him now— Wait - ing to - day,
4 *Je - sus is plead - ing, O hear now His voice—* *Hear Him to - day,*

1 call - ing to - day; Why from the sun - shine of love will you roam
2 *call - ing to - day; Bring Him your bur - den and you shall be blest—*
3 wait - ing to - day; Come with your sins, at His feet low - ly bow—
4 *hear Him to - day; They who be - lieve on His name shall re - joice—*

1 Far - ther and far - ther a - way?
2 *He will not turn you a - way.*
3 Come, and no long - er de - lay.
4 *Quick - ly a - rise and a - way.*

Call - ing to - day,

Call - ing to - day,

Je - sus is

call - ing, Is ten - der - ly call - ing to - day.

INVITATION

The Savior Is Waiting

435

Today if ye hear His voice harden not your heart.
— Hebrews 3:7,8

Ralph Carmichael

CARMICHAEL
Ralph Carmichael

1 The Sav-ior is wait-ing to en-ter your heart, Why don't you
2 If you'll take one step toward the Sav-ior, my friend, You'll find His

1 let Him come in? There's noth-ing in this world to keep you a-
2 arms o-pen wide; Re-ceive Him, and all of your dark-ness will

1 part, What is your an-swer to Him?
2 end, With-in your heart He'll a-bide.

Time af-ter time He has

wait-ed be-fore, And now He is wait-ing a-gain To see

if you're will-ing to o-pen the door: O how He wants to come in.

INVITATION

436 For Those Tears I Died

But whosoever drinketh of the water that I shall give him shall never thirst.

— John 4:14

Marsha Stevens

CHILDREN OF THE DAY
Marsha Stevens

1 You said You'd come and share all my sor-rows,
2 *Your good-ness so great I can't un - der - stand,* And
3 Je - sus, I give you my heart and my soul, I

1 You said You'd be there for all my to - mor-rows; I came so
2 *dear Lord, I know that all this was planned; I know You're*
3 know that with - out God I'd nev - er be whole; Sav-ior, You

1 close to send-ing You a - way, But just like You prom-ised You
2 *here now, and al - ways will be, Your love loosed my chains and*
3 o - pened all the right doors, And I thank You, and praise You from

1 came there to stay — I just had to pray.
2 *in You I'm free — But Je - sus, why me?*
3 earth's hum-ble shores — Take me, I'm Yours.

INVITATION

And Je-sus said, "Come to the wa-ter, stand by my side; I know you are thirst-y, you won't be de-nied. I felt ev-ery tear-drop when in dark-ness you cried, And I strove to re-mind you that for those tears I died."

INVITATION

437

Almost Persuaded

I would to God that not only thou, . . . but all . . .
were both almost and altogether such as I am . . . — Acts 26:29

Philip P. Bliss

ALMOST
Philip P. Bliss

1 "Al-most per-suad-ed" now to be-lieve; "Al-most per-suad-ed"
2 *"Al-most per-suad-ed," come, come to-day;* *"Al-most per-suad-ed,"*
3 "Al-most per-suad-ed," har-vest is past! "Al-most per-suad-ed,"

1 Christ to re-ceive: Seems now some soul will say, "Go, Spir-it,
2 *turn not a-way:* *Je - sus in-vites you here,* *An - gels are*
3 doom comes at last! "Al - most" can-not a-vail, "Al-most" is

1 go Thy way; Some more con-ven-ient day On Thee I'll call."
2 *lin-gering near, Prayers rise from hearts so dear,* *O wan-der-er, come.*
3 but to fail! Sad, sad, that bit-ter wail, "Al-most," but lost!

438

Psalm 144

O God, it is difficult to understand how You can regard man with such high regard and
show him so much concern.

His years upon this earth are so few.

He is little more than a wisp of wind in the time and space of Your great universe.

You created him as the object of Your love—only to see him turn from You to play with his
foolish toys.

You tried to teach him to love his fellowman—only to see him express his fear and suspicion
and hate through cruel acts of violence and war.

You showered upon him Your abundant gifts—only to see him make them his ultimate
concern.

Still You continue to love him and seek incessantly to save him from destroying himself
and the world You have placed in his hands.

Even while he rejects You, You reach out to draw him back to Yourself.

Even while he suffers the painful consequences of his rank rebelliousness, You offer to him
Your healing and demonstrate Your desire to restore him to love and joy.

And when he finally turns to You, he finds You waiting for him, ready to forgive his sins
and to reunite him to Your life and purposes once more.

That man who returns to his God is happy indeed!

He will forever be the object of God's love and blessings.

—Leslie Brandt

Sweet Hour of Prayer

Now Peter and John went up together . . . at the hour of prayer.
— Acts 3:1

William W. Walford

SWEET HOUR
William B. Bradbury

1 Sweet hour of prayer, sweet hour of prayer, That calls me from a world of care,
2 *Sweet hour of prayer, sweet hour of prayer, Thy wings shall my pe - ti - tion bear*

1 And bids me at my Fa - ther's throne Make all my wants and wish-es known:
2 *To Him whose truth and faith - ful - ness En - gage the wait - ing soul to bless:*

1 In sea - sons of dis - tress and grief My soul has oft - en found re-lief,
2 *And since He bids me seek His face, Be - lieve His Word, and trust His grace,*

1 And oft es - caped the tempt-er's snare By thy re-turn, sweet hour of prayer.
2 *I'll cast on Him my ev - ery care, And wait for thee, sweet hour of prayer.*

PRAYER AND INTERCESSION

440 The Lord's Prayer

And when thou hast shut thy door, pray to the Father... — Matthew 6:6

MALOTTE
Albert Hay Malotte
Arranged by Fred Bock

Matthew 6:9-13

Our Fa - ther, which art in heav - en, hal - low - ed

be Thy name. Thy king-dom come,

Thy will be done on earth as it is in

heav - en. Give us this day our dai - ly

PRAYER AND INTERCESSION

bread,   and for - give   us   our debts   as   we   for-give our

debt-ors. And lead us not   in-to temp-ta-tion, but de - liv-er us   from

e - vil,   for Thine   is the King-dom   and the Pow-er   and the

Glo - ry, for - ev - er.   A - men.

441 ***Prayer***

More things are wrought by prayer
Than this world dreams of. Wherefore, let thy voice
Rise like a fountain for me night and day.
For what are men better than sheep or goats
That nourish a blind life within the brain,
If, knowing God, they lift not hands of prayer
Both for themselves and those who call them friends,
For so the whole round earth is every way
Bound by gold chains about the feet of God.

—Alfred Lord Tennyson

442 O Master, Let Me Walk with Thee

He that loseth his life for My sake shall find it. — Matthew 10:39

Washington Gladden

MARYTON
H. Percy Smith

1 O Mas-ter, let me walk with Thee In low-ly
2 *Help me the slow of heart to move By some clear,*
3 Teach me Thy pa-tience: still with Thee In clos-er,
4 *In hope that sends a shin-ing ray Far down the*

1 paths of serv-ice free; Tell me Thy se-cret—help me
2 *win-ning word of love; Teach me the way-ward feet to*
3 dear-er com-pa-ny, In work that keeps faith sweet and
4 *fu-ture's broad-ening way, In peace that on-ly Thou canst*

1 bear The strain of toil, the fret of care.
2 *stay, And guide them in the home-ward way.*
3 strong, In trust that tri-umphs o-ver wrong.
4 *give, With Thee, O Mas-ter, let me live.* A-men.

I Need Thee Every Hour

Your Father knoweth what things ye have need of before ye ask.
— Matthew 6:8

Annie S. Hawks
Robert Lowry

NEED
Robert Lowry

443

1 I need Thee ev - ery hour, Most gra - cious Lord;
2 *I need Thee ev - ery hour, Stay Thou near by;*
3 I need Thee ev - ery hour, In joy or pain;
4 *I need Thee ev - ery hour, Teach me Thy will,*

1 No ten - der voice like Thine Can peace af - ford.
2 *Temp - ta - tions lose their power When Thou art nigh.*
3 Come quick - ly, and a - bide, Or life is vain.
4 *And Thy rich prom - is - es In me ful - fill.*

I need Thee, O I need Thee; Ev - ery hour I need Thee!

O bless me now, my Sav - ior— I come to Thee. A - men.

PRAYER AND INTERCESSION

Speak, Lord, in the Stillness

E. May Grimes

And the Lord came, and stood, and called .... Then Samuel answered, Speak Lord, for thy servant heareth. — I Samuel 3:10

QUIETUDE
Harold Green

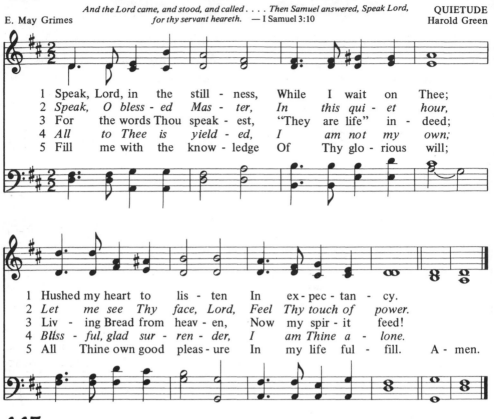

1 Speak, Lord, in the still - ness, While I wait on Thee;
2 *Speak, O bless - ed Mas - ter, In this qui - et hour,*
3 For the words Thou speak - est, "They are life" in - deed;
4 *All to Thee is yield - ed, I am not my own;*
5 Fill me with the know - ledge Of Thy glo - rious will;

1 Hushed my heart to lis - ten In ex - pec - tan - cy.
2 *Let me see Thy face, Lord, Feel Thy touch of power.*
3 Liv - ing Bread from heav - en, Now my spir - it feed!
4 *Bliss - ful, glad sur - ren - der, I am Thine a - lone.*
5 All Thine own good pleas - ure In my life ful - fill. A - men.

445   Colossians 1:11-20

We are praying, too, that you will be filled with His mighty, glorious strength so that you can keep going no matter what happens—always full of the joy of the Lord, and always thankful to the Father who has made us fit to share all the wonderful things that belong to those who live in the kingdom of light. For He has rescued us out of the darkness and gloom of Satan's kingdom and brought us into the kingdom of His dear Son, who bought our freedom with His blood and forgave us all our sins.

Christ is the exact likeness of the unseen God. He existed before God made anything at all, and, in fact, Christ Himself is the Creator who made everything in heaven and earth, the things we can see and the things we can't; the spirit world with its kings and kingdoms, its rulers and authorities; all were made by Christ for His own use and glory. He was before all else began and it is His power that holds everything together. He is the Head of the body made up of His people—that is, His church—which He began; and

He is the Leader of all those who arise from the dead, so that He is first in everything; for God wanted all of Himself to be in His Son.

It was through what His Son did that God cleared a path for everything to come to Him—all things in heaven and on earth—for Christ's death on the cross has made peace with God for all by His blood.

—(LB)

Prayer Is the Soul's Sincere Desire 446

. . . One of His disciples said unto Him, Lord, teach us to pray. . . . — Luke 11:1

SINCERE DESIRE

James Montgomery

William A. Schulthes

1 Prayer is the soul's sin - cere de - sire, Ut - tered or un - ex -
2 *Prayer is the Chris - tian's vi - tal breath, The Chris - tian's na - tive*
3 No prayer is made on earth a - lone, The Ho - ly Spir - it
4 *O Thou by whom we come to God, The Life, the Truth, the*

1 pressed; The mo - tion of a hid - den fire
2 *air, His watch-word at the gates of death:*
3 pleads; And Je - sus on th'e - ter - nal throne
4 *Way, The path of prayer Thy - self hast trod:*

1 That trem - bles in the breast.
2 *He en - ters heaven with prayer.*
3 For sin - ners in - ter - cedes.
4 *Lord, teach us how to pray.* A - men.

447 We Are Living, We Are Dwelling

Thou therefore endure hardness, as a good soldier of Jesus Christ. — II Timothy 2:3

Arthur C. Coxe

BLAENHAFREN
Welsh Melody

1 We are liv - ing, we are dwell - ing In a grand and awe-some time,
2 *Will ye play then? will ye dal - ly Far be-hind the bat-tle line?*
3 Sworn to yield, to wa - ver, nev - er, Con-se-crat - ed, born a - gain,

1 In an age on a - ges tell - ing— To be liv - ing is sub-lime.
2 *Up! it is Je - ho - vah's ral - ly— God's own arm hath need of thine.*
3 Sworn to be Christ's sol - diers ev - er, O for Christ at least be men!

1 Hark! the wak - ing up of na-tions, Hosts ad-vanc - ing to the fray;
2 *Worlds are charg - ing, heaven be-hold-ing—Thou hast but an hour to fight;*
3 O let all the soul with - in you For the truth's sake go a - broad!

1 Hark! what sound-eth is cre - a - tion's Groaning for the lat-ter day.
2 *Now, the bla-zoned cross un - fold - ing, On, right on-ward for the right!*
3 Strike! let ev - ery nerve and sin - ew Tell on a - ges, tell for God!

DEDICATION AND DEVOTION

In the year that King Uzziah died I saw the Lord sitting upon a throne, high and lifted up; and His train filled the temple. Above Him stood the seraphim; each had six wings: with two he covered his face, and with two he covered his feet, and with two he flew. And one called to another and said: "Holy, holy, holy is the Lord of hosts; the whole earth is full of His glory."

And the foundations of the thresholds shook at the voice of Him who called, and the house was filled with smoke. And I said: "Woe is me! For I am lost; for I am a man of unclean lips, and I dwell in the midst of a people of unclean lips; for my eyes have seen the King, the Lord of hosts!"

Then flew one of the seraphim to me, having in his hand a burning coal which he had taken with tongs from the altar. And he touched my mouth and said: "Behold, this has touched your lips; your guilt is taken away, and your sin is forgiven." And I heard the voice of the Lord saying, "Whom shall I send, and who will go for us?" Then I said, "Here am I! Send me."

—Isaiah 6:1-8 (RSV)

Psalms 122 & 123   449

How good it is to enter the sanctuary of the Lord!
   I know that God is not confined within man's four-walled creations,
   nor is He attached to altars and brass symbols.
      And yet, in the beauty and quietness of God's house
      I find His presence very real and fulfilling.

God is with me and about me
   even as I make my way through the concrete and steel jungles
      of the cold and unfriendly city.
He is present
   even behind the anonymous faces of the rushing crowds
     elbowing their way to their respective destinations.
   I find Him in the hearts and lives of His children
who infiltrate the urban masses and who are running His errands
     and fulfilling His purposes in the course of their daily duties.

I cannot outrun or evade my God.
   He goes before me and follows closely behind me.
  He will keep me and sustain me wherever I am.

     And yet I rejoice as I enter His sanctuary
and mingle with those who honor His name and seek His grace.
There, shielded from the screaming tensions and ear-splitting sounds of the city,
   in the company of those who love one another,
I happily open my heart to the loving mercy of God.

—Leslie Brandt

450 I Need Jesus

Bow down Thine ear, O Lord, and hear me; for I am poor and needy . . . — Psalm 86:1

George O. Webster

I NEED JESUS
Charles H. Gabriel

1 I need Je - sus: my need I now con - fess, No Friend like Him in
2 *I need Je - sus: I need a Friend like Him, A Friend to guide when*
3 I need Je - sus: I need Him to the end, No one like Him— He

1 times of deep dis - tress; I need Je - sus; the need I glad - ly
2 *paths of life are dim; I need Je - sus; when foes my soul as -*
3 is the sin - ners' Friend; I need Je - sus; no oth - er Friend will

1 own, Though some may bear their load a - lone, Yet I need Je - sus.
2 *sail, A - lone, I know I can but fail, So I need Je - sus.*
3 do, So con - stant, kind, so strong and true—Yes, I need Je - sus.

I need Je - sus; I need Je - sus. I need Je - sus ev - ery

day. Need Him in the sun - shine hour, need Him when the

DEDICATION AND DEVOTION

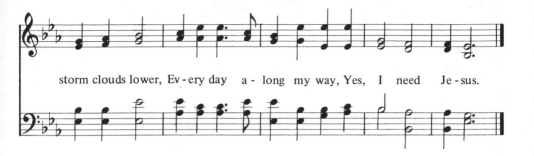

storm clouds lower, Ev-ery day a-long my way, Yes, I need Je-sus.

Jesus, Thou Joy of Loving Hearts 451

. . . Ye rejoice with joy unspeakable and full of glory. — I Peter 1:8

Attr. to Bernard of Clairvaux
Tr. by Ray Palmer

QUEBEC
Henry Baker

1 Je - sus, Thou joy of lov - ing hearts, Thou fount of
2 *Thy truth un - changed hath ev - er stood, Thou sav - est*
3 We taste Thee, O Thou liv - ing bread, And long to
4 *Our rest - less spir - its yearn for Thee, Wher-e'er our*
5 O Je - sus, ev - er with us stay, Make all our

1 life, Thou light of men, From the best bliss that
2 *those that on Thee call; To them that seek Thee*
3 feast up - on Thee still; We drink of Thee, the
4 *change - ful lot is cast: Glad when Thy gra - cious*
5 mo - ments calm and bright; Chase the dark night of

1 earth im - parts We turn un - filled to Thee a - gain.
2 *Thou art good, To them that find Thee all in all.*
3 foun-tain - head, And thirst our souls from Thee to fill.
4 *smile we see, Blest when our faith can hold Thee fast.*
5 sin a - way, Shed o'er the world Thy ho - ly light. A - men.

452 I Could Never Outlove the Lord

Give and it shall be given unto you; good measure, . . . and running over . . .

Gloria Gaither
William J. Gaither

— Luke 6:38

NEVER OUTLOVE
William J. Gaither

1 There've been times when giv-ing and lov-ing brought pain,
2 He showed us that on-ly through dy-ing we live,

1 And I prom-ised I would nev-er let it hap-pen a-gain;
2 And He gave when it seemed there was noth-ing to give;

1 But I found out that lov-ing was well worth the risk,
2 He loved when lov-ing brought heart-ache and loss,

1 And that e-ven in los-ing you win.
2 He for-gave from an old rug-ged cross.
I'm going to live the

way He wants me to live, I'm going to give un-til there's just

DEDICATION AND DEVOTION

no more to give; I'm going to love, love 'til there's just no more

love— I could nev-er, nev-er out-love the Lord.

I'll Live for Him

453

That they might live . . . unto Him who died for them. II Corinthians 5:15

Ralph E. Hudson

DUNBAR
C. R. Dunbar

1 My life, my love I give to Thee, Thou Lamb of God who died for me;
2 *I now be-lieve Thou dost re-ceive, For Thou hast died that I might live;*
3 O Thou who died on Cal-va-ry, To save my soul and make me free,
Ref. *I'll live for Him who died for me, How hap-py then my life shall be!*

D.C. Refrain

1 O may I ev-er faith-ful be, My Sav-ior and my God!
2 *And now hence-forth I'll trust in Thee, My Sav-ior and my God!*
3 I'll con-se-crate my life to Thee, My Sav-ior and my God!
Ref. *I'll live for Him who died for me, My Sav-ior and my God!*

454 Trust and Obey

To obey is better than sacrifice . . .
— I Samuel 15:22

James H. Sammis

TRUST AND OBEY
Daniel B. Towner

1 When we walk with the Lord In the light of His Word,
2 *Not a shad - ow can rise, Not a cloud in the skies,*
3 Not a bur - den we bear, Not a sor - row we share,
4 *Then in fel - low - ship sweet We will sit at His feet,*

1 What a glo - ry He sheds on our way! While we do His good will,
2 *But His smile quick - ly drives it a - way; Not a doubt or a fear,*
3 But our toil He doth rich - ly re - pay; Not a grief or a loss,
4 *Or we'll walk by His side in the way; What He says we will do,*

1 He a - bides with us still, And with all who will trust and o - bey.
2 *Not a sigh or a tear, Can re - main when we trust and o - bey.*
3 Not a frown or a cross, But is blest if we trust and o - bey.
4 *Where He sends we will go, Nev - er fear, on - ly trust and o - bey.*

Trust and o - bey, for there's no oth - er way

To be hap - py in Je - sus, but to trust and o - bey.

DEDICATION AND DEVOTION

I Am Thine, O Lord

. . . What would Thou have me to do?
— Acts 9:6

I AM THINE
William H. Doane

Fanny J. Crosby

1 I am Thine, O Lord— I have heard Thy voice, And it told Thy
2 *Con - se - crate me now to Thy serv - ice, Lord, By the power of*
3 O the pure de - light of a sin - gle hour That be - fore Thy
4 *There are depths of love that I can - not know 'Til I cross the*

1 love to me; But I long to rise in the arms of faith
2 *grace di - vine; Let my soul look up with a stead - fast hope*
3 throne I spend, When I kneel in prayer and with Thee, my God,
4 *nar - row sea; There are heights of joy that I may not reach*

1 And be clos - er drawn to Thee.
2 *And my will be lost in Thine.*
3 I com - mune as friend with friend.
4 *'Til I rest in peace with Thee.*

Draw me near - er, nearer, blessed Lord,

To the cross where Thou hast died; Draw me near - er, near - er,

near - er, bless - ed Lord, To Thy pre - cious, bleed - ing side. A - men.

DEDICATION AND DEVOTION

456 My Jesus, I Love Thee

We love Him because He first loved us.
— I John 4:19

William R. Featherston

GORDON
Adoniram J. Gordon

1 My Je-sus, I love Thee, I know Thou art mine; For Thee all the
2 *I love Thee be-cause Thou hast first lov-ed me, And pur-chased my*
3 I'll love Thee in life, I will love Thee in death, And praise Thee as
4 *In man-sions of glo-ry and end-less de-light, I'll ev-er a-*

1 fol- lies of sin I re-sign; My gra-cious Re-deem-er, my
2 *par- don on Cal-va-ry's tree; I love Thee for wear-ing the*
3 long as Thou lend-est me breath; And say when the death-dew lies
4 *dore Thee in heav-en so bright; I'll sing with the glit-ter-ing*

1 Sav- ior art Thou: If ev-er I loved Thee, my Je-sus, 'tis now.
2 *thorns on Thy brow: If ev-er I loved Thee, my Je-sus, 'tis now.*
3 cold on my brow: If ev-er I loved Thee, my Je-sus, 'tis now.
4 *crown on my brow: If ev-er I loved Thee, my Je-sus, 'tis now.* A-men.

457 Take Time to Be Holy

Because it is written: Be ye holy for I am holy. — I Peter 1:16

William D. Longstaff

LONGSTAFF
George C. Stebbins

1 Take time to be ho-ly, Speak oft-en with God; Find rest in Him
2 *Take time to be ho-ly, The world rush-es on; Much time spend in*
3 Take time to be ho-ly, Let Him be Thy guide, And run not be-

DEDICATION AND DEVOTION

1 al - ways, And feed on His Word. Make friends of God's chil - dren, Help
2 se - cret With Je - sus a - lone. By look - ing to Je - sus, Like
3 fore Him, What - ev - er be - tide. In joy or in sor - row, Still

1 those who are weak, For - get - ting in noth - ing His bless - ing to seek.
2 *Him Thou shalt be; Thy friends in thy con-duct His like-ness shall see.*
3 fol - low Thy Lord, And, look - ing to Je - sus, Still trust in His word.

Take My Life, and Let It Be Consecrated

458

Present your bodies a living sacrifice.
— Romans 12:1

HENDON

Frances R. Havergal

Henri A. César Malan

1 Take my life and let it be Con - se-crat-ed, Lord, to Thee; Take my hands and
2 *Take my feet and let them be Swift and beau-ti-ful for Thee; Take my voice and*
3 Take my lips and let them be Filled with mes-sa-ges for Thee; Take my sil - ver
4 *Take my love, my God, I pour At Thy feet its treas-ure store; Take my-self and*

1 let them move At the im-pulse of Thy love, At the im-pulse of Thy love.
2 *let me sing Al-ways, on-ly, for my King, Al-ways, on-ly for my King.*
3 and my gold, Not a mite would I with-hold, Not a mite would I with-hold.
4 *I will be Ev - er, on-ly, all for Thee, Ev-er, on-ly, all for Thee.*

459

All for Jesus

Ye are bought with a price; therefore glorify God in your body . . .

— I Corinthians 6:20

Mary D. James

CONSTANCY
Unknown

1 All for Je-sus, all for Je-sus! All my be-ing's ran-somed powers:
2 *Let my hands per-form His bid-ding, Let my feet run in His ways;*
3 Since my eyes were fixed on Je-sus, I've lost sight of all be-side,
4 *O what won-der! how a-maz-ing! Je-sus, glo-rious King of kings,*

1 All my thoughts and words and do-ings, All my days and all my hours:
2 *Let my eyes see Je-sus on-ly, Let my lips speak forth His praise:*
3 So en-rapt my spir-it's vi-sion, Look-ing at the Cru-ci-fied:
4 *Deigns to call me His be-lov-ed, Lets me rest be-neath His wings:*

1 All for Je-sus! all for Je-sus! All my days and all my hours;
2 *All for Je-sus! all for Je-sus! Let my lips speak forth His praise;*
3 All for Je-sus! all for Je-sus! Look-ing at the Cru-ci-fied;
4 *All for Je-sus! all for Je-sus! Rest-ing now be-neath His wings;*

1 All for Je-sus! all for Je-sus! All my days and all my hours.
2 *All for Je-sus! all for Je-sus! Let my lips speak forth His praise.*
3 All for Je-sus! all for Je-sus! Look-ing at the Cru-ci-fied.
4 *All for Je-sus! all for Je-sus! Rest-ing now be-neath His wings.*

DEDICATION AND DEVOTION

Prayer

Eternal Heavenly Father, we know that You are more eager to hear our prayers than we are to pray them, and more concerned to respond to them than we expect You to be. Forgive us now with that complete pardon that eases the troubled conscience and replaces its sharp torment with a permanent peace. This we ask that Your risen Son may be more alive among us. Amen.

—Bryan Jeffery Leech

Jesus, We Just Want to Thank You **461**

Gloria Gaither
William J. Gaither

Enter into His gates with thanksgiving and into His courts with praise.
— Psalm 100:4

THANK YOU
William J. Gaither

1 Je - sus, we just want to thank You, Je - sus, we just want to thank You, Je - sus, we just want to thank You, Thank You for be - ing so good.
2 *Je - sus, we just want to praise You, Je - sus, we just want to praise You, Je - sus, we just want to praise You, Praise You for be - ing so good.*
3 Je - sus, we just want to tell You, Je - sus, we just want to tell You, We love You for be - ing so good.
4 *Sav - ior, we just want to serve You, Sav - ior, we just want to serve You, Sav - ior, we just want to serve You, Serve You for be - ing so good.*
5 Je - sus, we know You are com - ing, Je - sus, we know You are com - ing, Take us to live in Your home.

DEDICATION AND DEVOTION

Living for Jesus

Present your bodies a living sacrifice, holy, . . . acceptable . . .
— Romans 12:1

Thomas O. Chisholm

LIVING
C. Harold Lowden

1 Liv-ing for Je-sus a life that is true, Striv-ing to please Him in
2 *Liv-ing for Je-sus who died in my place, Bear-ing on Cal-vary my*
3 Liv-ing for Je-sus wher-ev-er I am, Do-ing each du-ty in
4 *Liv-ing for Je-sus through earth's lit-tle while, My dear-est treas-ure, the*

1 all that I do; Yield-ing al - le-giance, glad-heart-ed and free,
2 sin and dis - grace; Such love con-strains me to an-swer His call,
3 His ho - ly name; Will - ing to suf-fer af - flic-tion and loss,
4 *light of His smile; Seek-ing the lost ones He died to re - deem,*

1 This is the path-way of bless-ing for me.
2 *Fol - low His lead-ing and give Him my all.*
3 Tak - ing each trial as a part of my cross.
4 *Bring-ing the wea-ry to find rest in Him.*

O Je - sus, Lord and

Sav-ior, I give my-self to Thee, For Thou, in Thy a - tone-ment, Didst

give Thy-self for me; I own no oth-er Mas-ter, My heart shall be Thy

DEDICATION AND DEVOTION

throne; My life I give, hence-forth to live, O Christ, for Thee a - lone.

The Example of Jesus Christ   **463**

With so many witnesses in a great cloud on every side of us, we too, then, should throw off everything that hinders us, especially the sin that clings so easily, and keep running steadily in the race we have started. Let us not lose sight of Jesus, who leads us in our faith and brings it to perfection: for the sake of the joy which was still in the future, He endured the cross, disregarding the shamefulness of it, and *from now on has taken His place at the right* of God's throne. Think of the way He stood such opposition from sinners and then you will not give up for want of courage. In the fight against sin, you have not yet had to keep fighting to the point of death.

Have you forgotten that encouraging text in which you are addressed as sons? *My son, when the Lord corrects you, do not treat it lightly; but do not get discouraged when He reprimands you. For the Lord trains the ones that He loves and He punishes all those that He acknowledges as His sons.* Suffering is part of your *training;* God is treating you as His *sons.* Has there ever been any *son* whose father did not *train* him? If you were not getting this training, as all of you are, then you would not be *sons* but bastards. Besides, we have all had our human fathers who punished us, and we respected them for it; we ought to be even more willing to submit ourselves to our spiritual Father, to be given life. Our human fathers were thinking of this short life when they punished us, and could only do what they thought best; but He does it all for our own good, so that we may share His own holiness. Of course, any punishment is most painful at the time, and far from pleasant; but later, in those on whom it has been used, it bears fruit in peace and goodness. So *hold up your limp arms and steady your trembling knees* and *smooth out the path you tread;* then the injured limb will not be wrenched, it will grow strong again.

—Hebrews 12:1-13 (JB)

464   Liberation from Materialism

· Forbid it, Lord, that our roots become too firmly attached to this earth, that we should fall in love with things.

Help us to understand that the pilgrimage of this life is but an introduction, a preface, a training school for what is to come.

Then shall we see all of life in its true perspective. Then shall we not fall in love with the things of time, but come to love the things that endure. Then shall we be saved from the tyranny of possessions which we have no leisure to enjoy, of property whose care becomes a burden. Give us, we pray, the courage to simplify our lives.

So may we be mature in our faith, childlike but never childish, humble but never cringing, understanding but never conceited.

So help us, O God, to live and not merely to exist, that we may have joy in our work. In Thy name, who alone can give us moderation and balance and zest for living, we pray.

Amen.

—Peter Marshall

465   Jesus, the Very Thought of Thee

Latin: 12th Century
Tr. by Edward Caswall

For me to live is Christ, and to die is gain. — Philippians 1:21

ST. AGNES
John B. Dykes

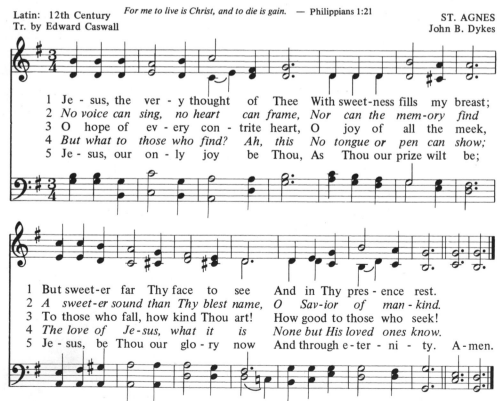

1 Je - sus, the ver - y thought of Thee With sweet-ness fills my breast;
2 *No voice can sing, no heart can frame, Nor can the mem-ory find*
3 O hope of ev - ery con - trite heart, O joy of all the meek,
4 *But what to those who find? Ah, this No tongue or pen can show;*
5 Je - sus, our on - ly joy be Thou, As Thou our prize wilt be;

1 But sweet-er far Thy face to see And in Thy pres - ence rest.
2 *A sweet-er sound than Thy blest name, O Sav-ior of man - kind.*
3 To those who fall, how kind Thou art! How good to those who seek!
4 *The love of Je-sus, what it is None but His loved ones know.*
5 Je - sus, be Thou our glo - ry now And through e - ter - ni - ty. A - men.

What a Friend We Have in Jesus

466

. . . In whom we have boldness and access with confidence by faith in Him.
— Ephesians 3:12

Joseph M. Scriven

ERIE
Charles C. Converse

1 What a friend we have in Je - sus, All our sins and griefs to bear!
2 *Have we tri - als and temp - ta - tions? Is there trou-ble an - y - where?*
3 Are we weak and heav - y - lad - en, Cum-bered with a load of care?

1 What a priv - i - lege to car - ry Ev - ery-thing to God in prayer!
2 *We should nev - er be dis - cour-aged— Take it to the Lord in prayer!*
3 Pre - cious Sav - ior, still our ref - uge— Take it to the Lord in prayer!

1 O what peace we oft - en for - feit, O what need-less pain we bear,
2 *Can we find a friend so faith - ful, Who will all our sor - rows share?*
3 Do thy friends de - spise, for - sake thee? Take it to the Lord in prayer!

1 All be - cause we do not car - ry Ev - ery-thing to God in prayer.
2 *Je - sus knows our ev - ery weak-ness— Take it to the Lord in prayer!*
3 In His arms He'll take and shield thee—Thou wilt find a sol - ace there.

DEDICATION AND DEVOTION

467 Take Thou Our Minds, Dear Lord

Let this mind be in you which is also in Christ Jesus.

— Philippians 2:5

William Hiram Foulkes

HALL
Calvin W. Laufer

1 Take Thou our minds, dear Lord, we hum - bly pray;
2 *Take Thou our hearts, O Christ — they are Thine own;*
3 Take Thou our wills, dear God! hold Thou full sway;
4 *Take Thou our - selves, O Lord, heart, mind, and will;*

1 Give us the mind of Christ through - out each day,
2 *Come Thou with - in our souls and claim Thy throne,*
3 Have in our in - most souls Thy per - fect way,
4 *Through our sur - ren - dered souls Thy plans ful - fill.*

1 Teach us to know the truth that sets us free;
2 *Help us to shed a - broad Thy gen - erous love;*
3 Guard Thou each sa - cred hour from self - ish ease;
4 *We yield our - selves to Thee— time, tal - ents, all;*

1 Grant us in all our thoughts to hon - or Thee.
2 *Use us to make the earth like heaven a - bove.*
3 Guide Thou our or - dered lives as Thou dost please.
4 *We hear, and hence - forth heed, Thy sov - ereign call.* A - men.

DEDICATION AND DEVOTION

Be Thou My Vision

468

Ancient Irish
Tr. by Mary Byrne
Versified by Eleanor Hull

Leave us not I pray thee . . . . and thou mayest be to us instead of eyes.
— Numbers 10:31

SLANE
Traditional Irish Melody
Harmonization by David Evans

Unison

1 Be Thou my Vi - sion, O Lord of my heart;
2 *Be Thou my Wis - dom, and Thou my true Word;*
3 Rich - es I heed not, nor man's emp - ty praise,
4 *High King of heav - en, my vic - to - ry won,*

1 Nought be all else to me, save that Thou art—
2 *I ev - er with Thee and Thou with me, Lord;*
3 Thou mine in - her - it - ance, now and al - ways:
4 *May I reach heav - en's joys, O bright heaven's Sun!*

1 Thou my best thought, by day or by night,
2 *Thou my great Fa - ther, I Thy true son;*
3 Thou and Thou on - ly, first in my heart,
4 *Heart of my own heart, what - ev - er be - fall,*

1 Wak - ing or sleep - ing, Thy pres - ence my light.
2 *Thou in me dwell - ing, and I with Thee one.*
3 High King of heav - en, my Treas - ure Thou art.
4 *Still be my Vi - sion, O Rul - er of all.* A - men.

Words used by permission of the Editor's Literary Estate, and Chatto & Windus, Ltd. Harmony copyright; from "The Church Hymnary," Revised Edition; used by permission of Oxford University Press.

ASPIRATION

469 Higher Ground

Lead me to the Rock that is higher than I . . . .
— Psalm 61:2

Johnson Oatman, Jr.

HIGHER GROUND
Charles H. Gabriel

1 I'm press-ing on the up-ward way, New heights I'm gain - ing ev - ery
2 *My heart has no de - sire to stay Where doubts a - rise and fears dis-*
3 I want to live a - bove the world, Though Sa-tan's darts at me are
4 *I want to scale the ut-most height And catch a gleam of glo - ry*

1 day; Still pray - ing as I'm on - ward bound, "Lord, plant my
2 *may; Though some may dwell where these a - bound, My prayer, my*
3 hurled; For faith has caught the joy - ful sound, The song of
4 *bright; But still I'll pray, 'til heaven I've found "Lord, lead me*

1 feet on high - er ground."
2 *aim is high - er ground.*
3 saints on high - er ground.
4 *on to high - er ground."*

Lord, lift me up and let me

stand By faith on heav - en's ta - ble - land, A high - er

plane than I have found: Lord, plant my feet on high - er ground.

ASPIRATION

"Are Ye Able", Said the Master

Are ye able to drink of the cup that I shall drink of. . . .
— Matthew 20:20

Earl Marlatt

BEACON HILL
Harry S. Mason

1 "Are ye a-ble," said the Mas-ter, "To be cru-ci-fied with Me?"
2 *"Are ye a-ble" to re-mem-ber, When a thief lifts up his eyes,*
3 "Are ye a-ble?" still the Mas-ter Whis-pers down e-ter-ni-ty,

1 "Yea," the stur-dy dream-ers an-swered, "To the death we fol-low Thee:"
2 *That his par-doned soul is wor-thy Of a place in par-a-dise?*
3 And he-ro-ic spir-its an-swer, Now, as then in Gal-i-lee:

"Lord, we are a-ble"— our spir-its are Thine; Re-mold them—

make us like Thee, di-vine. Thy guid-ing ra-diance a-

bove us shall be A bea-con to God, to love and loy-al-ty.

ASPIRATION

471 The Teacher

Lord, who am I to teach the way
To little children day by day,
So prone myself to go astray?

I teach them *knowledge,* but I know
How faint they flicker, and how low
The candles of my knowledge glow.

I teach them *power* to will and do,
But only now to learn anew
My own great weakness through and through.

I teach them *love* for all mankind
And all God's creatures, but I find
My love comes lagging far behind.

Lord, if their guide I still must be,
O let the little children see
The teacher leaning hard on Thee.

—Leslie Pinckney Hill

472 Teach Me Your Way, O Lord

Show me Thy way O Lord; teach me Thy way.
— Psalm 25:4, 5

B. Mansell Ramsey

CAMACHA
B. Mansell Ramsey

1 Teach me Your way, O Lord, Teach me Your way! Your guid-ing
2 *When I am sad at heart, Teach me Your way! When earth-ly*
3 When doubts and fears a-rise, Teach me Your way! When storm-clouds
4 *Long as my life shall last, Teach me Your way! Wher-e'er my*

1 grace af-ford—Teach me Your way! Help me to walk a-right, More by faith,
2 *joys de-part, Teach me Your way! In hours of lone-li-ness, In times of*
3 fill the skies, Teach me Your way! Shine thru the wind and rain, Thru sor-row,
4 *lot be cast, Teach me Your way! Un-til the race is run, Un-til the*

1 less by sight; Lead me with heaven-ly light— Teach me Your way!
2 *dire dis-tress, In fail-ure or suc-cess, Teach me Your way!*
3 grief and pain; Make now my path-way plain—Teach me Your way!
4 *jour-ney's done, Un-til the crown is won, Teach me Your way!* A-men.

Used by permission of George Taylor, The Cross Printing Works, Stainland, Halifax.
ASPIRATION

Make Me a Blessing

473

And I will make them and the places round about my hill a blessing....
— Ezekiel 34:26

Ira B. Wilson

SCHULER
George S. Schuler

1 Out in the high-ways and by-ways of life, Man-y are wea-ry and sad;
2 *Tell the sweet sto-ry of Christ and His love, Tell of His power to for - give;*
3 Give as 'twas giv-en to you in your need, Love as the Mas-ter loved you;

1 Car - ry the sun-shine where dark-ness is rife, Mak - ing the sor-row-ing glad.
2 *Oth-ers will trust Him if on - ly you prove True, ev - ery mo-ment you live.*
3 Be to the help-less a help - er in-deed, Un - to your mis-sion be true.

Make me a bless - ing, Make me a bless - ing — Out of my

life May Je - sus shine; Make me a bless - ing, O Sav - ior,

I pray, Make me a bless - ing to some - one to - day.

ASPIRATION

474 Eternal Life

The things which are not seen are eternal.

— II Corinthians 4:18

ETERNAL LIFE
Olive Dungan
Arranged by Fred Bock

St. Francis of Assisi

Lord, make me an in-stru-ment of Thy peace:

Where there is ha-tred, let me sow love; Where there is in-ju-ry, par-don;

Where there is doubt, faith; Where there is de-spair, hope;

Where there is dark-ness, light; Where there is sad-ness, joy.

DISCIPLESHIP

O Di-vine Mas - ter, grant that I may not so much seek

To be con-soled as to con - sole, To be un-der-stood as to un-der-stand,

To be loved as to love; For it is in giv - ing that we re -

ceive; It is in par-doning that we are par-doned; It

is in dy - ing that we are born to e - ter - nal life!

475

A Prayer

Lord Jesus Christ,

because You looked ahead to a future joy,

You were able to stand the agony of Your disgraceful death,

and as a result of this You now stand in the position of supreme and exalted rank.

Help me to follow You in this.

To look beyond my hardships as You did Yours.

To see in them a way through to maturity and ultimately to eternal reward.

Give me a determination like Yours to battle temptation and to give sin a wide berth.

Keep me from losing heart when the tension and pull away from You are the greatest.

Teach me how to learn from my sufferings

lest they make me embittered.

Lord, it really comforts me to know that in praying to You

I'm talking to the only one who can completely identify with me

where I am right now. Amen.

—Bryan Jeffery Leech

476 More Love to Thee, O Christ

And this I pray, that your love may abound more and more . . . . — Philippians 1:9

MORE LOVE TO THEE

Elizabeth P. Prentiss

William H. Doane

1 More love to Thee, O Christ, More love to Thee! Hear Thou the
2 *Once earth-ly joy I craved, Sought peace and rest; Now Thee a-*
3 Then shall my ev-ery breath Sing out Your praise; This be the

1 prayer I make On bend-ed knee; This is my ear-nest plea:
2 *lone I seek, Give what is best; This all my prayer shall be:*
3 on - ly song My heart shall raise; This still my prayer shall be:

More love, O Christ, to Thee, More love to Thee, More love to Thee! A-men.

ASPIRATION

More About Jesus Would I Know

477

But grow in grace in the knowledge of our Lord Jesus Christ
– 11 Peter 3:18

Eliza E Hewitt

SWENEY
John R. Sweney

1 More a-bout Je - sus would I know, More of His grace to oth - ers show;
2 *More a-bout Je - sus let me learn, More of His ho - ly will dis-cern;*
3 More a-bout Je - sus; in His word, Hold-ing com-mun-ion with my Lord;
4 *More a-bout Je - sus on His throne, Rich - es in glo - ry all His own;*

1 More of His sav - ing full - ness see, More of His love who died for me.
2 *Spir - it of God, my teach - er be, Show-ing the things of Christ to me.*
3 Hear - ing His voice in ev - ery line, Mak - ing each faith-ful say - ing mine.
4 *More of His king-dom's sure in-crease; More of His com - ing, Prince of Peace.*

More, more, a - bout Je - sus, More, more, a - bout Je - sus;

More of His sav - ing full - ness see, More of His love who died for me.

ASPIRATION

Blessed is the man who walks not in the counsel of the wicked,
> *nor stands in the way of sinners, nor sits in the seat of scoffers;*
but his delight is in the law of the Lord,
> *and on His law he meditates day and night.*
He is like a tree planted by streams of water,
> *that yields its fruit in its season,*
and its leaf does not wither.
> *In all that he does, he prospers.*

The wicked are not so,
> *but are like chaff which the wind drives away.*
Therefore the wicked will not stand in the judgment,
> *nor sinners in the congregation of the righteous;*
for the Lord knows the way of the righteous,
> *but the way of the wicked will perish.*

—(RSV)

479   Fill Thou My Life, O Lord My God

Now the Lord of hope fill you with all joy and peace. . . .
— Romans 15:13

Horatius Bonar

RICHMOND
Thomas Haweis

1 Fill Thou my life, O Lord my God, In ev-ery part with praise, That my whole be-ing may pro-claim Thy be-ing and Thy ways.
2 *Not for the lip of praise a-lone, Nor for the prais-ing heart— I ask Thee for a life made up Of praise in ev-ery part:*
3 Praise in the com-mon things of life, Its go-ings out and in; Praise in each du-ty and each deed, How-ev-er small and mean.
4 *Fill ev-ery part of me with praise: Let all my be-ing speak Of Thee and of Thy love, O Lord, Poor though I be, and weak.*
5 So shalt Thou, Lord, from e-ven me Re-ceive the glo-ry due; And so shall I be-gin on earth The song for-ev-er new.
6 *So shall no part of day or night From sa-cred-ness be free; But all my life, in ev-ery step, Be fel-low-ship with Thee. A-men.*

ASPIRATION

O To Be Like Thee

480

And every man that hath this hope in him purifieth himself, even as He is pure. —I John 3:3

CHRISTLIKE

Thomas O. Chisholm

William J. Kirkpatrick

1 O to be like Thee! Bless-ed Re-deem-er, This is my con-stant
2 *O to be like Thee! Full of com-pas-sion, Lov-ing, for-giv-ing,*
3 O to be like Thee! Low-ly in spir-it, Ho-ly and harm-less,
4 *O to be like Thee! Lord, I am com-ing, Now to re-ceive th'a-*
5 O to be like Thee! While I am plead-ing, Pour out Thy Spir-it,

1 long-ing and prayer; Glad-ly I'll for-feit all of earth's treas-ures,
2 *ten-der and kind, Help-ing the help-less, cheer-ing the faint-ing,*
3 pa-tient and brave; Meek-ly en-dur-ing cru-el re-proach-es,
4 *noint-ing di-vine; All that I am and have I am bring-ing.*
5 fill with Thy love; Make me a tem-ple deemed to re-ceive You:

1 Je-sus, Thy per-fect like-ness to wear.
2 *Seek-ing the wan-dering sin-ner to find!*
3 Will-ing to suf-fer oth-ers to save.
4 *Lord, from this mo-ment all shall be Thine.*
5 Fit me for life and heav-en a-bove.

O to be like Thee!

O to be like Thee, Bless-ed Re-deem-er, pure as Thou art! Come in Thy

sweet-ness, come in Thy full-ness; Stamp Thine own im-age deep on my heart.

ASPIRATION

481 Fill My Cup, Lord

I will take the cup of my salvation. . . . —Psalm 116:13

Richard Blanchard

FILL MY CUP
Richard Blanchard

1 Like the wom-an at the well I was seek-ing For things that
2 *There are mil-lions in this world who are crav-ing The pleas-ure*
3 So, my broth-er, if the things this world gave you Leave hun-gers

1 could not sat-is - fy; And then I heard my Sav-ior speak-ing: "Draw
2 *earth-ly things af - ford; But none can match the won-drous treas-ure*
3 that won't pass a - way, My bless - ed Lord will come and save you,

1 from My well that nev-er shall run dry."
2 *That I find in Je - sus Christ my Lord.* Fill my cup, Lord, I lift it
3 If you kneel to Him and hum-bly pray:

up, Lord! Come and quench this thirst-ing of my soul; Bread of heav-en,

feed me 'til I want no more—Fill my cup, fili it up and make me whole!

ASPIRATION

Deliver me, O God, from the enemies of my soul.
I am no longer afraid of men who stand in my way, even of those who obstruct Your pur-
poses and who deceive their fellowmen with their arrogant and clever cliches.
They anger me, but they do not frighten me.
My pain and confusion come by way of my own weaknesses and faithlessness.

I strive for success and am fractured by failure.
I reach for ecstacy and am clobbered with depression.
I wait for guidance and Your heavens are gray with silence.
I ask for infilling and am confronted with emptiness.
I seek opportunities and run into stone walls.

I overcome these pernicious demons in the morning—only to face them again when day
turns into night.
They refuse to die, these persistent devils.
They plague my days and haunt my nights and rob me of the peace and joy of God-moti-
vated living.

And yet, O Lord, You have surrounded my life like a great fortress.
There is nothing that can touch me save by Your loving permission.

—Leslie Brandt

May the Mind of Christ, My Savior　483

Let this mind be in you which is also in Christ Jesus . . . . — Philippians 2:5　　ST. LEONARDS

Kate B. Wilkinson　　　　　　　　　　　　　　　　　　　　　Cyril Barham-Gould

1 May the mind of Christ, my Sav-ior, Live in me from day to day,
2 *May the word of God dwell rich-ly In my heart from hour to hour,*
3 May the peace of God, my Fa-ther, Rule my life in ev-ery-thing,
4 *May the love of Je-sus fill me, As the wa-ters fill the sea;*
5 May I run the race be-fore me, Strong and brave to face the foe,
6 *May His beau-ty rest up-on me As I seek the lost to win,*

1 By His love and power con-trol-ling All I do and say.
2 *So that all may see I tri-umph On-ly through His power.*
3 That I may be calm to com-fort Sick and sor-row-ing.
4 *Him ex-alt-ing, self a-bas-ing— This is vic-to-ry.*
5 Look-ing on-ly un-to Je-sus As I on-ward go.
6 *And may they for-get the chan-nel, See-ing on-ly Him.*

ASPIRATION

484

Real Prayer

The prayer preceding all prayers is,
"May it be the real I who speaks.
May it be the real Thou
that I speak to."

—C. S. Lewis

485

Nearer, Still Nearer

Order my steps in Thy word and let not any iniquity have dominion over me. — Psalm 119:133

MORRIS

Lelia N. Morris

Lelia N. Morris

1 Near - er, still near - er, close to Thy heart, Draw me, my
2 *Near - er, still near - er, noth - ing I bring, Naught as an*
3 Near - er, still near - er, while life shall last, 'Til safe in

1 Sav - ior, so pre - cious Thou art; Fold me, O fold me
2 *of - fering to Je - sus my King; On - ly my sin - ful,*
3 glo - ry my an - chor is cast; Through end - less a - ges,

1 close to Thy breast, Shel - ter me safe in that "Ha - ven of
2 *now con - trite heart, Grant me the cleans - ing Thy blood doth im -*
3 ev - er to be, Near - er, my Sav - ior, still near - er to

1 Rest," Shel - ter me safe in that "Ha - ven of Rest."
2 *part, Grant me the cleans - ing Thy blood doth im - part.*
3 Thee, Near - er, my Sav - ior, still near - er to Thee. A - men.

ASPIRATION

Open My Eyes That I May See

486

Many prophets and kings have desired to see those things which ye see. — Luke 10:23-24

Clara H. Scott
Jeff Redd, alt.

OPEN MY EYES
Clara H. Scott

1 O-pen my eyes, that I may see Glimp-ses of truth You have for me;
2 *O-pen my ears, that I may hear Voic - es of truth so sharp and clear;*
3 O-pen my mouth, let me de-clare Words of as - sur - ance ev-ery-where;

1 Place in my hands the won-der-ful key That shall un-lock and set me free.
2 *And while the mes-sage sounds in my ear, Ev - ery-thing else will dis - ap-pear.*
3 O - pen my heart, and let me pre-pare Your lov-ing kind-ness-es to share.

Si-lent-ly now I wait for You, Read-y, my God, Your will to do;

1 O-pen my eyes, il - lu - mine me, Spir - it di - vine!
2 *O-pen my ears, il - lu - mine me, Spir - it di - vine!*
3 O-pen my heart, il - lu - mine me, Spir - it di - vine! A-men.

ASPIRATION

487 Prayer of Dedication

Lord, call us into the church.
Call us in often,
    and teach us the old words and old songs
    with their new meanings.
Lord, give us new words
    for the words we wear out.
Give us new songs
    for those that have lost their spirit.
Give us new reasons for coming in
    and for going out,
    into our streets and to our homes.
As the house of the Lord once moved
    like a tent through the wilderness,
    so keep our churches from being rigid.
Make our congregation alive and free.
Give us ideas we never had before,
    so that alleluia and gloria and amen
    are like the experiences we know in daily living.
Alleluia! O Lord, be praised!
In worship and in work, be praised! Amen.

—Herbert Brokering

488 We Are Climbing Jacob's Ladder

And behold, the Lord stood above it,
and said, I am the Lord, Thy God. . . . — Genesis 28:13

Traditional Spiritual

JACOB'S LADDER
Traditional Spiritual

1 We are climb-ing Ja-cob's lad-der. We are climb-ing Ja-cob's
2 Ev-ery round goes high-er, high-er. Ev-ery round goes high-er,
3 If you love Him, why not serve Him? If you love Him, why not
4 We are climb-ing high-er, high-er. We are climb-ing high-er,

1 lad-der. We are climb-ing Ja-cob's lad-der, Sol-diers of the cross.
2 high-er. Ev-ery round goes high-er, high-er, Sol-diers of the cross.
3 serve Him? If you love Him, why not serve Him? Sol-diers of the cross.
4 high-er. We are climb-ing high-er, high-er, Sol-diers of the cross.

ASPIRATION

In Heavenly Love Abiding

489

Abide in Me, and I in you, as the branch cannot bear fruit unless it abide in the vine . . .
— John 15:4

SEASONS

Anna L. Waring

Felix Mendelssohn

1 In heaven - ly love a - bid - ing, No change my heart shall fear;
2 *Wher - ev - er He may guide me, No fear shall turn me back;*
3 Green pas - tures are be - fore me, Which yet I have not seen;

1 And safe is such con - fid - ing, For noth - ing chan - ges here.
2 *My Shep-herd is be - side me, And noth - ing shall I lack.*
3 Bright skies will soon be o'er me, Where dark - est clouds have been.

1 The storm may roar with - out me, My heart may low be laid,
2 *His wis - dom ev - er wak - eth, His sight is nev - er dim;*
3 My hope I can - not meas - ure, My path to life is free;

1 But God is round a - bout me, And can I be dis - mayed?
2 *He knows the way He tak - eth, And I will walk with Him.*
3 My Sav - ior is my treas - ure, And He will walk with me.

INNER PEACE

I am so depressed tonight, O God.
I feel as if I am the sole target of an enemy barrage—that all the demons of hell are bent
upon damning my soul for eternity.

I remember Your precious promises, but I do not witness their fulfillment.
I talk to people about Your love, and they drown my zeal with scorn.
I step forth to carry out Your will, but I feel no sense of accomplishment.
I mouth words, wave my arms, and beat the air with fruitless endeavor.
Then I fall like a wounded warrior, bone-weary, defeated, and lonely.
And I wonder if You are truly my God, and if I am really Your child.

Consume, O God, these demons that depress, these enemies that plague my soul.
May the whirlwind of Your Spirit sweep them out of my life forever.
May I awaken in the morning with a heart full of joy, and with the strength and the courage
to walk straight and secure in the dangerous and difficult paths before me.

—Leslie Brandt

491 Peace, Perfect Peace

My peace I give unto you: not as the world giveth . . . – John 14:27

Edward H. Bickersteth

PAX TECUM
George T. Caldbeck

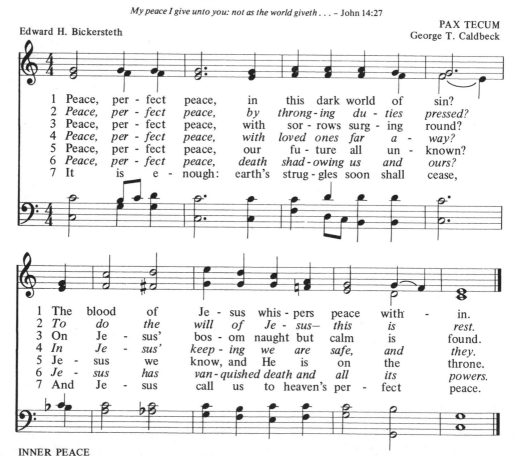

1 Peace, per-fect peace, in this dark world of sin?
2 *Peace, per-fect peace, by throng-ing du-ties pressed?*
3 Peace, per-fect peace, with sor-rows surg-ing round?
4 *Peace, per-fect peace, with loved ones far a-way?*
5 Peace, per-fect peace, our fu-ture all un-known?
6 *Peace, per-fect peace, death shad-ow-ing us and ours?*
7 It is e-nough: earth's strug-gles soon shall cease,

1 The blood of Je-sus whis-pers peace with-in.
2 *To do the will of Je-sus— this is rest.*
3 On Je-sus' bos-om naught but calm is found.
4 *In Je-sus' keep-ing we are safe, and they.*
5 Je-sus we know, and He is on the throne.
6 *Je-sus has van-quished death and all its powers.*
7 And Je-sus call us to heaven's per-fect peace.

INNER PEACE

Have no anxiety about anything, but in everything by prayer and supplication with thanksgiving let your requests be made known to God. And the peace of God, which passes all understanding, will keep your hearts and your minds in Christ Jesus.

–Philippians 4:6, 7 (RSV)

Thou Wilt Keep Him in Perfect Peace   **493**

. . . because he trusteth in Thee.

— Isaiah 26:3

Isaiah 26:3
Vivian Kretz

PERFECT PEACE
Vivian Kretz

"Thou wilt keep him in   per - fect peace whose mind is stayed on   Thee."

When the sha-dows come and dark-ness falls, He   giv - eth in - ward peace. O He

is   the on - ly per-fect rest - ing place, He   giv - eth per-fect   peace!

"Thou   wilt keep him in   per - fect peace whose mind   is stayed on   Thee."

INNER PEACE

494 Wonderful Peace

And the peace of God, which passeth all understanding shall keep your hearts and minds.
— Philippians 4:7

WONDERFUL PEACE

W. D. Cornell

W. G. Cooper

1 Far a - way in the depths of my spir - it to - night Rolls a
2 *What a treas - ure I have in this won - der - ful peace, Bur - ied*
3 I am rest - ing to - night in this won - der - ful peace, Rest - ing
4 *And I think when I rise to that cit - y of peace, Where the*
5 O my soul, are you here with - out com - fort or rest, March - ing

1 mel - o - dy sweet - er than psalm; In ce - les - tial-like strains it un -
2 *deep in the heart of my soul; So se - cure that no pow - er can*
3 sweet - ly in Je - sus' con - trol; For I'm kept from all dan - ger by
4 *au - thor of peace I shall see, That one strain of the song which the*
5 down the rough path-way of time? Make the Sav - ior your friend when the

1 ceas - ing - ly falls O'er my soul like an in - fi - nite calm.
2 *mine it a - way While the years of e - ter - ni - ty roll;*
3 night and by day, And His glo - ry is flood - ing my soul.
4 *ran-somed will sing, In that heav - en - ly king - dom shall be:*
5 shad-ows grow dark; O ac - cept this sweet peace so sub - lime.

Peace! Peace! won-der-ful peace, Coming down from the Fa-ther a - bove; Sweep

INNER PEACE

o-ver my spir-it for - ev-er, I pray, In fath-om-less bil-lows of love.

It Is Well with My Soul

495

Horatio G. Spafford

But God will redeem my soul from the power of death,
for He will receive me. —Psalm 49:15

VILLE DU HAVRE

Philip P. Bliss

1 When peace, like a riv-er, at-tend-eth my way, When sor-rows like
2 *My sin— O the joy of this glo-ri-ous thought—My sin, not in*
3 And, Lord, haste the day when my faith shall be sight, The clouds be rolled

1 sea bil-lows roll— What-ev-er my lot, Thou hast taught me to say,
2 *part, but the whole, Is nailed to the cross, and I bear it no more:*
3 back as a scroll: The trump shall re-sound and the Lord shall de-scend,

1 It is well, it is well with my soul.
2 *Praise the Lord, praise the Lord, O my soul!*
3 "E-ven so"— it is well with my soul.

It is well

It is well

with my soul,

with my soul,

It is well, it is well with my soul.

INNER PEACE

496

Security

We need not fear if the world and the mountains crumble into the sea.

— Psalm 46:2

Based on Isaiah 54:10
Lina Sandell
Tr. by E. Lincoln Pearson, stanzas 1, 4, alt.
Bryan Jeffery Leech, stanzas 2, 3

BERGEN MÅ VIKA
Source unknown

1 Great hills may trem - ble and moun - tains may crum - ble,
2 *Though peace be shat - tered by war's ag - i - ta - tion,*
3 Strong to pre - serve us in mo - ments of dan - ger,
4 *Teach us, O Lord, Thy com - mand-ments to pon - der,*

1 God's lov - ing - kind - ness re - main - eth se - cure;
2 *Though change and ten - sion give birth to great fears,*
3 Strong when frus - tra - tion and frail - ty in - crease;
4 *Help us to heed them wher - ev - er we roam,*

1 Peace He will give to the con - trite and hum - ble:
2 *God still re - mains an un - shak - en foun - da - tion,*
3 Strong to e - quip us for lov - ing the stran - ger,
4 *Wait - ing the day Thou shalt call us up yon - der,*

1 Thus saith the Lord— His prom - ise is sure.
2 *Strong to sup - port us through tur - bu - lent years;*
3 Strong where our hu - man re - sourc - es may cease.
4 *Trust - ing Thy prom - ise to car - ry us home.* A - men.

INNER PEACE

Like a River Glorious

497

Then had Thy peace been like a river and Thy righteousness as the waves . . . .
— Isaiah 48:18

Frances Ridley Havergal
Jeff Redd, alt., stanza 3

WYE VALLEY
James Mountain

1 Like a riv-er glo-rious Is God's per-fect peace, O-ver all vic-
2 *Hid-den in the hol-low Of His bless-ed hand, Nev-er foe can*
3 Ev-ery joy or test-ing Comes from God a-bove, Giv-en to His

1 to-rious In its bright in-crease; Per-fect, yet it flow-eth Full-er
2 *fol-low, Nev-er trai-tor stand; Not a surge of wor-ry, Not a*
3 chil-dren As an act of love; We may trust Him ful-ly All for

1 ev-ery day, Per-fect, yet it grow-eth Deep-er all the way.
2 *shade of care, Not a blast of hur-ry Touch the spir-it there.*
3 us to do— Those who trust Him whol-ly Find Him whol-ly true.

Trust-ing in Je-ho-vah, Hearts are ful-ly blest—

Find-ing, as He prom-ised, Per-fect peace and rest.

INNER PEACE

498 Through the Love of God, Our Savior

. . . I know that it shall be well with them that fear God.

— Ecclesiastes 8:12

Mary Peters

AR HYD Y NOS
Welsh melody

1 Through the love of God, our Sav - ior, All will be well;
2 *Though we pass through trib - u - la - tion, All will be well;*
3 We ex - pect a bright to - mor - row, All will be well;

1 Free and change-less is His fa - vor— All will be well.
2 *Ours is such a full sal - va - tion— All will be well.*
3 Faith can sing through days of sor - row, All will be well.

1 Pre-cious is the blood that healed us, Per - fect is the grace that sealed us,
2 *Hap-py when in God con -fid - ing, Fruit-ful if in Christ a - bid - ing,*
3 On our Fa-ther's love re - ly - ing, Je - sus ev - ery need sup- ply - ing

1 Strong the hand stretched out to shield us— All will be well.
2 *Ho - ly through the Spir - it's guid - ing— All will be well.*
3 In our liv - ing, in our dy - ing, All will be well.

INNER PEACE

I know not what I shall become: it seems to me that peace of soul and repose of spirit descend on me, even in sleep. To be without the sense of this peace, would be affliction indeed. . . .

I know not what God purposes with me, or keeps me for; I am in a calm so great that I fear naught. What can I fear, when I am with Him: and with Him, in His Presence, I hold myself the most I can. May all things praise Him. Amen.

—Brother Lawrence

Abide With Me   500

And now, . . . abide in Him, that when He shall appear we may have confidence, and not be ashamed . . . — 1 John 2:28

Henry F. Lyte   EVENTIDE   William H. Monk

1 A - bide with me— fast falls the e - ven - tide; The dark-ness deep-ens—
2 Swift to its close ebbs out life's lit - tle day; Earth's joys grow dim, its
3 I need Thy pres-ence ev - ery pass - ing hour; What but Thy grace can
4 I fear no foe, with Thee at hand to bless; Ills have no weight and
5 Hold Thou Thy cross be - fore my clos - ing eyes; Shine thru the gloom and

1 Lord, with me a - bide; When oth - er help - ers fail and com-forts
2 glo - ries pass a - way; Change and de - cay in all a-round I
3 foil the temp-ter's power? Who like Thy - self my guide and stay can
4 tears no bit - ter - ness; Where is death's sting? where, grave, thy vic - to -
5 point me to the skies; Heaven's morn-ing breaks and earth's vain shad-ows

1 flee, Help of the help-less, O a - bide with me.
2 see; O Thou who chang-est not, a - bide with me.
3 be? Through cloud and sun-shine, O a - bide with me.
4 ry? I tri - umph still if Thou a - bide with me.
5 flee; In life, in death, O Lord, a - bide with me. A-men.

INNER PEACE

501

'Til the Storm Passes By

A man shall be . . . like the shadow of a great rock in a weary land.
— Isaiah 32:2

LISTER
Mosie Lister

Mosie Lister

1 In the dark of the mid-night Have I oft hid my face,
2 *Man-y times Sa-tan whis-pered, "There is no use to try,*
3 When the long night has end-ed, And the storms come no more,

1 While the storms howl a - bove me, And there's no hid-ing place.
2 *For there's no end of sor-row, There's no hope by and by."*
3 Let me stand in Thy pres-ence On that bright, peace-ful shore.

1 'Mid the crash of the thun-der, Pre-cious Lord, hear my cry,
2 *But I know Thou art with me, And to - mor - row I'll rise*
3 In that land where the tem-pest Nev - er comes, Lord, may I

1 "Keep me safe 'til the storm pass - es by."
2 *Where the storms nev - er dark - en the skies.*
3 Dwell with Thee when the storm pass - es by.

INNER PEACE

'Til the storm pass-es o - ver, 'Til the thun - der sounds no more,

'Til the clouds roll for - ev - er from the sky,

Hold me fast, Let me stand in the hol - low of Thy hand;

Keep me safe 'til the storm pass - es by.

INNER PEACE

502 I'll Go Where You Want Me to Go

Paul, a servant of Jesus Christ . . . separated unto the Gospel of God. — Romans 1:1

Mary Brown, stanza 1
Charles E. Prior, stanzas 2, 3

I'LL GO
Carrie E. Rounsefell

1 It may not be on the moun-tain's height Or o-ver the storm-y sea,
2 *Per - haps to-day there are lov-ing words Which Je-sus would have me speak,*
3 There's sure-ly some-where a low-ly place In earth's har-vest fields so wide,

1 It may not be at the bat-tle-front My Lord will have need of me;
2 *There may be now, in the paths of sin, Some wan-der-er whom I should seek;*
3 Where I may la-bor thru life's short day For Je-sus the Cru-ci-fied;

1 But if by a still, small voice He calls To paths I do not know,
2 *O Sav - ior, if Thou wilt be my Guide, Tho dark and rug-ged the way,*
3 So, trust-ing my all un - to Thy care—I know Thou lov-est me—

1 I'll an-swer, dear Lord, with my hand in Thine, I'll go where You want me to go.
2 *My voice shall ech-o the mes-sage sweet, I'll say what You want me to say.*
3 I'll do Thy will with a heart sin-cere, I'll be what You want me to be.

I'll go where You want me to go, dear Lord, O'er moun-tain or plain or sea;

DISCIPLESHIP

I'll say what You want me to say, dear Lord, I'll be what You want me to be.

Glorifying God in the Everyday **503**

The wonder of the Incarnation slips into the Life of ordinary childhood; the marvel of the Transfiguration descends to the valley and the demon-possessed boy, and the glory of the Resurrection merges into Our Lord providing breakfast for His disciples on the sea shore in the early dawn. The tendency in early Christian experience is to look for the marvellous. We are apt to mistake the sense of the heroic for being heroes. It is one thing to go through a crisis grandly, but a different thing to go through every day glorifying God when there is no witness, no limelight, and no one paying the remotest attention to you. If we don't want medieval haloes, we want something that will make people say— What a wonderful man of prayer he is! What a pious, devoted woman she is! If anyone says that of you, you have not been loyal to God.

—Oswald Chambers

Must Jesus Bear the Cross Alone **504**

If any man come after Me let him . . .
take up his cross and follow . . . — Matthew 16:24

Thomas Shepherd

MAITLAND
George N. Allen

1 Must Je - sus bear the cross a - lone, And all the world go free?
2 *The con - se - crat - ed cross I'll bear, 'Til death shall set me free,*
3 O pre - cious cross! O glo - rious crown! O res - ur - rec - tion day!

1 No; there's a cross for ev - ery one, And there's a cross for me.
2 *And then go home my crown to wear, For there's a crown for me.*
3 Ye an - gels, from the stars come down, And take my soul a - way. A - men.

505 Your Cause Be Mine

For this cause was I born . . . that I should bear witness unto the truth.

— John 18:37

Bryan Jeffery Leech

RICHMOND BEACH
A. Royce Eckhardt

1 Your cause be mine, great Lord di - vine, Your aim be my am - bi - tion: For wast - ed is my great - est strength Un - less it find ex - pres - sion In love that gives it - self a - way, In life re - spon - sive to o -

2 *Your cause be mine, great Lord di - vine, This be my life's vo - ca - tion: To seek the prize when life is done— Your lov - ing ap - pro - ba - tion. Di - min - ish pride, in - crease my love, O may Your Spir - it now re -*

3 Your cause be mine, great Lord di - vine, The world's e - man - ci - pa - tion: To let Your light in - vade the dark In ev - ery sit - u - a - tion, To prove You in a thou - sand ways, To serve You well with zeal a -

DISCIPLESHIP

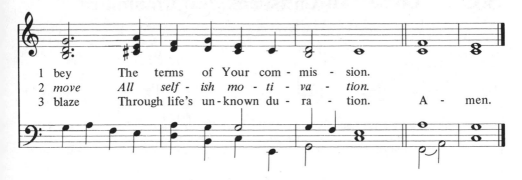

1 bey The terms of Your com - mis - sion.
2 *move* *All* *self* - *ish mo* - *ti* - *va* - *tion.*
3 blaze Through life's un-known du - ra - tion. A - men.

Make Us Worthy, Lord   506

Make us worthy, Lord,
to serve our fellow men throughout the world
who live and die in poverty and hunger.

Give them, through our hands, this day
their daily bread, and by our understanding love give Peace and Joy.

Lord, make a channel of Thy peace,

that where there is hatred I may bring love;

that where there is wrong, I may bring the spirit of forgiveness;

that where there is doubt, I may bring faith;

that where there is error, I may bring truth;

that where there is discord, I may bring harmony;

that where there is despair, I may bring hope;

that where there are shadows, I may bring light;

that where there is sadness, I may bring joy.

Lord,
grant that I may seek rather to comfort than to be comforted;

to understand than to be understood;

to love than to be loved;

for it is by forgetting self that one finds;

it is by dying that one awakens to eternal life.

Amen.

—*Mother Teresa*

507 Come, All Christians, Be Committed

No man having put his hand to the plow, and looking back is fit....
— Luke 9:62

Eva B. Lloyd

BEACH SPRING
"The Sacred Harp"
Harmonized by James H. Wood

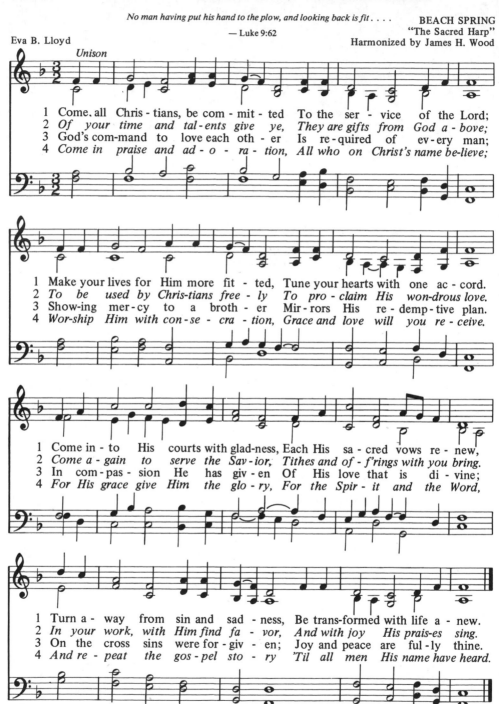

Unison

1 Come, all Chris - tians, be com - mit - ted To the ser - vice of the Lord;
2 *Of your time and tal - ents give ye, They are gifts from God a - bove;*
3 God's com - mand to love each oth - er Is re - quired of ev - ery man;
4 *Come in praise and ad - o - ra - tion, All who on Christ's name be - lieve;*

1 Make your lives for Him more fit - ted, Tune your hearts with one ac - cord.
2 *To be used by Chris - tians free - ly To pro - claim His won - drous love.*
3 Show - ing mer - cy to a broth - er Mir - rors His re - demp - tive plan.
4 *Wor - ship Him with con - se - cra - tion, Grace and love will you re - ceive.*

1 Come in - to His courts with glad - ness, Each His sa - cred vows re - new;
2 *Come a - gain to serve the Sav - ior, Tithes and of - f'rings with you bring.*
3 In com - pas - sion He has giv - en Of His love that is di - vine;
4 *For His grace give Him the glo - ry, For the Spir - it and the Word,*

1 Turn a - way from sin and sad - ness, Be trans - formed with life a - new.
2 *In your work, with Him find fa - vor, And with joy His prais - es sing.*
3 On the cross sins were for - giv - en; Joy and peace are ful - ly thine.
4 *And re - peat the gos - pel sto - ry 'Til all men His name have heard.*

DISCIPLESHIP

Give Me a Dream

Father,

once I had such big dreams, so much anticipation of the future.
Now no shimmering horizon beckons me; my days are lack-lustre
I see so little of lasting value in the daily round.

Where is Your plan for my life?

You have told us that without vision, we men perish. So, Father
in heaven, knowing that I can ask in confidence for what is Your
expressed will to give me, I ask You to deposit in my mind and heart
that particular dream, the special vision You have for my life.

And along with the dream, will You give me whatever graces,
patience, and stamina it takes to see the dream through to fruition?

I sense this may involve adventures I have not bargained for.

But I want to trust You
enough to follow even if You lead along new paths.

I admit to liking some of my ruts.

But I know that habit patterns
that seem like cozy nests from the inside,
from Your vantage point
may be prison cells.

Lord,
if You have to break down
any prisons of mine
before I can see the stars and catch the vision,
then, Lord, begin the process now.
In joyous expectation.
Amen.

—Catherine Marshall

My Eternal King

My God, I love Thee;
Not because I hope for heaven thereby,
Nor yet because who love Thee not
Must die eternally.

Thou, O my Jesus, Thou didst me
Upon the cross embrace,
For me didst bear the nails and spear,
And manifold disgrace.

Then why, O blessed Jesus Christ,
Should I not love Thee well?
Not for the hope of winning heaven,
Or of escaping hell.

E'en so I love Thee, and will love
And in Thy praise will sing,
Solely because Thou art my God,
And my eternal King!

—Francis Xavier
Tr. Edward Caswall

ASPIRATION

510 Glorious Is Thy Name, Most Holy

We love Him because He first loved us . . . — I John 4:19

Ruth Elliot

HOLY MANNA
William Moore

1 Glo - rious is Thy name, Most Ho - ly, God and Fa - ther of us all;
2 *For our world of need and an - guish We would lift to Thee our prayer.*
3 In the midst of time we jour - ney, From Thy hand comes each new day;

1 We Thy ser - vants bow be - fore Thee, Strive to an - swer ev - ery call.
2 *Faith-ful stew - ards of Thy boun - ty, May we with our broth-ers share.*
3 We would use it in Thy ser - vice, Hum - bly, wise - ly, while we may.

1 Thou with life's great good hast blest us, Cared for us from ear - liest years;
2 *In the name of Christ our Sav - ior, Who re - deems and sets us free,*
3 So to Thee, Lord and Cre - a - tor, Praise and hon - or we ac - cord,

1 Un - to Thee our thanks we ren - der; Thy deep love o'er-comes all fears.
2 *Gifts we bring of heart and trea - sure, That our lives may wor-thier be.*
3 Thine the earth and Thine the heav - ens, Through all the E - ter - nal Word.

STEWARDSHIP

Lord, we gather in comfort and security today, while many of Your children huddle in fear and die of starvation. We know that merely feeling guilty for our comfort does not minister to the needs of others. Lord, we want to be involved in helping, and serving, and healing. Help us this day to gain more understanding, to feel more deeply the hurt of others, to come to new commitments of ourselves and our substance to You. Amen.

—Gary W. Demarest

Little Is Much, When God Is in It 512

There is a small boy here with five loaves and two fishes.

Mrs. F. W. Suffield   — John 6:9   Mrs. F. W. Suffield

1 In the har-vest field now rip-ened, There's a work for all to do;
2 *Does the place you're called to la-bor Seem so small and lit-tle known?*
3 When the con-flict here is end-ed And our race on earth is run;

1 Hark, the voice of God is call-ing, To the har-vest call-ing you.
2 *It is great if God is in it, And He'll not for-get His own.*
3 He will say, if we are faith-ful, "Wel-come home, my child, well done."

Lit-tle is much when God is in it, La-bor not for wealth or fame;

There's a crown and you can win it, If you go in Je-sus' name.

STEWARDSHIP

513 God, Whose Giving Knows No Ending

A man can receive nothing except it be given to him from heaven.
— John 3:27

NETTLETON
Traditional American Melody
John Wyeth

Robert Lansing Edwards

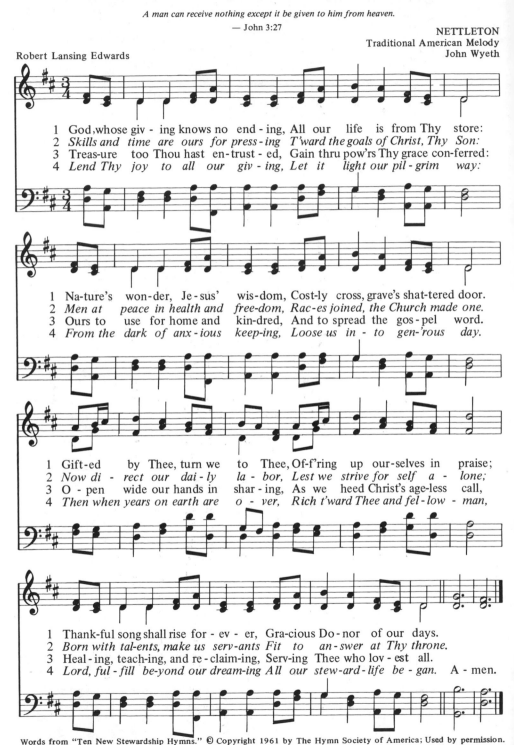

1 God, whose giv - ing knows no end - ing, All our life is from Thy store:
2 *Skills and time are ours for press - ing T'ward the goals of Christ, Thy Son:*
3 Treas - ure too Thou hast en - trust - ed, Gain thru pow'rs Thy grace con - ferred:
4 *Lend Thy joy to all our giv - ing, Let it light our pil - grim way:*

1 Na - ture's won - der, Je - sus' wis - dom, Cost - ly cross, grave's shat - tered door.
2 *Men at peace in health and free - dom, Rac - es joined, the Church made one.*
3 Ours to use for home and kin - dred, And to spread the gos - pel word.
4 *From the dark of anx - ious keep - ing, Loose us in - to gen - 'rous day.*

1 Gift - ed by Thee, turn we to Thee, Of - f'ring up our - selves in praise;
2 *Now di - rect our dai - ly la - bor, Lest we strive for self a - lone;*
3 O - pen wide our hands in shar - ing, As we heed Christ's age - less call,
4 *Then when years on earth are o - ver, Rich t'ward Thee and fel - low - man,*

1 Thank - ful song shall rise for - ev - er, Gra - cious Do - nor of our days.
2 *Born with tal - ents, make us serv - ants Fit to an - swer at Thy throne.*
3 Heal - ing, teach - ing, and re - claim - ing, Serv - ing Thee who lov - est all.
4 *Lord, ful - fill be - yond our dream - ing All our stew - ard - life be - gan. A - men.*

STEWARDSHIP

C. S. Lewis didn't talk about percentage giving.

He said the only safe rule is to give more than we can spare.

Our charities should pinch and hamper us.

If we live at the same level of affluence

as other people who have our level of income,

we are probably giving away too little.

Obstacles to charity include

greed for luxurious living,

greed for money itself,

fear of financial insecurity,

and showy pride.

—Kathryn Ann Lindskoog

We Give Thee but Thine Own   515

Of thine own have we given Thee. — I Chronicles 29:14

William W. How

SCHUMANN
Mason and Webb's *Cantica Laudis*

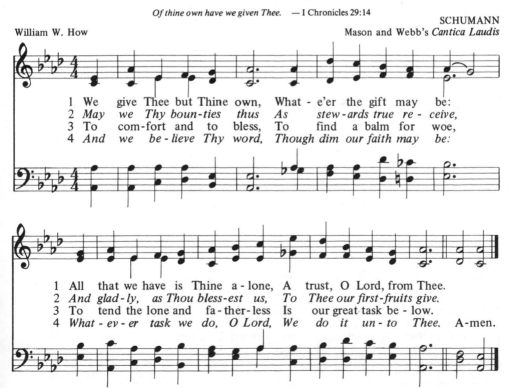

1 We give Thee but Thine own, What - e'er the gift may be:
2 *May we Thy boun-ties thus As stew-ards true re - ceive,*
3 To com-fort and to bless, To find a balm for woe,
4 *And we be-lieve Thy word, Though dim our faith may be:*

1 All that we have is Thine a - lone, A trust, O Lord, from Thee.
2 *And glad-ly, as Thou bless-est us, To Thee our first-fruits give.*
3 To tend the lone and fa-ther-less Is our great task be - low.
4 *What-ev-er task we do, O Lord, We do it un-to Thee.* A-men.

516 Give of Your Best to the Master

Ye are My friends if ye do whatsoever I command you.

— John 15:14

Howard B. Grose

BARNARD
Charlotte A. Barnard

1 Give of your best to the Mas - ter, Give of the strength of your youth;
2 *Give of your best to the Mas - ter, Give Him first place in your heart;*
3 Give of your best to the Mas - ter, Naught else is wor - thy His love;

Refrain: Give of your best to the Mas - ter; Give of the strength of your youth;

Fine

1 Throw your soul's fresh, glowing ar - dor In - to the bat - tle for truth.
2 *Give Him first place in your ser - vice; Con-se-crate ev - ery part.*
3 He gave him-self for your ran - som, Gave up His glo - ry a - bove;

Clad in sal - va-tion's full ar - mor, Join in the bat-tle for truth.

1 Je - sus has set the ex - am - ple - Daunt-less was He, young and brave;
2 *Give, and to you shall be giv - en. - God His be - lov - ed Son gave;*
3 Laid down His life with-out mur - mur, You from sin's ru - in to save;

D.C.

1 Give Him your loy - al de - vo - tion, Give Him the best that you have.
2 *Grate-ful-ly seek-ing to serve Him, Give Him the best that you have.*
3 Give Him your heart's ad-o - ra - tion, Give Him the best that you have.

STEWARDSHIP

O Lord my God, I thank Thee that Thou
hast brought this day to a close;
I thank Thee that Thou hast given me peace
in body and in soul.
Thy hand has been over me and has protected
and preserved me,

Forgive my puny faith,
the ill that I this day have done,
and help me to forgive all who
have wronged me.

Grant me a quiet night's sleep beneath
Thy tender care.
And defend me from all the temptations
of darkness.

Into Thy hands I commend my loved ones,
and all who dwell in this house;
I commend my body and soul.

—Dietrich Bonhoeffer

All Praise to Thee, My God 518

My praise shall be of Thee in the great congregation; — Psalm 22:25

TALLIS' CANON
Thomas Ken
Thomas Tallis

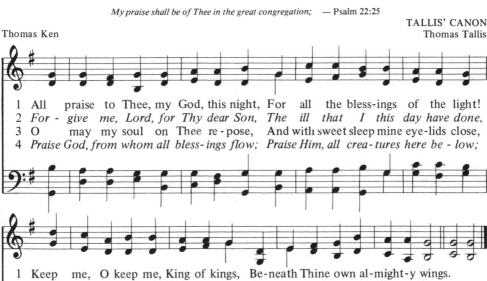

1 All praise to Thee, my God, this night, For all the bless-ings of the light!
2 For - give me, Lord, for Thy dear Son, The ill that I this day have done,
3 O may my soul on Thee re - pose, And with sweet sleep mine eye-lids close,
4 Praise God, from whom all bless-ings flow; Praise Him, all crea-tures here be - low;

1 Keep me, O keep me, King of kings, Be-neath Thine own al-might-y wings.
2 That with the world, my-self, and Thee, I, when I sleep, at peace may be.
3 Sleep that may me more vig-orous make To serve my God when I a-wake.
4 Praise Him a-bove, ye heaven-ly host; Praise Fa-ther, Son, and Ho-ly Ghost. A-men.

519

Savior, Again to Thy Dear Name We Raise

And when they had sung a hymn they went out . . . .
— Matthew 26:30

John Ellerton

ELLERS
Edward J. Hopkins

1 Sav - ior, a - gain to Thy dear name we raise
2 *Grant us Thy peace up - on our home-ward way;*
3 Grant us Thy peace, Lord, through the com - ing night;
4 *Grant us Thy peace through - out our earth - ly life,*

1 With one ac - cord our part - ing hymn of praise:
2 *With Thee be - gan, with Thee shall end the day;*
3 Turn Thou for us its dark - ness in - to light:
4 *Our joy in sor - row, and our strength in strife;*

1 Once more we pray be - fore our wor - ship cease;
2 *Guard Thou the lips from sin, the hearts from shame,*
3 From harm and dan - ger keep Thy chil - dren free,
4 *Then, when Thy voice shall bid our con - flict cease,*

1 That Thou wilt grant to us Thy word of peace.
2 *That in this house have called up - on Thy name.*
3 For dark and light are both a - like to Thee.
4 *Call us, O Lord, to Thine e - ter - nal peace.* A-men.

Lord, Dismiss Us with Your Blessing 520

Salvation belongeth to the Lord; Thy blessing is upon Thy people.

— Psalm 3:8

John Fawcett

SICILIAN MARINERS
Tattersall's *Psalmody*

1 Lord, dis - miss us with Your bless - ing, Fill our hearts with
2 *Thanks we give and ad - o - ra - tion For Your gos - pel's*

1 joy and peace; Let us each, Your love pos - sess - ing,
2 *joy - ful sound; May the fruits of Your sal - va - tion*

1 Tri - umph in re - deem - ing grace. O re - fresh us,
2 *In our hearts and lives a - bound. Ev - er faith - ful,*

1 O re - fresh us, Trav - eling through this wil - der - ness.
2 *ev - er faith - ful To the truth may we be found.* A - men.

521

A Prayer

God be in my head, and in my understanding;

God be in mine eyes and in my looking;

God be in my mouth, and in my speaking;

God be in my heart, and in my thinking;

God be at mine end, and at my departing. Amen.

—Ancient Prayer

522 **The Lord Bless You and Keep You**

The Lord bless thee and keep thee, . . . and make His face to shine upon thee . . . .   BENEDICTION

Numbers 6:24-26   — Numbers 6:24, 25   Peter C. Lutkin

The Lord bless you and keep you; The Lord lift His coun-te-nance up-

on you, and give you peace, and give you peace; The Lord

and give you peace, and give you peace;

Lord make His

make His face to shine up-on you, And be gra - cious un-to

And be gra-cious

you, be gra-cious, The Lord be gra-cious, gra-cious un-to you. A - men.

and be gra-cious,

God Be with You 'Til We Meet Again 523

May the Lord watch between me and thee . . . . — Genesis 31:49

GOD BE WITH YOU
William G. Tomer

Jeremiah E. Rankin

1 God be with you 'til we meet a-gain, By His coun-sels guide, up-hold you,
2 *God be with you 'til we meet a-gain, 'Neath His wings protecting hide you,*
3 God be with you 'til we meet a-gain, If life's tri-als should con-found you,
4 *God be with you 'til we meet a-gain, Keep love's banner floating o'er you,*

1 With His sheep se-cure-ly fold you: God be with you 'til we meet a-gain.
2 *Dai - ly man-na still pro-vide you: God be with you 'til we meet a-gain.*
3 God will put His arms a-round you: God be with you 'til we meet a-gain.
4 *Smite death's threat'ning wave before you: God be with you 'til we meet a-gain.*

Benediction   524

May the Lord take from you all resistance to His will.

May He give to you the fullness of His life

and the sufficiency of His practical, daily help.

May the Lord send you during this week to come to those

He can only serve through your unique experience of life

and your very special abilities.

May the Lord bring us together even when we are apart,

as we learn to be supportive of one another in our prayers

and our service. Amen.

—Bryan Jeffery Leech

525 Now Thank We All Our God

Our God, we thank Thee and praise Thy glorious name.
— I Chronicles 29:13

Martin Rinkart
Tr. by Catherine Winkworth

NUN DANKET
Johann Crüger
Harmonized by Felix Mendelssohn

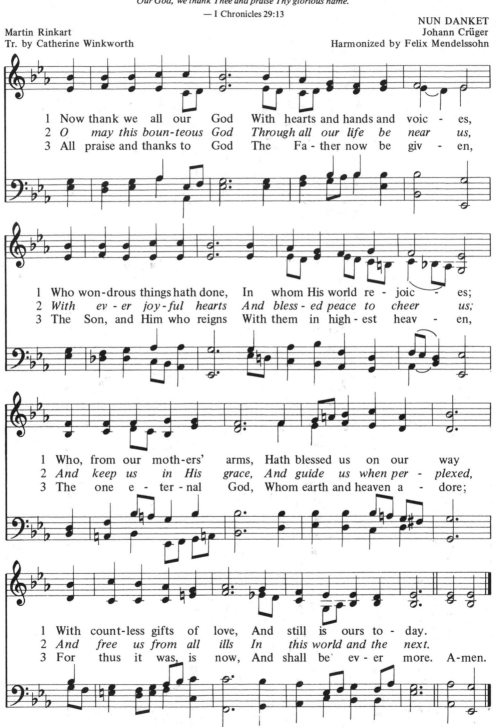

1 Now thank we all our God With hearts and hands and voic - es,
2 *O may this boun-teous God Through all our life be near us,*
3 All praise and thanks to God The Fa - ther now be giv - en,

1 Who won-drous things hath done, In whom His world re - joic - es;
2 *With ev - er joy-ful hearts And bless - ed peace to cheer us;*
3 The Son, and Him who reigns With them in high - est heav - en,

1 Who, from our moth-ers' arms, Hath blessed us on our way
2 *And keep us in His grace, And guide us when per - plexed,*
3 The one e - ter - nal God, Whom earth and heaven a - dore;

1 With count-less gifts of love, And still is ours to - day.
2 *And free us from all ills In this world and the next.*
3 For thus it was, is now, And shall be' ev - er more. A-men.

HERITAGE

Our Love
for the Family of God

526

Faith of Our Fathers

. . . You should earnestly contend for the faith which was once delivered unto the saints.
— Jude 1:3

ST. CATHERINE
Henri F. Hemy
Descant by Bob Burroughs

Frederick W. Faber

Descant

3 Faith of our fa - thers, we will love Both friend and foe in

1 Faith of our   fa - thers, liv - ing still In spite of dun - geon,
2 *Faith of our   fa - thers, God's great power Shall win all   na - tions*
3 Faith of our   fa - thers, we will love Both friend and foe in

all   our strife,   And preach thee, love knows how,

1 fire, and sword, O how our hearts beat high with joy
2 *un - to thee, And through the truth that comes from God*
3 all   our strife, And preach thee too as love knows how,

By kind - ly words, and vir - tuous life.   Faith of our

1 When-e'er we hear that glo - rious word! Faith of our fa - thers,
2 *Man - kind shall then in - deed be free. Faith of our fa - thers,*
3 By kind - ly words and vir - tuous life. Faith of our fa - thers,

HERITAGE

fa - thers, ho-ly   faith,   We will be true 'til   death.   A - men.

1 ho - ly faith,   We will be   true   to thee 'til death.
2 *ho - ly faith,   We will be   true   to thee 'til death.*
3 ho - ly faith,   We will be true   to thee 'til death.   A - men.

Answered Prayer   527

I asked God for strength,
    that I might achieve,
  I was made weak,
      that I might learn humbly to obey . . .
I asked for health,
    that I might do greater things,
  I was given infirmity,
      that I might do better things . . .
I asked for riches,
    that I might be happy,
  I was given poverty,
      that I might be wise . . .
I asked for power,
    that I might have the praise of men,
  I was given weakness,
      that I might feel the need of God . . .
I asked for all things,
    that I might enjoy life,
  I was given life,
      that I might enjoy all things . . .
I got nothing that I asked for—
but everything I had hoped for;
    Almost despite myself,
    my unspoken prayers were answered.
      I am among all men most richly blessed.

—Unknown Confederate Soldier

HERITAGE

528 God of Grace and God of Glory

Put on the whole armour of God that ye may be able to stand. — Ephesians 6:11

CWM RHONDDA

Harry Emerson Fosdick

John Hughes

1 God of grace and God of glo - ry, On Thy peo - ple
2 Lo! the hosts of e - vil round us Scorn Thy Christ, as -
3 Cure Thy chil - dren's war - ring mad - ness; Bend our pride to
4 Set our feet on loft - y plac - es, Gird our lives that

1 pour Thy power; Crown Thine an - cient church's sto - ry, Bring her bud to
2 sail His ways! From the fears that long have bound us, Free our hearts to
3 Thy con - trol; Shame our wan - ton, self - ish glad - ness, Rich in things and
4 they may be Ar - mored with all Christ-like grac - es In the fight to

1 glo - rious flower. Grant us wis - dom, Grant us cour - age,
2 faith and praise. Grant us wis - dom, Grant us cour - age,
3 poor in soul. Grant us wis - dom, Grant us cour - age,
4 set men free. Grant us wis - dom, Grant us cour - age,

1 For the fac - ing of this hour, For the fac - ing of this hour.
2 For the liv - ing of these days, For the liv - ing of these days.
3 Lest we miss Thy kingdom's goal, Lest we miss Thy king - dom's goal.
4 That we fail not man nor Thee, That we fail not man nor Thee. A-men.

HERITAGE

Arranged by Robert Elmore

4 Set our feet on loft - y plac - es, Gird our lives that they may be

Ar-mored with all Christ - like grac - es In the fight to set men free.

Grant us wis-dom, Grant us cour-age, That we fail not man nor

(TPT.)

Thee, That we fail not man nor Thee. A-men.

HERITAGE

529

As male and female we look to the Spirit.
He makes us stewards of life
to plan its beginning,
to live its living,
to care in its dying.
He makes us the stewards of marriage
with its lifelong commitment to love;
yet He knows our frailty of heart.

—*"Our Song of Hope"*

530

O Perfect Love

A man shall cleave unto his wife; and they shall be one flesh. — Genesis 2:24

O PERFECT LOVE

Dorothy Gurney

Joseph Barnby

1 O per-fect Love, all hu-man thought tran-scend-ing, Low - ly we kneel
2 *O per-fect Life, be Thou their full as - sur-ance Of ten - der char-*
3 Grant them the joy which bright-ens earth - ly sor - row, Grant them the peace

1 in prayer be - fore Thy throne, That theirs may be the love which knows no
2 *i - ty and stead-fast faith, Of pa - tient hope, and qui - et, brave en -*
3 which calms all earth - ly strife, And to life's day the glo-rious un-known

1 end - ing, Whom Thou for ev - er - more dost join in one.
2 *dur - ance, With child-like trust that fears nor pain nor death.*
3 mor - row That dawns up - on e - ter - nal love and life. A - men.

MARRIAGE

If you can find a truly good wife, she is worth more than precious gems.

Her husband can trust her, and she will richly satisfy his needs. She will not hinder him, but help him all his life.

She finds wool and flax and busily spins it. She buys imported foods, brought by ship from distant ports.

She gets up before dawn to prepare breakfast for her household, and plans the day's work for her servant girls.

She goes out to inspect a field, and buys it; with her own hands she plants a vineyard. She is energetic, a hard worker, and watches for bargains. She works far into the night!

She sews for the poor, and generously gives to the needy. She has no fear of winter for her household, for she has made warm clothes for all of them.

Her husband is well known, for he sits in the council chamber with the other civic leaders.

She is a woman of strength and dignity, and has no fear of old age.

When she speaks, her words are wise, and kindness is the rule for everything she says.

She watches carefully all that goes on throughout her household, and is never lazy.

Her children stand and bless her; so does her husband. He praises her with these words: "There are many fine women in the world, but you are the best of them all."

Charm can be deceptive and beauty doesn't last, but a woman who fears and reverences God shall be greatly praised.

—Proverbs 31:10-21, 23, 25-30 (LB)

Men and boys:

THE WORLD NEEDS MEN

. . . who cannot be bought;

. . . whose word is their bond;

. . . who put character above wealth;

. . . who are larger than their vocations;

. . . who do not hesitate to take chances;

. . . who will not lose their identity in a crowd;

. . . who will be as honest in small things as in great things;

. . . who will make no compromise with wrong;

. . . whose ambitions are not confined to their own selfish desires;

. . . who will not say they do it "because everybody else does it;"

. . . who are true to their friends through good report and evil report, in adversity as well as in prosperity;

. . . who do not believe that shrewdness and cunning are the best qualities for winning success;

. . . who are not ashamed to stand for the truth when it is unpopular;

. . . who can say "no" with emphasis, although the rest of the world say "yes."

God, make *me* this kind of man.

—Leonard Wagner

Minister: *We have heard it said that the Home is the heart of our society. If this is true, our society is in trouble.*

People: *Lord, help us to build strong Christian homes. Help children to develop a sense of responsibility and personal discipline which will bring honor to Christ and happiness to the family. Help parents to love one another as You love them and outdo one another in acts of kindness, generosity and thoughtfulness.*

In Jesus' name. Amen.

—Donn Moomaw

534 The Parents' Creed

I believe that my children are a gift of God—the hope of a new tomorrow.

I believe that immeasurable possibilities lie slumbering in each son and daughter.

I believe that God has planned a perfect plan for their future, and that His love shall always surround them; and so

I believe that they shall grow up!—first creeping, then toddling, then standing, stretching skyward for a decade and a half—until they reach full stature—a man and a woman!

I believe that they can and will be molded and shaped between infancy and adulthood—as a tree is shaped by the gardener, and the clay vessel in the potter's hand, or the shoreline of the sea under the watery hand of the mighty waves; by home and church; by school and street, through sights and sounds and the touch of my hand on their hand and Christ's spirit on their heart! So,

I believe that they shall mature as only people can—through laughter and tears, through trial and error, by reward and punishment, through affection and discipline, until they stretch their wings and leave their nest to fly!

O God — I believe in my children. Help me so to live that they may always believe in me—and so in Thee.

—Robert H. Schuller

In the Circle of Each Home

535

And all thy children shall be taught of the Lord; and great shall be the peace of thy children.
— Isaiah 54:13

BEL AIR

Bryan Jeffery Leech

Bryan Jeffery Leech

1 In the cir-cle of each home, Lord, Your love is need-ed;
2 *In the cir-cle of each home, Be our strong foun-da-tion;*
3 In the cir-cle of each home, Lord, Your love is want-ed
4 *In the cir-cle of each home, Is af-fec-tion grow-ing?*

1 For that fra-gile cir-cle bends When You are un-heed-ed.
2 *Lord, we need Your wis-dom there In each sit-u-a-tion.*
3 So that we'll not take Your grace And our life for grant-ed.
4 *Are there fruits of char-ac-ter From a care-ful sow-ing?*

1 For that hu-man cir-cle breaks With our pro-longed de-fi-ance,
2 *If we have Your sur-er pace, We'll march as to a drum-mer.*
3 Should our chil-dren fail to see The proofs of what we've taught them,
4 *Do we praise the good we see, And par-don oth-ers' sin-ning?*

1 And we stand like win-ter trees Made bare by self re-li-ance.
2 *Then our lives will fruit-ful be, Like trees we see in sum-mer.*
3 Then we'll lack au-thor-i-ty, And fade like trees in au-tumn.
4 *Are our branch-es blos-som-filled Like trees at spring's be-gin-ning?*

FAMILY AND HOME

536 Children As a Trust

We don't own our children: we hold them in trust for God, who gave them to us. The eighteen or twenty years of provision and oversight and training that we normally have, represent our fulfillment of that trust.

—Joseph Bayly

537 The Wise May Bring Their Learning

Then Peter said, "Silver and gold have I none, but such as I have, I give unto you. — Acts 3:6

Anonymous, in *The Book of Praise for Children*

FOREST GREEN
Arranged by Ralph Vaughan Williams

1 The wise may bring their learn - ing, The rich may bring their wealth,
2 *We'll bring Him hearts that love Him; We'll bring Him thank-ful praise,*
3 We'll come and show the Sav - ior The things we do each day;

1 And some may bring their bril - liance, And some bring strength and health;
2 *And young souls hum-bly striv - ing To walk in ho - ly ways:*
3 We'll try our best to please Him At home, at school or play:

1 We too, would bring our trea - sures To of - fer to the King;
2 *And these shall be our trea - sures We of - fer to the King,*
3 And bet - ter are these trea - sures To of - fer to our King

1 We have no gifts de - serv - ing: What shall we chil - dren bring?
2 *And these are gifts that ev - en The young-est child may bring.*
3 Than rich - est gifts with - out them: Yet these a child may bring. A-men.

FAMILY AND HOME

A Christian Home

538

Train up a child in the way he should go, and when he is old he will not depart from it.
— Proverbs 22:6

Barbara B. Hart

FINLANDIA
Jean Sibelius

1 O give us homes built firm up-on the Sav-ior, Where Christ is
2 O give us homes with god-ly fa-thers, moth-ers, Who al-ways
3 O Lord, our God, our homes are Thine for-ev-er! We trust to

1 Head and Coun-sel-lor and Guide; Where ev-ery child is
2 place their hope and trust in Him; Whose ten-der pa-tience
3 Thee their prob-lems, toil, and care; Their bonds of love no

1 taught His love and fa-vor And gives his heart to Christ, the cru-ci-
2 tur-moil nev-er both-ers, Whose calm and cour-age trou-ble can-not
3 en-e-my can sev-er If Thou art al-ways Lord and Mas-ter

1 fied: How sweet to know that though his foot-steps wa-ver
2 dim; A home where each finds joy in serv-ing oth-ers,
3 there: Be Thou the cen-ter of our least en-deav-or—

1 His faith-ful Lord is walk-ing by his side!
2 And love still shines, tho days be dark and grim.
3 Be Thou our Guest, our hearts and homes to share. A-men.

FAMILY AND HOME

Lord, I Want to Remember

"Lord, I want to remember that my children are not my children. Let me let them manage themselves at the right pace. May they have the self-respect which comes from a growing self-government. Free them from unnecessary resentment.

"From infancy up, may they know how to love because they have seen love at its best. Here in our home may they be taught that they are children of God. And may they sense the Divine in others also.

"May they know the joy of work well done. Early may they learn what they need for discipline and staying power. As they tie into the problems of society, may they be angry when they should, as they should.

"For the future of all, this is my prayer."

—Charlie W. Shedd

540 Happy the Home When God Is There

When I call to remembrance the . . . faith that is in thee, which dwelt first in thy grandmother, . . . and thy mother. — II Timothy 1:5

Henry Ware, Jr.
Bryan Jeffery Leech, alt.

ST. AGNES
John B. Dykes

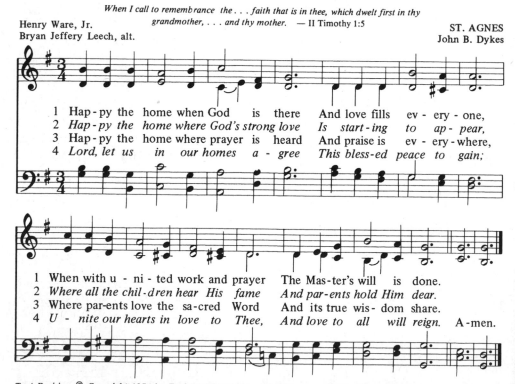

1 Hap-py the home when God is there And love fills ev-ery-one,
2 *Hap-py the home where God's strong love Is start-ing to ap-pear,*
3 Hap-py the home where prayer is heard And praise is ev-ery-where,
4 *Lord, let us in our homes a-gree This bless-ed peace to gain;*

1 When with u-ni-ted work and prayer The Mas-ter's will is done.
2 *Where all the chil-dren hear His fame And par-ents hold Him dear.*
3 Where par-ents love the sa-cred Word And its true wis-dom share.
4 *U-nite our hearts in love to Thee, And love to all will reign.* A-men.

FAMILY AND HOME

For this reason I kneel before the Father, from whom the whole family of believers in heaven and on earth derives its name. I pray that out of His glorious riches He may strengthen you with power through His Spirit in your inner being, so that Christ may dwell in your hearts through faith. And I pray that you, being rooted and established in love, may have power, together with all the saints, to grasp how wide and long and high and deep is the love of Christ, and to know this love that surpasses knowledge—that you may be filled to the measure of all the fullness of God.

Now to Him who is able to do immeasurably more than all we ask or imagine, according to His power that is at work within us, to Him be glory in the church and in Christ Jesus throughout all generations, for ever and ever!

As a prisoner for the Lord, then, I urge you to live a life worthy of the calling you have received. Be completely humble and gentle; be patient, bearing with one another in love. Make every effort to keep the unity of the Spirit through the bond of peace. There is one body and one Spirit—just as you were called to one hope when you were called—one Lord, one faith, one baptism; one God and Father of all, who is over all and through all and in all.

—(NIV)

Prayer   **542**

Lord,
All around us we see brokenness, and we are aware of the fragility of life.

There is a child's delicate trust and sense of wonder which can be so easily trampled and broken.

There is a teenager's sense of self-worth which can be completely shattered by a word or simply by a disapproving look.

There is a family's unit of love, respect, and closeness which can be marred by criticism or misunderstandings, dividing family members into torn and fragmented individuals.

There is a marriage (we all thought was so whole and sturdy) which can splinter into pieces before our eyes.

There is an old man, a young boy, and a middle-aged woman who all suffer from the crushing effects of daily pressures. Their minds are emotionally disturbed and frail.

O dear Lord, be the glue that holds our fragmented hearts and minds together and never let us forget Your words:

"I am leaving you with a gift—peace of mind and heart! And the peace I give isn't fragile like the peace the world gives. So don't be troubled or afraid."

Thank You, Lord, for that because these *are* very fragile times and sometimes we *are* afraid.

—Joyce Landorf

543 The Family of God

Gloria Gaither
William J. Gaither

FAMILY OF GOD
William J. Gaither

*And God said, I will dwell in them . . . and they shall be My people;
. . . and ye shall be My sons and daughters.* — II Corinthians 6:16, 18

I'm so glad I'm a part of the fam-ily of God— I've been washed in the foun-tain, cleansed by His blood! Joint heirs with Je-sus as we trav-el this sod, For I'm part of the fam-i-ly, the fam-i-ly of

Fine

God.

1 You will no-tice we say "broth-er and sis-ter" 'round
2 *From the door of an or-phanage to the house of the*

1 here— It's be-cause we're a fam-i-ly and these folks are so near;
2 *King— No long-er an out-cast, a new song I sing;*

THE CHURCH—FAMILY OF BELIEVERS

1 When one has a heart-ache we all share the tears,
2 From rags un-to rich-es, from the weak to the strong,

D.C.

1 And re-joice in each vic-tory In this fam-i-ly so dear.
2 I'm not wor-thy to be here, But, praise God, I be-long!

The Bond of Love

544

By this shall all men know that ye are My disciples — if ye love one another.
— John 13:35

Otis Skillings

BOND OF LOVE
Otis Skillings

1 We are one in the bond of love, We are one in the
2 Let us sing now, ev-ery-one, Let us feel His

1 bond of love; We have joined our spir-it with the
2 love be-gun; Let us join our hands that the

1 Spir-it of God, We are one in the bond of love.
2 world will know We are one in the bond of love.

THE CHURCH—FAMILY OF BELIEVERS

545 I Love Your Kingdom, Lord

The Kingdom of God is . . . righteousness and peace, and joy in the Holy Spirit.

Based on Psalm 26:8   — Romans 14:17

Timothy Dwight

ST. THOMAS
Williams' *New Universal Psalmodist*

1 I love Your king-dom, Lord, The house of Your a-bode,
2 *I love Your Church, O God— Her walls be-fore Your stand,*
3 For her my tears shall fall, For her my prayers as-cend,
4 *Sure as Your truth shall last, To Zi-on shall be given*

1 The Church our blest Re-deem-er saved With His own pre-cious blood.
2 *Dear as the ap-ple of Your eye, And held with-in Your hand.*
3 To her my cares and toils be given 'Til all con-cerns shall end.
4 *The bright-est glo-ries earth can yield, And bright-er joys of heaven. A-men.*

Handbell descant by Darlene Lawrence

THE CHURCH—FAMILY OF BELIEVERS

We Are God's People

546

We are His people, and the sheep of His pastures.
— Psalm 100:3

SYMPHONY
Johannes Brahms
Arranged by Fred Bock

Bryan Jeffery Leech

Unison

1 We are God's peo - ple, the cho - sen of the Lord,
2 *We are God's loved ones, the Bride of Christ our Lord,*
3 We are the Bod - y of which the Lord is Head,
4 *We are a Tem - ple, the Spir - it's dwell - ing place,*

1 Born of His Spir - it, es - tab - lished by His Word; Our
2 *For we have known it, the love of God out - poured; Now*
3 Called to o - bey Him, now ris - en from the dead; He
4 *Formed in great weak - ness, a cup to hold God's grace; We*

1 cor - ner-stone is Christ a-lone, And strong in Him we stand: O let us
2 *let us learn how to re-turn The gift of love once given: O let us*
3 wills us be a fam-i - ly Di-verse yet tru - ly one: O let us
4 *die a-lone, for on its own Each em-ber los - es fire; Yet joined in*

1 live trans - par - ent - ly, And walk heart to heart and hand in hand.
2 *share each joy and care, And live with a zeal that pleas-es Heaven.*
3 give our gifts to God, And so shall His work on earth be done.
4 *one the flame burns on To give warmth and light, and to in - spire.*

THE CHURCH—FAMILY OF BELIEVERS

547 The Church's One Foundation

Other foundation can no man lay than is laid . . . Jesus Christ.

— I Corinthians 3:11

Samuel J. Stone

AURELIA
Samuel S. Wesley

1 The Church-'s one foun - da - tion Is Je - sus Christ her Lord,
2 E - lect from ev - ery na - tion, Yet one o'er all the earth,
3 'Mid toil and trib - u - la - tion, And tu - mult of her war,
4 Yet she on earth hath un - ion With God, the Three in One,

1 She is His new cre - a - tion By wa - ter and the word;
2 Her char - ter of sal - va - tion, One Lord, one faith, one birth;
3 She waits the con - sum - ma - tion Of peace for ev - er - more;
4 And mys - tic sweet com - mun - ion With those whose rest is won;

1 From heaven He came and sought her To be His ho - ly bride;
2 One ho - ly name she bless - es, Par - takes one ho - ly food,
3 Till with the vi - sion glo - rious, Her long - ing eyes are blest,
4 O hap - py ones and ho - ly! Lord, give us grace that we

1 With His own blood He bought her, And for her life He died.
2 And to one hope she press - es, With ev - ery grace en - dued.
3 And the great Church vic - to - rious Shall be the Church at rest.
4 Like them, the meek and low - ly, On high may dwell with Thee. A - men.

THE CHURCH—FAMILY OF BELIEVERS

Arranged by Eric Thiman

4 Yet she on earth hath un - ion With God, the Three in One,

And mys-tic sweet com-mun - ion With those whose rest is won;

O hap-py ones and ho - ly! Lord, give us grace that we

Like them, the meek and low - ly, On high may dwell with Thee. A-men.

THE CHURCH—FAMILY OF BELIEVERS

548 Getting Used to the Family of God

"But you are . . . a people set apart to sing the praises of God."
— I Peter 2:9

Gloria Gaither
William J. Gaither

TOGETHER
William J. Gaither

1 Climb-ing the moun-tains, cross-ing the plains, Ford-ing the
2 *Reach-ing our hands to a broth-er that's new, Learn-ing to*

1 riv-ers, shar-ing the pains; Some-times the loss-es and
2 *say that I real-ly love you; Learn-ing to walk as the*

1 some-times the gain, Get-ting used to the fam-'ly of God.
2 *Mas-ter would do,*

Go-ing to-geth-er, en-joy-ing the trip, Get-ting used to the

fam-'ly I'll spend e-ter-ni-ty with; Learn-ing to love you, how

THE CHURCH—FAMILY OF BELIEVERS

eas - y it is, Get-ting used to the fam-'ly of God.

Prayer for Unity

549

*Our Father, we thank You for the privilege of being together
    at this time and in this place.*

*As Your people, we pray that Your love will unite us into a
    fellowship of discovery.*

*Cleanse us of everything that would sap our strength for
    togetherness.*

Unravel the knots in our spirits.
Cleanse the error of our minds.
Free us from the bondage of our negative imaginations.
*Break down the barriers that sometimes keep us apart and
    cause us to drift along without a dream.*

As we go from here—
Explode in us new possibilities for service.
*Kindle within us the fires of Your compassion so that we
    may not wait too long to learn to love.*

May we be a people with loving purposes—
Reaching out . . .
Breaking walls . . .
Building bridges . . .
Let us be Your alleluia in a joyless, fragmented world.

In the name of our Lord, we pray.
Amen.

—Champ Traylor

550 Come, We that Love the Lord

Ye are come unto Mount Zion, and unto the city of the living God . . . . — Hebrews 12:22

Isaac Watts
Robert Lowry

MARCHING TO ZION
Robert Lowry

1 Come, we that love the Lord, And let our joys be known; Join
2 *Let those re - fuse to sing Who nev - er knew our God;* But
3 Then let our songs a-bound And ev - ery tear be dry; We're

1 in a song with sweet ac-cord, Join in a song with sweet ac - cord
2 *chil - dren of the heaven - ly King, But chil - dren of the heaven - ly King*
3 march-ing thru Em-man-uel's ground, We're march-ing thru Em-man-uel's ground

1 And thus sur - round the throne, And thus sur - round the throne.
2 *May speak their joys a - broad, May speak their joys a - broad.*
3 To fair - er worlds on high, To fair - er worlds on high.

We're march - ing to Zi - on, Beau - ti - ful, beau - ti - ful Zi - on; We're

march - ing up - ward to Zi - on, The beau - ti - ful cit - y of God.

THE CHURCH—FAMILY OF BELIEVERS

There's a Church Within Us, O Lord   551

Behold, the Kingdom of God is within you.
— Luke 17:21

THE CHURCH WITHIN US
Kent E. Schneider

Kent E. Schneider

1 There's a church with - in us, O Lord,
2 *There's po - ten - tial with - in us, O Lord;*
3 There's a fire with - in us, O Lord;
4 *There's some build-ing to be done, O Lord,*
5 There's the church with - in us, O Lord,

1 There's a church with - in us, O Lord.
2 *Some-thing's stir - ring with - in us, O Lord.*
3 A new life's a - burn - in', O Lord.
4 *There's some build - ing to be done, O Lord.*
5 There's the church with - in us, O Lord.

1 Not a build - ing, but a soul, Not a por - tion, but a
2 *Some-thing's strain-ing to have birth, To be vis - i - ble on*
3 A fire for new life, Com - bat - ing pres - ent
4 *Not with steel, not with stone, But with lives which are our*
5 Not a build - ing, but one soul, Not a por - tion, but one

1 whole— There's a church with - in us, O Lord.
2 *earth— There's po - ten - tial with - in us, O Lord.*
3 strife— There's a fire with - in us, O Lord.
4 *own— There's the church to be built, O Lord.*
5 whole— We are your church in the world.

THE CHURCH - FAMILY OF BELIEVERS

552 Plenty of Room in the Family

Once you were not a people . . . now you are the people of God.

Gloria Gaither
William J. Gaither

— I Peter 2:10a

PLENTY OF ROOM
William J. Gaither

Plen-ty of room in the fam - ily, Room for the young and the old;

Plen-ty of hap - pi-ness, plen-ty of love, Plen-ty of room in the fold.

Fine

1 There's plen-ty of food at the ta - ble, No
2 *There's lots to be done in the fam - ily,* A
3 If you're lone-ly and look - ing for friend - ship, If you're

1 need to e-con - o-mize there; There's all you can hold and there's
2 *job that will fit ev-ery man;* There's car-ing and lift - ing and
3 lost and you want to be found, There's plen-ty of room in the

THE CHURCH—FAMILY OF BELIEVERS

1 plen - ty be - sides, The store-house will nev - er be bare.
2 *lov - ing to do,* *So pitch in and do* *all you can.*
3 fam - ily of God, There's plen - ty of love to go 'round.

Psalm 15   553

Who is the one, O Lord, that remains a part
of Your kingdom?
What are the prerequisites for membership
in Your family?

It is that one who walks circumspectly—
and in obedience to Your precepts and principles.
He must be open and honest before God and man.
He must speak and act in love toward his neighbor.
He cannot condone that which is evil
and must not participate in that
which promotes injustice.
He must listen to his brother's griefs
and complaints.
He must seek to lighten his burden
and to share in his sorrow and pain.
He must reach out to heal rather than to hurt,
to be kind and gentle to all who cross his path.

Those who lovingly relate to God and fellowman
will never be separated from the family of God.

—Leslie Brandt

Hear Our Prayer, O Lord   554

Hear our prayer, O Lord;

Incline Thine ear to us

And grant us Thy peace. Amen.

—Traditional

THE CHURCH—FAMILY OF BELIEVERS

555 Built on the Rock

. . . they drank of the Spiritual Rock . . . and that Rock is Christ. — I Corinthians 10:4

Nicolai F. S. Grundtvig
Tr. by Carl Doving
Revised by Fred C. M. Hansen

KIRKEN
Ludwig M. Lindeman

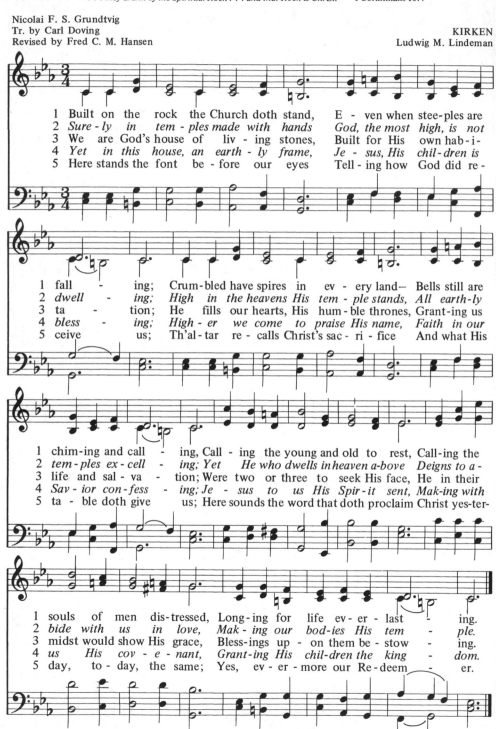

1 Built on the rock the Church doth stand, E - ven when stee-ples are
2 *Sure - ly in tem - ples made with hands God, the most high, is not*
3 We are God's house of liv - ing stones, Built for His own hab - i -
4 *Yet in this house, an earth - ly frame, Je - sus, His chil-dren is*
5 Here stands the font be - fore our eyes Tell - ing how God did re -

1 fall - ing; Crum-bled have spires in ev - ery land— Bells still are
2 *dwell - ing; High in the heavens His tem - ple stands, All earth-ly*
3 ta - tion; He fills our hearts, His hum - ble thrones, Grant-ing us
4 *bless - ing; High - er we come to praise His name, Faith in our*
5 ceive us; Th'al - tar re - calls Christ's sac - ri - fice And what His

1 chim-ing and call - ing, Call - ing the young and old to rest, Call-ing the
2 *tem - ples ex - cell - ing; Yet He who dwells in heaven a-bove Deigns to a -*
3 life and sal - va - tion; Were two or three to seek His face, He in their
4 *Sav - ior con - fess - ing; Je - sus to us His Spir-it sent, Mak-ing with*
5 ta - ble doth give us; Here sounds the word that doth proclaim Christ yes-ter-

1 souls of men dis-tressed, Long-ing for life ev - er - last - ing.
2 *bide with us in love, Mak - ing our bod-ies His tem - ple.*
3 midst would show His grace, Bless-ings up - on them be - stow - ing.
4 *us His cov - e - nant, Grant-ing His chil-dren the king - dom.*
5 day, to - day, the same; Yes, ev - er - more our Re-deem - er.

There's a Quiet Understanding

556

I will pray with the understanding, . . . also, I will sing with the understanding. . . . —I Corinthians 14:15

QUIET UNDERSTANDING

Tedd Smith

Tedd Smith

1 There's a qui - et un - der-stand-ing When we're gath-ered
2 And we know when we're to-geth-er, shar - ing love and

1 in the Spir - it, It's a prom - ise that He gives us,
2 un - der-stand-ing, That our broth-ers and our sis - ters

1 When we gath-er in His name. There's a love we feel in Je-sus,
2 Feel the one-ness that He brings. Thank You, thank You, thank You, Je-sus,

1 There's a man - na that He feeds us, It's a prom - ise
2 For the way You love and feed us, For the man - y

1 that He gives us When we gath-er in His name.
2 ways You lead us,

Thank You, thank You, Lord.

THE CHURCH—FAMILY OF BELIEVERS

557 Christ Is Made the Sure Foundation

And built upon the foundation . . . Jesus Christ himself being the chief cornerstone.

—Ephesians 2:20

Latin: 7th Century
Tr. by John M. Neale

REGENT SQUARE
Henry T. Smart

1 Christ is made the sure foun-da-tion, Christ the head and
2 *To this tem - ple, where we call Thee, Come, O Lord of*
3 Here vouch-safe to all Thy serv-ants What they ask of
4 *Laud and hon-or to the Fa-ther, Laud and hon-or*

1 cor - ner - stone, Chos - en of the Lord and prec - ious,
2 *hosts, to - day; With ac - cus - tomed lov - ing - kind - ness*
3 Thee to gain, What they gain from Thee for - ev - er
4 *to the Son, Laud and hon-or to the Spir - it,*

1 Bind - ing all the Church in one, Ho - ly Zi - on's
2 *Hear Thy peo - ple as they pray, And Thy full - est*
3 With the bless - ed to re - tain, And here-aft - er
4 *Ev - er three and ev - er one, One in might and*

1 help for-ev - er, And her con - fi - dence a - lone.
2 *ben - e - dic - tion Shed with - in its walls al - way.*
3 in Thy glo - ry Ev - er - more with Thee to reign.
4 *one in glo - ry, While un - end - ing a - ges run. A-men.*

THE CHURCH—FAMILY OF BELIEVERS

The People of God 558

My dear people, let us love one another since love comes from God and everyone who loves is begotten by God and knows God. Anyone who fails to love can never have known God, because God is love. God's love for us was revealed when God sent into the world His only Son so that we could have life through Him; this is the love I mean: not our love for God, but God's love for us when He sent His Son to be the sacrifice that takes our sins away. My dear people, since God has loved us so much, we too should love one another. No one has ever seen God; but as long as we love one another God will live in us and His love will be complete in us. We can know that we are living in Him and He is living in us because He lets us share His Spirit.

We ourselves saw and we testify that the Father sent His Son as Savior of the world. If anyone acknowledges that Jesus is the Son of God, God lives in Him, and He in God. We ourselves have known and put our faith in God's love towards ourselves. God is love and anyone who lives in love lives in God, and God lives in Him. Love will come to its perfection in us when we can face the day of judgement without fear; because even in this world we have become as He is. In love there can be no fear, but fear is driven out by perfect love: because to fear is to expect punishment, and anyone who is afraid is still imperfect in love. We are to love, then because He loved us first. Anyone who says, "I love God", and hates his brother, is a liar, since a man who does not love the brother that he can see cannot love God, whom he has never seen. So this is the commandment that He has given us, that anyone who loves God must also love his brother.

— 1 John 4:7-21 (JB)

Come, Holy Spirit, Dove Divine 559

We are buried with Him in baptism. — Romans 6:4

MARYTON
Adoniram Judson
H. Percy Smith

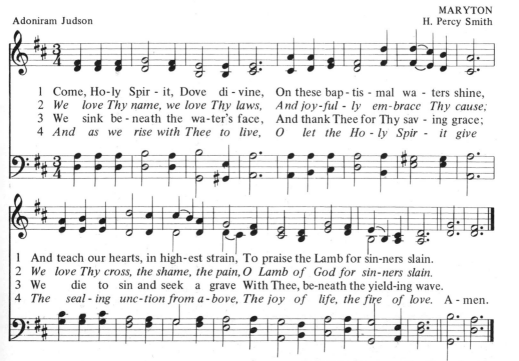

1 Come, Ho-ly Spir-it, Dove di-vine, On these bap-tis-mal wa-ters shine,
2 *We love Thy name, we love Thy laws, And joy-ful-ly em-brace Thy cause;*
3 We sink be-neath the wa-ter's face, And thank Thee for Thy sav-ing grace;
4 *And as we rise with Thee to live, O let the Ho-ly Spir-it give*

1 And teach our hearts, in high-est strain, To praise the Lamb for sin-ners slain.
2 *We love Thy cross, the shame, the pain, O Lamb of God for sin-ners slain.*
3 We die to sin and seek a grave With Thee, be-neath the yield-ing wave.
4 *The seal-ing unc-tion from a-bove, The joy of life, the fire of love.* A-men.

THE CHURCH—FAMILY OF BELIEVERS

560   Blest Be the Tie That Binds

Ye are the body of Christ and members in particular . . . . — I Corinthians 12:27

DENNIS
Johann G. Naegeli
Arranged by Lowell Mason

John Fawcett

1 Blest be the tie that binds Our hearts in Chris - tian love;
2 *Be - fore our Fa - ther's throne We pour our ar - dent prayers;*
3 We share each oth - er's woes, Each oth - er's bur - dens bear;
4 *From sor - row, toil, and pain, And sin we shall be free;*

1 The fel - low-ship of kin - dred minds Is like to that a - bove.
2 *Our fears, our hopes, our aims are one, Our com - forts and our cares.*
3 And oft - en for each oth - er flows The sym - pa - thiz - ing tear.
4 *And per - fect love and joy shall reign Through all e - ter - ni - ty.*   A - men.

561   Thanksgiving

Thank You, Father, for Your magnificence in nature.
Thank You, Father, for the inner promptings of Your Spirit.
Thank You, Father, for fresh truth to live by.
Thank You, Father, for people whose lives illustrate Your word.
Thank You, Father, for this church to which I belong,

       for those who help me,
       intercede for me,
       support me,
       love me,
       inspire me.

Lord, I cannot live as a Christian without them, for I need that part of Yourself that You
       have placed within them.
And they cannot live without me, because they need the gifts that You have deposited in
       me.
Lord, free us of the selfishness, the self-centeredness, the ego-trips, the independence of
       spirit that keeps us from binding ourselves into one.

Lord, help us to think first of those things which will benefit others before we begin listing
       our own needs.
Give us grace to live in such a way that we *draw* attention to You. Amen.

—Bryan Jeffery Leech

THE CHURCH—FAMILY OF BELIEVERS

Two Communion Readings

I Corinthians 11:17-29   **562**

The teaching I gave you
was given me personally by the Lord Himself,
and it was this:

the Lord Jesus,
in the same night in which He was betrayed,
took bread and when He had given thanks
He broke it and said,
"This is My body — and it is for you.
Do this in remembrance of Me."

Similarly, when supper was ended,
He took the cup saying,
"This cup is the new agreement made by My blood:
do this, whenever you drink it,
in remembrance of Me."

This can only mean that whenever you eat this bread and drink this cup,
you are proclaiming the Lord's death until He comes again.

So that, whoever eats the bread or drinks the cup of the Lord
without proper reverence
is sinning against the body and blood of the Lord.

No, a man should thoroughly examine himself,
and only then
should he eat the bread or drink of the cup.
He that eats and drinks carelessly
is eating and drinking a condemnation of himself,
for he is blind to the presence of the Body.

—(J.B. Phillips)

Revelation 22:16-17   **563**

"I, Jesus,
have sent my angel to you with this testimony for the churches.
I am the root and the offspring of David,
the bright morning star."

The Spirit and the Bride say, "Come."
And let him who hears say, "Come."
And let him who is thirsty come,
let him who desires
take the water of life without price.

—(RSV)

THE CHURCH—FAMILY OF BELIEVERS

564 Let Us Break Bread Together

He took bread and blessed it, and brake, and gave to them.
— Luke 24:30

American Folk Hymn

LET US BREAK BREAD
American Folk Melody

1 Let us break bread to - geth-er on our knees;
2 *Let us drink wine to - geth-er on our knees;*
3 Let us praise God to - geth-er on our knees;

1 Let us break bread to - geth-er on our knees;
2 *Let us drink wine to - geth-er on our knees;*
3 Let us praise God to - geth-er on our knees;

When I fall on my knees, With my face to the ris - ing sun,

O Lord, have mer - cy on me.

COMMUNION

A Hymn of Joy We Sing

565

. . . I went with them to the house of God with . . . joy and praise. — Psalm 42:4

Based on Matthew 26:30
Aaron R. Wolfe

SCHUMANN
Mason and Webb's *Cantica Laudis*

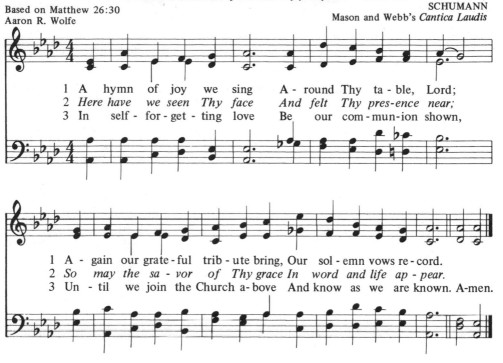

1 A hymn of joy we sing A - round Thy ta - ble, Lord;
2 *Here have we seen Thy face And felt Thy pres-ence near;*
3 In self - for - get - ting love Be our com - mun-ion shown,

1 A - gain our grate-ful trib - ute bring, Our sol - emn vows re-cord.
2 *So may the sa - vor of Thy grace In word and life ap - pear.*
3 Un - til we join the Church a-bove And know as we are known. A-men.

One Solitary Life

566

Born in an obscure village, He was the child of a peasant woman. He worked in a carpenter shop until He was thirty years old, and then for three years He travelled around the country, stopping long enough to talk and to listen to people, and help where He could. He never wrote a book, He never had a hit record, He never went to college, He never ran for public office, He never had a family, or owned a house. He never did any of the things that usually accompany greatness. He had no credentials but Himself. But when He was only thirty-three years old, the tide of public opinion turned against Him, and His friends all rejected Him. When He was arrested, very few wanted anything to do with Him. After the trial, He was executed by the State along with admitted thieves. Only because a generous friend offered his own cemetery plot was there any place to bury Him. This all happened nineteen centuries ago, and yet today He is the leading figure of the human race, and the ultimate example of love. Now it is no exaggeration to say that all the armies that have ever marched, all the navies that have ever set sail, all the rulers that have ever ruled, all the kings that have ever reigned on this earth, all put together have not affected the life of man on earth like this One Solitary Life.

—Fred Bock (alt.)

567

Here, O My Lord, I See Thee Face to Face

Horatius Bonar

Thy Face, Lord, will I seek. —Psalm 27:8

PENITENTIA
Edward Dearle

1 Here, O my Lord, I see Thee face to face,
2 *Here would I feed upon the bread of God,*
3 I have no help but Thine, nor do I need
4 *Mine is the sin, but Thine the right-eous-ness,*

1 Here would I touch and han-dle things un-seen;
2 *Here drink with Thee the roy-al wine of heaven;*
3 An-oth-er arm save Thine to lean up-on;
4 *Mine is the guilt, but Thine the cleans-ing blood;*

1 Here grasp with firm-er hand e-ter-nal grace,
2 *Here would I lay a-side each earth-ly load,*
3 It is e-nough, my Lord, e-nough in-deed—
4 *Here is my robe, my ref-uge, and my peace—*

1 And all my wea-ri-ness up-on Thee lean.
2 *Here taste a-fresh the calm of sin for-giv'n.*
3 My strength is in Thy might, Thy might a-lone.
4 *Thy blood, Thy right-eous-ness, O Lord, my God.* A-men.

COMMUNION

We Dedicate This Temple

568

I have built a house of habitation for thee. — II Chronicles 6:2a

AURELIA
Samuel S. Wesley

Ernest K. Emurian

1 We ded-i-cate this tem-ple, O Fa-ther, un-to Thee,
2 *We ded-i-cate this tem-ple To Christ, the Lord of love,*
3 We ded-i-cate this tem-ple, O Spir-it from on high,
4 *We ded-i-cate this tem-ple, This la-bor of our hands,*

1 The God of an-cient a-ges And a-ges yet to be:
2 *Who brought God's rev-e-la-tion, The king-dom from a-bove:*
3 To Thee, in our thanks-giv-ing That Thou art al-ways nigh
4 *To Fa-ther, Son and Spir-it, Whose tem-ple ev-er stands*

1 That here our hearts may wor-ship And here our songs as-cend
2 *That we may learn His good-ness, His god-li-ness and grace,*
3 To com-fort us in sor-row, To strength-en in dis-tress:
4 *In hearts that learn to love Thee And minds that com-pre-hend,*

1 In lov-ing ad-o-ra-tion And praise that knows no end.
2 *Who holds all men and na-tions With-in His love's em-brace.*
3 That we, through truth and mer-cy, May walk in ho-li-ness.
4 *In wills em-powered to wit-ness Thy king-dom with-out end!* A-men.

DEDICATION SERVICES

ᶜWelcoming a Child

The Child's Parents: Lord, You have trusted us with one of Your priceless treasures, a human child. You have allowed us to share with You in the miracle of creation and now that miracle has become flesh—and we hold it in our arms. We are excited and full of joy! But we are also fearful. O, Lord, we are imperfect parents in such an imperfect world. Speak to us. Assure us of Your nearness—now, as we wait with this child, speak to us.

Minister: *Unless you are converted and become as little children, you shall not enter into the kingdom of heaven. Whosoever shall humble himself as this little child, the same is the greatest in the kingdom of heaven. And whoever shall receive one such little child in My name receives Me.* [1]

Choir: Train up a child in the way he should go: and when he is old, he will not depart from it. [2] I am the Way, the Truth, and the Life. [3]

Minister: *And all thy children shall be taught of the Lord, and great shall be the peace of your children.* [4]

Choir: Cast all your cares upon Him for He cares for you.

People: *Trust in the Lord with all your heart; and lean not to your own understanding. In all your ways acknowledge Him, and He shall direct your paths.* [5]

Prayer by Layman: Lord, we have here in our church family a new child, a new person, a new soul. The responsibility for this little person is too much for any two parents alone. They need the loving support of the fellowship of believers as they train and guide and nurture little _(name)_ . We give ourselves today, Lord, to that task. We accept the responsibility of helping to bring _(name)_ to maturity in You. We will uphold him (her) with our love, teach him (her) the word of God, encourage him (her) when he (she) fails, and we will be careful not to bruise this tender bud by harsh words, quick judgments, and cruel criticism. For truly, Father, this is our child, and we want to protect and teach him (her) and to bring him (her) to the moment when he (she) will choose for himself (herself) to know You as Savior and Lord of his (her) life. Amen.

— Gloria Gaither

1. Matthew 18:3-5
2. Proverbs 22:6
3. John 14:6
4. Isaiah 54:13
5. Proverbs 3:5 (KJV)

Thank God for Children

570

Children possess an uncanny ability to cut to the core of the issue, to expose life to the bone, and strip away the barnacles that cling to the hull of our too sophisticated pseudo-civilization. One reason for this, I believe, is that children have not mastered our fine art of deception, that we call "finesse." Another is that they are so "lately come from God" that faith and trust are second nature to them. They have not acquired the obstructions to faith that come with education; they possess instead unrefined wisdom, a gift from God.

—Gloria Gaither

This Child We Dedicate to Thee

571

And Hannah prayed . . . and the child Samuel grew on, and was in favor with God . . . and man.
— I Samuel 2:1 & 26

From the German
Tr. by Samuel Gilman

FEDERAL STREET
Henry K. Oliver

1 This child we ded - i - cate to Thee, O God of
2 O may Thy Spir - it gen - tly draw Its will - ing

1 grace and pu - ri - ty! In Thy great love its life pro -
2 soul to keep Thy law; May vir - tue, pi - e - ty, and

1 long, Shield it, we pray, from sin and wrong.
2 truth Dawn e - ven with its dawn - ing youth. A - men.

DEDICATION SERVICES

572

Renew Thy Church, Her Ministries Restore

. . . Thou hath lost thy first love. — Revelation 2:4

Kenneth Lorne Cober

ALL IS WELL
J. T. White's "Sacred Harp"

1 Re-new Thy church, her min-is-tries re-store: Both to serve and a-dore.
2 *Teach us Thy Word, re-veal its truth di-vine; On our path let it shine.*
3 Teach us to pray, for Thou art ev-er near; Thy still voice let us hear.
4 *Teach us to love, with strength of heart and mind, Ev-ery-one, all man-kind.*

1 Make her a-gain as salt through-out the land, And as light from a stand.
2 *Tell of Thy works, Thy might-y acts of grace; From each page show Thy face.*
3 Our souls are rest-less till they rest in Thee: This our glad des-ti-ny.
4 *Break down old walls of pre-ju-dice and hate; Leave us not to our fate.*

1 'Mid som-ber shad-ows of the night Where greed and hatred spread their blight,
2 *As Thou hast loved us, sent Thy Son, And our sal-va-tion now is won,*
3 Be-fore Thy pres-ence keep us still, That we may find for us Thy will
4 *As Thou hast loved and given Thy life To end hos-til-i-ty and strife,*

1 O send us forth with power en-dued: Help us, Lord, be re-newed!
2 *O let our hearts with love be stirred: Help us, Lord, know Thy Word!*
3 And seek Thy guid-ance ev-ery day: Teach us, Lord, how to pray!
4 *O share Thy grace from heaven a-bove: Teach us, Lord, how to love!* A-men.

RENEWAL AND REVIVAL

Renewal 573

Renewal begins

when a person is exposed to the forces that will stretch him
and help him to discover the power of Christ
in the relationships where he feels least secure.
A church discovers renewal when it preaches and acts
in a way which motivates the members to move from their specialties
into other dimensions of life.

—Keith Miller & Bruce Larson

Revive Us Again 574

Wilt Thou not revive us again; that Thy people may rejoice in Thee? — Psalm 85:6

REVIVE US AGAIN

William P. Mackay

John J. Husband

1 We praise Thee, O God, for the Son of Thy love,
2 We praise Thee, O God, for Thy Spir - it of light,
3 All glo - ry and praise to the Lamb that was slain,
4 Re - vive us a - gain— fill each heart with Thy love;

1 For Je - sus who died and is now gone a - bove.
2 Who has shown us our Sav - ior and ban - ished our night.
3 Who has tak - en our sins and has cleansed ev - ery stain.
4 May each soul be re - kin - dled with fire from a - bove.

Hal - le - lu - jah, Thine the glo - ry! Hal - le - lu - jah, a - men! Hal - le -

lu - jah, Thine the glo - ry! Re - vive us a - gain. A - men.

RENEWAL AND REVIVAL

575 If My People Will Pray

If My people . . . pray and seek My face . . . I will forgive . . . — II Chronicles 7:14

Based on II Chronicles 7:14

CHRONICLES
Jimmy Owens

If My peo-ple which are called by My name, Shall

hum-ble them-selves, shall hum-ble them-selves and pray;

If My peo-ple who are called by My name, Shall

seek my face and turn from their wick-ed ways;

Then will I hear from heav-en, Then will I hear from heav-en,

RENEWAL AND REVIVAL

RENEWAL AND REVIVAL

576 Thou, Whose Purpose Is to Kindle

But who may abide the day of His coming? . . . for He is a refiner's fire.
— Malachi 3:2, 3

Based on Luke 12:49
David Elton Trueblood

HYFRYDOL
Rowland H. Prichard

1 Thou, whose pur-pose is to kin-dle: Now ig-nite us
2 Thou, who in Thy ho-ly gos-pel Will that man should
3 Thou, who still a sword de-liv-ers Ra-ther than a

1 with Thy fire; While the earth a-waits Thy burn-ing
2 tru-ly live: Make us sense our share of fail-ure,
3 pla-cid peace: With Thy sharp-ened word dis-turb us,

1 With Thy pas-sion us in-spire. O-ver-come our sin-ful
2 Our tran-quil-li-ty for-give. Teach us cour-age as we
3 From com-pla-cen-cy re-lease! Save us now from sat-is-

1 calm-ness, Rouse us with re-demp-tive shame; Bap-tize with Thy
2 strug-gle In all lib-er-a-ting strife; Lift the small-ness
3 fac-tion When we pri-vate-ly are free, Yet are un-dis-

1 fie-ry Spir-it, Crown our lives with tongues of flame.
2 of our vis-ion By Thine own a-bun-dant life.
3 turbed in spir-it By our broth-er's mis-er-y.

RENEWAL AND REVIVAL

Jesus Christ is unique, and one cannot be in His presence and not reveal the man he really is. Jesus pulls each person from behind his mask. In the exposure of that bleeding love on the cross, men become what they really are.

You may think you are wonderful until you stand in the presence of the One who is purity itself. It is the pure light of God that pierces a man. You can keep up your pretense of being holy until you stand in that light. Then immediately there is nowhere to hide, all your masks are torn away, all your hollow smiles fade.

Revival means to be exposed for what we are. The presence of the Lord is revealing.

—*Festo Kivengere*

II Chronicles 7:8-18   **578**

For the next seven days, they celebrated the Tabernacle Festival, with large crowds coming in from all over Israel; they arrived from as far away as Hamath at one end of the country to the brook of Egypt at the other. A final religious service was held on the eighth day. Then, on October 7, he sent the people home, joyful and happy because the Lord had been so good to David and Solomon and to His people Israel.

So Solomon finished building the Temple as well as his own palace. He completed what he had planned to do.

One night the Lord appeared to Solomon and told him, "I have heard your prayer and have chosen this Temple as the place where I want you to sacrifice to Me. If I shut up the heavens so that there is no rain, or if I command the locust swarms to eat up all of your crops, or if I send an epidemic among you, then if my people will humble themselves and pray, and search for me, and turn from their wicked ways, I will hear them from heaven and forgive their sins and heal their land. I will listen, wide awake, to every prayer made in this place. For I have chosen this Temple and sanctified it to be my home forever; my eyes and my heart shall always be here.

As for yourself, if you will follow me as your father David did, then I will see to it that you and your descendants will always be kings of Israel.

—(LB)

579 O Breath of Life

. . . He breathed on them and saith unto them: Receive Ye the Holy Ghost. — John 20:22

BLOMQVIST

Bessie Porter Head

Joel Blomqvist

1 O Breath of Life, come sweep-ing through us,
2 O Wind of God, come bend us, break us,
3 O Breath of Love, come breathe with-in us,
4 O Heart of Christ, once bro-ken for us,
5 Re-vive us, Lord! Is zeal a-bat-ing

1 Re-vive Your Church with life and power;
2 'Til hum-bly we con-fess our need;
3 Re-new-ing thought and will and heart;
4 In You we find our strength and rest;
5 While har-vest fields are vast and white?

1 O Breath of Life, come, cleanse, re-new us,
2 Then in Your ten-der-ness re-make us,
3 Come, love of Christ, a-fresh to win us,
4 Our bro-ken con-trite hearts now sol-ace,
5 Re-vive us, Lord— the world is wait-ing!

1 And fit Your Church to meet this hour.
2 Re-vive, re-store— for this we plead.
3 Re-vive Your Church in ev-ery part.
4 And let Your wait-ing Church be blest.
5 E-quip Your Church to spread the light. A-men.

RENEWAL AND REVIVAL

There Shall Be Showers of Blessing

Who hath blessed us with all spiritual blessings. — Ezekiel 34:26

SHOWERS OF BLESSING

Daniel W. Whittle

James McGranahan

1 There shall be show-ers of bless-ing: This is the prom-ise of love;
2 *There shall be show-ers of bless-ing— Pre-cious re-viv-ing a-gain;*
3 There shall be show-ers of bless-ing: Send them up-on us, O Lord;
4 *There shall be show-ers of bless-ing: O, that to-day they might fall,*

1 There shall be sea-sons re-fresh-ing, Sent from the Sav-ior a-bove.
2 *O-ver the hills and the val-leys, Sound of a-bun-dance of rain.*
3 Grant to us now a re-fresh-ing, Come, and now hon-or Thy Word.
4 *Now as to God we're con-fess-ing, Now, as on Je-sus we call!*

Show — ers of bless-ing, Show-ers of bless-ing we need:

Mer-cy-drops 'round us are fall-ing, But for the show-ers we plead.

RENEWAL AND REVIVAL

581 It Is No Secret

For I am persuaded that none of these things are hidden . . .
for this thing was not done in a corner. — Acts 26:26

IT IS NO SECRET
Stuart Hamblen

Stuart Hamblen

1 The chimes of time ring out the news; An - oth - er day is through.
2 *There is no night, for in His light You'll nev - er walk a - lone.*

1 Some-one slipped and fell. Was that some-one you? You may have longed for
2 *Al - ways feel at home where-ev-er you may roam. There is no power can*

1 add - ed strength, your cour - age to re - new. Do not be dis -
2 *con - quer you, while God is on your side. Just take Him at His*

1 heart-ened, for I bring hope to you. It is no se - cret
2 *prom-ise; Don't run a - way and hide.*

what God can do. What He's done for oth - ers, He'll do for

ENCOURAGEMENT

you.   With arms wide   o - pen,   He'll par - don   you,

It   is   no   se - cret   what God can   do.

Jeremiah's Hope
Within Hopelessness

582

Jerusalem had been devastated by Nebuchadnezzar.

He was boxed-in with gloom,—a proud city destroyed,—friends taken captive,—once-beautiful people left rotting in the streets,—infants with parched tongues cleaving to roofs of mouths,—some so hungry they turned to cannibalism. He penned his lamentation.

But then in his "Easter Eve" of the human soul, when all is lost, he senses *hope* within *hopelessness.* This soul weighed down by God's judgment springs forth with a confidence in the Lord's unconquerable mercy.

"And therefore I have hope: The steadfast love of the Lord never ceases. His mercies never come to an end!" Praise be to God for such hope!

—John A. Huffman, Jr.
Lamentations 3:21, 22

ENCOURAGEMENT

583 God's Power in Our Weakness

Worship Leader: *And He said unto me, My grace is sufficient for thee: for My strength is made perfect in weakness.*

People: He said . . . "I am with you; that is all you need. My power shows up best in weak people."

Worship Leader: *Most gladly will I glory in my infirmities that the power of Christ may rest upon me.*

People: Now I am glad to boast about how weak I am; I am glad to be a living demonstration of Christ's power, instead of showing off my own power and abilities.

Worship Leader: *For when I am weak, then am I strong.*

People: For when I am weak, then I am strong—the less I have, the more I depend on Him!

All: Yes. God's power shows up best in weak people. So I boast of my weakness, for because of it others are able to know for sure that the power and glory they see in me has got to be the *power of God*—and if that power can be present in one such as I, it surely is available to them as well!

—Gloria Gaither

584 God Is at Work Within You

Philippians 2:13

For it is God who worketh in you . . . — Philippians 2:13

TOPEKA
Fred Bock

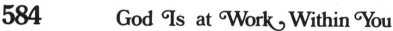

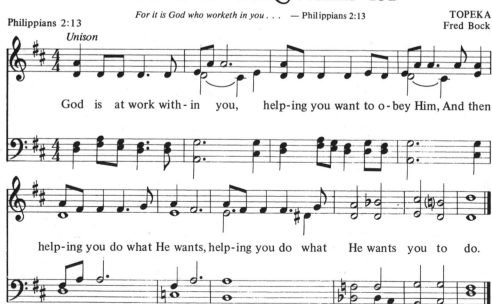

God is at work with-in you, help-ing you want to o-bey Him, And then

help-ing you do what He wants, help-ing you do what He wants you to do.

Text used by permission of Tyndale House Foundation.

ENCOURAGEMENT

Only Believe

585

It is Thy Father's good pleasure to give you the kingdom.
— Luke 12:32

Paul Rader

ONLY BELIEVE
Paul Rader

1 Fear not, lit-tle flock, from the cross to the throne, From death in-to
2 *Fear not, lit-tle flock, He go-eth a-head, Your Shep-herd se-*
3 Fear not, lit-tle flock, what-ev-er your lot; He en-ters all

1 life He went for His own; All pow-er in earth, all pow-er a-
2 *lect-eth the path you must tread; The wa-ters of Ma-rah He'll sweeten for*
3 rooms, "the doors be-ing shut." He nev-er for-sakes, He nev-er is

1 bove, Is giv-en to Him for the flock of His love.
2 *thee— He drank all the bit-ter in Geth-sem-a-ne.* On-ly be-lieve,
3 gone—So count on His pres-ence in dark-ness and dawn.

on-ly be-lieve; All things are pos-si-ble, on-ly be-lieve;

On-ly be-lieve, on-ly be-lieve; All things are pos-si-ble, on-ly be-lieve.

ENCOURAGEMENT

You, my brothers, were called to be free. But do not use your freedom to indulge your sinful nature; rather, serve one another in love. The entire law is summed up in a single command: "Love your neighbor as yourself." If you keep on biting and devouring each other, watch out or you will be destroyed by each other.

So I say, live by the Spirit, and you will not gratify the desires of your sinful nature. For the sinful nature desires what is contrary to the Spirit, and the Spirit what is contrary to the sinful nature. They are in conflict with each other, so that you do not do what you want. But if you are led by the Spirit, you are not under law.

The acts of the sinful nature are obvious: sexual immorality, impurity and debauchery; idolatry and witchcraft; hatred, discord, jealousy, fits of rage, selfish ambition, dissensions, factions and envy; drunkenness, orgies, and the like. I warn you, as I did before, that those who live like this will not inherit the kingdom of God.

But the fruit of the Spirit is love, joy, peace, patience, kindness, goodness, faithfulness, gentleness and self-control. Against such things there is no law. Those who belong to Christ Jesus have crucified their sinful nature with its passions and desires. Since we live by the Spirit, let us keep in step with the Spirit. Let us not become conceited, provoking and envying each other.

Brothers, if a man is trapped in some sin, you who are spiritual should restore him gently. But watch yourself; you also may be tempted. Carry each other's burdens, and in this way you will fulfill the law of Christ.

—(NIV)

ENCOURAGEMENT

He Keeps Me Singing

587

Speaking . . . in psalms, and hymns, and . . .
songs, making melody in your hearts . . . — Ephesians 5:19

Luther B. Bridgers

SWEETEST NAME
Luther B. Bridgers

1 There's with-in my heart a mel - o - dy— Je - sus whis - pers sweet and low,
2 *All my life was wrecked by sin and strife; Dis - cord filled my heart with pain;*
3 Feast-ing on the rich - es of His grace, Rest - ing 'neath His shelt'ring wing,
4 *Tho sometimes He leads thru wa - ters deep, Tri - als fall a - cross the way,*
5 Soon He's com-ing back to wel-come me, Far be - yond the star - ry sky;

1 "Fear not, I am with Thee—peace be still," In all of life's ebb and flow.
2 *Je - sus swept a - cross the bro-ken strings, Stirred the slumb'ring chords again.*
3 Al - ways look-ing on His smil-ing face— That is why I shout and sing.
4 *Tho sometimes the path seems rough and steep, See His foot-prints all the way.*
5 I shall wing my flight to worlds un-known, I shall reign with Him on high.

Je - sus, Je - sus, Je - sus— Sweet-est name I know,

Fills my ev - ery long - ing, Keeps me sing-ing as I go.

© Copyright 1910. Renewal 1937 Broadman Press. All rights reserved. Used by permission.© Copyright 1910. Renewal 1937 Broadman Press. All rights reserved. Used by permission.

FELLOWSHIP WITH GOD

588 In the Garden

And they heard the voice of the Lord walking in the garden. . .
— Genesis 3:8

C. Austin Miles

GARDEN
C. Austin Miles

1 I come to the gar-den a-lone, While the dew is still on the
2 *He speaks, and the sound of His voice Is so sweet the birds hush their*
3 I'd stay in the gar-den with Him Though the night a-round me be

1 ros-es; And the voice I hear, fall-ing on my ear, The
2 *sing-ing, And the mel-o-dy that He gave to me With-*
3 fall-ing, But He bids me go; through the voice of woe, His

1 Son of God dis-clos-es.
2 *in my heart is ring-ing.* And He walks with me, and He
3 voice to me is call-ing.

talks with me, And He tells me I am His own; And the

joy we share as we tar-ry there, None oth-er has ev-er known.

FELLOWSHIP WITH GOD

*N*ow when He saw the crowds,
He went up on a mountainside
and sat down.
His disciples came to Him,
and He began to teach them,
saying:

"Blessed are the poor in spirit,
for theirs is the kingdom of heaven.
Blessed are those who mourn,
for they will be comforted.
Blessed are the meek,
for they will inherit the earth.
Blessed are those who hunger
and thirst for righteousness,
for they will be filled.
Blessed are the merciful,
for they will be shown mercy.
Blessed are the pure in heart,
for they will see God.
Blessed are the peacemakers,
for they will be called sons of God.
Blessed are those who are persecuted
because of righteousness,
for theirs is
the kingdom of heaven.

Blessed are you when people insult you,
persecute you and falsely say
all kinds of evil against you
because of Me.
Rejoice and be glad,
because great is your reward in heaven,
for in the same way
they persecuted the prophets
who were before you."

—Matthew 5:1-12 (NIV)

590 I Am His and He Is Mine

. . . Yea, I have loved you with an everlasting love;
with loving kindness have I drawn thee.
— Jeremiah 31:3

George Robinson

EVERLASTING LOVE
James Mountain

1 Loved with ev - er - last - ing love, Led by grace that love to know—
2 *Heaven a - bove is soft - er blue, Earth a - round is sweet - er green;*
3 Things that once were wild a - larms Can - not now dis - turb my rest;
4 *His for - ev - er, on - ly His— Who the Lord and me shall part?*

1 Spir - it breath - ing from a - bove, Thou hast taught me it is so!
2 *Some-thing lives in ev - ery hue Christ-less eyes have nev - er seen!*
3 Closed in ev - er - last - ing arms, Pil - lowed on the lov - ing breast!
4 *Ah, with what a rest of bliss Christ can fill the lov - ing heart!*

1 O this full and per - fect peace From His pres - ence all di - vine—
2 *Birds in song His glo - ries show, Flow'rs with deep - er beau - ties shine,*
3 O to lie for - ev - er here, Doubt and care and self re - sign,
4 *Heav'n and earth may fade and flee, First-born light in gloom de - cline,*

1 In a love which can-not cease, I am His and He is mine; mine.
2 *Since I know, as now I know, I am His and He is mine; mine.*
3 While He whis - pers in my ear— I am His and He is mine; mine.
4 *But while God and I shall be, I am His and He is mine; mine.*

Just a Closer Walk with Thee
591

For we also are weak in Him, but we shall live with Him by the power of God.
— II Corinthians 13:4

Unknown

CLOSER WALK
Traditional Folk Song

1 I am weak but Thou art strong; Je - sus, keep me from all wrong;
2 *Through this world of toil and snares,* *If I fal - ter, Lord, who cares?*
3 When my fee - ble life is o'er, Time for me will be no more;
Refrain: Just a clos - er walk with Thee, Grant it, Je - sus, is my plea,

D.C. for Refrain

1 I'll be sat - is - fied as long As I walk, let me walk close to Thee.
2 *Who with me my bur - den shares?* *None but Thee, dear Lord, none but Thee.*
3 Guide me gent - ly, safe - ly o'er To Thy king - dom shore, to Thy shore.
Refrain: Dai - ly walk-ing close to Thee, Let it be, dear Lord, let it be.

John 14 : 24 -30
592

If anyone loves Me he will keep My word, and My Father will love him, and
we shall come to him, and make our home with him.

Those who do not love Me do not keep My words.

And My word is not My own: it is the word of the One who sent Me.

I have said these things to you while still with you; but the Advocate, the
Holy Spirit, whom the Father will send in My name, will teach you
everything and remind you of all I have said to you.

Peace I bequeath to you, My own peace I give you, a peace the world cannot
give, this is My gift to you.

Do not let your hearts be troubled or afraid.

You heard Me say: I am going away, and shall return.

If you loved Me you would have been glad to know that I am going to the
Father, for the Father is greater than I.

I have told you this now before it happens, so that when it does happen you
may believe.

I shall not talk with you any longer.

—(JB)

FELLOWSHIP WITH GOD

Take His Peace

Congregation:	*When the whirlwinds of doubt*
	Churn their way into your soul,
Minister:	Take His peace.
Congregation:	*When your world's reduced to ashes,*
	Leaving nothing firm and whole,
Minister:	Take His peace.
Minister:	There amidst the broken wreckage
	In the midnight of your day,
	In the apex of the stormcloud,
	He's the quiet place to stay,
Congregation & Minister:	**Take His peace, take His peace.**
Congregation:	*When your mind gropes for answers*
	To the questions that you face,
Minister:	Take His peace.
Congregation:	*When your past comes back to haunt you*
	And you need amazing grace,
Minister:	Take His peace.
Minister:	There's an answer beyond question,
	It's the truth for which you yearn:
	There's forgiveness without merit,
	There's a love you needn't earn,
Congregation & Minister:	**Take His peace, take His peace.**
Congregation:	*When your're weary of the struggle*
	And you need a place to rest,
Minister:	Take His peace.
Congregation:	*When you lose more than you're winning*
	And you're failing every test,
Minister:	Take His peace.
Minister:	There's no need to win a battle
	That's been fought and won before;
	You can lay back in the Victory,
	Freely share His boundless store,
Congregation & Minister:	**Take His peace, take His peace.**
Congregation:	*When you're worried and you're fearful*
	For the children you hold dear,
Minister:	Take His peace.
Congregation:	*Let a loving Heavenly Father*
	Share each joy and dry each tear,
Minister:	Take His peace.
Minister:	God has promised if we teach them
	And we guide them from the start,
	Then the seed of truth and peace
	Shall find rich soil in their hearts,
Congregation & Minister:	**Claim His peace, claim His peace!**

–Gloria Gaither
William J. Gaither

FELLOWSHIP WITH GOD

Anywhere with Jesus

594

... *He led them. . . by a cloudy pillar; . . . and by a pillar of fire ...*
— Nehemiah 9:12

Jessie B. Pounds
Adapted by Helen C. Dixon

SECURITY
Daniel B. Towner

1 An-y-where with Je-sus I can safe-ly go, An-y-where He
2 *An-y-where with Je-sus I am not a-lone, Oth-er friends may*
3 An-y-where with Je-sus o-ver land and sea, Tell-ing souls in

1 leads me in this world be-low; An-y-where with-out Him dear-est
2 *fail me, He is still my own; Though His hand may lead me o-ver*
3 dark-ness of sal-va-tion free; Read-y as He sum-mons me to

1 joys would fade, An-y-where with Je-sus I am not a-fraid.
2 *drear-y ways, An-y-where with Je-sus is a house of praise.*
3 go or stay, An-y-where with Je-sus when He points the way.

An-y-where! an-y-where! Fear I can-not know;

An-y-where with Je-sus I can safe-ly go.

GUIDANCE

595 Lead On, O King Eternal

If the Lord be God, follow Him . . . . — I Kings 18:21

Ernest W. Shurtleff

LANCASHIRE
Henry T. Smart
Descant by John Ness Beck

Descant

3 Lead on, Lead on, O King e-ter-nal,

1 Lead on, O King e - ter - nal, The day of march has come;
2 *Lead on, O King e - ter - nal, Till sin's fierce war shall cease,*
3 Lead on, O King e - ter - nal, We fol - low not with fears,

For glad - ness breaks like morn-ing Wher-e'er Thy face ap - pears.

1 Hence-forth in fields of con - quest Thy tents shall be our home.
2 *And ho - li - ness shall whis - per The sweet a - men of peace.*
3 For glad - ness breaks like morn - ing Wher - e'er Thy face ap - pears.

Thy cross is lift - ed o'er us, We jour - ney in its light;

1 Through days of prep - a - ra - tion Thy grace has made us strong, And
2 *For not with swords' loud clash - ing, Nor roll of stir - ring drums—With*
3 Thy cross is lift - ed o'er us, We jour - ney in its light; The

GUIDANCE

The crown awaits the con-quest: Lead on, O God of might. Lead on! A - men.

1 now, O King e - ter - nal, We lift our bat - tle song.
2 *deeds of love and mer - cy The heaven-ly king-dom comes.*
3 crown a - waits the con-quest: Lead on, O God of might. A - men.

Alternate Last Verse Harmonization

Arranged by John Ness Beck

3 Lead on, O King e - ter - nal, we fol - low, not with fears, For

glad - ness breaks like morn - ing Where - e'er Thy face ap - pears. Thy

cross is lift - ed o'er us, We jour - ney in its light; The

crown a - waits the con-quest: Lead on, O God of might. A - men.

GUIDANCE

596
Gentle Shepherd

I am the good Shepherd and know My sheep . . . .
— John 10:14

Gloria Gaither
William J. Gaither

GENTLE SHEPHERD
William J. Gaither

Gen-tle Shep-herd, come and lead us, For we need You to help us find our way. Gen-tle Shep-herd, come and feed us, For we need Your strength from day to day. There's no oth-er we can turn to Who can help us face an-oth-er day; Gen-tle Shep-herd, come and lead us, For we need You to help us find our way.

GUIDANCE

God Leads Us Along

597

*. . . And the sheep hear His voice;
and He calls His own sheep by name, and He leadeth them out. — John 10:3*

G. A. Young

GOD LEADS US
G. A. Young

1 In shad-y, green pas-tures, so rich and so sweet, God leads His dear
2 Some-times on the mount where the sun shines so bright, God leads His dear
3 Though sor-rows be-fall us and e-vils op-pose, God leads His dear

1 chil-dren a-long; Where the wa-ter's cool flow bathes the wea-ry one's feet,
2 chil-dren a-long; Some-times in the val-ley, in dark-est of night,
3 chil-dren a-long; Thru grace we can con-quer, de-feat all our foes,

God leads His dear children a-long. Some thru the wa-ters, some thru the

flood, Some thru the fire, but all thru the blood; Some thru great sor-row, but

God gives a song, In the night sea-son and all the day long.

GUIDANCE

598 All the Way My Savior Leads Me

I have glorified Thee; . . . I have finished the work which thou gavest me.
— John 17:4

Fanny J. Crosby

ALL THE WAY
Robert Lowry

1 All the way   my Sav-ior leads me— What have   I   to ask be - side?
2 *All the   way   my Sav-ior   leads me— Cheers each wind - ing path I   tread,*
3 All the   way   my Sav-ior leads me— O   the   full - ness of His   love!

1 Can   I   doubt His ten - der mer - cy, Who through life   has been my guide?
2 *Gives me grace   for ev - ery   tri - al, Feeds me   with   the liv - ing bread.*
3 Per - fect rest   to me   is prom - ised In   my   Fa - ther's house a - bove.

1 Heaven-ly   peace, di - vin - est com - fort, Here   by   faith   in Him to dwell!
2 *Though my   wea - ry steps may fal - ter And my   soul   a-thirst may be,*
3 When my   spir - it, clothed im - mor - tal, Wings its   flight   to realms of day,

1 For   I   know, what - e'er be - fall   me, Je - sus   do - eth all   things   well;
2 *Gush-ing from   the Rock be - fore   me, Lo! a   spring of joy   I   see;*
3 This my   song through end-less a - ges: Je - sus   led me all   the   way;

1 For I know, what-e'er be - fall me, Je - sus do-eth all things well.
2 *Gush - ing from the Rock be - fore me, Lo! a spring of joy I see.*
3 This my song through end-less a - ges: Je - sus led me all the way.

Freedom of the Will 599

We remember how Jesus said, ". . . I have finished the work which Thou gavest me to do" (John 17:4). That statement reveals that God had a definite plan for Jesus' life, that He could and did know what that plan was, and that it was possible for Him to accomplish it. That was true for Christ; it is also true for each one of us. No one of us is here by accident nor by chance. God has a plan for your life—of that you can be sure.

However, God gave to each person power of choice and free-dom of will. We remember how our Lord prayed, ". . . neverthe-less not my will, but Thine be done" (Luke 22:42). That prayer teaches two very important truths: first, one might have a will for his own life that is contrary to God's will for him. Second, it is possible to follow your own will and turn your back on God's will for you. Were those two facts not true, then Christ's prayer would have been mockery.

—Charles L. Allen

600
Take Thou My Hand, O Father

Teach me Thy Way, O Lord; Lead me in a plain path....
— Psalm 27:11

Julie Katharina Hausmann
Tr. by Herman Brückner
Jeff Redd, alt.

SO NIMM DENN MEINE HÄNDE
Friedrich Silcher

1 Take Thou my hand, O Fa - ther, And lead Thou me,
2 O cov - er with Thy mer - cy My poor, weak heart!
3 Lord, make my heart re - spon - sive, And stir my soul,

1 Un - til I and my jour - ney, and heav - en see.
2 *Let ev - ery thought re - bel - lious From me de - part.*
3 Un - til through all the dark - ness, I reach my goal.

1 A - lone I would not wan - der One sin - gle day;
2 *Per - mit Thy child to lin - ger Here at Thy feet,*
3 Then take my hand, O Fa - ther, And lead Thou me

1 Be Thou my true com - pan - ion And with me stay.
2 *To ful - ly trust Thy good - ness With faith com - plete.*
3 Un - til I end my jour - ney, and hea - ven see. A - men.

GUIDANCE

Savior, Like a Shepherd Lead Us

601

. . . . That great shepherd of the sheep . . . make you perfect in every good work.

— Hebrews 13:20-21

Attributed to Dorothy A. Thrupp

BRADBURY
William B. Bradbury

1 Sav - ior, like a Shep-herd lead us, Much we need Thy ten-der care;
2 *We are Thine; do Thou be - friend us; Be the guard-ian of our way;*
3 Ear - ly let us seek Thy fa - vor; Ear - ly let us do Thy will;

1 In Thy pleas-ant pas-tures feed us; For our use Thy folds pre-pare.
2 *Keep Thy flock; from sin de - fend us; Seek us when we go a - stray.*
3 Bless-ed Lord and on - ly Sav - ior, With Thy love our bos-oms fill.

1 Bless-ed Je - sus, Bless-ed Je - sus, Thou hast bought us, Thine we are;
2 *Bless-ed Je - sus, Bless-ed Je - sus, Hear Thy chil-dren when they pray;*
3 Bless-ed Je - sus, Bless-ed Je - sus, Thou hast loved us, love us still;

1 Bless-ed Je - sus, Bless-ed Je - sus, Thou hast bought us, Thine we are.
2 *Bless-ed Je - sus, Bless-ed Je - sus, Hear Thy chil-dren when they pray.*
3 Bless-ed Je - sus, Bless-ed Je - sus, Thou hast loved us, love us still. A-men.

GUIDANCE

602 · James 1:5-8

If there is any one of you who needs wisdom, he must ask God, who gives to all freely and ungrudgingly; it will be given to him. But he must ask with faith, and no trace of doubt, because a person who has doubts is like the waves thrown up in the sea when the wind drives. That sort of person, in two minds, wavering between going different ways, must not expect that the Lord will give him anything.

—(JB)

603 · God Moves in a Mysterious Way

Heaven is my throne and the earth is my footstool — Isaiah 66:1

William Cowper

DUNDEE
Scottish Psalter

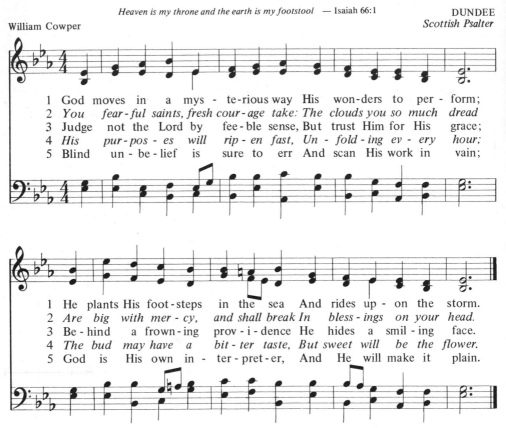

1 God moves in a mys - te-rious way His won-ders to per - form;
2 *You   fear-ful saints, fresh cour-age take: The clouds you so much   dread*
3 Judge   not the Lord by   fee - ble sense, But trust Him for His   grace;
4 *His   pur-pos - es   will   rip - en fast, Un - fold - ing ev - ery   hour;*
5 Blind   un - be - lief is   sure to   err And scan His work in   vain;

1 He plants His foot-steps in the sea And rides up - on the storm.
2 *Are big   with mer - cy,   and shall break In   bless-ings on your head.*
3 Be - hind   a frown-ing prov - i - dence He hides a smil - ing face.
4 *The bud   may have a   bit - ter taste, But sweet will be the flower.*
5 God is His own in - ter - pret-er, And He will make it plain.

604 · The Tangle of the Mind

To seek the meaning of things and God's will does not spare us either from error or from doubt; nor does it solve all the mysteries of our destiny, all the insoluble problems which are set us by any event of Nature or in our lives; nevertheless, it does give a new meaning to our lives.

—Paul Tournier

If You Will Only Let God Guide You

605

Howbeit, when He, the spirit of truth is come,
He will guide you into all truth. — John 16:13

Georg Neumark
Tr. by Catherine Winkworth
Jeff Redd, alt.

NEUMARK
Georg Neumark

1 If you will on-ly let God guide you And hope in Him through
2 *On-ly be still and wait His leis-ure In cheer-ful hope, with*
3 Sing, pray and keep His ways un-swerv-ing— So do your own part

1 all your ways, He'll give you strength what-ev-er hap-pens
2 *heart con-tent. Take all as part of God's good pleas-ure*
3 faith-ful-ly; And trust His word, its ev-ery prom-ise

1 And take you through the e-vil days; Who trusts in God's un-
2 *Which His all-car-ing love has sent; For all our in-most*
3 Shows forth our God's in-teg-ri-ty; God nev-er yet for-

1 chang-ing love Builds on the rock that can-not move.
2 *wants are known To Him who chose us for His own.*
3 sook the need Of one who trust-ed Him to lead. A-men.

GUIDANCE

606 He Leadeth Me, O Blessed Thought

He leadeth me in the paths of righteousness. — Psalm 23:3

HE LEADETH ME
William B. Bradbury
Descant by Tom Fettke

Joseph H. Gilmore

Descant

3 And when my task on earth is done, When by Thy grace the vic-tory's won,

1 He lead - eth me, O blessed thought! O words with heav'nly comfort fraught!
2 Lord, *I would clasp Thy hand in mine, Nor ev - er mur-mur nor re-pine;*
3 And when my task on earth is done, When by Thy grace the vic-t'ry's won,

E'en death's cold wave I will not flee, Since God thru Jor-dan lead-eth me.

1 What-e'er I do, where-e'er I be, Still 'tis God's hand that lead-eth me.
2 *Con-tent what-ev - er lot I see, Since 'tis my God that lead-eth me.*
3 E'en death's cold wave I will not flee, Still God through Jor-dan lead-eth me.

He lead - eth, lead-eth me, By His own hand He lead-eth me;

He lead-eth me, He lead - eth me, By His own hand He lead-eth me;

GUIDANCE

His faith-ful fol-lower I would be, For by His hand He lead-eth me.

His faith-ful fol-lower I would be, For by His hand He lead-eth me.

Where He Leads Me

607

Master, I will follow Thee whithersoever Thou goest.
— Matthew 8:19

E. W. Blandy

NORRIS
John S. Norris

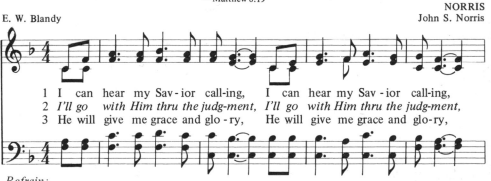

1 I can hear my Sav-ior call-ing, I can hear my Sav-ior call-ing,
2 *I'll go with Him thru the judg-ment, I'll go with Him thru the judg-ment,*
3 He will give me grace and glo-ry, He will give me grace and glo-ry,

Refrain:

Where He leads me I will fol-low, Where He leads me I will fol-low,

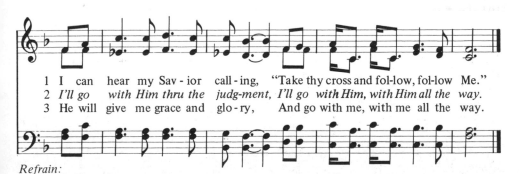

1 I can hear my Sav-ior call-ing, "Take thy cross and fol-low, fol-low Me."
2 *I'll go with Him thru the judg-ment, I'll go with Him, with Him all the way.*
3 He will give me grace and glo-ry, And go with me, with me all the way.

Refrain:

Where He leads me I will fol-low— I'll go with Him, with Him all the way.

GUIDANCE

608 Guide Me, O Thou Great Jehovah

He will guide us even unto death. — Psalm 48:14

William Williams
Tr. by Peter Williams

CWM RHONDDA
John Hughes

1 Guide me, O Thou great Je - ho - vah, Pil - grim through this
2 O - pen now the crys - tal foun - tain, Whence the heal - ing
3 When I reach the riv - er Jor - dan, Bid my anx - ious

1 bar - ren land; I am weak, but Thou art might - y— Hold me with Thy
2 *stream doth flow; Let the fire and cloud - y pil - lar Lead me all my*
3 fears sub - side; Bear me through the swell - ing cur - rent, Land me safe on

1 power - ful hand: Bread of heav - en, Bread of heav - en,
2 *jour - ney through: Strong De - liv - er - er, strong De - liv - er - er,*
3 Ca - naan's side: Songs of prais - es, songs of prais - es

1 Feed me 'til I want no more, Feed me 'til I want no more.
2 *Be Thou still my strength and shield, Be Thou still my strength and shield.*
3 I will ev - er give to Thee, I will ev - er give to Thee. A - men.

GUIDANCE

Jesus Will Walk with Me

609

But if we walk in the light as He is in the light . . . .

— John 1: 7

JESUS WILL WALK WITH ME
Haldor Lillenas

Haldor Lillenas

1 Je - sus will walk with me down thru the val - ley, Je - sus will walk with me
2 *Je - sus will walk with me when I am tempt-ed,* *Giv-ing me strength as my*
3 Je - sus will walk with me, guarding me ev - er, Giv-ing me vic-tory thru
4 *Je - sus will walk with me in life's fair morn-ing,* *And when the shadows of*

1 o - ver the plain; When in the shad-ow or when in the sun-shine,
2 *need may de - mand; When in af - flic - tion His pres - ence is near me,*
3 storm and thru strife; He is my Com-fort-er, Coun - sel - or, Lead-er,
4 *eve - ning must come; Liv - ing or dy - ing, He will not for-sake me.*

1 If He goes with me I shall not com-plain.
2 *I am up - held by His al - might - y hand.* Je - sus will
3 O - ver the un - e - ven jour - ney of life.
4 *Je - sus will walk with me all the way home.*

walk with me, He will talk with me; He will walk with me; In joy or in

sor - row, to - day and to-mor-row, I know He will walk with me.

GUIDANCE

610 Prayer

Give us

A pure heart

That we may see Thee,

A humble heart

That we may hear Thee,

A heart of love

That we may serve Thee,

A heart of faith

That we may live Thee.

—Dag Hammarskjöld

611 Precious Lord, Take My Hand

Thou wilt show me the path of life:
at Thy right hand there are pleasures for evermore.
— Psalm 6:11

Thomas A. Dorsey

PRECIOUS LORD
Arranged by Thomas A. Dorsey

1 Pre-cious Lord, take my hand, Lead me on, help me stand; I am
2 *When my way grows drear, Pre-cious Lord, lin-ger near; When my*

1 tired, I am weak, I am worn; Thru the storm, thru the night, Lead me
2 *life is al-most gone, Hear my cry, hear my call, Hold my*

1 on to the light, Take my hand, pre-cious Lord, lead me home.
2 *hand lest I fall; Take my hand, pre-cious Lord, lead me home.*

GUIDANCE

Finally then, find your strength in the Lord, in His mighty power. Put on all the armour which God provides, so that you may be able to stand firm against the devices of the devil. For our fight is not against human foes, but against cosmic powers, against the authorities and potentates of this dark world, against the superhuman forces of evil in the heavens. Therefore, take up God's armour; then you will be able to stand your ground when things are at their worst, to complete every task and still to stand. Stand firm, I say. Fasten on the belt of truth; for coat of mail put on integrity; let the shoes on your feet be the gospel of peace, to give you firm footing; and, with all these, take up the great shield of faith, with which you will be able to quench all the flaming arrows of the evil one. Take salvation for helmet; for sword, take that which the Spirit gives you—the words that come from God. Give yourselves wholly to prayer and entreaty; pray on every occasion in the power of the Spirit. To this end keep watch and persevere, always interceding for all God's people; and pray for me, that I may be granted the right words when I open my mouth, and may boldly and freely make known His hidden purpose, for which I am an ambassador—in chains. Pray that I may speak of it boldly, as it is my duty to speak.   —(NEB)

Fight the Good Fight   **613**

Fight the good fight of faith. — 1 Timothy 6:12

John S. B. Monsell

PENTECOST
William Boyd

1 Fight the good fight with all thy might! Christ is thy
2 *Run the straight race through God's good grace; Lift up thine*
3 Cast care a - side, lean on thy guide; His bound - less
4 *Faint not nor fear, His arms are near; He chang - eth*

1 strength, and Christ thy right. Lay hold on life, and
2 *eyes, and seek His face. Life with its way be -*
3 mer - cy will pro - vide. Trust, and thy trust - ing
4 *not, and thou art dear. On - ly be - lieve, and*

1 it shall be Thy joy and crown e - ter - nal - ly.
2 *fore us lies; Christ is the path, and Christ the prize.*
3 soul shall prove Christ is its life, and Christ its love.
4 *thou shalt see That Christ is all in all to thee. A-men.*

LOYALTY AND COURAGE

614

For All the Saints

God is not ashamed to be called their God; for He hath prepared for them a city.
— Hebrews 11:16

SINE NOMINE

William W. How

Ralph Vaughan Williams

Unison

1 For all the saints who from their la-bors rest, Who
2 *Thou wast their rock, their for-tress, and their might, Thou,*
3 O may Thy sol - diers, faith - ful, true, and bold,
4 O blest com - mu - nion, fel - low - ship di - vine!
5 But lo! there breaks a yet more glo - rious day; The
6 *From earth's wide bounds, from o - cean's far - thest coast, Through*

1 Thee by faith be - fore the world con - fessed, Thy
2 *Lord, their cap - tain in the well - fought fight;*
3 Fight as the saints who no - bly fought of old, And
4 *We fee - bly strug - gle, they in glo - ry shine; Yet*
5 saints tri - um - phant rise in bright ar - ray; The
6 *gates of pearl streams in the count - less host,*

1 name, O Je - sus, be for - ev - er blest:
2 *Thou, in the dark - ness drear, their one true light:*
3 win with them the vic - tor's crown of gold:
4 *all are one in Thee, for all are Thine:*
5 King of glo - ry pass - es on His way:
6 *Sing - ing to Fa - ther, Son, and Ho - ly Ghost:*

Music from "The English Hymnal" by permission of Oxford University Press.

LOYALTY AND COURAGE

Al - le-lu - ia! Al - le-lu - ia! A-men.

The Temptation to Quit 615

The program of God through history is like a relay race. Let one runner drop out and the whole team loses. Let one runner lose the baton and the whole team is eliminated. Let one runner break the rules and the whole team is disqualified. The work of no runner counts until every runner does his share and the anchor man has hit the tape at the finish line.

The phrase "let us keep our eyes fixed on Jesus" is the key. The idea is clear. There are lots of distractions as we run. Bypaths beckon us; false goals attract us; competition discourages us; opposition causes us to falter. Jesus, however, a tried and trusted leader who blazed the trail of faith by His own obedience and perseverance and who finished the course in a burst of glory is both our guide and our goal. We look away from everything else to Him, if we want to run well.

—David Hubbard

616 Stand Up, Stand Up for Jesus

Watch ye, stand fast in the faith. — I Corinthians 16:13

George Duffield

WEBB
George J. Webb

1 Stand up, stand up for Je - sus, Ye sol - diers of the cross;
2 *Stand up, stand up for Je - sus, The trum - pet call o - bey;*
3 Stand up, stand up for Je - sus, Stand in His strength a - lone;
4 *Stand up, stand up for Je - sus, The strife will not be long;*

1 Lift high His roy - al ban - ner, It must not suf - fer loss.
2 *Forth to the might - y con - flict, In this His glo - rious day.*
3 The arm of flesh will fail you, Ye dare not trust your own.
4 *This day the noise of bat - tle, The next the vic - tor's song.*

1 From vic - t'ry un - to vic - t'ry His ar - my shall He lead,
2 *Ye that are men now serve Him A - gainst un - num-bered foes;*
3 Put on the gos - pel ar - mor, Each piece put on with prayer;
4 *To him that o - ver - com - eth A crown of life shall be:*

1 'Til ev - ery foe is con - quered And Christ is Lord in - deed.
2 *Let cour - age rise with dan - ger And strength to strength op - pose.*
3 Where du - ty calls, or dan - ger Be nev - er want - ing there.
4 *He with the King of glo - ry Shall reign e - ter - nal - ly.*

LOYALTY AND COURAGE

Onward, Christian Soldiers

617

Thou therefore endure hardness as a good soldier . . . — II Timothy 2:3

Sabine Baring-Gould

ST. GERTRUDE
Arthur S. Sullivan

1 On - ward, Chris-tian sol - diers, march-ing as to war. With the cross of
2 *Like a might - y ar - my moves the Church of God; Broth-ers, we are*
3 Crowns and thrones may per - ish, king - doms rise and wane, But the Church of
4 *On - ward, then, ye peo - ple, join our hap - py throng; Blend with ours your*

1 Je - sus go - ing on be - fore: Christ, the roy-al Mas - ter, leads a -
2 *tread-ing where the saints have trod, We are not di - vid - ed, all one*
3 Je - sus con - stant will re - main, Gates of hell can nev - er 'gainst that
4 *voic - es in the tri - umph song, Glo - ry, laud, and hon - or un - to*

1 gainst the foe; For - ward in - to bat - tle, see His ban - ners go.
2 *bod - y we: One in hope and doc - trine, one in char - i - ty.*
3 Church pre-vail; We have Christ's own prom-ise, and that can - not fail.
4 *Christ the King: This through countless a - ges men and an - gels sing.*

On-ward, Chris-tian sol - diers, march-ing as to war,

With the cross of Je - sus go - ing on be - fore.

LOYALTY AND COURAGE

618 I Will Sing the Wondrous Story

Rejoice with me, for I have found my sheep which was lost. — Luke 15:6

Francis H. Rowley

WONDROUS STORY
Peter P. Bilhorn

1 I will sing the won-drous sto - ry Of the Christ who died for me,
2 *I was lost but Je - sus found me, Found the sheep that went a - stray,*
3 I was bruised but Je - sus healed me, Faint was I from man-y a fall;
4 *Days of dark - ness still come o'er me, Sor - row's paths I oft - en tread,*

1 How He left His home in glo - ry For the cross of Cal - va - ry.
2 *Threw His lov - ing arms a - round me, Drew me back in - to His way.*
3 Sight was gone, and fears pos-sessed me, But He freed me from them all.
4 *But the Sav - ior still is with me, By His hand I'm safe - ly led.*

Yes, I'll sing the won-drous sto - ry Of the Christ who died for

me, Sing it with the saints in glo - ry Gath-ered by the crys-tal sea.

TESTIMONY, WITNESS AND EVANGELISM

Our
Love for Others

619 I Love to Tell the Story

. . . They that were scattered abroad went everywhere preaching the word.

— Acts 8:4

Katherine Hankey

HANKEY
William G. Fischer

1 I love to tell the sto - ry Of un-seen things a - bove,
2 *I love to tell the sto - ry— More won-der-ful it seems*
3 I love to tell the sto - ry— 'Tis pleas-ant to re - peat
4 *I love to tell the sto - ry— For those who know it best*

1 Of Je - sus and His glo - ry, Of Je - sus and His love;
2 *Than all the gold-en fan - cies Of all our gold-en dreams;*
3 What seems, each time I tell it, More won-der-ful-ly sweet;
4 *Seem hun-ger-ing and thirst-ing To hear it like the rest;*

1 I love to tell the sto - ry— Be - cause I know 'tis true,
2 *I love to tell the sto - ry— It did so much for me,*
3 I love to tell the sto - ry— For some have nev - er heard
4 *And when in scenes of glo - ry I sing the new, new song,*

1 It sat - is - fies my long - ings As noth - ing else can do.
2 *And that is just the rea - son I tell it now to Thee.*
3 The mes - sage of sal - va - tion From God's own ho - ly word.
4 *'Twill be the old, old sto - ry That I have loved so long.*

TESTIMONY, WITNESS AND EVANGELISM

I love to tell the sto - ry! 'Twill be my theme in glo - ry—

To tell the old, old sto - ry Of Je - sus and His love.

I Stand by the Door

620

I stand by the door.

I neither go too far in, nor stay too far out,

The door is the most important door in the world—

It is the door through which men walk when they find God.

There's no use my going way inside, and staying there,

When so many are still outside and they, as much as I,

Crave to know where the door is.

And all that so many ever find

Is only the wall where a door ought to be.

They creep along the wall like blind men,

With outstretched, groping hands;

Feeling for a door, knowing there must be a door,

Yet they never find it . . .

So I stand by the door.

—Samuel Shoemaker

621 Turn Your Eyes upon Jesus

I am come that they might have life, and that they might have it more abundantly. — John 10:10   LEMMEL

Helen H. Lemmel   Helen H. Lemmel

1 O soul, are you wea - ry and trou - bled? No light in the
2 *Through death in - to life ev - er - last - ing He passed, and we*
3 His word shall not fail you—He prom - ised; Be - lieve Him, and

1 dark - ness you see? There's light for a look at the Sav - ior, And
2 *fol - low Him there; O - ver us sin no more hath do - min - ion— For*
3 all will be well: Then go to a world that is dy - ing, His

1 life more a - bun-dant and free!
2 *more than con-querors we are!*
3 per - fect sal - va - tion to tell!

Turn your eyes up-on Je - sus,

Look full in His won-der-ful face,

And the things of

earth will grow strange - ly dim In the light of His glo-ry and grace.

TESTIMONY, WITNESS AND EVANGELISM

O How He Loves You and Me

622

As the Father hath loved Me, so I have loved you;
— John 15:9

Kurt Kaiser

HE LOVES YOU AND ME
Kurt Kaiser

1 O how He loves you and me.
2 Je - sus to Cal - vary did go,

1 O how He loves you and me;
2 His love for man - kind to show;

1 He gave His life, what more could He give:
2 What He did there brought hope from de - spair:

1 O how He loves you, O, how He loves me,
2 O how He loves you, O, how He loves me,

1 O how He loves you and me.
2 O how He loves you and me.

TESTIMONY, WITNESS AND EVANGELISM

623

The Longer I Serve Him

. . . He that loseth his life for My sake shall find it.
— Matthew 10:39

William J. Gaither

THE SWEETER HE GROWS
William J. Gaither

1 Since I start-ed for the King-dom, Since my life He con-
2 *Ev - ery need He is sup-ply-ing, Plen-teous grace He be-*

1 trols, Since I gave my heart to Je-sus, The long-er I
2 *stows; Ev - ery day my way gets bright-er, The long-er I*

1 serve Him, the sweet-er He grows. The long-er I serve Him the sweet-er
2 *serve Him, the sweet-er He grows.*

He grows, The more that I love Him, more love He be-stows; Each day is like

heav-en, my heart o-ver-flows, The long-er I serve Him the sweet-er He grows.

TESTIMONY, WITNESS AND EVANGELISM

Lord, remind us that Your call is not just to the treasured time of worship or to those peaceful moments of prayer, but, because of the resurrection, it is to move with courage into the encounters and arenas of life where many have not heard the Gospel's call. Help us to speak when it is not easy, to act when it is safer to just go along with wrong. Help us to know that in the day of Jesus Christ, His kingdom will come; and let us, O God, be bound by a love amazing and divine, and then go out and embrace a weary and despairing world and lift that world to You. Amen.

—Kenneth Working

Lord, Speak to Me
625

And He that searcheth the hearts knoweth what is in the mind of the Spirit.
— Romans 8:27

Frances Ridley Havergal

CANONBURY
Robert Schumann

1 Lord, speak to me, that I may speak In living echoes of Thy tone; As Thou hast sought, so let me seek Thy erring children lost and lone.

2 O lead me, Lord, that I may lead The wandering and the wavering feet; O feed me, Lord, that I may feed Thy hungering ones with manna sweet.

3 O teach me, Lord, that I may teach The precious things Thou dost impart; And wing my words, that they may reach The hidden depths of many a heart.

4 O fill me with Thy fullness, Lord, Until my very heart o'er flow In kindling thought and glowing word, Thy love to tell, Thy praise to show.

5 O use me, Lord, use even me, Just as Thou wilt, and when, and where, Until Thy blessed face I see— Thy rest, Thy joy, Thy glory share. A-men.

TESTIMONY, WITNESS AND EVANGELISM

626 It Took a Miracle

If any man be in Christ he is a new creature . . . — II Corinthians 5:17

John W. Peterson

MONTROSE
John W. Peterson

1 My Father is om-nip-o-tent, And that you can't de-ny;
2 *Though here His glo-ry has been shown, We still can't ful-ly see*
3 The Bi-ble tells us of His power And wis-dom all way through,

1 A God of might and mir-a-cles— 'Tis writ-ten in the sky.
2 *The won-ders of His might, His throne—'Twill take e-ter-ni-ty.*
3 And ev-ery lit-tle bird and flower Are tes-ti-mo-nies too.

It took a mir-a-cle to put the stars in place, It took a

mir-a-cle to hang the world in space; But when He saved my soul,

Cleansed and made me whole, It took a mir-a-cle of love and grace!

TESTIMONY, WITNESS AND EVANGELISM

Jesus Is All the World to Me

627

Greater love hath no man than this . . . . — John 15:13

Will L. Thompson

ELIZABETH
Will L. Thompson

1 Je - sus is all the world to me, My life, my joy, my all;
2 *Je - sus is all the world to me, My Friend in tri - als sore;*
3 Je - sus is all the world to me, And true to Him I'll be;
4 *Je - sus is all the world to me, I want no bet - ter friend;*

1 He is my strength from day to day, With - out Him I would fall.
2 *I go to Him for bless - ings, and He gives them o'er and o'er.*
3 O how could I this Friend de - ny, When He's so true to me?
4 *I trust Him now, I'll trust Him when Life's fleet - ing days shall end.*

1 When I am sad to Him I go, No oth - er one can cheer me so;
2 *He sends the sun - shine and the rain, He sends the har - vest's gold - en grain;*
3 Fol - low - ing Him I know I'm right, He watch - es o'er me day and night;
4 *Beau - ti - ful life with such a Friend; Beau - ti - ful life that has no end;*

1 When I am sad He makes me glad, He's my Friend.
2 *Sun - shine and rain, har - vest of grain, He's my Friend.*
3 Fol - low - ing Him by day and night, He's my Friend.
4 *E - ter - nal life, e - ter - nal joy, He's my Friend.*

TESTIMONY, WITNESS AND EVANGELISM

628 He Touched Me

And Jesus put forth His hand and touched him, saying, I will; be thou clean.
— Matthew 8:3

William J. Gaither

HE TOUCHED ME
William J. Gaither

1 Shack - led by a heav - y bur - den, 'Neath a load of
2 Since I met this bless - ed Sav - ior, Since He cleansed and

1 guilt and shame — Then the hand of Je - sus touched me,
2 made me whole, I will nev - er cease to praise Him —

1 And now I am no long - er the same. He touched me, O He
2 I'll shout it while e - ter - ni - ty rolls.

touched me, And O the joy that floods my soul; Some - thing

TESTIMONY, WITNESS AND EVANGELISM

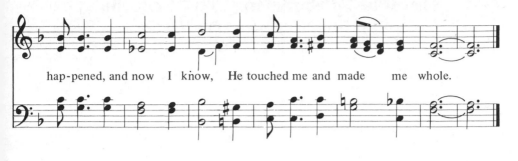

hap-pened, and now I know, He touched me and made me whole.

Only Trust Him

629

Trust ye in the Lord forever; for in the Lord . . . is everlasting strength. — Isaiah 26:4

MINERVA

John H. Stockton

John H. Stockton

1 Come, ev - ery soul by sin op-pressed, There's mer-cy with the Lord;
2 *For Je - sus shed His pre - cious blood, Rich bless-ings to be - stow;*
3 Yes, Je - sus is the Truth, the Way, That leads you in - to rest:

1 And He will sure-ly give you rest By trust-ing in His word.
2 *He of - fers now the crim-son flood To wash us white as snow.*
3 Be - lieve in Him with-out de-lay, And you are ful-ly blest.

On - ly trust Him, on - ly trust Him, On - ly trust Him now;

He will save you, He will save you, He will save you now.

TESTIMONY, WITNESS AND EVANGELISM

630 There Is Sunshine in My Soul Today

For God who commanded light to shine out of darkness hath shined in our hearts.

— II Corinthians 4:6

SUNSHINE

Eliza E. Hewitt

John R. Sweney

1 There is sun-shine in my soul to - day, More glo - ri - ous and bright
2 *There is mu - sic in my soul to - day, A car - ol to my King,*
3 There is spring-time in my soul to - day, For when the Lord is near
4 *There is glad-ness in my soul to - day, And hope and praise and love,*

1 Than glows in an - y earth - ly sky, For Je - sus is my light.
2 *And Je - sus, lis - ten-ing can hear The songs I can - not sing.*
3 The dove of peace sings in my heart, The flowers of grace ap - pear.
4 *For bless - ings which He gives me now, For joys laid up a - bove.*

O there's sun-shine, bless - ed sun-shine, When the peace-ful, hap - py mo-ments

roll; When Je-sus shows His smil - ing face, There is sun-shine in my soul.

TESTIMONY, WITNESS AND EVANGELISM

I Know Whom I Have Believed

631

. . . He is able to keep that which I have committed unto Him . . .

Based on II Timothy 1:12
Daniel W. Whittle

— II Timothy 1:12

EL NATHAN
James McGranahan

1 I know not why God's won-drous grace To me He hath made known,
2 I know not how this sav - ing faith To me He did im - part,
3 I know not how the Spir - it moves, Con- vinc - ing men of sin,
4 I know not when my Lord may come, At night or noon-day fair,

1 Nor why, un-wor-thy, Christ in love Re - deemed me for His own.
2 Nor how be-liev - ing in His word Wrought peace with-in my heart.
3 Re - veal - ing Je - sus through the word, Cre - at - ing faith in Him.
4 Nor if I walk the vale with Him, Or meet Him in the air.

But "I know whom I have be - liev - ed, and am per - suad - ed that He is

a - ble To keep that which I've com-mit-ted Un - to Him a-gainst that day."

TESTIMONY, WITNESS AND EVANGELISM

632 He's Everything to Me

... What is man that Thou art mindful of him? — Psalm 8:4

WOODLAND HILLS
Ralph Carmichael

Ralph Carmichael

1 In the stars His hand-i - work I see, On the
2 I will cel - e - brate na - tiv - i - ty, For it

1 wind He speaks with maj - es - ty; Though He rul - eth o - ver
2 has a place in his - to - ry; Sure, He came to set His

1
1 land and sea, What is that to me?
2 peo - ple free,

2
What is that to me? 'Til by faith I met Him

face to face And I felt the won-der of His grace,

TESTIMONY, WITNESS AND EVANGELISM

Then I knew that He was more than just a God who did - n't
care, who lived a - way out there, And now He walks be - side me
day by day, Ev - er watch - ing o'er me lest I stray,
Help - ing me to find that nar - row way, He's ev - ery - thing to
me. He's ev - ery - thing to me.

633 In My Heart There Rings A Melody

Serve the Lord with gladness: come before His presence with singing.
— Psalm 100:2

Elton M. Roth

HEART MELODY
Elton M. Roth

1 I have a song that Je - sus gave me, It was sent from
2 *I love the Christ who died on Cal - vary, For He washed my*
3 'Twill be my end - less theme in glo - ry, With the an - gels

1 heaven a - bove; There nev - er was a sweet - er mel - o - dy, 'Tis a
2 *sins a - way; He put with - in my heart a mel - o - dy, And I*
3 I will sing; 'Twill be a song with glo - rious har - mo - ny, When the

1 mel - o - dy of love.
2 *know it's there to stay.*
3 courts of heav - en ring.

In my heart there rings a mel - o - dy, There

rings a mel - o - dy with heav - en's har - mo - ny; In my heart there

rings a mel - o - dy, There rings a mel - o - dy of love.

TESTIMONY, WITNESS AND EVANGELISM

O, How I Love Jesus

He that loveth not knoweth not God; for He is love. — I John 4:8

O, HOW I LOVE JESUS
American Melody
Descant by Ralph H. Good Pasteur

Frederick Whitfield

1 There is a name I love to hear, I love to sing its worth;
2 It tells me of a Sav-ior's love, Who died to set me free;
3 It tells of One whose lov-ing heart Can feel my deep-est woe,

1 It sounds like mu - sic in my ear, The sweet - est name on earth.
2 It tells me of His pre-cious blood, The sin - ner's per - fect plea.
3 Who in each sor - row bears a part That none can bear be - low.

Descant: To

me, it's won-der-ful, To me, it's won-der-ful! To

O, how I love Je - sus, O, how I love Je - sus,

me, it's won-der-ful To know that Je-sus is mine!

O, how I love Je - sus— Be-cause He first loved me!

TESTIMONY, WITNESS AND EVANGELISM

635 Why Do I Sing About Jesus?

I live by the faith of the Son of God who loved me and gave Himself for me. — Galatians 2:21

Albert A. Ketchum

KETCHUM
Albert A. Ketchum

1 Deep in my heart there's a glad - ness — Je - sus has saved me from
2 *On - ly a glimpse of His good - ness, That was suf - fi - cient for*
3 He is the fair - est of fair ones, He is the Lil - y, the

1 sin! Praise to His name, what a Sav - ior! Cleans - ing with-
2 *me; On - ly one look at the Sav - ior, Then was my*
3 Rose; Riv - ers of mer - cy sur - round Him, Grace, love, and

1 out and with - in!
2 *spir - it set free.* Why do I sing a - bout Je - sus?
3 pit - y He shows.

Why is He pre - cious to me? He is my Lord and my

Sav - ior: Dy - ing, He set me free!

TESTIMONY, WITNESS AND EVANGELISM

The Light of the World Is Jesus 636

Christ shall give thee light. — Ephesians 5:14

LIGHT OF THE WORLD

Philip P. Bliss

Philip P. Bliss

1 The whole world was lost in the dark-ness of sin— The Light of the
2 *No dark - ness have we who in Je - sus a - bide— The Light of the*
3 No need of the sun - light in heav - en, we're told— The Light of that

1 world is Je - sus; Like sun - shine at noon-day His glo - ry shone in—
2 *world is Je - sus; We walk in the Light when we fol - low our Guide—*
3 world is Je - sus; The Lamb is the Light in the Cit - y of Gold—

1 The Light of the world is Je - sus.
2 *The Light of the world is Je - sus.* Come to the Light, 'tis
3 The Light of that world is Je - sus.

shin - ing for thee! Sweet - ly the Light has dawned up-on me; Once I was

blind, but now I can see— The Light of the world is Je - sus.

TESTIMONY, WITNESS AND EVANGELISM

637 Now I Belong to Jesus

Abide in Me, and I in you. — John 15:4

Norman J. Clayton

ELLSWORTH
Norman J. Clayton

1 Je-sus my Lord will love me for-ev-er, From Him no power of
2 *Once I was lost in sin's deg-ra-da-tion, Je-sus came down to*
3 Joy floods my soul for Je-sus has saved me, Freed me from sin that

1 e-vil can sev-er, He gave His life to ran-som my soul,
2 *bring me sal-va-tion, Lift-ed me up from sor-row and shame,*
3 long had en-slaved me; His pre-cious blood He gave to re-deem,

1 Now I be-long to Him;
2 *Now I be-long to Him;* Now I be-long to
3 Now I be-long to Him;

Je-sus, Je-sus be-longs to me, Not for the

years of time a-lone, But for e-ter-ni-ty.

TESTIMONY, WITNESS AND EVANGELISM

Something Worth Living For

638

He hath sent me to heal the brokenhearted;
to preach deliverance to the captives . . . . — Isaiah 61:1

Dale Oldham

SOMETHING MORE
William J. Gaither

1 Life was shat-tered and hope was gone— Crush-ing the load that I
2 *There, with life at its low - est ebb, Who could heal and re -*
3 O the joy of sins for - given— Noth - ing's the same as be -

1 bore; Then out of the depths I cried, "O God,
2 *store? Then He came and mend - ed my bro - ken heart—*
3 fore; My life o - ver - flows since Je - sus came

1 Give me some-thing worth liv - ing for."
2 *He gave me some-thing worth liv - ing for.* Some-thing more than my
3 And gave me some-thing worth liv - ing for.

yes - ter - days, More than I had be - fore, Some-thing more than

wealth or fame— He gave me some-thing worth liv - ing for.

TESTIMONY, WITNESS AND EVANGELISM

639 Since Jesus Came Into My Heart

But the fruit of the spirit is love, joy, peace, ... — Galatians 5:22

Rufus H. McDaniel

McDANIEL
Charles H. Gabriel

1 What a won-der-ful change in my life has been wrought Since Je-sus came
2 *I have ceased from my wan-dering and go-ing a-stray, Since Je-sus came*
3 I shall go there to dwell in that Cit-y, I know, Since Je-sus came

1 in-to my heart! I have light in my soul for which long I have sought,
2 *in-to my heart! And my sins, which were man-y, are all washed a-way,*
3 in-to my heart! And I'm hap-py, so hap-py, as on-ward I go,

Since Je-sus came in-to my heart! Since Je-sus came in-to my

heart, Since Je-sus came in-to my heart, Floods of joy o'er my

soul like the sea bil-lows roll, Since Je-sus came in-to my heart.

TESTIMONY, WITNESS AND EVANGELISM

Forgiveness

640

I went very unwillingly to a society in Aldersgate Street, where one was reading Luther's preface to the *Epistle to the Romans*. While he was describing the change which God makes in the heart through faith in Christ, I felt my heart strangely warmed. I felt I did trust in Christ, Christ alone for salvation; and an assurance was given me that He had taken away *my* sins, even *mine,* and saved *me* from the law of sin and death.

—John Wesley

Pass It On

641

PASS IT ON

Kurt Kaiser

If God so loved us we ought also to love one another. — 1 John 4:11

Kurt Kaiser

1 It only takes a spark to get a fire go - ing,
2 *What a won-drous time is spring—when all the trees are bud - ding,*
3 I wish for you, my friend, this hap - pi-ness that I've found—

1 And soon all those a - round can warm up in its glow - ing;
2 *The birds be-gin to sing, the flow - ers start their bloom-ing;*
3 You can de-pend on Him, it mat - ters not where you're bound;

1 That's how it is with God's love, once you've ex - per - i - enced it:
2 *That's how it is with God's love, once you've ex - per - i - enced it:*
3 I'll shout it from the moun-tain top, I want my world to know:

1 You spread His love to ev - ery - one, you want to pass it on.
2 *You want to sing, it's fresh like spring, you want to pass it on.*
3 The Lord of love has come to me, I want to pass it on.

TESTIMONY, WITNESS AND EVANGELISM

642 If I Gained the World

For what is a man profited if he gain the whole world and lose his own soul? — Matthew 16:26

Anna Ölander
Tr. composite

TRUE RICHES
Swedish Melody

1 If I gained the world but lost the Sav - ior, Were my life worth
2 *Had I wealth and love in full - est meas - ure, And a name re -*
3 O what emp - ti - ness with - out the Sav - ior Mid the sins and
4 *O the joy of hav - ing all in Je - sus! What a balm the*

1 liv - ing for a day? Could my yearn - ing heart find rest and
2 *vered both far and near, Yet no hope be - yond, no har - bor*
3 sor - rows here be - low! And e - ter - ni - ty, how dark with -
4 *bro - ken heart to heal! Ne'er a sin so great but He'll for -*

1 com - fort In the things that soon must pass a - way? If I
2 *wait - ing Where my storm-tossed ves - sel I could steer— If I*
3 out Him— On - ly night and tears and end - less woe! What though
4 *give it, Nor a sor - row that He does not feel! If I*

1 gained the world, but lost the Sav - ior, Would my gain be
2 *gained the world, but lost the Sav - ior, Who en - dured the*
3 I might live with - out the Sav - ior, When I come to
4 *have but Je - sus, on - ly Je - sus, Noth - ing else in*

TESTIMONY, WITNESS AND EVANGELISM

1 worth the life - long strife? Are all earth - ly pleas - ures worth com -
2 *cross and died for me,* *Could then all the world af - ford a*
3 die, how would it be? O to face the val - ley's gloom with -
4 *all the world be - side,* *O then ev - ery - thing is mine in*

1 par - ing For a mo - ment with a Christ - filled life?
2 *ref - uge, Whith - er in my an - guish I might flee?*
3 out Him! And with - out Him all e - ter - ni - ty!
4 *Je - sus— For my needs and more He will pro - vide.*

Christ Be with Me · 643

I arise today
Through God's strength to pilot me:
God's might to uphold me,
God's wisdom to guide me,
God's eye to look before me,
God's ear to hear me,
God's word to speak for me,
God's hand to guard me,
God's way to lie before me,
God's shield to protect me.

Christ be with me, Christ before me, Christ behind me,
Christ in me, Christ beneath me, Christ above me,
Christ on my right, Christ on my left,
Christ when I lie down, Christ when I sit down, Christ when I arise,
Christ in the heart of every man who thinks of me,
Christ in the mouth of every one who speaks of me,
Christ in every eye that sees me,
Christ in every ear that hears me.

—St. Patrick

644 Since I Have Been Redeemed

I know that my redeemer liveth. . . . — Job 19:25

Edwin O. Excell

OTHELLO
Edwin O. Excell

1 I have a song I love to sing, Since I have been re-deemed,
2 *I have a Christ that sat - is - fies, Since I have been re-deemed,*
3 I have a wit - ness bright and clear, Since I have been re-deemed,
4 *I have a home pre - pared for me, Since I have been re-deemed,*

1 Of my Re-deem-er, Sav - ior, King— Since I have been re - deemed.
2 *To do His will my high - est prize— Since I have been re - deemed.*
3 Dis - pell - ing ev - ery doubt and fear— Since I have been re - deemed.
4 *Where I shall dwell e - ter - nal - ly— Since I have been re - deemed.*

Since I have been redeemed, Since I have been redeemed, I will glo-ry in His name:

Since I have been re-deemed, I will glo-ry in my Sav-ior's name.

TESTIMONY, WITNESS AND EVANGELISM

There's Room at the Cross

. . . While we were yet sinners, Christ died for us. — Romans 5:8

645

STANPHILL

Ira F. Stanphill

Ira F. Stanphill

1 The cross up-on which Je-sus died Is a shel-ter in
2 *Though mil-lions have found Him a friend And have turned from the*
3 The hand of my Sav-ior is strong, And the love of my

1 which we can hide; And its grace so free is suf-
2 *sins they have sinned, The Sav-ior still waits to*
3 Sav-ior is long; Through sun-shine or rain, through

1 fi-cient for me, And deep is its foun-tain— as wide as the sea.
2 *o-pen the gates And wel-come a sin-ner be-fore it's too late.*
3 loss or in gain, The blood flows from Cal-vary to cleanse ev-ery stain.

There's room at the cross for you, There's room at the cross for you; Though

millions have come, There's still room for one—Yes, there's room at the cross for you.

TESTIMONY, WITNESS AND EVANGELISM

646 Redeemed

Let the redeemed of the Lord say so . . . . — Psalm 107:2

Fanny J. Crosby

REDEEMED
William J. Kirkpatrick

1 Redeemed—how I love to pro-claim it! Redeemed by the blood of the Lamb;
2 *Redeemed and so hap-py in Je-sus, No lan-guage my rap-ture can tell;*
3 I think of my bless-ed Re-deem-er, I think of Him all the day long;
4 *I know I shall see in His beau-ty The King in whose law I de-light;*

1 Redeemed through His in-fi-nite mer-cy, His child, and for-ev-er, I am.
2 *I know that the light of His pres-ence With me shall con-tin-ual-ly dwell.*
3 I sing, for I can-not be si-lent; His love is the theme of my song.
4 *Who lov-ing-ly guards ev-ery foot-step, And gives me a song in the night.*

Re-deemed, re-deemed, Re-deemed by the blood of the Lamb.

Re-deemed, re-deemed, His child, and for-ev-er, I am.

TESTIMONY, WITNESS AND EVANGELISM

O Happy Day! 647

Let the wicked forsake his way for He will abundantly pardon. — Isaiah 55:7

Philip Doddridge
Gloria Gaither, stanza 4, alt.

HAPPY DAY
Edward F. Rimbault

1 O hap-py day that fixed my choice On Thee, my Sav-ior and my God!
2 *O hap-py bond that seals my vows To Him who mer-its all my love!*
3 It's done, the great trans-ac-tion's done—I am my Lord's and He is mine;
4 *At peace, my long-di-vid-ed heart, Can in this calm as-sur-ance rest;*

1 Well may this glow-ing heart re-joice And tell its rap-tures all a-broad.
2 *Let cheer-ful an-thems fill His house, While to that sa-cred shrine I move.*
3 He drew me, and I fol-lowed on, Thrilled to con-fess the voice di-vine.
4 *There is no power can make me part From Love by which I've been pos-sessed.*

Hap-py day, hap-py day, When Je-sus washed my sins a-way!

He taught me how to watch and pray And live re-joic-ing ev-ery day;

Hap-py day, hap-py day, When Je-sus washed my sins a-way!

TESTIMONY, WITNESS AND EVANGELISM

648 I'll Tell the World That I'm A Christian

For I am not ashamed of the gospel of Christ . . . — Romans 1:16

Baynard L. Fox

TUCKER
Baynard L. Fox

1 I'll tell the world that I'm a Chris-tian— I'm not a-shamed His name to
2 *I'll tell the world that He is com-ing— It may be near or far a-*

1 bear; I'll tell the world that I'm a Chris-tian— I'll take Him with me
2 *way; But we must live as if His com-ing Would be to-mor-row*

1 an-y-where. I'll tell the world how Je-sus saved me, And how He
2 *or to-day. For when He comes and life is o-ver, For those who*

1 gave me a life brand-new; And I know that if you trust Him
2 *love Him there's more to be; Eyes have nev-er seen the won-ders*

1 That all He gave me He'll give to you. I'll tell the world
2 *That He's pre-par-ing for you and me. O tell the world*

TESTIMONY, WITNESS AND EVANGELISM

1 that He's my Sav - ior, No oth - er one could love me so; My life, my
2 *that you're a Chris - tian, Be not a - shamed His name to bear; O tell the*

1 all is His for - ev - er, And where He leads me I will go.
2 *world that you're a Chris - tian, And take Him with you ev - er - y - where.*

Where Has All the Witness Gone ? 649

Lord, we admit to ourselves and to You that we have often enjoyed our faith and the privilege of being Your people, while avoiding the responsibility for making our spiritual discoveries known to others.

Our lives should be living illustration of the truth, but they are frequently hard to read and even sometimes misleading.

We are frequently too busy to think through our faith and to be prepared to give a defense of our position and an introduction to the Savior.

We are fearful of rejection and even of being thought different.

We consign to professional people in the church the task that belongs to us all, of recommending the Master to the man in the street.

We are unwilling to suffer even slight inconvenience that someone else may turn from a meaningless existence to purposeful living. And sometimes with lop-sided concern we pray too much for our loved ones and insufficiently for Your loved ones—the poor, the defenseless, the neglected little people of the world. Too often, Lord, we try to predict who will respond and who will not, and we recommend with presumptive rashness when and how You are to fulfill our prayers for the salvation of others. Father, forgive these wrong and unhealthy attitudes.

Help us to love You so ardently and so courageously that, with tact and a sense of humor and great graciousness, we may begin to find all sorts of opportunities to recommend You to those who desperately need You. Amen.

—Bryan Jeffery Leech

650 I'd Rather Have Jesus

. . . but as for me and my house, we will serve the Lord. — Joshua 24:15b

I'D RATHER HAVE JESUS

Rhea F. Miller

George Beverly Shea

1 I'd rath-er have Je-sus than sil-ver or gold, I'd rath-er be
2 *I'd rath-er have Je-sus than men's ap - plause, I'd rath-er be*
3 He's fair-er than lil-ies of rar-est bloom, He's sweet-er than

1 His than have rich-es un - told; I'd rath-er have Je-sus than
2 *faith-ful to His dear cause; I'd rath-er have Je-sus than*
3 hon-ey from out the comb; He's all that my hun-ger-ing

1 hous-es or lands, I'd rath-er be led by His nail-pierced hand.
2 *world-wide fame, I'd rath-er be true to His ho-ly name.*
3 spir-it needs, I'd rath-er have Je-sus and let Him lead.

Than to be the king of a vast do-main Or be held in sin's dread sway;

I'd rath-er have Je-sus than an-y-thing This world af-fords to-day.

TESTIMONY, WITNESS AND EVANGELISM

Jesus Never Fails

*Heaven and earth will pass away
but My words shall not . . . . — Matthew 24:35*

Arthur A. Luther

JESUS NEVER FAILS
Arthur A. Luther

1 Earth - ly friends may prove un - true, Doubts and fears as - sail;
2 *Though the sky be dark and drear, Fierce and strong the gale,*
3 In life's dark and bit - ter hour Love will still pre - vail;

1 One still loves and cares for you, One who will not fail.
2 *Just re - mem - ber He is near, And He will not fail.*
3 Trust His ev - er - last - ing power— Je - sus will not fail.

Je - sus nev - er fails, Je - sus nev - er fails;

Heaven and earth may pass a - way, But Je - sus nev - er fails.

TESTIMONY, WITNESS AND EVANGELISM

652

Get All Excited

And He hath on His vesture and on His thigh a name written:
KING OF KINGS, and LORD OF LORDS. — Revelation 19:16

William J. Gaither

GET ALL EXCITED
William J. Gaither

Get all ex-cit - ed, go tell ev-ery-bod - y that Je - sus

Christ is King! Get all ex-cit - ed, go tell ev-ery-bod - y that

Je - sus Christ is King! Get all ex-cit - ed, go tell

ev - ery - bod - y that Je - sus Christ is King,

Fine

Je - sus Christ is still the King of kings, King of kings!

TESTIMONY, WITNESS AND EVANGELISM

D.C. al Fine

You talk a-bout peo-ple, you talk a-bout things that real-ly aren't im-port-ant at all, You talk a-bout weath-er, you talk a-bout prob-lems we have here at home and a-broad; But, friend, I'm ex-cit - ed a-bout a so-lu - tion for the world—I'm going to shout and sing, "Je-sus Christ is still the King of kings, King of kings!

TESTIMONY, WITNESS AND EVANGELISM

653 He Lifted Me

He brought me up out of a horrible pit . . . — Psalm 40:2

Charles H. Gabriel

HE LIFTED ME
Charles H. Gabriel

1 In lov-ing-kind - ness Je-sus came My soul in mer - cy to re-claim,
2 *He called me long be - fore I heard, Be - fore my sin - ful heart was stirred,*
3 His brow was pierced with man-y a thorn, His hands by cru - el nails were torn,
4 *Now on a high - er plane I dwell, And with my soul I know 'tis well;*

1 And from the depths of sin and shame Through grace He lift - ed me.
2 *But when I took Him at His word, For - given He lift - ed me.*
3 When from my guilt and grief, for - lorn, In love He lift - ed me.
4 *Yet how or why, I can - not tell, He should have lift - ed me.*

From sink-ing sand He lift-ed me, With ten-der hand He lift - ed me;

From shades of night to plains of light, O praise His name, He lift - ed me!

TESTIMONY, WITNESS AND EVANGELISM

Have You Any Room For Jesus?

Behold, I stand at the door and knock . . . — Revelation 3:20

ANY ROOM
C. C. Williams

Unknown

1 Have you an-y room for Je-sus, He who bore your load of sin?
2 *Room for pleas-ure, room for busi-ness—But, for Christ the cru-ci-fied,*
3 Have you an-y room for Je-sus, As in grace He calls a-gain?
4 *Room and time now give to Je-sus, Soon will pass God's day of grace;*

1 As He knocks and asks ad-mis-sion, Will you ev-er let Him in?
2 *Not a place that He can en-ter, In the heart for which He died?*
3 Here to-day is time ac-cept-ed, To-mor-row you may call in vain.
4 *Soon thy heart left cold and si-lent, And thy Sav-ior's plead-ing cease.*

Room for Je-sus, King of glo-ry! Has-ten now, His word o-bey;

Swing your heart's door wide-ly o-pen, Bid Him en-ter while you may.

655 Reach Out and Touch

. . . And as many as touched became perfectly whole. — Matthew 14:36

Charles F. Brown

REACH OUT
Charles F. Brown

1 Reach out and touch a soul that is hun-gry, Reach out and touch a
2 *Reach out and touch a friend who is wea-ry, Reach out and touch a*

1 spir - it in de - spair, Reach out and touch a life torn and
2 *seek - er un - a - ware, Reach out and touch, though touch-ing means*

1 dirt - y, A man who is lone-ly— If you care! Reach out and
2 *los - ing A part of your own self— If you dare! Reach out and*

1 touch that neigh-bor who hates you, Reach out and touch that stran-ger who
2 *give your love to the love-less, Reach out and make a home for the*

1 meets you, Reach out and touch the broth-er who needs you, Reach out
2 *home-less, Reach out and shed God's light in the dark-ness, Reach out*

TESTIMONY, WITNESS AND EVANGELISM

1 and let the smile of God touch thru you.
2 *and let the smile of God touch thru* *you.*

Something Beautiful 656

There is therefore now no condemnation
to them that are in Christ Jesus . . . . — Romans 8:1

Gloria Gaither

SOMETHING BEAUTIFUL
William J. Gaither

Some - thing beau - ti - ful, some - thing good;

All my con - fu - sion He un - der - stood;

All I had to of - fer Him was bro - ken - ness and

strife, But He made some - thing beau - ti - ful of my life.

TESTIMONY, WITNESS AND EVANGELISM

657

Heaven Came Down and Glory Filled My Soul

And suddenly there shone round about Him a light from Heaven; — Acts 9:3

HEAVEN CAME DOWN

John W. Peterson

John W. Peterson

1 O what a won-der-ful, won-der-ful day— Day I will nev-er for-
2 *Born of the Spir-it with life from a-bove In-to God's fam-i-ly di-*
3 Now I've a hope that will sure-ly en-dure Aft-er the pass-ing of

1 get; Aft-er I'd wan-dered in dark-ness a-way, Je - sus my
2 *vine, Jus-ti-fied ful-ly through Cal-va-ry's love, O what a*
3 time; I have a fu-ture in heav-en for sure, There in those

1 Sav-ior I met. O what a ten-der, com-pas-sion-ate friend—
2 *stand-ing is mine! And the trans-ac-tion so quick-ly was made*
3 man-sions sub-lime. And it's be-cause of that won-der-ful day

1 He met the need of my heart; Shad-ows dis-pel-ling, With
2 *When as a sin-ner I came, Took of the of-fer Of*
3 When at the cross I be-lieved; Rich-es e-ter-nal And

TESTIMONY, WITNESS AND EVANGELISM

1 joy   I am tell - ing, He made all the dark - ness de - part!
2 *grace He did prof-fer— He saved me, O praise His dear name!*
3 bless-ings su - per - nal From His pre-cious hand I re - ceived.

Heav-en came down and glo-ry filled my soul,

When at the cross the Sav - ior made me whole;   My

sins were washed a - way   And my night was turned to day—

Heav - en came down and glo - ry filled my soul!

658

O Zion, Haste, Thy Mission High Fulfilling

Go ye therefore, and teach all nations . . . . — Matthew 28:19

Mary A. Thomson

TIDINGS

James Walch

1 O Zi - on, haste, thy mis-sion high ful - fill - ing, To tell to
2 *Pro - claim to ev - ery peo - ple, tongue, and na - tion That God in*
3 Give of thy sons to bear the mes-sage glo - rious, Give of thy

1 all the world that God is light; That He who made all na - tions
2 *whom they live and move is love; Tell how He stooped to save His*
3 wealth to speed them on their way; Pour out thy soul for them in

1 is not will - ing One soul should per - ish, lost in shades of night.
2 *lost cre - a - tion, And died on earth that man might live a - bove.*
3 prayer vic - to - rious, And haste the com - ing of the glo - rious day.

Pub - lish glad ti - dings, ti - dings of peace,

Ti - dings of Je - sus, re - demp-tion, and re - lease. A - men.

MISSIONS

Arranged by Eugene Butler

3 Give of thy sons to bear the mes-sage glo - rious, Give of thy

wealth to speed them on their way; Pour out thy soul for

them in prayer vic - to - rious, And haste the com - ing of the glo-rious

day. Pub - lish glad ti - dings, ti - dings of peace,

Ti - dings of Je - sus, re - demption, and re - lease. A - men.

MISSIONS

659 We've a Story to Tell to the Nations

Go ye, therefore, and teach all nations. . . . — Matthew 28:19

MESSAGE

H. Ernest Nichol

H. Ernest Nichol

1 We've a sto - ry to tell to the na - tions That shall turn their
2 *We've a song to be sung to the na - tions That shall lift their*
3 We've a mes - sage to give to the na - tions—That the Lord who
4 *We've a Sav - ior to show to the na - tions Who the path of*

1 hearts to the right, A sto - ry of truth and mer - cy, A
2 *hearts to the Lord, A song that shall con - quer e - vil And*
3 reign - eth a - bove Hath sent us His Son to save us And
4 *sor - row hath trod, That all of the world's great peo - ples Might*

1 sto - ry of peace and light, A sto - ry of peace and light.
2 *shat - ter the spear and sword, And shat - ter the spear and sword.*
3 show us that God is love, And show us that God is love.
4 *come to the truth of God, Might come to the truth of God.*

For the dark-ness shall turn to dawn-ing, And the dawn-ing to noon-day bright,

And Christ's great king-dom shall come on earth, The king-dom of love and light.

Acts 17:22-31

660

"Men of Athens! I see that in every way you are very religious. For as I walked around and observed your objects of worship, I found even an altar with this inscription: TO AN UNKNOWN GOD. Now what you worship as something unknown I am going to proclaim to you.

"The God who made the world and everything in it is the Lord of heaven and earth and does not live in temples built by hands. And He is not served by human hands, as if He needed anything, because He Himself gives all men life and breath and everything else. From one man He made every nation of men, that they should inhabit the whole earth; and He determined the times set for them and the exact places where they should live. God did this so that men would seek Him and perhaps reach out for Him and find Him, though He is not far from each one of us. For in Him we live and move and have our being. As some of your own poets have said, 'We are His children.'

"Therefore since we are God's children, we should not think that the Divine Being is like gold or silver or stone—an image made by man's design and skill. In the past God overlooked such ignorance, but now He commands all people everywhere to repent. For He has set a day when He will judge the world with justice by the man He has appointed. He has given proof of this to all men by raising Him from the dead."

—(NIV)

661 Rescue the Perishing

And His disciples came to Him. . . , saying, Lord, save us, we perish. — Matthew 8:25

Fanny J. Crosby

RESCUE

William H. Doane

1 Res - cue the per - ish - ing, Care for the dy - ing, Snatch them in pit-y from
2 *Tho they are slight-ing Him, Still He is wait - ing, Wait - ing the pen-i-tent*
3 Down in the hu-man heart, Crushed by the tempt-er, Feel - ings lie bur-ied that
4 *Res - cue the per - ish - ing— Du - ty de-mands it! Strength for thy la-bor the*

1 sin and the grave; Weep o'er the err - ing one, Lift up the fall - en,
2 *child to re - ceive; Plead with them ear-nest-ly, Plead with them gen-tly,*
3 grace can re-store; Touched by a lov - ing heart, Wak-ened by kind - ness,
4 *Lord will pro-vide; Back to the nar - row way Pa - tient-ly win them,*

1 Tell them of Je - sus, the might - y to save.
2 *He will for - give if they on - ly be - lieve.*
3 Chords that are bro-ken will vi - brate once more.
4 *Tell the poor wan-derer a Sav - ior has died.*

Res - cue the per - ish-ing,

Care for the dy - ing; Je - sus is mer - ci - ful, Je - sus will save.

MISSIONS

Let Your Heart Be Broken

662

A vessel unto honor . . . for the Master's use. — II Timothy 2:21

BJORKLUND MAJOR
Bryan Jeffery Leech
Arranged by Fred Bock

Bryan Jeffery Leech

Unison

1 Let your heart be bro - ken For a world in need:
2 *Here on earth ap - ply - ing Prin - ci - ples of love,*
3 Blest to be a bless - ing, Priv - i - leged to care,
4 *Add to your be - liev - ing Deeds that prove it true,*
5 Let your heart be ten - der And your vi - sion clear;

1 Feed the mouths that hun - ger, Soothe the wounds that bleed,
2 *Vis - i - ble ex - pres - sion— God still rules a - bove—*
3 Chal-lenged by the need— Ap - par - ent ev - ery - where.
4 *Know - ing Christ as Sav - ior, Make Him Mas - ter, too.*
5 See man-kind as God sees, Serve Him far and near.

1 Give the cup of wa - ter And the loaf of bread—
2 *Liv - ing il - lus - tra - tion Of the Liv - ing Word*
3 Where man-kind is want - ing, Fill the va - cant place.
4 *Fol - low in His foot - steps, Go where He has trod;*
5 Let your heart be bro - ken By a broth - er's pain;

1 Be the hands of Je - sus, Serv - ing in His stead.
2 *To the minds of all who've Nev - er seen or heard.*
3 Be the means through which the Lord re - veals His grace.
4 *In the world's great trou - ble Risk your - self for God.*
5 Share your rich re - sourc - es, Give and give a - gain.

MISSIONS

663 Send the Light

For God who commanded the light to shine out of darkness,
hath shined in our hearts.... — II Corinthians 4:6

Charles H. Gabriel

McCABE
Charles H. Gabriel

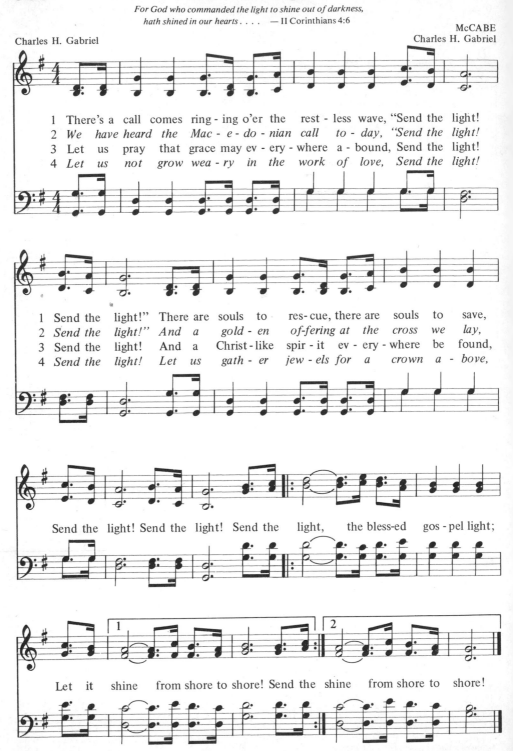

1 There's a call comes ring-ing o'er the rest-less wave, "Send the light!
2 *We have heard the Mac-e-do-nian call to-day, "Send the light!*
3 Let us pray that grace may ev-ery-where a-bound, Send the light!
4 *Let us not grow wea-ry in the work of love, Send the light!*

1 Send the light!" There are souls to res-cue, there are souls to save,
2 *Send the light!" And a gold-en of-fering at the cross we lay,*
3 Send the light! And a Christ-like spir-it ev-ery-where be found,
4 *Send the light! Let us gath-er jew-els for a crown a-bove,*

Send the light! Send the light! Send the light, the bless-ed gos-pel light;

Let it shine from shore to shore! Send the shine from shore to shore!

MISSIONS

So Send I You

664

Peace be unto you; as My Father hath sent me, even also send I you. — John 20:21

Based on John 20:21
E. Margaret Clarkson

SO SEND I YOU
John W. Peterson

1 So send I you— by grace made strong to tri - umph O'er hosts of
2 *So send I you— to take to souls in bond - age The word of*
3 So send I you— My strength to know in weak - ness, My joy in
4 *So send I you— to bear My cross with pa - tience, And then one*

1 hell, o'er dark - ness, death and sin, My name to bear, and in that
2 *truth that sets the cap - tive free, To break the bonds of sin, to*
3 grief, My per - fect peace in pain, To prove My power, My grace, My
4 *day with joy to lay it down, To hear My voice, "Well done, My*

Sts. 1,2,3

1 name to con - quer—So send I you, my vic - to - ry to win.
2 *loose death's fet - ters— So send I you, to bring the lost to me.*
3 prom-ised pres - ence—So send I you, e - ter - nal fruit to gain.
4 *faith - ful serv - ant— Come, share My throne, my king-dom and My*

St. 4

crown!" "As the Fa - ther hath sent Me, So send I you."

MISSIONS

665 Where Cross the Crowded Ways of Life

And unto you which believe He is precious . . . . — I Peter 2:7

Frank M. North

GERMANY
William Gardiner's *Sacred Melodies*

1 Where cross the crowd-ed ways of life, Where sound the cries of race and clan,
2 *In haunts of wretch-ed-ness and need, On shad-owed thresh-olds dark with fears,*
3 The cup of wa - ter given for Thee Still holds the fresh-ness of Thy grace;
4 *O Mas-ter, from the moun-tain side, Make haste to heal these hearts of pain,*
5 'Til sons of men shall learn Thy love And fol-low where Thy feet have trod:

1 A - bove the noise of self-ish strife, We hear Thy voice, O Son of man!
2 *From paths where hide the lures of greed, We catch the vi - sion of Thy tears.*
3 Yet long these mul - ti - tudes to see The sweet com-pas-sion of Thy face.
4 *A - mong these rest - less throngs a-bide, O tread the cit - y's streets a-gain;*
5 'Til glo-rious from Thy heaven a-bove Shall come the cit-y of our God. A-men.

666 Vision

1st Reader: After this I looked, and behold, a great multitude which no man could number, from every nation, from all tribes and peoples and tongues, standing before the throne and before the Lamb, clothed in white robes, with palm branches in their hands, and crying out with a loud voice,

People: *"Salvation belongs to our God who sits upon the throne and to the Lamb!"*

1st Reader: And all the angels stood round the throne and round the elders and the four living creatures, and they fell on their faces before the throne and worshipped God, saying,

PEOPLE: *"Amen! Blessing and glory and wisdom and thanksgiving and honor and power and might be to our God for ever and ever! Amen."*

1st Reader: Then one of the elders addressed me, saying,

2nd Reader: "Who are these, clothed in white robes, and whence have they come?"

1st Reader: I said to him, "Sir, you know." And he said to me,

2nd Reader: "These are they who have come out of the great tribulation; they have washed their robes and made them white in the blood of the Lamb. Therefore are they before the throne of God, and serve Him day and night within His temple; and He who sits upon the throne will shelter them with His presence . . . and God will wipe every tear from their eyes.

—Revelation 7:9-17 (RSV)

MISSIONS

Jesus Saves!

. . . Joy shall be in heaven over one sinner that repenteth . . . . — Luke 15:7

JESUS SAVES

Priscilla J. Owens

William J. Kirkpatrick

1 We have heard the joy - ful sound: Je - sus saves! Je - sus saves!
2 *Waft it on the roll - ing tide:* Je - sus saves! Je - sus saves!
3 Sing a - bove the bat - tle strife: Je - sus saves! Je - sus saves!
4 *Give the winds a might - y voice:* Je - sus saves! Je - sus saves!

1 Spread the ti - dings all a - round: Je - sus saves! Je - sus saves!
2 *Tell to sin - ners far and wide:* Je - sus saves! Je - sus saves!
3 By His death and end - less life: Je - sus saves! Je - sus saves!
4 *Let the na - tions now re - joice:* Je - sus saves! Je - sus saves!

1 Bear the news to ev - ery land, Climb the steeps and cross the waves;
2 *Sing, ye is - lands of the sea; Ech - o back, ye o - cean caves;*
3 Sing it soft - ly through the gloom, When the heart for mer - cy craves;
4 *Shout sal - va - tion full and free, High - est hills and deep - est caves;*

1 On - ward! 'tis our Lord's com - mand; Je - sus saves! Je - sus saves!
2 *Earth shall keep her ju - bi - lee: Je - sus saves! Je - sus saves!*
3 Sing in tri - umph o'er the tomb: Je - sus saves! Je - sus saves!
4 *This our song of vic - to - ry: Je - sus saves! Je - sus saves!*

MISSIONS

668 Macedonia

And the word of the Lord was published throughout all the region. — Acts 13:49

Anne Ortlund

ALL SAINTS, NEW
Henry S. Cutler

1 The vi - sion of a dy - ing world Is vast be - fore our eyes;
2 *The sav - age hugs his god of stone And fears de - scent of night;*
3 To - day, as un - der - stand - ing's bounds Are stretched on ev - ery hand,
4 *The warn - ing bell of judg - ment tolls, A - bove us looms the cross;*

1 We feel the heart - beat of its need, We hear its fee - ble cries:
2 *The cit - y dwell - er cring - es lone A - mid the gar - ish light:*
3 O clothe Thy Word in bright, new sounds, And speed it o'er the land;
4 *A - round are ev - er - dy - ing souls— How great, how great the loss!*

1 Lord Je - sus Christ, re - vive Thy church In this, her cru - cial hour!
2 *Lord Je - sus Christ, a - rouse Thy church To see their mute dis - tress!*
3 Lord Je - sus Christ, em - pow - er us To preach by ev - ery means!
4 *O Lord, con - strain and move Thy church, The glad news to im - part!*

1 Lord Je - sus Christ, a - wake Thy church With Spir - it - giv - en power.
2 *Lord Je - sus Christ, e - quip Thy church With love and ten - der - ness.*
3 Lord Je - sus Christ, em - bold - en us In near and dis - tant scenes.
4 *And Lord, as Thou dost stir Thy church, Be - gin with - in my heart.* A - men.

MISSIONS

Hear the Voice of Jesus Calling 669

They will not believe in Him unless they have heard of Him. — Romans 10:14b

Daniel March
Bryan Jeffery Leech, alt.

RIPLEY
Gregorian Chant
Adapted by Lowell Mason

1 Hear the voice of Je-sus call-ing, "Who will go and work to-day?"
2 *If you do not cross the o-cean And a dis-tant land ex-plore,*
3 If you can-not be a watch-man Stand-ing high on Zi-on's wall,
4 *Nev-er find your-self re-peat-ing, "There is noth-ing I can do;"*

1 Fields are white and har-vests read-y, Who will bear the sheaves a-way?
2 *You can give a lov-ing wit-ness, heal-ing those whose hearts are sore.*
3 Point-ing men to find the Sav-ior, Who is life and peace to all,
4 *While a world of men is dy-ing, There's a work God calls you to.*

1 Loud and long the Mas-ter calls you, Rich re-ward He of-fers free;
2 *Though your tal-ents may be mea-ger, Of-fer up the things you can,*
3 With your gifts and in-ter-ces-sions You can do as He com-mands,
4 *Glad-ly take the task He gives you, Let His will your pleas-ure be;*

1 Who will an-swer, glad-ly say-ing, "Here am I, send me, send me."
2 *All that you can do for Je-sus Will be use-ful in His hand.*
3 Join-ing with all faith-ful spokes-men Serv-ing Him in dis-tant lands.
4 *An-swer quick-ly, when He calls you, "Here am I, send me, send me."*

MISSIONS

670 Once to Every Man and Nation

Choose you this day whom ye will serve. — Joshua 24:15

James Russell Lowell

EBENEZER
Thomas J. Williams

1 Once to every man and nation Comes the moment to decide, In the strife of truth with falsehood, For the good or evil side; Some great cause, God's new Messiah, Offering

2 Then to side with truth is noble, When we share her wretched crust, Ere her cause bring fame and profit And 'tis prosperous to be just; Then it is the brave man chooses, While the

3 By the light of burning martyrs, Christ, Thy bleeding feet we track, Toiling up new Calvaries ever With the cross that turns not back; New occasions teach new duties, Time makes

4 Though the cause of evil prosper, Yet 'tis truth alone is strong; Though her portion be the scaffold And upon the throne be wrong; Yet that scaffold sways the future, And, be-

MISSIONS

1 each the bloom or blight, And the choice goes
2 *cow - ard stands a - side, Till the mul - ti -*
3 an - cient good un - couth: They must up - ward
4 *hind the dim un - known, Stand - eth God with -*

1 by for - ev - er 'Twixt that dark - ness and that light.
2 *tude make vir - tue Of the faith they had de - nied.*
3 still, and on - ward, Who would keep a - breast of truth.
4 *in the shad - ow, Keep - ing watch a - bove His own.*

Indifference   **671**

When Jesus came to Golgotha they hanged Him on a tree,
They drove great nails through hands and feet, and made a Calvary;
They crowned Him with a crown of thorns, red were His wounds and deep,
For those were crude and cruel days, and human flesh was cheap.

When Jesus came to our town, they simply passed Him by,
They never hurt a hair of Him, they only let Him die;
For men had grown more tender, and they would not give Him pain,
They only just passed down the street, and left Him in the rain.

Still Jesus cried, "Forgive them, for they know not what they do,"
And still it rained the winter rain that drenched Him through and through;
The crowds went home and left the streets without a soul to see,
And Jesus crouched against a wall and cried for Calvary.

—G. A. Studdert-Kennedy

672 Through All the World

And it shall be to Me a name of joy, a praise and honor before all the nations. — Jeremiah 33:9

CONRAD

Bryan Jeffery Leech

Paul F. Liljestrand

1 Through all the world let ev-ery na-tion sing To God, the King!
2 *Through all the world let ev-ery man ex-press True righ-teous-ness!*
3 Through all the world let ev-ery man em-brace The gift of grace!
4 *If all the world in ev-ery part shall hear And God re-vere,*

1 As Lord may Christ pre-side Where now He is de-fied,
2 *May Christ be now the norm To which all men con-form,*
3 May Christ's great light con-sume Our cit-ies' dark-est gloom,
4 *We must be moved to care And in His name to share*

1 And sov-ereign place His throne In hearts not yet His own.
2 *His pas-sion cure the sin That fes-ters from with-in.*
3 May Christ's great love ef-face Hos-til-i-ties of race.
4 *The lib-er-at-ing Word Which must be told a-broad.*

MISSIONS

1 Through all the world let ev-ery na-tion sing To God, the King!
2 *Through all the world let ev-ery man ex - press True righ - teous - ness!*
3 Through all the world let ev-ery man em - brace The gift of grace!
4 *Then all the world in ev-ery part shall hear And God re - vere!*

Precious in God's Sight   673

    In God's sight a person is the most precious of all values. This truth possessed Jesus and never let Him go. He thought it, taught it, and lived it with full devotion. He illustrated it with stories of the lost sheep, the lost coin, and the lost son.

    Every individual is inherently worthful to the Father—every child everywhere, of every race, of every condition. Love requires response, and parenthood craves companionship and cooperation. Therefore every human being on this globe is indispensable to God, indispensable in the sense that God can never be fully Himself without loving comradeship, and He can never complete His work without faithful cooperation from every individual everywhere.

    Jesus taught and lived the twin truths that man needs God and God needs man, which is to say, parents and child are so bound together that cleavage is disastrous. No idea could be further from the mind of our Lord than the persistent doctrine that God is so transcendent, so holy, so sovereign that He is unknowable, inaccessible, and unresponsive. In the prayer which He taught His disciples, Jesus makes it clear that men should carry all their needs to the Father, even a petition for the satisfaction of daily bodily requirements. Jesus knew men to be frail, sinful, easily corrupted, sometimes monstrously depraved, capable of cruel and atrocious behavior—but always, always, always a child of God, and, even when a prodigal, indispensable to the lonely and yearning heart of the Father.

                                     —Kirby Page

674
Far, Far Away in Sin and Darkness Dwelling

Then said I, Here am I; send me. — Isaiah 6:8

Based on Matthew 28:18-20
James McGranahan

GO YE
James McGranahan

1 Far, far a - way, in sin and dark-ness dwell-ing, Mil - lions of souls for-
2 *See o'er the world wide o - pen doors in - vit - ing, Sol - diers of Christ, a -*
3 "Why will ye die?" the voice of God is call - ing, "Why will ye die?" re -
4 *God speed the day, when those of ev - ery na - tion "Glo - ry to God!" tri -*

1 ev - er may be lost; Who then will go, sal - va-tion's sto-ry tell - ing,
2 *rise and en - ter in! Chris - tians, a - wake! your forc-es all u - nit - ing,*
3 ech - o in His name; Je - sus hath died to save from death ap-pall-ing,
4 *um-phant-ly shall ring; Ran-somed, re-deemed, re - joic-ing in sal - va - tion,*

1 Look - ing to Je - sus, mind-ing not the cost?
2 *Send forth the gos - pel, break the chains of sin.* "All power is
3 Life and sal - va - tion there-fore go pro - claim.
4 *Shout Hal - le - lu - jah, for the Lord is King.*

giv - en un - to Me, All power is giv - en un - to Me, Go ye in - to

all the world and preach the gos-pel, And lo, I am with you al - way,"

MISSIONS

*F*ather, help me to talk like a Christian:
> to speak in such a way that I build up another person's confidence in himself, instead of tearing down his reputation.

Father, help me to drive like a Christian:
> to be watchful and careful lest I cause harm to someone else on the highways.

Father, help me to give like a Christian:
> without thought of return, without anyone knowing what I do, and with Your approval as sufficient reward.

Father, help me to dress like a Christian:
> by not attracting attention to myself for being too fashionable or too casual; and help me to show by my appearance that I want people to know me for what I am inside myself.

Father, help me to sleep like a Christian:
> at peace with myself because sin is forgiven; and at peace with others because I do not allow my anger to last through a day.

Father, help me to eat like a Christian:
> to eat healthily, to eat moderately, to eat gratefully, giving thanks to You who provide my food, and for the one who prepares my food.

Father, keep me from being so pious that I keep You out of the practical areas of life. Be with me when I am alone, and when I shed my inhibitions, lest in those moments I cancel out all that I seem to be when I'm on my best behavior.

Father, I ask this because I follow a Master who was never guilty of the slightest wrong-doing, and who always showed His love in the small details of living. Amen.

—Bryan Jeffery Leech

676 I Am Praying for You

We give thanks . . . praying always for you. — Colossians 1:3

S. O'Maley Cluff

INTERCESSION
Ira D. Sankey

1 I have a Savior—He's plead-ing in glo-ry, A dear, lov-ing
2 *I have a Fa-ther—to me He has giv-en A hope for e-*
3 I have a robe; 'tis re-splen-dent in white-ness, A-wait-ing in
4 *When He has found you—tell oth-ers the sto-ry, That my lov-ing*

1 Sav-ior, though earth-friends be few; And now He is watch-ing in
2 *ter-ni-ty, bless-ed and true; And soon He will call me to*
3 glo-ry my won-der-ing view; O, when I re-ceive it all
4 *Sav-ior is your Sav-ior, too; Then pray that your Sav-ior will*

1 ten-der-ness o'er me, But O that my Sav-ior were your Sav-ior, too.
2 *meet Him in heav-en, But O that He'd let me bring you with me, too!*
3 shin-ing in bright-ness, Dear friend, could I see you re-ceiv-ing one, too!
4 *bring them to glo-ry, And prayer will be an-swered—'twas an-swered for you!*

For you I am pray-ing, For you I am pray-ing, For

you I am pray-ing, I'm pray-ing for you.

CONCERN FOR OTHERS

They'll Know We Are Christians by Our Love

677

Based on John 13:35
Peter Scholtes

. . . that they may be one, even as We are one . . . . — John 17:22

ST. BRENDAN'S
Peter Scholtes

Unison

1 We are one in the Spir - it, we are one in the Lord,
2 *We will walk with each oth - er, we will walk hand in hand,*
3 We will work with each oth - er, we will work side by side,
4 *All praise to the Fa - ther, from whom all things come,*

1 We are one in the Spir - it, we are one in the Lord,
2 *We will walk with each oth - er, we will walk hand in hand,*
3 We will work with each oth - er, we will work side by side,
4 *And all praise to Christ Je - sus, His on - ly Son,*

1 And we pray that all u - ni - ty may one day be re - stored:
2 *And to - geth - er we'll spread the news that God is in our land:*
3 And we'll guard each man's dig - ni - ty and save each man's pride:
4 *And all praise to the Spir - it, who makes us one:*

And they'll know we are Christ-ians by our love, by our love,

Yes, they'll know we are Christ-ians by our love.

CONCERN FOR OTHERS

678 The Hungry Man & I

To allow the hungry man to remain hungry would be blasphemy against God and one's neighbor, for what is nearest to God is precisely the need of one's neighbor. It is for the love of Christ, which belongs as much to the hungry man as to myself, that I share my bread with him and that I share my dwelling with the homeless. If the hungry man does not attain to faith, then the fault falls on those who refused him bread. To provide the hungry man with bread is to prepare the way for the coming of grace.

Dietrich Bonhoeffer

679 Eternal Father, Strong to Save

For the Lord knoweth how to deliver . . . — II Peter 2:9

William Whiting, stanzas 1, 4
Robert Nelson Spencer, stanzas 2, 3

MELITA
John Bacchus Dykes

1 E - ter - nal Fa - ther, strong to save, Whose arm hath bound the
2 O Christ, the Lord of hill and plain O'er which our traf - fic
3 O Spir - it, whom the Fa - ther sent To spread a - broad the
4 O Trin - i - ty of love and power, Our breth - ren shield in

1 rest - less wave, Who bids the might - y o - cean deep Its
2 runs a - main By moun - tain pass or val - ley low: Wher -
3 fir - ma - ment: O wind of heav - en, by Thy might Save
4 dan - ger's hour; From rock and tem - pest, fire and foe, Pro -

1 own ap - point - ed lim - its keep: O hear us when we
2 ev - er, Lord, our breth - ren go, Pro - tect them by Thy
3 all who dare the ea - gle's flight, And keep them by Thy
4 tect them where - so - e'er they go; Thus ev - er - more shall

The words to St. 2 & 3 used by permission of Parish Press.

CONCERN FOR OTHERS

1 cry to Thee For those in per - il on the sea.
2 guard - ing hand From ev - ery per - il on the land.
3 watch - ful care From ev - ery per - il in the air.
4 rise to Thee Glad praise from air and land and sea. A - men.

Can This World Be Fed? 680

Everything I know and understand causes me to come down on the optimistic side of this question. It can be done.

Not easily.
Not inexpensively.
Certainly not without some changes.
But it can be done.

It is not the way that is lacking. It is the will. The more you understand about basic causes of hunger in the world today, the more you cannot avoid the conclusion that God has given man and the earth the capacity to conquer and control it.

If we treated all humanity with the dignity and love they are due as the offspring of God, if we acted toward our environment as its caretakers and not its ravishers, if we viewed the mandate to "tend and dress" the earth as the Creator's orders to us, men could live together in peace and the earth would bring forth its abundance.

THAT WAS GOD'S PLAN.

Anything short of that is the result of man's sin—his sin against God, against his fellow man, against his environment.

It is history.
And it is prophecy.

. . . If we have the capacity to relieve suffering and save life—and we do—and refuse to do it, that will undoubtedly be a part of our judgment.

—W. Stanley Mooneyham

681 Let There Be Peace on Earth

Peace, I leave with you, My peace I give unto you . . . . — John 14:27

WORLD PEACE
Sy Miller
Jill Jackson

Sy Miller
Jill Jackson

Let there be peace on earth, and let it be - gin with me. Let there be peace on earth, the peace that was meant to be. With God as our Fa - ther, bro - thers all are we. Let me walk with my bro - ther in per - fect har - mon - y.

BROTHERHOOD and WORLD PEACE

Let peace be - gin with me; let this be the mo - ment now. With ev - ery step I take, let this be my sol - emn vow: To take each mo-ment, and live each mo - ment in peace e - ter - nal - ly! Let there be peace on earth, and let it be - gin with me.

BROTHERHOOD and WORLD PEACE

682 A Song of Peace

. . . My peace I give unto you; not as the world giveth . . . . — John 14:27

Lloyd Stone, stanzas 1, 2
Georgia Harkness, stanza 3
Bryan Jeffery Leech, stanza 4

FINLANDIA
Jean Sibelius

Unison

1 This is my song, O God of all the na-tions,
2 *My coun-try's skies are blu-er than the o-cean,*
3 This is my prayer, O Lord of all earth's king-doms,
4 *This is my song, O God of all the na-tions,*

1 A song of peace for lands a-far and mine; This is my
2 *And sun-light beams on clo-ver-leaf and pine; But oth-er*
3 Thy king-dom come— on earth Thy will be done; Let Christ be
4 *A song of peace for men in ev-ery place; And yet I*

1 home, the coun-try where my heart is; Here are my hopes, my
2 *lands have sun-light too, and clo-ver, And skies are ev-ery-*
3 lift-ed up 'til all men serve Him, And hearts u-nit-ed
4 *pray for my be-lov-ed coun-try The re-as-sur-ance*

1 dreams, my ho-ly shrine: But oth-er hearts in oth-er lands are
2 *where as blue as mine: O, hear my song, Thou God of all the*
3 learn to live as one: O, hear my prayer, Thou God of all the
4 *of con-tin-ued grace: Lord, help us find our one-ness in the*

BROTHERHOOD AND WORLD PEACE

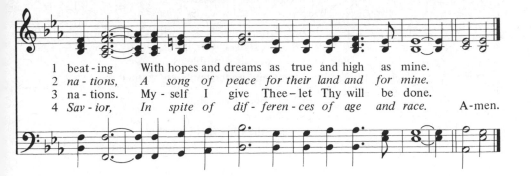

1 beat-ing	With hopes and dreams as	true and high	as	mine.
2 *na - tions,*	*A song of peace for their land and*	*for*	*mine.*
3 na - tions.	My - self I give Thee – let Thy will	be	done.
4 *Sav - ior,*	*In spite of dif - feren - ces of age*	*and race.*	A-men.

1 Corinthians 13:1-13   683

If I speak in the tongues of men and of angels, but have not love, I am only a resounding gong or a clanging cymbal. If I have the gift of prophecy, and can fathom all mysteries and all knowledge, and if I have a faith that can move mountains, but have not love, I am nothing. If I give all I possess to the poor and surrender my body to the flames, but have not love, I gain nothing.

Love is patient, love is kind. It does not envy, it does not boast, it is not proud. It is not rude, it is not self-seeking, it is not easily angered, it keeps no record of wrongs. Love does not delight in evil but rejoices in the truth. It always protects, always trusts, always hopes, always perseveres.

Love never fails. But where there are prophecies, they will cease; where there are tongues, they will be stilled; where there is knowledge, it will pass away. For we know in part and we prophesy in part, but when perfection comes, the imperfect disappears. When I was a child, I talked like a child, I thought like a child, I reasoned like a child. When I became a man, I put childish ways behind me. Now we see but a poor reflection; then we shall see face to face. Now I know in part; then I shall know fully, even as I am fully known.

And now these three remain: faith, hope and love. But the greatest of these is love.

— (NIV)

Within the Church

There is no color barrier with God.
He is color-blind.
There are many practical problems
which still have to be wisely and understandingly worked out.

But one thing is certain,
that the color barrier
and the Christian Church
cannot go together.

It was the world which God so loved,
and within the Church
it is the world which is
the family of God.

—William Barclay

685   In Christ There Is No East or West

. . . In every nation he that feareth Him, and worketh righteousness, is accepted with Him. — Acts 10:35

ST. PETER
Alexander R. Reinagle

John Oxenham

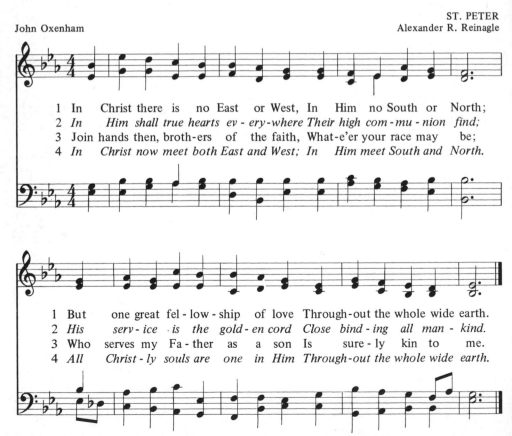

1 In   Christ there is   no East   or West, In   Him   no South or   North;
2 *In   Him shall true hearts ev - ery-where Their high com - mu - nion find;*
3 Join hands then, broth-ers of   the faith, What-e'er your race may   be;
4 *In   Christ now meet both East and West; In   Him meet South and North.*

1 But   one great fel - low - ship of love Through-out the whole wide earth.
2 *His   serv - ice - is the gold - en cord Close bind - ing all man - kind.*
3 Who   serves my Fa - ther as   a son Is   sure - ly kin to   me.
4 *All   Christ - ly souls are   one in Him Through-out the whole wide earth.*

BROTHERHOOD AND WORLD PEACE

Christ For the World We Sing

Acquaint thyself with Him and be at peace. — Job 22:21

ITALIAN HYMN

Samuel Wolcott

Felice de Giardini

1 Christ for the world we sing; The world to Christ we bring With loving zeal— The poor and them that mourn, The faint and o - ver-borne, Sin - sick and sor - row-worn, For Christ to heal.

2 *Christ for the world we sing; The world to Christ we bring With fervent prayer— The way - ward and the lost, By rest - less pas - sions tossed, Re - deemed at count - less cost From dark de - spair.*

3 Christ for the world we sing; The world to Christ we bring With one ac - cord— With us the work to share, With us re - proach to dare, With us the cross to bear, For Christ our Lord.

4 *Christ for the world we sing; The world to Christ we bring With joy - ful song— The new - born souls whose days, Re - claimed from er - ror's ways, In - spired with hope and praise, To Christ be - long. A - men.*

BROTHERHOOD AND WORLD PEACE

687 God of Our Fathers

The Lord of hosts is with us, the God of Jacob is our refuge. — Psalm 48:7

Daniel C. Roberts

NATIONAL HYMN
George W. Warren

Trumpets before each stanza

1 God of our fa-thers, whose al-might-y hand
2 *Thy love di-vine hath led us in the past,*
3 From war's a-larms, from dead-ly pes-ti-lence,
4 *Re-fresh Thy peo-ple on their toil-some way,*

1 Leads forth in beau-ty all the star-ry band
2 *In this free land by Thee our lot is cast;*
3 Be Thy strong arm our ev-er sure de-fense;
4 *Lead us from night to nev-er end-ing day;*

1 Of shin-ing worlds in splen-dor through the skies,
2 *Be Thou our rul-er, guard-ian, guide, and stay,*
3 Thy true re-li-gion in our hearts in-crease,
4 *Fill all our lives with love and grace di-vine,*

1 Our grate-ful songs be-fore Thy throne a-rise.
2 *Thy word our law, Thy paths our cho-sen way.*
3 Thy boun-teous good-ness nour-ish us in peace.
4 *And glo-ry, laud, and praise be ev-er Thine!* A-men.

PATRIOTIC

Alternate Last Verse Harmonization

Arranged by Fred Bock

f

4 Re-fresh Thy peo - ple on their toil-some way, Lead us from night to nev - er end-ing day; Fill all our lives with love and grace di - vine, And glo - ry, laud, and praise be ev - er Thine! A - men.

PATRIOTIC

688 The Star-Spangled Banner

... And on Mine arm shall they trust. — Isaiah 51:5

Francis Scott Key

NATIONAL ANTHEM
John Stafford Smith

1 O say, can you see, by the dawn's ear - ly light, What so
2 O thus be it ev - er, when free men shall stand Be -

1 proud - ly we hailed at the twi-light's last gleam - ing, Whose broad
2 tween their loved homes and the war's des - o - la - tion! Blest with

1 stripes and bright stars, through the per - il - ous fight, O'er the ram - parts we
2 vic - tory and peace, may the heaven-res-cued land Praise the Power that hath

1 watched, were so gal - lant - ly stream - ing? And the rock-ets' red glare, the bombs
2 made and pre-served us a na - tion! Then con-quer we must, when our

1 burst-ing in air, Gave proof through the night that our flag was still
2 cause it is just; And this be our mot - to: "In God is our

1 there.	O	say does that	star-span-gled	ban-ner	yet	wave
2 trust!"	And the star-span-gled	ban-ner	in	tri-umph shall	wave

1 O'er the land	of the	free	and	the home	of the	brave?
2 O'er the land	of the	free	and	the home	of the	brave?

## Before an Election	689

Lord Jesus, we ask Thee to guide the people of this nation as they exercise their dearly bought privilege of franchise. May it neither be ignored unthinkingly nor undertaken lightyly. As citizens all over this land go to the ballot boxes, give them a sense of high privilege and joyous responsibility.

Help those who are about to be elected to public office to come to understand the real source of their mandate—a mandate given by no party machine, received at no polling booth, but given by God; a mandate to represent God and truth at the heart of the nation; a mandate to do good in the name of Him under whom this country was established.

We ask Thee to lead our country in the paths where Thou wouldst have her walk, to do the tasks which Thou hast laid before her. So may we together seek happiness for all our citizens in the name of Him who created us all equal in His sight, and therefore brothers. Amen.

—Peter Marshall

690 America, the Beautiful

But in every nation He that feareth Him,
and worketh righteousness is accepted by Him. — Acts 10:35

MATERNA
Samuel A. Ward
Descant by Fred Bock

Katharine Lee Bates

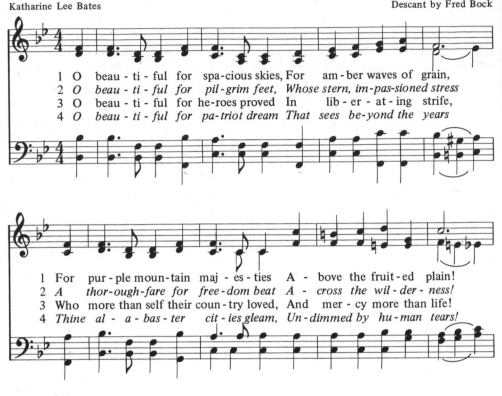

1 O beau-ti-ful for spa-cious skies, For am-ber waves of grain,
2 *O beau-ti-ful for pil-grim feet, Whose stern, im-pas-sioned stress*
3 O beau-ti-ful for he-roes proved In lib-er-at-ing strife,
4 *O beau-ti-ful for pa-triot dream That sees be-yond the years*

1 For pur-ple moun-tain maj-es-ties A-bove the fruit-ed plain!
2 *A thor-ough-fare for free-dom beat A-cross the wil-der-ness!*
3 Who more than self their coun-try loved, And mer-cy more than life!
4 *Thine al-a-bas-ter cit-ies gleam, Un-dimmed by hu-man tears!*

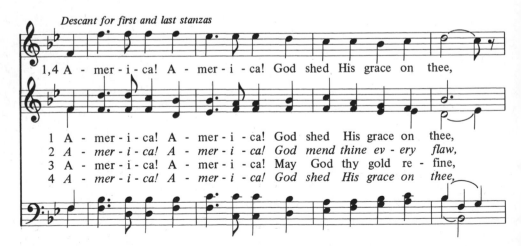

Descant for first and last stanzas

1,4 A-mer-i-ca! A-mer-i-ca! God shed His grace on thee,

1 A-mer-i-ca! A-mer-i-ca! God shed His grace on thee,
2 *A-mer-i-ca! A-mer-i-ca! God mend thine ev-ery flaw,*
3 A-mer-i-ca! A-mer-i-ca! May God thy gold re-fine,
4 *A-mer-i-ca! A-mer-i-ca! God shed His grace on thee,*

PATRIOTIC

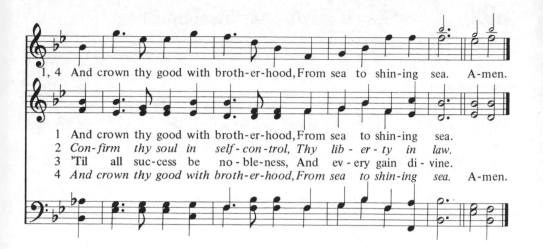

1, 4 And crown thy good with broth-er-hood, From sea to shin-ing sea. A-men.

1 And crown thy good with broth-er-hood, From sea to shin-ing sea.
2 Con-firm thy soul in self-con-trol, Thy lib-er-ty in law.
3 'Til all suc-cess be no-ble-ness, And ev-ery gain di-vine.
4 And crown thy good with broth-er-hood, From sea to shin-ing sea. A-men.

The Social Obligations of a Christian

691

The Bible teaches that the Christian should be law-abiding. The Bible also teaches loyalty to country. A loyalty and love of country does not mean that we cannot criticize certain unjust laws that may discriminate against special groups. The Bible says that God is no respecter of persons. All should have equal opportunities. The government of God is to be our model.

The Bible also teaches that we are to co-operate with the government. Jesus was asked, "Is it lawful to give tribute?" Jesus set the example forever by paying taxes. It takes money to run a government and to maintain law and order. The tax dodger is a civic parasite and an actual thief. No true Christian will be a tax dodger. Jesus said, we are to "render to Caesar the things that are Caesar's." We ought to be more than taxpayers. To be simply law-abiding is not enough. We ought to seek and work for the good of our country. Sometimes we may be called upon to die for it. We are to do it gladly—as unto God. We are to be conscientious in our work as good citizens.

—Billy Graham

692 Battle Hymn of the Republic

If the trumpet give an uncertain sound who shall prepare himself for the battle? — I Corinthians 14:8

BATTLE HYMN OF THE REPUBLIC
American Melody
Introductory fanfare by Roy Ringwald
Descant by Fred Bock

Julia Ward Howe

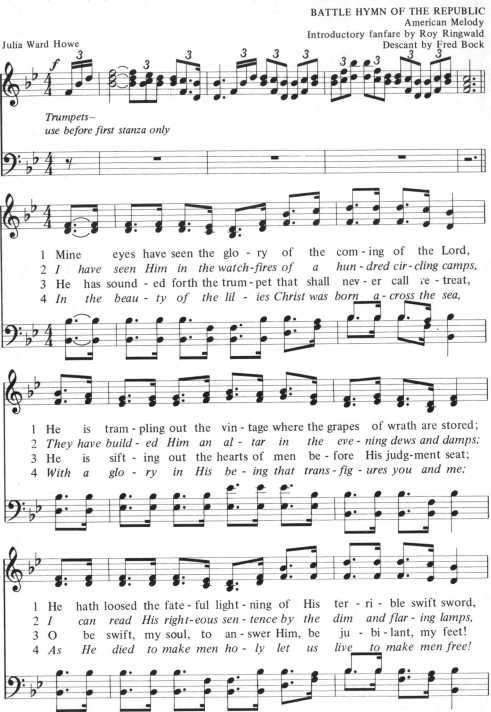

Trumpets—
use before first stanza only

1 Mine eyes have seen the glo - ry of the com - ing of the Lord,
2 *I have seen Him in the watch-fires of a hun - dred cir - cling camps,*
3 He has sound - ed forth the trum - pet that shall nev - er call re - treat,
4 *In the beau - ty of the lil - ies Christ was born a - cross the sea,*

1 He is tram - pling out the vin - tage where the grapes of wrath are stored;
2 *They have build - ed Him an al - tar in the eve - ning dews and damps;*
3 He is sift - ing out the hearts of men be - fore His judg-ment seat;
4 *With a glo - ry in His be - ing that trans - fig - ures you and me;*

1 He hath loosed the fate - ful light - ning of His ter - ri - ble swift sword,
2 *I can read His right-eous sen - tence by the dim and flar - ing lamps,*
3 O be swift, my soul, to an - swer Him, be ju - bi - lant, my feet!
4 *As He died to make men ho - ly let us live to make men free!*

PATRIOTIC

Descant for Refrain

Glo - ry! Hal - le -

1 His truth is march - ing on.
2 *His day is march - ing on.*
3 Our God is march - ing on.
4 *While God is march - ing on.*

Glo - ry! glo - ry! Hal - le -

lu - jah! Glo - ry! Hal - le - lu - jah!

lu - jah! Glo - ry! glo - ry! Hal - le - lu - jah!

Glo - ry! Hal - le - lu - jah! His truth is march - ing on!

Glo - ry! glo - ry! Hal - le - lu - jah! His truth is march - ing on!

PATRIOTIC

693   # This Is My Country

. . . In every nation he that feareth Him, and worketh righteousness is accepted by Him.
— Acts 10:35

Don Raye

MY COUNTRY
Al Jacobs

Unison

This is my coun-try, Land of my birth;

This is my coun-try, Grand-est on earth!

I pledge thee my al-le-giance, A-mer-i-ca, the bold;

For this is my coun-try to have and to hold!

PATRIOTIC

America, Our Heritage

694

Mountains, and all hills, fruitful trees, fowls . . . let them praise the name of the Lord. — Psalm 148:9

OUR HERITAGE
Helen Steele

Helen Steele

1 High tower-ing moun-tains, fields gold with grain, Rich, fer - tile farm-lands,
2 *Wide roll - ing prai - ries, lakes deep and broad, Can - yons ma - jes - tic,*
3 Stout hearts and true, hold fast what is ours, God give us cour-age

1 flocks on the plain, Homes blest with peace, with love, with - out
2 *fash - ioned by God, Life lived in peace, con - tent - ed and*
3 through dark - est hours, God give us strength and guide with Thy

1, 2
1 fears: This is the her - i - tage we've kept through the years.
2 *free: This is the her - i - tage for - ev - er to be.*

3
3 hand A - mer - i - ca, our her - i - tage, our home - land. A - men.

PATRIOTIC

695 My Country, 'Tis of Thee

Blessed is that nation whose God is the Lord. — Psalm 33:12

AMERICA
Henry Carey
Descant by Mary E. Caldwell

Samuel F. Smith

Descant
4 Our fa - thers' God, to Thee, Au - thor of lib - er - ty,

1 My coun - try, 'tis of thee, Sweet land of lib - er - ty,
2 My na - tive coun - try, thee, Land of the no - ble, free,
3 Let mu - sic swell the breeze, And ring from all the trees
4 Our fa - thers' God, to Thee, Au - thor of lib - er - ty,

To Thee we sing: Long may our land be bright With free-dom's

1 Of thee I sing: Land where my fa - thers died, Land of the
2 Thy name I love. I love thy rocks and rills, Thy woods and
3 Sweet free-dom's song. Let mor - tal tongues a-wake; Let all that
4 To Thee we sing: Long may our land be bright With free-dom's

ho - ly light; Pro - tect us by Thy might, Great God, our King!

1 Pil - grims' pride. From ev - ery moun - tain-side Let free - dom ring!
2 tem - pled hills; My heart with rap - ture thrills Like that a - bove.
3 breathe par-take; Let rocks their si - lence break, The sound pro - long.
4 ho - ly light; Pro - tect us by Thy might, Great God, our King!

PATRIOTIC

Amen 696

Louis Bourgeois

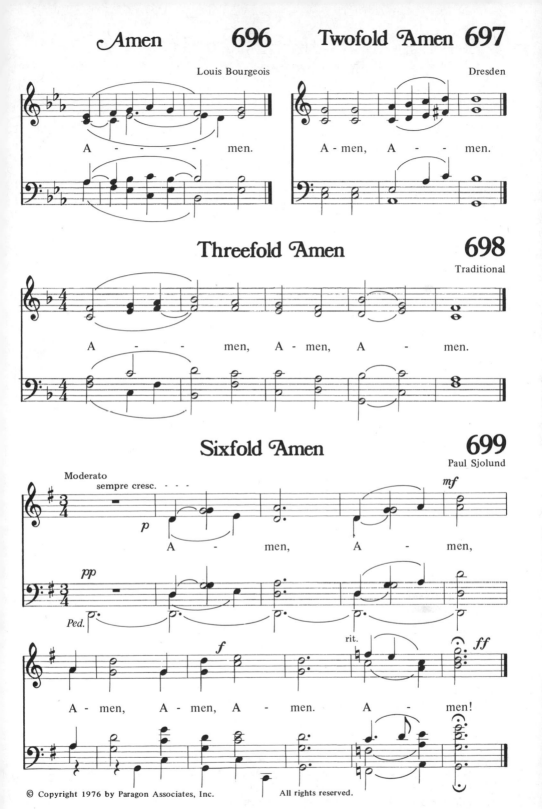

A - - - - men.

Twofold Amen 697

Dresden

A - men, A - men.

Threefold Amen 698

Traditional

A - - men, A - men, A - - men.

Sixfold Amen 699

Paul Sjolund

Moderato
sempre cresc. - - - -

mf

p

A - - men, A - men,

pp

Ped.

f

rit.

ff

A - men, A - men, A - men. A - - men!

This page has been prepared for future hymnal inserts.

This page has been prepared for future hymnal inserts.

This page has been prepared for future hymnal inserts.

Indexes

Copyright Acknowledgements

SOURCES OF READINGS AND PRAYERS

NOTE:

Alphabetical Index of Authors (readings)

Alphabetical Index of Readings

Scriptural Allusions in Hymns

OLD TESTAMENT:

Numbers 6:24-26	522	The Lord bless you and keep you
II Chronicles 7:14	575	If My people will pray
Nehemiah 8:10	354	The joy of the Lord
Psalm 23	61	Like a lamb who needs the Shepherd
Psalm 23	66	My Shepherd will supply my need
Psalm 23	40, 42	The Lord's my Shepherd, I'll not want
Psalm 24:7	239	Lift up your heads, ye mighty gates
Psalm 26:8	545	I love your kingdom, Lord
Psalm 46	118	A mighty fortress is our God
Psalm 55:22	53	Cast thy burden upon the Lord
Psalm 72	238	Jesus shall reign, where'er the sun
Psalm 87:3	376	Glorious things of Thee are spoken
Psalm 90	370	O God, our help in ages past
Psalm 92	330	It is good to sing Thy praises
Psalm 98	171	Joy to the world!
Psalm 103	379	Bless His holy name
Psalm 103	379	Bless the Lord, o my soul
Psalm 150	373	Praise the Lord, His glories show
Isaiah 26:3	493	Thou wilt keep him in perfect peace
Isaiah 33:20,21	376	Glorious things of Thee are spoken
Isaiah 40:31	52	They that wait upon the Lord
Isaiah 43:1,2	32	How firm a foundation
Isaiah 54:10	496	Great hills may tremble
Isaiah 54:10	496	Security
Lamentations 3:22, 23	98	Great is Thy faithfulness

NEW TESTAMENT:

Matthew 6:9-13	440	The Lord's prayer
Matthew 14:19	30	Break Thou the bread of life
Matthew 21:5-11	250	Ride on! Ride on in majesty!
Matthew 21:15,16	248	Hosanna, loud hosanna
Matthew 26:30	565	A hymn of joy we sing
Matthew 28:18-20	674	All power is given unto Me
Matthew 28:18-20	674	Far, far away in sin and darkness
Mark 10:13-15	213	I think when I read that sweet story
Luke 12:49	576	Thou, whose purpose is to kindle
John 3:16	315	For God so loved the world
John 3:16,17	20	God so loved the world
John 13:35	677	They'll know we are Christians by our love
John 13:35	677	We are one in the Spirit
Philippians 2:5-11	351	At the name of Jesus
Philippians 2:13	234	He is Lord
Philippians 2:13	584	God is at work within you
Philippians 4:4	374	Rejoice, the Lord is king
II Timothy 1:12	631	I know Whom I have believed
II Timothy 2:19	32	How firm a foundation
Hebrews 13:5	32	How firm a foundation

$\mathcal{A}$lphabetical $\mathcal{I}$ndex
of $\mathcal{H}$ymn $\mathcal{T}$itles and $\mathcal{F}$irst $\mathcal{L}$ines